MASTERED BY THE CLOCK

Mark M. Smith

THE FRED W. MORRISON SERIES IN SOUTHERN STUDIES

Mastered by the Clock

Time, Slavery, and Freedom in the American South

The
University
of North
Carolina
Press

Chapel Hill
& London

© 1997 The University of North Carolina Press

All rights reserved

Manufactured in the United States of America

Designed by April Leidig-Higgins

Set in Minion by Keystone Typesetting, Inc.

The paper in this book meets the guidelines for permanence and durability of the Committee on Production Guidelines for Book Longevity of the Council on Library Resources.

Material from my article, "Time, Slavery and Plantation Capitalism in the Ante-Bellum American South," *Past and Present: A Journal of Historical Studies* 150 (February 1996): 142–68, is used by permission from The Past and Present Society, Oxford, England.

A version of Chapter 1 first appeared as "Counting Clocks, Owning Time: Detailing and Interpreting Clock and Watch Ownership in the Antebellum South, 1739–1865," *Time and Society: An International Interdisciplinary Journal* 3 (October 1994): 321–40; used by permission of SAGE Publications.

01 00 99 98 97   5 4 3 2 1

Library of Congress Cataloging-in-Publication Data

Smith, Mark M. (Mark Michael), 1968–

Mastered by the clock: time, slavery, and freedom in the American South / Mark M. Smith. p. cm.—(Fred W. Morrison series in Southern studies)

Includes bibliographical references (p.   ) and index.

ISBN 0-8078-2344-9 (cloth: alk. paper).— ISBN 0-8078-4693-7 (pbk.: alk. paper)

1. Slavery—Southern States—History—18th century. 2. Slavery—Southern States—History—19th century. 3. Time—Social aspects—Southern States—History—18th century. 4. Time—Social aspects—Southern States—History—19th century. 5. Plantation life—Southern States—History—18th century. 6. Plantation life—Southern States—History—19th century. 7. Southern States—Social conditions. I. Title. II. Series.

E446.S65   1997   97-7045

975'.00496—dc21   CIP

FOR MARGARET J. SMITH AND MICHAEL J. LEA;

IN MEMORY OF E. F. GOODCHILD

CONTENTS

ILLUSTRATIONS

FIGURES

TABLES

ACKNOWLEDGMENTS

IN A WORLD where time is increasingly precious and academics in particular seem to have less of it, one is always fortunate to find exceptionally fine minds to read entire manuscripts. I count myself especially lucky to have found several. Joyce Chaplin and Clyde Wilson gave generously of their time and knowledge. They provided some crucial, often face-saving advice, and offered trenchant criticisms and inspiring suggestions. With the speed of a man who has mastered time, Stanley Engerman devoured the manuscript, cajoled its author, and helped tighten and improve the work in many ways. I am very grateful for his guidance. James Oakes kindly took time to give the entire manuscript a thorough going over. As I anticipated, it did not remain unscathed. The book has benefited tremendously from his exceptionally incisive comments. His suggestions were characteristically encouraging, extremely thoughtful, and very useful. Eugene D. Genovese has always loomed large in the formulation and writing of this study, and he loomed even larger once he had read it. As I hope he knows, I am more than grateful for his gracious comments, helpful advice, tough questions, and splendid example. He has proven inspirational.

Robert M. Weir, Jennifer Ring, and Thavolia Glymph were the readers of this book in dissertation form. Collectively, they probed the text and prodded its author. Individually, they have done much to improve this work. Jennifer Ring's mastery of political theory was put to good use in a study that deals with time and draws from Marx. Thavolia Glymph has been a wonderful critic and friend, and I am extremely thankful for her continued support and thorough, rigorous critique of my work. Robert M. Weir deserves special thanks. Not only was he instrumental in putting me on the road to southern history, but he was the first to hear my ideas about time consciousness in the South. I am in his debt for allowing me to test my ideas in his colonial history seminar and for his characteristically careful, imaginative, and intelligent reading of the manuscript.

Lacy K. Ford Jr. directed the dissertation from which this book is drawn. Always encouraging of an ostensibly offbeat topic, Lacy proved wonderfully supportive. He has been generous with his counsel and ruthless in his demands for the highest standards. Lacy dealt with the logistical and intellectual problems that accompanied this study with fortitude, grace, and kindness.

Michael O'Malley kindly read a version of Chapter 1 and for this, his support, and his own pioneering work on the history of American time consciousness, I thank him. John Oldfield, always a tireless supporter, read part of the manuscript and gave much needed encouragement as did Dean Kinzley, Lou Ferleger, and Carlene Stephens. Ron Atkinson's astute reading of the introduction proved valuable. For this, his friendship, and continuing support, I am grateful. Parts of the present work have been published in *Time and Society*, *Past and Present*, and the *American Historical Review*. The editors and anonymous reviewers of these journals forced me to think hard about what I was trying to say and I appreciate their wise counsel. In addition, I thank the *American Historical Review* and the American Historical Association for permission to use small portions of my article "Old South Time in Comparative Perspective," published in vol. 101 (December 1996): 1432–69.

When parts of this book have been presented publicly, commentators and audience alike proved generous with useful advice and suggestions. Wayne K. Durrill had encouraging things to say about my views on the dialectic of time in the slave-master relationship at the Third Social History Conference held at the University of Cincinnati in October 1993. Charles Joyner and Mechal Sobel provided useful suggestions on a paper presented at the Southern Historical Association annual meeting in Louisville, Kentucky, in November 1994. I should also like to thank Tony Badger for the invitation to present a synopsis of this study to the American History Research Seminar at Sidney Sussex College, Cambridge, in February 1995.

My former colleagues at the University of Birmingham, England, took sincere interest in my work. Andy Miles and Rob Lewis read parts of the manuscript or alerted me to evidence I would have otherwise overlooked, and Peter Cain gave me the benefit of his redoubtable wisdom on more than one occasion. Conversations with graduate students are often the most fruitful: ones with Liese Perrin and Richard Sheldon at Birmingham were no exception.

Benton Calmes's continued and valued friendship as well as his sharp intellect have helped improve this study in numerous ways. I trust he knows how grateful I am. Alex Byrd, Jim Tidd, Trenton Hizer, and R. Randall Moore have variously thrown tidbits of information my way and have always been willing to listen to and comment on this project. Tina Manley trudged the streets of Charleston to get some of the photographs for this book. For her patience, considerable talent, and general kindness, I am in her debt. Lewis Bateman and Pamela Upton of the University of North Carolina Press have been wonderfully supportive not only in procuring the manuscript but in seeing it through to completion. Trudie Calvert's copyediting was superb, and she helped improve the book considerably. I am particularly indebted to the press's anonymous readers of the manuscript who offered me some excellent advice. Having thanked the aforementioned, I should also add that the usual disclaimers apply.

Simple hospitality was important to the completion of this study. Michael and Cheryl Bell kindly put me up during my stays in Richmond, and Michael listened patiently to my interminable musings on time. Grant Hamby and his late wife, Carolyn, put me up and up with me in Chapel Hill. For buying me time, I am extremely grateful; for having lost my friend, deeply saddened.

Financial support was critical to the formulation and completion of this work. Two Andrew W. Mellon Research Fellowships at the Virginia Historical Society, Richmond, in the summers of 1993 and 1994; a British Academy Personal Research Grant for 1995–96; a Madelyn Moeller Research Fellowship from the Museum of Early Southern Decorative Arts in Winston-Salem, North Carolina, during the summer of 1993; and generous financial assistance from the Graduate Council at the University of South Carolina, Columbia, and the School of Social Sciences, University of Birmingham, England, helped immeasurably. I am particularly grateful to the University of South Carolina's Institute for Southern Studies and its director, Walter B. Edgar. He and his staff made my various stays there as a Research Fellow most enjoyable and very productive.

The library staff at many research institutions provided timely and efficient assistance. I would especially like to thank those of the Virginia Historical Society, Richmond; the South Caroliniana Library, Columbia; and the Government Documents Room, Thomas Cooper Library, Columbia. Brad Rauschenberg and the staff at the MESDA Research Center, the Museum of Early Southern Decorative Arts, Winston-Salem, were extraordinarily supportive, and I am grateful for their generosity, help, and hospitality.

Permission to quote from the following works is acknowledged: Eugene D. Genovese, *Roll, Jordan, Roll: The World the Slaves Made* (New York: Vintage Books, 1976); and Charles L. Perdue Jr., Thomas E. Barden, and Robert K. Phillips, eds., *Weevils in the Wheat: Interviews with Virginia Ex-Slaves* (Charlottesville: University Press of Virginia, 1976). And for permission to quote from the appropriate collections held at the following institutions, I am grateful: the Virginia Historical Society, Richmond; the Georgia Historical Society, Savannah; the South Caroliniana Library, University of South Carolina, Columbia; the South Carolina Historical Society, Charleston; the MESDA Research Center, Museum of Early Southern Decorative Arts, Winston-Salem, North Carolina; the Southern Historical Collection, Wilson Library, University of North Carolina at Chapel Hill; the South Carolina Department of Archives and History, Columbia; and the Special Collections Library, Duke University, Durham, North Carolina.

Catherine knows more about time in the South than she would probably want to admit. For poring over the pages, for ironing out the numerous rough spots, and, most important, for making each minute count, I am indebted to her. Now that I am emancipated, albeit temporarily, from time, I hope we will have more of it to share.

My parents, Margaret J. Smith and Michael J. Lea, have given their son every advantage they could afford. They and my late grandfather, E. F. Goodchild, have been my most valued teachers. For always reminding me of the value and beauty of work while they themselves were inured to labor, I am humbled and supremely thankful. If I have learned an iota of what they have tried to impart, I am immeasurably wiser. For this, for everything, I am forever grateful.

MASTERED BY THE CLOCK

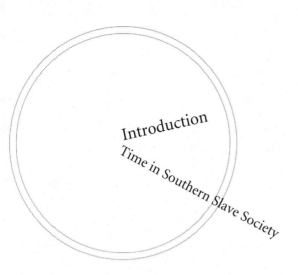

Introduction

Time in Southern Slave Society

In . . . plantations—where commercial speculations figure from the start and production is intended for the world market, the capitalist mode of production exists, although only in a formal sense, since the slavery of Negroes precludes free wage-labour, which is the basis of capitalist production. But the business in which slaves are used is conducted by *capitalists*. The method of production which they introduce has not arisen out of slavery but is grafted on to it.

—Karl Marx, *Theories of Surplus-Value*

Capitalist characteristics may also occur *sporadically*, as something which does not dominate society, at isolated points within earlier social formations.

—Karl Marx, *Capital: A Critique of Political Economy*, vol. 1

In the old steam boating days the typical Southerner was pictured as a ranting, roving blade, who wore a broad-brimmed Panama hat and a great watch-fob.

—Henry Watterson, "Oddities of Southern Life," 1882

Time was on the tongues of the four men waiting to take the stage-coach through South Carolina in 1853. Among them was the northerner Frederick Law Olmsted, at once a patient observer of the antebellum South and impatient traveler through it. The horses hushed, a fascinating debate over time took place. Having "took out a large silver hunting-watch," the driver asked his passengers "what time it was." "Quarter past eleven," said one of the men. "Twelve minutes past," countered another. "Well, fourteen, only, I am," offered the third. Olmsted proved correct. "Thirteen," he said. The driver agreed, and they were on their way.

Could this mild argument over the minute be carried on in the antebellum period by people other than northerners? Olmsted thought not and took satisfaction in discovering that all four men originated north of Mason and Dixon's line. For surely this concern with punctuality, this recognition of the timepiece as the true arbiter of time, could be born only of the most modern and progressive nineteenth-century society? And surely that society was the industrializing, free-wage-labor North, not the agricultural, slave South? But Olmsted himself revealed the fiction of such assumptions. Once his punctilious driver had delivered him in the Palmetto State's rice district, Olmsted, his eye always trained for detail, found the watch being applied to slave labor. "The ploughing gang," he observed of low-country slaves, "was superintended by a driver, who was provided with a watch; and while we were looking at them he called out that it was twelve o'clock. The mules were immediately taken from the ploughs, and the plough-boys mounting them, leapt the ditches, and cantered off to the stables, to feed them."[1] Certainly, the slaves, unlike the coach passengers, had little opportunity to debate the time, and, equally certain, the watch was northern made and as imported as the idea of clock time itself. But here it was: clock-regulated slave labor. That it appeared to be in, not of, the slave South hardly seemed to matter to the slaves, the driver, or the observer. How clock time came to be in the South, its impact on master and slave, and its meaning for our assessment of the Old South are, broadly, the subjects of this book.

Conversations about time, similar in both substance and meaning to the one recounted by Olmsted, were carried out throughout the nineteenth-century world. From Britain to South Africa, from the American North to Australia, industrial and urban managers and workers conceived of and used clock time as if it had "melted into the interstices of practical consciousness," as, indeed, it had.[2] Of all nineteenth-century societies, the literature suggests, only the American free-wage-labor North managed to inspire country dwellers to adopt, and in turn promote, clock consciousness.[3] But southern slaves and their masters were in advance of most of these societies because, along with their bucolic northern brethren, they were one of the few agricultural peoples in the nineteenth-century world to embrace clock time.

Writing on the historical evolution of time awareness has generally identified several key historical forces that served to promote a time consciousness among eighteenth- and nineteenth-century rural and, especially, industrial-urban managers and workers. With few exceptions, observers have viewed the emergence of time discipline and clock-regulated work as being intimately bound up with the emergence of capitalism.[4] If we accept the basic and relatively uncontroversial point that the larger forces of time's rationalization and commodification provided the cultural, intellectual, and economic impetus behind the rise of modern time discipline, then the specific historical developments that created a time consciousness among workers and managers in the nineteenth century probably consisted of the following. First was the dissemination of a mercantile conception of time stressing that while some time was God's, time was also money and that, as such, it should be saved, not wasted, for reasons sacred and, increasingly, secular.[5] Second, urban and factory clocks were increasingly used to regulate and coordinate personal, social, and economic temporal activity. Third, the number of clocks and watches in any given population increased. Finally, the advent of technologies such as the railroads disseminated urban, industrial, wage-labor time to the countryside and helped heighten a preexisting, though relatively vague, idea that clock time should be obeyed and that punctuality was a civic and personal virtue. In other words, these forces, which may have operated at different times and with differing degrees and potency in various constituencies, are the same ones that David Landes sketched in his explanation of the emergence of a modern clock consciousness.[6] These forces, it seems, increased in potency when articulated with the nineteenth century's belief in the legitimacy of free wage labor and so helped produce a world increasingly governed by the clock.

If such agencies behind the nineteenth century's drive toward clock time can be found in the antebellum South, can we assume that these forces in and of themselves were sufficient (for, plainly, they were necessary) to push the non-wage slave South toward the adoption of clock time? If so, was it just these forces alone that urged antebellum southern planters to put the clock in the field? Or was there something in the nature of antebellum slavery that encouraged planters to adopt time discipline and urged their bondpeople to do likewise?

Before reviewing the historical and theoretical literature on time consciousness in the slave South, it might be helpful to explain the essential premise of this study. At its simplest, this book views the antebellum slave South as containing important contradictions that, ostensibly at least, set it apart from the burgeoning nineteenth-century capitalist world marketplace. Thanks to several pioneering works, most notably those by Eugene D. Genovese, these contradictory impulses are well known. The slave-master paternalist relationship as well as the nature of the Old South's relationship to merchant capitalism were, according to Genovese, the main reasons why profit-oriented southern planters were forced to remain noncapitalist in an increasingly free-wage-labor, capitalist world.[7] Other equally excellent work, however, has shown that southern slavery contained seeds of modernist rationalization.[8] Southern planters were, by these accounts, not simply profit-motivated; they were successful at making money.[9] Even if we grant that they were less than wholly successful in making healthy profits, we may still argue that in their desire to make a profit from their chattel, antebellum southern planters were as capitalist-minded as bourgeois Yankees. As an economic system, slavery had always been based on commodity production and thus had always harbored commercial tendencies. Consequently, slavery's acquisitive aspect readily passed into profit maximization under modern, nineteenth-century world market conditions. But there is a real sense in which the social and political relations that were an integral part of this profit-oriented society set the region outside of modern capitalism. Although slave owners embraced a profit-oriented culture, they simultaneously retained an organic and hierarchical view of human relations. Fearful of what they perceived to be the mobocratic and anarchic tendencies of free wage labor and its eighteenth- and nineteenth-century handmaiden, liberal democracy, masters chose to retain slavery, eventually with a suicidal passion.

Planters, then, were caught in a dilemma.[10] They wanted to be perceived as modern, and they wanted to make money. This was true from the day those who became planters landed on colonial shores, and it explains why they grew the profitable staples that they did. But such men could not escape the fact that slavery was as much about social control as it was about economic profit. In short, slavery satisfied the demands of profit-oriented capitalism, but also, and just as important, it preserved planters' organic and hierarchical social order.

By the 1830s, however, the South's peculiar institution was coming under increasingly vitriolic attack by northern free-wage-labor advocates, usually in the guise of abolitionists. Slavery was attacked because it was perceived to be immoral, archaic, and out of step with nineteenth-century liberal capitalist forces. Short of jettisoning slavery as a social system, slaveholders were faced with a problem: how to modernize slavery so that it still satisfied the old capitalist-planter concerns with profit maximization, the preservation of strict social hierarchy, and their claim to modernity without inviting the dangerous democratic tendencies associated with modernization into their society.[11]

Historians have given several brilliant answers to this question. This book is a modest effort to add an answer to the list. It aims to show that planters' adoption of clock time during and after the 1830s as a legitimate arbiter of work and social organization satisfied simultaneously their drive for profit, their desire for discipline and social order, and, in the context of the first half of the nineteenth century, their claim to modernity. Because the clock could be used to regulate labor both socially and economically, it satisfied masters' profit culture and gave them a substantial base from which to describe themselves as modern. Clock time and the obedience and regularity it inspired among workers and their managers were, after all, among the litmus tests of modernity in all industrializing, free-wage-labor, capitalist societies. To share in this formulation of work and time meant that slave owners could also share in the title of modern and, by importing the clock, could accomplish all this without embracing a reckless and potentially dangerous free-wage-labor ideology. Slaveholders reckoned that, used properly, clock time could inspire discipline and obedience in a slave workforce that was always trying to upset plantation order and jeopardize planters' profits through individual and collective acts of resistance. Simultaneously tyrannical, modern, and profit-oriented, the nineteenth-century clock and its attendant ability to rationalize and order the behavior of human beings became the planters' weapon of choice in their ongoing battle with their chattel.

Of course, because slavery was not free wage labor, even clock-regulated antebellum slavery cannot lay a wholly convincing claim to the title of capitalist. In some respects, planters' use of clock time was more akin to what sociologist Chris Nyland has identified as the conception of time embodied in eighteenth-century mercantilist orthodoxy. According to Nyland, mercantilist theory stressed that the regulation of work time was of critical importance for economic prosperity because workers, like slaves, were "innately slothful, working only if forced to." Classical economists such as Adam Smith, however, reformulated work time conceptions by arguing that workers specifically, humans generally, "were not naturally lazy and that if they behaved as if they were it was because of insufficient motivation to do otherwise." Hence classical economists, the progenitors of free-wage-labor capitalism, could equate time with wage because they entertained a benign, liberal view of human nature whereby workers could be both regulated and motivated by time because they shared in the acquisitive spirit. Planters, in contrast, seem to have retained a more mercantilist notion of time primarily because they viewed slaves and laboring classes generally as indolent and because wages were irrelevant, indeed antithetical, to their society. But what should be stressed here is that mercantilist and free-wage-labor assessments of the use and role of time differed in form rather than substance. Mercantilism was a capitalist system, and it differed from Smithian liberalism only inasmuch as it held a more pessimistic view of human nature. Planters' time conceptions, then, were not precapitalist in this sense; they were merely preclassical.[12]

Historical reality, of course, rarely accords precisely with theoretical formulations, and the planter-as-preclassical one is no exception. Not only was the shift from mercantilist orthodoxy to classical economic thought protracted, tortured, and much debated with many precursors and just as many vestiges; not only did some of the antebellum South's most famous proslavery thinkers actually find something of value in Smith's *Wealth of Nations*, but no few northern and British industrial capitalists remained as skeptical of their laborers' work ethic as slaveholders did of their slaves'.[13] Although there is evidence to suggest that antebellum masters introduced incentive and bonus systems to their plantations (thus qualifying their essential distrust of slaves' ability to develop an acquisitive ethic), it seems that eighteenth- and nineteenth-century industrial capitalists occasionally shared slaveholders' fundamental view of workers as inherently slothful and reluctant to labor unless forced to.[14] Certainly, the earliest British factory managers (those operating before the general ascendancy of Smithian political economy) timed their workers but did so out of a profound distrust. The "Law Book" of the Crowley Iron Works from 1700, for example, "ordered that no person upon the account doth reckon by any other clock, bell, watch or dyall but the Monitor's, which clock is never to be altered but by the clock-keeper."[15] These earliest industrial capitalists, then, were as reluctant as antebellum masters to allow their workers the freedom to negotiate that most precious of commodities, time. Crowley's owners thought workers did not respect time, would not respond positively to time-wage incentives, and so were hardly entitled to participate in its everyday application and formulation. Indeed, as David Brody has shown, the practice of managers monopolizing time in northern factories and prohibiting workers from bargaining over time was not uncommon even during the antebellum period.[16] On some important points, then, industrial capitalists and antebellum slave owners sometimes agreed: both harbored, to varying degrees, a distrust and suspicion of workers, slave and free. Neither laborer, so it seemed, would work diligently unless coerced to some extent, and a monopoly over time, who owned it, and who set its value helped ensure this control.[17] As owners of capital, the slave-owning and industrial classes held much in common, and any differences are best measured in degrees, not absolutes.[18]

This is not to suggest, however, that the degrees separating masters of capital, North and South, should be ignored. They were, after all, sufficient to put both classes on very different political trajectories. While southern masters occasionally treated their slaves as likely to respond to incentives, most often they clung to a preclassical view of workers, black ones especially. And while northern managers no doubt harbored a distrust of their wage slaves, they erred on the side of believing that laborers shared in a work ethic that embodied "the prospect of quick profit [which] would do more 'to reduce a People to a habit of Prudence and Industry than is possible to be effected by Whip, or Hunger or by all the penal laws, that can be Invented for the Suppressing of Idleness.' "[19] Although this guarded optimism was a thin veneer that barely concealed managers' ultimate willingness to punish the tardy where it hurt most (in the pocket and, by extension, the stomach), all too readily this essentially late eighteenth-century, Smithian view of human nature found sustenance in the emergence of northern democratizing capitalism in and after the 1830s. In the last three decades of the antebellum period especially, northern factory managers seemed more willing than ever to negotiate with their newly enfranchised workforce about time, its relationship to wages, and its essential worth and definition. Northern industrial capitalism began to be conceived by managers and, albeit reluctantly, by workers, as the freedom to sell one's labor power.[20] Managers, then, in adopting clock time as a measure of labor, imposed on themselves an obligation to debate the worth of their workers' time. But as E. P. Thompson demonstrated for industrializing England, managers benefited from engaging in such negotiations. By debating clock time and its implicit equation with wage, workers came to legitimize the capitalist argument that labor power could be reduced to clock time and all the efficiency gains that that reduction entailed. Time-wage negotiations essentially brought the watch-owning and clock-listening working class under the ideological umbrella of industrial capitalism by teaching them the language and worth of clock time.[21]

But here antebellum northern industrialists and southern masters parted otherwise close company. Masters, because they wanted capitalism without democracy (at least in its northern guise), refused, insofar as they were able, to negotiate the worth of their slaves' time. Time, after all, was the master's, as it had to be in a slave society. Clock- and watch-owning slaves would too easily become time-negotiating workers, and so, planters feared, the thin edge of the mobocratic wedge would make its way south. Alternatively, slaveholders aimed to make their bondpeople obey clock time without straddling the time-negotiating line that had been breached by the northern bourgeoisie. In other words, southern masters aimed simply to impose clock time, as the managers of the Crowley Iron Works had done in 1700. The next step, when workers "formed their short-time committees in the ten-hour movement," looked distinctly dangerous, the point at which laborers "struck for overtime or time-and-a-half" positively anarchic. Moreover, if we are to credit the sincerity of some proslavery ideologues, it was not healthy for the slaves either.[22] Of course, the price to pay for remaining preclassical, for, as it were, stopping at Crowley, was that slaveholders were required to develop alternative ways to render bondpeople as clock obedient as free workers were clock disciplined. Many of their answers were drawn, simultaneously, from the safety of the past and cherry-picked, carefully and gingerly, from their present. And these alternatives answered their dilemma fairly successfully.

If we step back from the larger theoretical debate over what constitutes capitalism, we see a slave society that used the clock, the time it kept, and the rational obedience it enforced among its workers to such practical effect that the actual distance between, say, nineteenth-century northern modernity and antebellum planter capitalism was more apparent than real. To be sure, premodern impulses remained in the slave South as they did in every modernizing nineteenth-century society; hence the gerund. Because modernization was a process, premodern legacies and modern innovations lived side by side as, in fact, one would expect and as, indeed, E. P. Thompson demonstrated some while ago.[23] But in the final analysis, southern slaves and, later, freedpeople, as well as their antebellum masters and New South employers, acted so much like time-obedient workers and clock-conscious capitalists that, with but a few qualifications, they may justly be called modernizing, if not modern. If the Old South was not capitalist in the strictest, free-wage-labor sense, it was nonetheless modern in its commitment to, and understanding of, clock time.

When they have considered the matter at all, historians of the American slave South have judged southerners' attitudes toward time to be task-oriented, naturally derived, and hence premodern. By most accounts, eighteenth- and nineteenth-century southerners considered nature's rhythms, not the clock, the legitimate arbiter of work and social organization. There is a general, if rarely articulated, belief that if nineteenth-century Americans experienced anything like the protracted shift to a clock discipline apparent in other industrializing nations, they were to be found in northern factories, not on southern plantations. In his seminal 1974 study, *Roll, Jordan, Roll*, Eugene Genovese explained why:

> The planters' problem came to this: . . . How could they instill factorylike discipline into a working population engaged in a rural system that, for all

its tendencies toward modern discipline, remained bound to the rhythms of nature and to traditional ideas of work, time, and leisure? . . . The slaves could and did work hard, as their African ancestors had before them. . . . But they resisted that regularity and routine which became the *sine qua non* for industrial society and which the planters, despite their own rejection of so much of the bourgeois work ethic, tried to impose upon them.

But if slaveholders did attempt to instill a "factorylike" time discipline in their bondpeople, if slaves did manage successfully to resist clock time regularity and routine, Genovese and those who have accepted his interpretation have provided scant documentation to illustrate how and why.[24]

This oversight is especially unfortunate because it has tended to create the impression that there was precious little clock consciousness in the antebellum South. Although much excellent scholarship has recently been produced on time conceptions and the historical, often protracted interfacing of clock-regulated and seasonal labor for several other countries, the historical study of time in the South still rests on the tacit assumption that clock time was alien to the region.[25]

Why this should be the case is not altogether clear. I would, however, hazard to suggest five reasons why historians of the Old South, like Genovese, have insisted that colonial and antebellum southerners embraced a premodern and largely natural time orientation. First, because Genovese's larger concern was to demonstrate that slaves' various strategies of resistance successfully prevented progress-minded planters from joining the burgeoning capitalist marketplace and because slaveholders were forced to remain merely *in* not *of* the capitalist Atlantic system, Genovese may well have assumed that the whole question of time, how planters used and defined it, how slaves resisted it, and what this meant for the antebellum South's economic development, fitted the contours of his larger thesis. In *Roll, Jordan, Roll*, Genovese assumes (but, uncharacteristically, does not demonstrate) that although planters themselves entertained a modern conception of time, slaves' resistance to its imposition rendered clock time, for southerners as a whole, irrelevant. Genovese contends that the southern plantation "setting remained rural, and the rhythms of work followed seasonal fluctuations. Nature remained the temporal reference point for the slaves."[26] He also argues: "The black work ethic grew up within a wider Protestant Euro-American community with a work ethic of its own. The black ethic represented at once a defense against an enforced system of economic exploitation and an autonomous assertion of value generally associated with preindustrial values. As such, it formed part of a more general southern work ethic, which developed in antagonism to that of the wider American society."[27]

Genovese then concludes that planters' appeal to clock time convinced neither themselves nor their slaves: "The slaveholders operated in a capitalist world market, they presided over the production of commodities, and they had to pay attention to profit-and-loss statements. Consequently, they developed a strong commitment to the Puritan work ethic—but only so far as their slaves were concerned. Slaves ought to be steady, regular, continent, disciplined clock-punchers." Convinced of blacks' innate indolence, however, masters "decided that blacks could not work steadily and so concluded that they ought not expect them to."[28]

The second reason behind southern historians' apparent acceptance of this thesis may be found in their reliance on E. P. Thompson's seminal essay, "Time, Work-Discipline and Industrial Capitalism," which led them to apply a model of the emergence of a modern time sensibility and its relationship to capitalism that does not fit the slave South very well.[29] Thompson, after all, detailed the dialectical battle between nineteenth-century English factory workers' preindustrial, natural time consciousness with a modern, factory-inspired time discipline. He argued that because factory workers came to own watches and because they were co-opted by managers' ministrations concerning the relationship between time and wage, workers reluctantly relinquished their natural time sensibility, replacing it with a modern, internalized respect for time, or a clock discipline that nurtured an "inward notation of time."[30] We must be careful, however, not to apply wholesale Thompson's pioneering but brittle task-orientation/time-discipline model to a slave society in which it is not always clear whether there were any Puritan-inspired managers, work was to no small degree seasonal and diurnal, and the workers had no access to mechanical timepieces which, according to both Thompson and Genovese, is an important prerequisite for internalizing a time discipline. As Genovese put it: "However much the slaveholders might have wished to transform their slaves into clock-punchers, they could not, for in a variety of senses both literal and metaphoric, there were no clocks to punch."[31]

The belief that mechanical timepieces were nonexistent in the antebellum South leads to the third reason why the idea of a predominantly natural southern time consciousness has persisted in historical writings. Although the mechanical timepiece itself is no guarantor of time discipline, clocks and watches are nonetheless necessary for the accurate timing of labor generally and unskilled work especially.[32] While the cultural attitude toward time and ideas about its application distinguishes different types of time conceptions, the characteristic of time under capitalism is that clocks, watches, and a rational economic use of time are necessary for time discipline to exist. In noncapitalist modes of production, where substantial numbers of people may feasibly own clocks and watches, the timepiece can represent any number of phenomena without necessarily indicating a belief in the clock or watch as the legitimate arbiter of time and work. But as Karl Marx suggested, under capitalism, the mechanical timepiece takes on added significance. Mechanically regulated time acquires a fetishistic quality and the communicator of mechanical time, the bell, develops a despotic, commanding power.[33] Under capitalism, the town clock still denotes piety to many, and people buy clocks to assert a kind of hearth-based morality. But cobbled on to these notions is an ever more potent conviction that time is also a secular and decontextualized phenomenon; that the clock and watch can represent labor, money, and a means to increase the level and rate of exploitation. The aim of the capitalist is to ensure workers' respect for the clock as the true judge of work and time, something that, in E. P. Thompson's view, requires the annihilation of workers' commitment to old-style time consciousness, which derives its legitimacy primarily from nature and a task-oriented view of labor. The process of grafting an internalized respect for the clock or time discipline onto a noncapitalist, task-oriented temporal consciousness hints at a predetermined victory for clock time, even though that victory may never be absolute. In industrializing England, for instance, this victory was won by clock-conscious factory managers who successfully promoted a respect for the clock among a nascent proletariat through exhortations concerning time thrift, wage incentives, and fines for clock-defined lateness. Although the battle over time in the American South shared some of these characteristics, it was, for a variety of reasons, different. Masters, in short, owned time, clocks, and watches; slaves did not.

Fourth, although it is misleading to characterize antebellum southerners' attitude toward time as predominantly natural, observers of the colonial South are far nearer the truth when they make such claims.[34] But treating colonial and antebellum southern time sensibilities as monolithic has, perhaps, blinkered us to the emergence of a southern clock-defined time awareness that matured from its dormant state in the eighteenth century to an energized and germinated form during and after the 1830s.

Finally, the point needs to be stressed that the presence or even predominance of natural time in a society does not necessarily preclude the existence of a potent and powerful mechanical conception of time. The South was, without doubt, a society born in nature's diurnal womb and suckled on her agricultural and crop-producing climate and geography. But clock time and natural time were never mutually exclusive in the South. Rather, they were complementary. As Michael O'Malley has pointed out, the clock itself can be viewed as nature's motif, as embodying seasonal rhythms and epitomizing celestial piety, and seasonal agriculture can resemble the push against time and engender the frenetic work habits usually associated with industrial time discipline.[35] Some observers, however, have overlooked the intimacy shared by the clock and nature. Richard D. Brown's perspective, for example, is revealing. He writes of seventeenth-century New England farmers: "Old seasonal routines characterized most farm activities. . . . Only during harvest times were the hours lengthy. . . . Racing against the sun and the rain, communities turned out to bring in the crop." Despite acknowledging the push against time inherent in nature, Brown nevertheless insists that "concepts of efficiency, of 'time thrift,' seem to have been almost entirely alien to gentlemen, merchants, artisans, and farmers, whether Anglican or Puritan." If Brown is right, his historical actors frequently behaved in ways they either did not understand or decided to ignore. Men and women less romantically inclined knew too well the need for the best use of time against nature's seasonal push. This, in short, is why they "raced" against time.[36] Once people began to pace themselves against natural time, the tendency to race against clock time was a logical step requiring no great conceptual or intellectual revolution. What it would require, however, was the presence of clocks and watches and, equally as important, new ideas concerning their use and application. The real battle would take place on the literal and metaphoric field of indoctrination, inculcating this clock-defined conception of time in others who were committed to naturally defined and culturally specific time. And it was in the very essence of this battle that ideas about who owned time, who defined time, and, ultimately, who was free from and slave to time, took place.

Once it is allowed that nature's diurnal round can be frenetic and driving, it takes no leap of faith to believe that clock time can be readily accommodated to, and incorporated in, this broader temporal rhythm. This accommodation in turn can serve to reduce nature's rhythm to smaller units of time that people can understand and apply at the everyday level of social and economic interaction. What was previously defined by the sun's movement across the sky is broken up into smaller fragments by the mechanical timepiece. Pristine solar time becomes, in other words, measurable and reducible to mechanical time; nature-bound work rhythms are freed, joined, and ultimately enveloped by the clock's. The solar day still exists in both physical reality and peoples' minds and consciousness. What the clock and watch add to this broader, natural time awareness is a more minute and measurable unit of time that exists, surrogatelike, within natural time. Very likely, without the presence of solar time, the clock finds no niche in which to fit, which perhaps explains why industrial clock time necessarily leads on from a long-held familiarity with natural time.[37] In other words, if we are to delineate the emergence of a mechanical time sensibility in any setting, we must be as sensitive to the presence and essence of natural time rhythms as we are to the appearance and social significance of clocks and watches.

Precisely how the two forms of time measurement gel and coexist depends on the social and economic relations extant in a particular society. Under conventional industrial capitalism, natural time appears to be subordinated to clock time because artificial light and enclosed factory buildings are almost independent of nature. Accordingly, the types of time regulators used in such settings are also less contingent on nature.[38] In a predominantly agricultural society that, for various reasons, adopts clock time, natural and mechanical time are inevitably more interdependent because agricultural production is reliant on sun and season even though the labor employed in this mode of production might well be partly clock regulated. Because historians of the slave South have slighted this interdependency of clock and sun, because they have followed the theoretical frameworks constructed by historians concerned with the much more rapid and comparatively more straightforward ascendancy of clock time in conventionally capitalist societies, they have paid much attention to the presence of natural time. In doing so, they have assumed that because the slave South was agricultural and necessarily seasonal the region did not embrace mechanical time, that southerners did not use clocks, and, ergo, that the region was doomed to remain merely in, not of, the capitalist marketplace. What, after all, it is implied, would a southern cotton planter want with clocks and watches? This logic, in turn, has led observers to assume that clocks and watches at any time of the South's history were rare; the modern, clock-dependent personality even rarer.

But such assumptions ignore the history of the human battles over time and its definition that took place in the South. If the conflict between task orientation and time discipline, between natural and clock time as defined, instigated, and acted out by men and women is to emerge in any historical context or to have any historical meaning, then at least some of the actors involved in the conflict must own timepieces and have the intellectual wherewithal to use them as tools of power.[39] Moreover, at the larger, ontological level, it is widely agreed that the modern compulsion to obey time has been instigated by the mechanical timepiece, not just by nature. For the modern tyranny of time to exist, in other words, clocks and watches must exist either in conjunction with or in attempted defiance of natural time rhythms.[40] And the reason for this is simple and strikes at the heart of why clock time was so very important to a slave society.

All that the invention and subsequent use of clocks did was bestow a conditional and highly contingent power on man over nature. By setting events against the clock and, in fact, setting the clock itself, people could insinuate their own temporal definitions within nature's round. This ability to define clock time has, to complacent modern eyes, set man over nature. Not so from the viewpoints of eighteenth- and, especially, nineteenth-century southern masters, however. People of those eras understood that mechanical time was always employed within a diurnal round that could upset events defined by the clock. But what the ownership and understanding of the clock did bestow was power: specifically, the power to set the actions of others, even the behavior of oneself, against artificial, mechanical time. Like every other propertied class, masters coveted both profit and the social control of labor, and thus any additional forms or tools of power would always be welcome in the ongoing effort to regulate the behavior and productivity of chattel. Nature, after all, controlled master and slave. If masters could interpose and create another, albeit conditional, tool to control the slave without jeopardizing their own power and independence, then plainly the disparity between free and unfree, between master and slave, would be further accentuated. In this process of accentuation, the master's freedom would be more crisply defined, his power consolidated, and his workforce rendered more efficient and obedient. And if the use of the clock gave nineteenth-century slave owners the added bonus of being considered modern, this was all to the good.

But the power-hungry often make mistakes and pay hidden costs in their quest for mastery. Southern slaveholders were no exception. Once they had introduced clock time to their society, once mechanical time was added to nature as another, legitimate arbiter of social and economic organization, southern masters came to find themselves threatened not only by the forces that helped them embrace clock time but also by the mental and corporeal clock they had invented. By the mid-nineteenth century, rushing against the clock had become a way of life for most white southerners. It was a dependency their own experience as masters made them acutely aware of. In some respects, their great experiment backfired. They were determined to regulate the labor and behavior of slaves by the clock, but the introduction of the infernal machine into their organic society had some unintended consequences. Because no master could seriously countenance the widespread ownership of clocks and watches among slaves, because slaves' time was, by definition, masters' time, masters somehow had to invent a method to regulate a slave workforce that had no watches. In this instance, their efforts succeeded. Certainly slave culture and behavior in the late antebellum period were more attuned to clock time than in previous years. But the sun and stars were still apparent in the minds of bondpeople as, indeed, they were in the minds of masters themselves. The difference between masters' and slaves' time conceptions, however, was in degrees, not absolutes. For watch and clock ownership had both created and reinforced among masters a time discipline, an internal sense of time that commanded that they act in accordance with the clock. For slaves, clock time was important but, during the antebellum period at least, it was not internalized. Ironically, while they may have obeyed the sound of clock time, African Americans' internalization of clock time had to await freedom. Masters, however, had much earlier become enslaved by a power they themselves had helped create for the purposes of furthering their profits and their mastery. By 1860 they would have sympathized with Georg Lukács's assessment of the tyrannical nature of clock time in the twentieth century: "Through the subordination of man to the machine the situation arises in which men are effaced by their labor; in which the pendulum of the clock has become as accurate a measure of the relative activity of two workers as it is of the speed of two locomotives. . . . Time is everything, man is nothing; he is at the most the incarnation of time." Delight though they did in leisurely pursuits, masters did so in a context defined increasingly by the clock.[41] In a very real sense, then, this study is as much about the clock's mastery of masters and southerners generally as it is about masters' mastery of slaves through the clock.

Certain assumptions concerning southerners' understanding of time, then, not only have hampered the study of time in the slave South but have tended to deny that study altogether. Because the southern application of clock time to labor was necessarily different from the form instigated by, say, industrial capitalists in northern and British free-wage-labor factories and because, as Marx pointed out, the imperatives of free-wage-labor capitalism dictate that only identical duplicates of its pristine model can be considered truly capitalist, the southern slave owners' version of plantation clock time was either overlooked by contemporaries and, later, historians, or dismissed as something alien to and more primitive than capitalism.[42] But, as I will argue, flawed and idiosyncratic though it necessarily was, the southern application of clock time and the practical effects it instigated were akin to the type of time employed under nineteenth-century industrial capitalism.

To explain why this was the case, this study of the emergence of a modern, clock-dependent time sensibility among antebellum southerners generally, planters particularly, and how this in turn affected slaves' perceptions of time begins by articulating Thompson's model with one that notes the continued and enduring presence of a natural time understanding coupled not to a time discipline but to something which may be termed time obedience. Used here, time obedience refers to a respect for mechanical time among workers that, unlike time discipline, is not internalized but rather enforced or imposed by time-conscious planter-managers through the threat or use of violence or through the constant repetition of mechanically defined time through sound as with the chiming of clock-regulated bells. Whereas industrial time discipline was the product of a protracted fight between managers' efforts to get clock- and watch-owning workers to internalize a Puritan-inspired respect for the clock, time obedience was characteristic of the slave South, its presence revealing an ongoing if at times one-sided battle to force slaves to respect, at least outwardly, mechanically regulated time. Just as medieval European church clocks had "regulated the movements of the town with militant imperiousness," so southern slave owners of the antebellum period came to apply an essentially preindustrial association of time with sound to their plantations for the capitalist purpose of promoting social order and economic efficiency.[43] Southern bondpeople, very much like nineteenth-century industrial workers, found themselves either timed directly by the planter's field watch or, just as effectively, by the sound of a clock-regulated plantation bell. Unlike factory workers, however, southern slaves were denied access to the mechanical time-piece, which was to have important implications for their understanding of and resistance to clock time.

This study, then, urges a reevaluation of the usefulness of the concept of time discipline and its relationship to the changing contours of nascent capitalism, attempts to heighten our sensitivity to the assimilated, engrafted nature of capitalism in the South, and, in the process, reevaluates our understanding of southern time sensibilities.[44] I argue, in effect, that the slave South was one of the few rural regions of the nineteenth-century world to be affected by a modern clock consciousness with only parts of the rural North having a similarly advanced understanding of time.[45] The reasons for this are twofold. First, the slave South either shared or imported all the forces that had promoted time discipline in other nineteenth-century societies. Second, what it did not import, what it refused to share—free wage labor in factory or agricultural form—did not matter as much as we have perhaps assumed. The impulses inherent in late antebellum slavery were both necessary and sufficient to push both masters and their chattel toward a clock consciousness and time obedience that was little different from and in some ways more advanced than the free-wage-labor form.[46] The whip and the sound of time proved just as effective in the South as the Puritan work ethic/free-wage-labor/industrial combination had been elsewhere in rendering master and slave obedient to and cognizant of clock time.

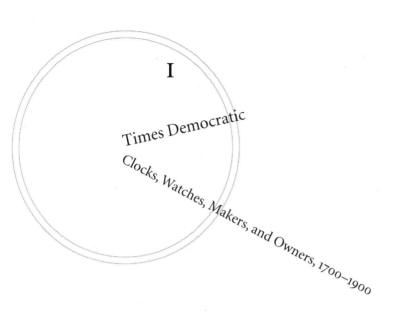

I

Times Democratic

Clocks, Watches, Makers, and Owners, 1700–1900

The principal churches are those of St. Philip and St. Michael of
the Anglicans, adorned by towers with clocks.
—*Luigi Castiglioni's Viaggio*, 1785–87

You often hear people say, "This watch cost me ten hogsheads of
tobacco."
—Marquis de Chastellux, 1782

It is said that the house of every substantial farmer in the days
following the Revolution had three ornaments—a polyglot
bible, a tin reflector and a wooden clock.
—Richardson Wright, *Hawkers and Walkers*, 1927

B urdened still by the legacy of slavery, by popular misconceptions concerning southerners' putative indifference toward clock time, and by the stereotype of Colored Peoples' Time, the antebellum American South is often portrayed as preindustrial and task oriented, a place where slavery, the absence of extensive wage-labor relations, and the predominance of agriculture and nature's attendant diurnal round conspired to render southerners either apathetic toward or unable to institute clock time.[1] Even historians who see southern slave owners as efficiency-minded planter-capitalists have not countenanced the possibility that the use of clocks and watches may have been one means used to achieve that end.[2] This oversight is unfortunate not only because it has tended to preclude the study of time in the South but also because it has denied the existence of one of the South's most democratic and universal features: the presence of publicly accessible time and an increasing shift toward the ownership of private time in the form of clocks and watches.

Before entering into any discussion of how clocks and watches were used and applied in the South we must know how available such technology was to southerners over time and place.[3] This chapter demonstrates, albeit for a geographically circumscribed area, that substantial numbers of white southerners did own affordable mechanical timepieces and examines the ways in which clocks and watches, public and private, were made available.[4]

Both before and during the period when significant numbers of southerners came to own clocks and watches, they also had access to public sources of time. Even slaves, who ordinarily did not own clocks or watches, had access to public time, the presence of which constituted one of the South's most democratic features, not just in cities but in the countryside.[5] Church clocks and the bells used to communicate this time were the South's most accessible form of public time. Although pinpointing the origins of the region's first church clocks is difficult, it is believed that in "1720, the first clocks were introduced to be placed in churches, the hour glass having been previously used."[6] Evidence suggests that a modest but significant number of eighteenth-century southern churches had bells and clocks installed. Of the sixty colonial South Carolina churches built before 1800, for example, we know that at least four had bells and that three housed bells and clocks.[7]

Public clocks, North and South, were, even by modern standards, considered well made and reasonably accurate. One Nantucket clock displaying not just the time but also the declination of sun and moon showed but a ten-day error "after 40 years." Of an eighteenth-century clock found in Yorktown in 1894 it was said, "Despite its 112 years the old clock keeps good time. It strikes

12 sometimes when it should strike 1. . . . Modern clocks have been known to be as erratic."[8]

Colonial and antebellum southern cities and ports, as might be expected, had the greatest share of church clocks. Bells and a clock, for example, were ordered for Charleston's St. Michael's in 1764 from London. And in 1849 the city's St. Philip's Episcopal Church, "through the liberality of a wealthy and benevolent donor," was "furnished with a clock and chimes."[9] In fact, St. Philip's had bells as early as 1710, and, according to a report in the *Gentleman's Magazine* in 1753, the church also sported a multifaceted clock. In 1766 itinerant Anglican minister Charles Woodmason described the church as having "a Cupola of 50 feet, with two Bells, and a Clock and Bell." Fire in 1835 and the Civil War divested the church of clock and bells but only temporarily.[10] Nor were Charleston's Anglican churches the only ones to have clocks. On June 26, 1804, James Badger was paid "for Cleaning & Varnishing and Gilding Work to the Dial Clock of the Old Church now fixed in the New Independent Congregational Church" in Charleston. On October 10 of that year Bethel Threadcraft was paid to repair the clock.[11] And landscape drawings and paintings of Charleston from the nineteenth century depict church clocks dominating the skyline of the city.[12]

Church clocks were not confined to Charleston. They were to be found throughout the eighteenth and nineteenth centuries in both rural and urban regions of the South.[13] Although the number of colonial and antebellum southern churches with clocks and bells is unclear, the little work that has been done on the subject generally suggests that church clocks and bells were not uncommon.[14] At the very least, rural churches often had bells with which to communicate either private watch or clock time to their congregations. Of the thirty-one churches built in Laurens County, South Carolina, from 1706 to 1882, for example, four, or 13 percent, had bells installed.[15]

Although less common, sundials provided another source of public time. Admittedly, there does not appear to have been an abundance of sundials in the South. Few, for example, were advertised in the region's newspapers or agricultural journals. One surviving sundial from Norfolk, Virginia, dated 1709 might explain why. It was made in England but for reading at a latitude of thirty-seven degrees—precisely the latitude of Norfolk. Plainly it was easier to export clocks and watches that were independent of varying colonial latitudes rather than manufacture a multiplicity of sundials with individual latitude engravings for each colonial outpost. Only by the late 1850s did America begin to manufacture its own sundials. Again, however, the market must have been small given the ready availability of domestic and foreign clocks and watches.[16]

Secular sources of public time were provided by the South's county court-

St. Michael's Church and clock,
Charleston, South Carolina
(© Tina Manley, 1996)

houses. In Charleston in 1806, bids were invited for "making and fixing on the front of the Court-House in this City, a complete *South Vertical* SUN DIAL."[17] Most of Virginia's colonial and antebellum courthouses had bells and cupolas and most, at one time or another, housed public clocks. Courthouse clocks existed in Essex, Prince William, Culpeper, Loudon, Pittsylvania, and Botetourt County courthouses dating from the seventeenth and eighteenth centuries.[18] So too elsewhere. The Hillsborough County, North Carolina, courthouse housed a British clock in 1805. The clock had been moved from nearby St. Matthew's Church, where it had been kept since 1764.[19] And Richmond's "Bell Tower," like other secular structures, was refurbished during the 1850s and was "summounted by a Clock and Bell."[20]

If public sources of clock time were available to eighteenth- and nineteenth-century southerners, so, too, increasingly were privately owned clocks and watches. Much, too much perhaps, has been made of the social and cultural value often attached to clock or watch ownership. While colonial southerners may have been more concerned with the ornamental than were their antebellum counterparts, when it came to clocks and watches, the mechanical timepiece was always aesthetic but functional.[21] In short, though it has been argued that the mechanical timepiece "was first a mechanical curiosity, then a toy, bauble, or article of adornment, and finally, at long last, a serious time-piece," in the American South the clock or watch was always a statement of fashion, a talisman of cultural capital and social status, and, simultaneously, an instrument of precision and of necessity. Rolex owners of the twentieth cen-tury no doubt understand this dual significance.[22]

That clock and watch ownership always had a cultural dimension and status value is clear from advertisements by colonial jewelers. In 1752, for example, James Rutherford, "a regular-bred gold and silver smith," arrived in Charles-ton, South Carolina, offering to make and mend watches "after the best and newest fashions." Rutherford stressed his European background in his sales pitch.[23] And English clock makers understood well Americans' penchant for the aesthetic timepiece. As London merchant Thomas Slater explained to Charleston planter John Ball Sr. in 1812: "I have seen a Clock maker who has informed me he can make you a very good Clock of the best materials & workmanship . . . but he dont recommend it to shew the Moons-age—but the time & day of the month only, he says such Clocks are only made for shew & Exportation."[24]

Clocks and watches never lost their aesthetic and cultural value. Watches were advertised during the 1770s as "elegant," as "used in the politest places in England," being "all new-fashioned, and highly finished."[25] Likewise, in 1782, Alexander Hamilton proposed to tax "clocks, watches and other similar items of luxury," as did Congress in 1815.[26] "A handsome sixteen day Clock, of the newest fashion," and "an elegant Gold Watch" were peddled in 1806, as were "elegant" watch seals and "an elegant Eight Day Clock" in 1820. By the 1830s "Fancy hard-Ware" stores were still stocking elegant chronometers.[27]

Elegant, fashionable, and genteel though they were, timepieces also became precise, especially after the invention of the lever watch escapement by Thomas Mudge in 1750 which rendered mechanical timekeeping more accurate than it had been with the use of the comparatively simpler cylinder escapement.[28] As early as the 1750s, for instance, almanacs offered elaborate explanations of how to reset watches and clocks that had run down using the sun and various astronomical tables.[29] Advertisements by jewelers are also suggestive of an increasing concern with accurate time telling. John Clayton of Charleston told readers that he would "clean, mend, repair . . . either plain or repeating . . . clocks and watches." Significantly, he guaranteed his work.[30] New adjectives to describe timepieces also entered advertising parlance. As always, clocks and watches were elegant and "of the latest fashion," but descriptions conveying precision as well as good taste began to appear in the 1750s. "A good eight-day clock" was peddled in January 1752, and a eulogy to George Graham, "clock and watch maker," in the April 20, 1752, *South Carolina Gazette* suggests that advertisements touting watches as "Graham's make" were not only indicative of high-brow taste but also of high-quality chronometers. John Paul Grimké's advertisement of one such Graham watch in August 1752, for example, takes on additional meaning when it is apparent that colonial southerners respected Graham's timepieces not only for their beauty but for their "degree of perfection [in] the mensuration [*sic*] of time . . . never before attained."[31]

In the 1760s, advertisements stressing both the ornamentation and accuracy of watches were still common.[32] The reason is straightforward: white southerners were anxious that their watches worked, kept good time, and could be repaired when necessary. When, in March 1774, Philip Vickers Fithian of Virginia awoke to find "the Main Spring of my Watch either unhook'd or broke," he complained, "As there is no oppertunity [*sic*] here of having her refitted, I seem in considerable difficulty." Similarly, William Ancrum, Charleston merchant, was obliged to inform his backcountry overseer that the watch he had sent him to be repaired in 1777 "is not yet in proper Order."[33]

Needless to say, this penchant for aesthetic but accurate and reliable timepieces was hardly likely to abate by the early national or antebellum periods. By the late 1850s, in fact, the burgeoning American watch manufacturing industry pioneered by the Waltham Watch Company in Massachusetts took the position that its products were superior to foreign ones precisely because they were not luxurious. As one advertisement had it: "THE ONLY ENTIRELY SATISFACTORY PROOF OF A GOOD WATCH IS THAT IT TELLS CORRECTLY, AND WITHOUT INTERRUPTION, THE TRUE TIME OF DAY. All other tests are illusory."[34]

That colonial and antebellum southerners had access to mechanical timepieces at all was attributable first to the region's merchants, who imported a variety of clocks and watches to the South from Europe and the North throughout the colonial and antebellum periods, and, second, to nineteenth-century clock and watch peddlers.

Colonial newspaper advertisements reveal the high level of importation of timepieces from Europe in the eighteenth century. Jeweler John Paul Grimké of Charleston dealt with European makers directly and advertised silver watches "just imported from London" throughout 1743.[35] Similarly, general merchants included orders for clocks, watches, and timepiece paraphernalia in their wholesale orders to Europe. Georgia merchants Russell & Clayton ordered two watch keys for planter William Gibbons in 1764, for example. For fixing his clocks and watches, however, Gibbons appears to have employed local artisans, including one craftsman who "Mend[ed] a Clock at Plantation."[36] Similarly, in 1774, Charleston merchant Josiah Smith ordered a watch directly from London. For Smith it was a worthwhile purchase because "it seems to keep time and I hope will hold out my lifetime."[37] Northern-made or imported watches were also exported or reexported to the South. In 1796, for instance, John Ball Sr. of Charleston District paid $125.50 for a gold watch from New York.[38] And early nineteenth-century merchants in Fredericktown, Maryland, imported clock parts from the North and Europe presumably for local repairers or assemblers.[39]

The South's dependency on foreign- and, increasingly, northern-made watches and clocks continued into the antebellum period. Marlboro County, South Carolina, merchant James Barentine, for example, imported "1 Watch Gard" for Malcolm McRae in 1852.[40] Between March 27 and December 24, 1817, general merchant John Rodgers, of Unionville, South Carolina, ordered a total of nine watch keys and seals for his up-country clients either from Charleston wholesalers or from northern watch manufacturers.[41]

By the 1850s, rural general store owners were providing similar services. G. D. Smith of Newberry, South Carolina, for example, made a total of twenty-two transactions with local customers for clocks and watches between August 1, 1858, and July 20, 1859. Of these, exactly half were for purchasing watches, the other half for miscellaneous watch equipment such as guards and keys.[42] And from their plantations, planters found it convenient to include clocks and watches in their orders to their factors. Virginia planter Richard Eppes, for example, asked his Petersburg factors to get him a clock in December 1851.[43]

By the early nineteenth century, southern merchants began to encounter stiff competition from transplanted Yankee peddlers who roamed southern towns and hamlets selling and repairing foreign and northern timepieces. These itinerant journeymen were perhaps most responsible for making clocks and watches available to nineteenth-century rural settlers, planters, and farmers. By the late 1800s, these men still serviced the South's rural communities.[44]

Peddlers and various import taxes notwithstanding, nineteenth-century southerners still imported considerable numbers of timepieces from Europe. Taxes on timepieces at both the local and international levels were apparently common in the nineteenth century. One 1815 North Carolina statute placed a two dollar tax on every gold watch in individual possession, a dollar on each silver one.[45] But tariffs on foreign timepieces hardly lessened the flood or the domestic demand for clocks and watches. Despite the provisions of the tariff of 1842, which added clocks and watches to its ad valorem duties, Americans imported $30,806 worth of "chronometers and clocks" in 1845, most of them from Britain.[46] In a further effort to protect the North's nascent timepiece industry, the 1846 tariff upped the duties on "clocks and parts of clocks."[47] In the short run at least, it did not work. The value of chronometer and clock imports rose to $31,494 in 1846, as did imports of "Watches & parts of watches." In 1845 the gross value of these articles exported to the United States was $1,106,543; in 1846 it had risen to $1,265,393. By contrast, American reexports of northern-assembled European clock and watch parts remained comparatively small during the 1840s. In 1845 the value of such goods was just $8,445, a year later, $1,902.[48] Even as late as 1851, France exported $59,404 worth of clocks to the United States, $1,757,502 worth of watches, and $14,771 of watch crystals.[49]

But the 1850s were also the decade of American clock and watch manufacturing. New Haven clock makers perfected the division of labor in the manufacturing process, and some New England companies exported over half of their clocks to Britain.[50] As a result, America began to import fewer clocks in the mid-1850s although the value of imported watches appears to have increased threefold. Only by the 1880s did America export more watches than it imported.[51]

The South never had an indigenous clock and watch manufacturing industry.[52] Although colonial and antebellum southern newspapers are replete with advertisements for timepieces by "Clock and Watch Makers," such pronouncements are grossly misleading. Few, probably less than fifty, of the thousand or so people who advertised themselves as clock and watch makers from around 1650 to the beginning of the Civil War actually made timepieces. If they did, they made them in small workshops or at home where much of their business was taken up merely with the mending or cleaning of imported northern or European clocks and watches rather than with the making of genuine southern timepieces.[53]

The disparity between rhetoric and reality in the southern clock "making" trade may be seen in the business activities of Benjamin Barton of Alexandria, Virginia. By his own account, he was in the "clock and watch making business." His business transactions, 1853–56, tell a different story. Between these years, Barton wrote or received seventeen business letters, only four of which indicate that he either cleaned or repaired a clock or watch. He was never commissioned to manufacture a timepiece.[54]

The daybook for 1836 of "Watchmaker" John D. Smith of Fairfield County, South Carolina, records a total of 167 transactions with local customers. Of this total, 97 (58 percent) concerned the repairing and cleaning of clocks and watches and the procuring of watch crystals and keys. On 12 occasions he imported timepieces for his clients. The remaining 58 transactions (about 35 percent) involved silversmithing, gun repair, jewelry alterations, and fixing miscellaneous items such as umbrellas. Not once did Smith make a watch.[55]

The work performed by southern craftsmen who advertised themselves as clock and watch makers did not change in future years. As late as 1888, for example, P. A. Gardener, Spartanburg, South Carolina, "Watchmaker," devoted 27 percent of his work to clock and watch repair, 15 percent to importing northern and foreign timepieces, and 58 percent to silversmithing and non-timepiece-related work. His hands never fabricated a clock or watch.[56]

Actual makers of clocks and watches in the South, then, were very rare, so rare, in fact, that those few who did exist have been well documented by historians.[57] Philip Whitney estimates that of the sixty or so people who advertised themselves as clock and watch makers in the Shenandoah Valley in the eighteenth and nineteenth centuries, only sixteen actually made an entire clock.[58] Other, though hardly categorical, evidence points to the fabricating of timepieces by a handful of other southern artisans. William Steffins of New Orleans paraded himself as a "Practical Watch Maker" and "Maker of the One Year Time Piece" in 1851.[59] But even the one North Carolina establishment which in 1820 had "1 bellows 1 plating mill 1 watch & clock engine" and various other equipment with which to manufacture watches spent half its time repairing watches as well as manufacturing them.[60]

The tendency for watch repairers to put their own watch papers into watches they fixed but did not make adds to the confusion regarding actual numbers.[61] Photographic evidence suggests that John Fessler's Maryland watch papers are reliable evidence of his own watchmaking.[62] And Roberts, Dutton & Company of Richmond certainly seem to have made clocks or gone to the bother of affixing their own labels to clocks they may or may not have made in the 1810s.[63] Similarly, John McKee of Chester, South Carolina, appears to have been a genuine maker of both clocks and their casings in the 1840s because the cherry and pine wood of which they are made are native to the South Carolina up-country. Even McKee, however, was not above placing his own name on northern-manufactured clocks. Certainly his manufacturing label inside his tall case clocks proclaiming that they were made "At J. M'Kee's CLOCK FACTORY, CHESTER COURT HOUSE, (S.C.)" is a little hard to swallow.[64]

That southerners repaired rather than manufactured clocks and watches is also apparent from nineteenth-century census data. Although incomplete, these data show that the annual value of watches and clocks made in all southern states in 1860 amounted to $64,375. The corresponding figure for northern and middle states was about twenty times greater at $1,233,150. Conversely, the total value of clocks and watches repaired in the South in 1870 was estimated at $295,587; the respective estimate for the northern and middle states was only three times greater at $909,873. In 1860 the South had only five watchmaking establishments, each employing an average of 1.2 hands. The northern and middle states, by contrast, had three times as many businesses which, on average, employed 8.6 hands per establishment.[65]

If for "maker" we read "repairer, possibly maker," it is clear that American clock and watch makers were always located primarily outside of the South. Between 1650 and 1750, only 21 percent of clock and watch makers, more probably repairers, lived in the South. Between 1801 and the 1860s, this proportion dropped to 8 percent. Conversely, gains were made in both the northern and western states, thus explaining the need for southerners to import their timepieces throughout the colonial and antebellum periods.[66]

Plainly, however, the South had large numbers of artisans who could at least repair and, very occasionally, make timepieces. In the late seventeenth to mid-eighteenth centuries, the southern clock and watch making and mending industry was dominated by South Carolina, where 64 percent of all southern timepiece makers lived and worked. During the nineteenth century, the Palmetto State lost ground to Virginia especially but also to North Carolina and Georgia, the proportion of southern clock and watch makers living in these states being 49, 14, and 16 percent respectively. This, however, denoted only a proportional decrease for South Carolina because the numbers of clock and watch repairers and makers in the South as a whole increased between 1666 and 1881.[67] Certainly, cities tended to dominate the clock and watch trade, but makers and repairers were not unknown in rural localities and villages. Although Charleston, South Carolina, was home to most of the region's colonial and antebellum makers and repairers, such craftsmen could also be found in many of the state's rural counties and districts by the mid-nineteenth century.[68]

The presence and socioeconomic characteristics of southern makers tell us much about the wider importance of timepieces in the eighteenth- and nineteenth-century South. Once southern clock and watch repairers had settled in a particular location, they tended to remain there, especially during the seventeenth and eighteenth centuries and in the longer established colonies like Virginia and South Carolina. Younger colonies like Georgia, which preserved a more itinerant, frontier culture into the early nineteenth century, tended to have a more geographically mobile clock and watch maker population. Between 1801 and 1881, for example, only 3 percent of South Carolina's timepiece makers and repairers and 2 percent of Virginia's had worked at three or more separate establishments in their lives, compared to 10 percent in Georgia and 5 percent in North Carolina.[69]

Given what we know about colonial immigration patterns, it is hardly surprising that the number of southern-born timepiece makers and repairers increased between 1666 and 1881. Between 1666 and 1750, 70 percent of these men were native to the South. The respective proportions for 1751–1800 and 1800–1881 were 76 and 84 percent. At any one time less than 6 percent of the South's clock and watch repairs were performed by transplanted northerners. Between 30 and 10 percent of the work was done by European immigrants from 1666 to 1881.[70] Immigrant English clock makers, not surprisingly, predominated, especially in the colonial period. Eighteenth-century newspaper reports from London support the statistical evidence: "It is a fact, that a great number of agents are now employed in seducing the artificers of this metropolis, and particularly those in the watch and clock making branches, to emigrate to America. Yesterday morning three watch and two clock makers, set out from Clerkenwell to take shipping for America."[71] Moreover, if few northerners came to the South to work in this field, then even fewer southerners left the region to mend clocks and watches in the North or Europe, thus suggesting that their limited skills of mending and repairing were peculiarly suited to the South and not competitive in regions that had many qualified, genuine clock and watch makers.[72]

Some regional variation within the South notwithstanding, most of those who advertised themselves as clock and watch makers tended to specialize in their trade. Less than 15 percent of all clock and watch makers in Georgia, Virginia, and the Carolinas, for example, pursued other trades unrelated or only marginally connected with clock and watch making and repairing during the period 1666–1881. With the exception of South Carolina, roughly half of the South's timepiece makers and repairers tended to branch into jewelry, silversmithing, and engraving in addition to their work with clocks and watches. Overall, between 76 and 41 percent devoted all of their attention to clock and watch repairing and making, 1666–1881, with the proportion decreasing by the late nineteenth century. Significantly, however, this drop in the numbers of highly specialized clock and watch makers owed more to their limited diversification into related fields than to an increase in the numbers of dabblers in the clock and watch industry.[73]

For the South generally, between 1666 and 1881 one-man clock and watch establishments remained the most popular, although partnerships in the trade became increasingly common.[74] Evidence suggests that if not in actual partnership, timepiece makers occasionally hired out some aspects of their work. James Jacks of Charleston, for example, not only advertised an "elegant assortment of . . . gold, silver, and gilt watches" in 1791 but also offered a "warranted" repair service. But Jacks employed others to add the elegance to the clocks he imported while he concentrated on their repairs. Throughout the 1790s, for example, Jacks entrusted Alexander Crawford, painter and glazier, to construct the cases of the clocks he imported and repaired.[75]

Southern clock and watch makers and repairers could exist in such numbers only because white southerners provided them plenty of business. Southerners apparently took advantage of the benefits of preventive maintenance and got their timepieces cleaned on a regular basis, thus suggesting the importance they attached to accurate timepieces. On June 15, 1773, for example, planter William Cabell of Amherst County, Virginia, noted in his diary, "paid Mr. Patterson 12/6 for cleaning my watch &C."[76] Repairers apparently made house calls, too. On January 23, 1854, Lunenburg, Virginia, farmer William Haynie Hatchett "got home to dinner found old Mr. McIntyre the clock man fixing my clock."[77] "An Ohio Yankee came along to day," noted Alabama planter William Proctor Gould in his diary in June 1852, "and fixed our old clock—He says it will run fifty years longer—paid him $2. Bought a Silver watch of him, which I intend to keep."[78]

Nor were repairs to the comparatively fragile and temperamental antebellum watches once in a lifetime affairs. Between 1846 and 1861, South Carolina planter James R. Sparkman had his watch repaired eight times by various local artisans. Although the average cost for each repair was not cheap (about three dollars), Sparkman obviously thought it necessary. Planter David Gavin sent his watch to be repaired by two different makers a total of six times between 1857 and 1861 at a total cost of $16.60.[79] Sometimes watch repair, especially of exotic and complicated timepieces, required the intervention of community elites to ensure that the job was done properly. In 1856, for example, Mitchell King, Charleston judge and lawyer, received the following appeal:

> The accompanying watch will be handed to you by Mr Wm Frapman a mercantile Gentleman of our City was made two years ago to order by Mr French of the Royal Exchange and has never proved satisfactory.
>
> It was last Year sent to him by the same Gentleman for [repair] and arrangement but without any improvement.
>
> This watch was ordered by my son for a friend and its failing to answer the requirements is a source of much mystification to him. He is under the impression that as the watch is undoubtedly of a superior workmanship Mr French would be induced to give it more special attention . . . in its adjustment if it were handed to him by any one of known influence in your Community therefore &C.[80]

Even though there were plenty of repairers in the South, some planters still preferred to have their northern watches fixed by northern workmen. Heyward Manigault's trip north in 1847 provided planter John Berkley Grimball with such an opportunity: "I sent my watch by Manigault to have the case fixed in New York and gave him $10 to pay the expense of the work."[81]

Certainly the numbers of clock and watch makers present in the eighteenth- and nineteenth-century South, the region's importation of foreign and northern clocks and watches, and the full use southerners made of repair services suggest that timepiece ownership in the region was considerable. Statistics alone, however, can tell us the levels of ownership and the socioeconomic characteristics of southern clock and watch owners.

The following data, based on an analysis of over two thousand probate inventory records for two regions of that quintessential southern state, South Carolina, not only detail the growth and extent of clock and watch ownership over time (1739–1865) but attempt to make meaningful comparisons between rural and urban timepiece ownership. Also examined are ownership levels according to inventoried wealth, incidence of slaveholding, and the relative cost of owning a timepiece over time and region.

In its racial composition, its radical political heritage, its geopolitical characteristics, and its dependency on high numbers of slaves for its economic and political power, pre-1865 South Carolina in many ways approximates what historians mean when they talk about the slave South.[82] Although largely an agricultural society dependent on a variety of staple crops, South Carolina boasted one of the largest colonial and antebellum seaports in North America: Charleston.[83] As the main conduit for locally grown indigo, cotton, and rice, the city of Charleston was nestled among some of the South's largest plantations. Together, city and neighboring plantations formed Charleston District. According to census figures, Charleston District, with its amalgam of urban and rural slaveholders, merchants, and artisans, was the most populous of South Carolina's districts with more than seventy-two thousand inhabitants in 1850. Slaves accounted for a little over forty-four thousand of this total, thus making free blacks (a tiny fraction) and whites a minority of about twenty-eight thousand, or 39 percent.[84] Because wealthy planters tended to maintain both a house in the city and a plantation household, the proportion of exclusively city dwellers is difficult to determine with any accuracy.[85] Nevertheless, the social, political, and economic influence wielded by Charleston, the city, over Charleston, the district, gave the district as a whole a distinctive urban coloring during the eighteenth and nineteenth centuries.[86]

By contrast, Laurens County, located in the later settled region of South Carolina's up-country, was more typical of the agricultural South.[87] It was poorer than its coastal cousin, its planters owned fewer slaves and less land, and it had no real urban center.[88] The ratio of enslaved to free was roughly even (11,953:11,454) and its population smaller (23,407) than Charleston's in 1850.[89] Meaningful urban-rural comparisons, then, can be made between the two regions.

Historians of colonial and antebellum America are well versed in the use of probate inventories—the listing of property individuals own at death—to estimate wealth and other socioeconomic characteristics of a given population.[90] As with any historical document, such records can be used in many ways. Here, clocks and watches recorded in the probate inventories for Charleston District and Laurens County were counted according to four criteria: chronological time, inventoried material wealth, estimated cost of clocks and watches, and number of slaves owned.[91]

Figure 1 charts the broad contours of clock and watch ownership in Charleston District and Laurens County over the 126-year period, 1739 to 1865.[92] Between 1783 and 1865, the proportion of clock- and/or watch-owning inhabitants in Laurens County went from 10 to 71 percent.[93] Because the incidence of timepiece ownership was higher at an earlier date, figures for Charleston District are less dramatic but still denote a significant increase of 43 percentage points. By 1865, 66 percent of Charleston's population owned a timepiece, which, though 5 percent less than that of Laurens, nonetheless demonstrates that two-thirds of the inhabitants in both regions owned at least one mechanical timepiece.

When divided into three time cohorts, 1739 to 1809/10, 1805–9/10 to 1839–43/44, and 1839–43/44 to 1865, it becomes apparent that timepiece ownership increased at different rates and at different times in the rural and urban regions. While Laurens experienced only a 4 percent increase in the numbers owning clocks and watches from 1783 to 1809, Charleston from 1739 to 1810 witnessed a 25 percent gain. That there was such an increase in Charleston is not surprising given the predilection of British troops for pillaging Charleston's gold and silver watches during the Revolutionary War (the British evacuated Charleston, taking their booty with them in 1782).[94] Qualitative evidence supports the statistics. In 1767, Peter Manigault informed a friend from Philadelphia that he was unable to sell his "Gold enameled Watch" for him in Charleston because the "Jewelers in Town . . . have all agreed that they can afford to sell it here much cheaper than the Price you have fixed." He counseled: "I would advise by no means to send such things of this sort to Carolina again, for you may depend upon it you will always be a Looser by them." It was a sentiment echoed by merchant Henry Laurens that same year. "Your watch is not sold," he told James Habersham, because "their [sic] is such a super-

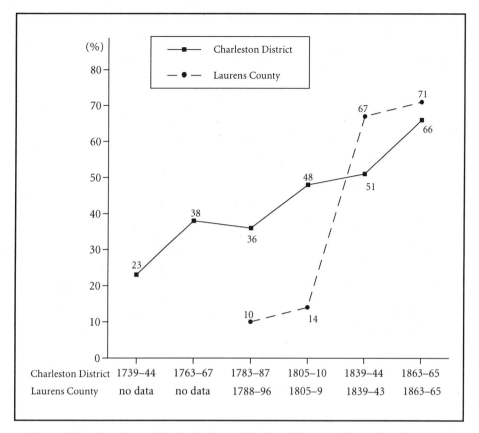

Figure 1. Timepiece Ownership in Charleston District and Laurens County, South Carolina, 1739–1865

abundance of Watches, jewelry, &ca. imported here that the Sales are become slower than I had imagined."[95]

Laurens County's 53 percent increase in timepiece ownership came in the 1805–9 to 1839–43 period. In the same period, timepiece ownership in Charleston plateaued out to a 3 percent gain. From 1839 to the end of the Civil War in 1865, gains in both regions were modest to fair (4 percent in Laurens, 15 percent in Charleston), suggesting that both rural and urban South Carolinians responded to an increase in the supply of timepieces (clocks especially) from Europe and the northern states between 1810 and 1840.[96]

Perhaps most intriguing, the evidence presented in Figure 2 suggests that nonslaveholders were sometimes just as, and occasionally more, responsible for this overall increase in clock and watch ownership through the entire period.[97] While both rural and urban slave owners were caught up in the larger trend toward timepiece ownership, the rural increase is due more to clock and

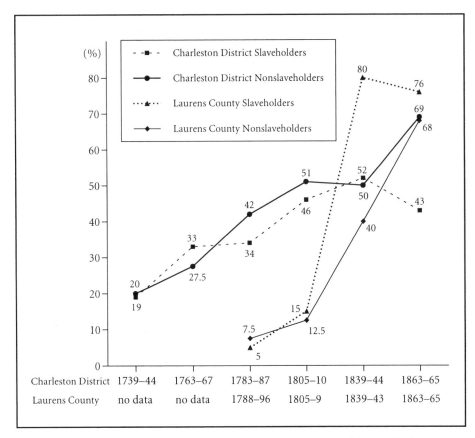

Figure 2. Timepiece Ownership among Slaveholders and Nonslaveholders in Charleston District and Laurens County, South Carolina, 1739–1865

watch ownership among slave owners whereas Charleston's increase is primarily, though not exclusively, among nonslaveholding whites, probably slaveless merchants and petty property owners. The period 1805–44 saw slight changes in this trend. By 1839–44, timepiece ownership among Charleston slaveholders edged that of nonslaveholders by a margin of 2 percent. Laurens County slaveholders, in contrast, made truly phenomenal gains in timepiece ownership from 1805 to 1843, and their nonslaveholding brethren maintained a more modest rate of increase. Timepiece ownership among Laurens County slave owners reached 80 percent by 1843, dwarfing both slave-owning and non-slave-owning urban timepiece owners, about 50 percent of whom possessed clocks and watches.

   In the final cohort, 1839–65, slave-owning urbanites, no doubt fearful of a Union invasion during the Civil War (many watches were hidden and thus do not appear in the 1863–65 inventories), possessed fewer timepieces than they did from 1805 to 1844.[98] Curiously, this is not the case with non-slave-owning Charlestonians who, although also presumably anxious about a Union invasion, increased their level of timepiece ownership to almost 70 percent. By contrast, all Laurens County denizens, in less danger from rampaging Union forces, either maintained or increased their high levels of timepiece possession.[99]

Among other things, this analysis of probate inventories correlates timepiece ownership with wealth levels, incidence of slave owning, and the relative and absolute cost of clocks and watches for the two regions between 1739 and 1865.[100] Typically, wealth and slave owning proved exponential and, on the whole, the wealthier the cohort, the higher the average value of the clock or watch.[101] And like other regions in nineteenth-century America, rural inhabitants were less affluent than urban ones.[102] Most revealing, perhaps, the figures suggest that when considered as a percentage of total inventoried material wealth, timepieces were not as costly as some historians have assumed.[103]

Between 1739 and 1810, non-slave-owning Charlestonians devoted progressively less of their wealth to owning a timepiece, spending an average of 3.3 percent of their total wealth on such items over the seventy-one-year period. This is not to say that timepieces were cheap or that less affluent, non-slave-owning urban dwellers did not have to exercise opportunity cost choices when purchasing a clock or watch. Because mass-produced clocks were not available until after the 1820s at the earliest and because eighteenth-century Europe, Britain especially, exported relatively large numbers of watches to colonial America, watches were, on average, 22 percent cheaper than clocks during the 1739–1810 period.[104] Accordingly, thrifty and economically rational men in both Laurens and Charleston bought the less expensive and more available watches (see Table 1). Wealthier though they were, slave-owning Charlestonians also demonstrated prudence when buying timepieces by similarly opting for watches. Differences within Charleston's slaveholding class were contingent on wealth and number of slaves owned, and the smallest slaveholders (owning one to five bondpeople) devoted proportionally more of their wealth to timepiece ownership than other slaveholders. In any case, the financial sacrifice for owning a timepiece, for slaveholders as a group especially but for non-slave-owning urbanites too, though not insignificant, was often minimal.

The data for Laurens are more sketchy. Laurens had few very large slaveholders (twenty-one or more slaves) in the 1788–1809 period.[105] Nevertheless, among those few who bought timepieces, both slave owners and nonowners usually devoted about 2 percent or less of their wealth to the purchase of a clock and/or watch.

This situation, however, was to alter with two changes in the first half of the nineteenth century which increased the supply of clocks and watches and

Table 1. Clock and Watch Ownership and Average Values of Both in Charleston District, 1739–1865, and Laurens County, South Carolina, 1788–1865

| | Type of Timepiece Owned (%) | | | | | | | | | | |
| | Watch(es) Only | | Clock(s) Only | | Clock(s) and Watch(es) | | Totals | | | Average Values | |
	1	2	1	2	1	2	Ws	Cs	Both	Ws	Cs
Charleston											
1739–44	68	16	9	0	5	2	84	9	7	£ 27	£56
1763–67	67	13	11	0	8	1	80	11	9	£ 31	£48
1783–87	49	12	24	2	12	2	61	26	14	£ 10	£15
1805–10	46	32	15	3	3	0.5	78	18	3.5	$ 31	$27
1839–44	24	29	25	7	13	2	53	32	15	$ 34	$18
1863–65	9	15	3	67	3	3	24	70	6	$ 63	$27
Laurens											
1788–96	33	33	33	0	0	0	66	33	0	£ 1	£ 1
1805–9	55	45	0	0	0	0	100	0	0	$ 14	$ 0
1839–43	8	0	67	18	6	1	8	85	7	$ 27	$19
1863–65	9	13	22	42	8	6	22	64	14	$143	$31

Source: Compiled from Charleston District Inventories, 1739–1865, and Laurens District Inventories, 1783–1865, SCDAH.

Legend: 1 = slaveholder; 2 = nonslaveholder

Note: All values derived from the assessor's estimate of the timepiece's monetary worth at owner's time of death.

lowered their relative and absolute cost. The first of these changes was the mechanization of timepiece making (clocks especially) in parts of Europe and, more significant, in the North.[106] Second, the expansion of cotton production in South Carolina coupled with Britain's increased demand for the staple between 1800 and 1860 increased South Carolinians' buying power.[107] Not only do these larger trends help account for the general increase in timepiece ownership in Laurens and Charleston generally, but they also help explain why all those sampled devoted, on average, proportionally less wealth to timepiece ownership between 1809 and 1865 than they had from 1739 to 1810.

Trends first discernible in the eighteenth century were sometimes amplified in the nineteenth. As before, non-slave-owning Charlestonians and all groups in Laurens County seemingly demonstrated rational decision making when buying their timepieces: all chose the now less expensive clock. By 1865, clocks were roughly 44 percent cheaper than watches for urbanites and 73 percent less expensive for inhabitants of Laurens. All groups but one took advantage of the cost differential. Slave-owning Charlestonians, one of the wealthiest classes on the North American continent by the eve of the Civil War, apparently saw the cost of timepieces as largely incidental and so opted to buy the more expensive watch. For this most affluent of classes, cultural capital was no doubt at stake in their decisions to purchase the more expensive and publicly demonstrable watch.[108]

But whatever the specifics of clock and watch ownership in rural and urban South Carolina, it seems that, in comparative perspective, the South's level and incidence of timepiece ownership were roughly the same as the rates and levels of timepiece ownership elsewhere (see Table 2). And the basic reasons for increased watch and clock ownership in the South as in the North, were similar. If we agree with Martin Bruegel that northern timepiece ownership was in part a reflection of heightening personal time discipline, the same, as later chapters show, was true in the South.[109]

The foregoing emphasis on economic rationality as an explanation for southerners' decisions to buy either a clock or a watch may be more problematic and less clear-cut than the analysis suggests. As Michael O'Malley has pointed out in his examination of time consciousness in the antebellum North, the social and economic significance of owning a clock or a watch varied and was contingent on notions of public and private time, of household piety, and of market-oriented, economic behavior.[110] O'Malley's evidence suggests that the clock tended to regulate the home and, given the home's association with piety and morality, linked clocks with nature generally. In urban settings, so the argument goes, town clocks could be used to regulate public order, and their presence probably obviated the need for extensive watch ownership. Urbanites bought clocks simply to reaffirm a feeling of piety about time and order at home. The watch, by contrast, though it may have shared all the aforementioned qualities associated with the clock, was different because it regulated the owner wherever he or she might be and so would suit, for example, a slave owner who wanted to time slaves' labor in the fields. The rural slave owner, then, presumably bought watches because his time needed to be portable and, in the absence of town-based public time, his watch would be his only means of timekeeping.

In some respects, this line of reasoning applies to the contours of timepiece ownership in South Carolina, for example, the tendency for Charleston slave owners to choose watches over clocks for virtually the entire 1739–1865 period. At their town houses in Charleston, a clock would have sufficed to regulate order at home but was probably negated by the presence of public clocks, which were present in the city from about 1720 on. The question then remains,

Table 2. New York and South Carolina Timepiece Ownership Compared, 1739–1889

	No. of Inventories	Percent with Timepieces
Rural North		
Greene County, New York		
1801–10	27	25.9
1811–20	49	40.8
1821–30	46	63.0
1831–40	35	65.7
1841–50	41	73.2
Urban South		
Charleston District, South Carolina		
1739–44	166	23.0
1763–67	392	38.0
1783–87	509	36.0
1805–10	394	48.0
1839–44	107	51.0
1863–65	56	66.0
1866–67	105	55.0
1883–86	44	73.0
Rural South		
Laurens County, South Carolina		
1788–96	62	10.0
1805–09	73	14.0
1839–43	121	67.0
1863–65	125	71.0
1866–67	64	76.0
1880–89	42	83.0

Sources: Greene County, New York, figures are from Bruegel, " 'Time That Can Be Relied Upon,' " 551; South Carolina data compiled from Appendix, Tables A.11–A.24.

Why did Charleston slave owners prefer watches over clocks? Aside from the aesthetic value and cultural capital associated with watch ownership, Charleston District slave owners specifically, and southern masters generally, had very real reasons to own a watch.

Away from their city homes, these planters were often on their plantations, actively participating in the production of cotton and the ordering of their slave workforce. In this instance, O'Malley's argument seems to hold true: a clock would appear inappropriate for maintaining order on the plantation because only a watch could be taken into the fields. But O'Malley is right only if one agrees with his assumption that clock time is necessarily housebound. As will be shown, it was not. If, like Laurens County's slave owners, planters could not afford a watch, they could still recruit the sound of house-based clock time for purposes of agricultural production and preserving plantation order.[111]

Before any such experiments with clock-regulated plantation labor could take place, however, southerners had to embrace a new mentality, one that simultaneously espoused the value of timed labor and meshed with the older association of time with nature. Just such a development occurred during the 1830s and after.

Late antebellum southerners did not like relying on northern technology. They felt that importing northern-made goods, including clocks and watches, rendered them "dependent on the North." The "Southern planter," it was complained in 1851, "barters with the North the labor of three or four agricultural hands for that of two, at the most three, mechanics or manufacturing operatives" through importation. "Is it then to be wondered at, that the South does not keep pace with the North?"[112]

As sectional tensions heightened in the late 1850s, southerners became even more ambivalent about importing northern clocks and watches. On the one hand, they applauded "marvels of invention" like "an electric clock, which wakes you up, tells you what time it is, and lights a lamp for you at any time you please," while on the other, they had grave reservations about "what we pay New England to support her John Browns." By 1859, it was estimated, New England "sells annually to the South $60,000,000 of merchandise," including "clocks."[113]

But southerners, it seemed, could not help themselves for trying. Once they had bought northern and foreign watches, once they had made timepieces integral to the fabric of their social and economic existence, southerners found that they could not do without them. Planter-lawyer David Gavin explained the source of southern ambivalence in 1861:

The Legislature have taxed our own manufactures on their capital and the sales of the goods the same as the goods manufactured in the North or abolitionist States, They have seceded on account of Abolition sentiment and Legislation in the Northern states, but incourage them to bring their manufactured goods here, They are opposed to Abolition with their mouths, but their acts are in favour of it, for they incourage it by fostering their manufactures and importations. . . . It seems we are neither fish nor flesh—neither in nor out of the Union. The Legislature talks one way and acts another.[114]

Long before 1861, however, southern planters had begun to import far more than watches from the North and industrial capitalist societies generally. In addition to timepieces, southerners tried to embrace northern capitalist ideas on how to apply clock time to economic and social life. But this embrace was highly conditional. It was both repulsive and alluring to the southern mind. As it turned out, southerners' attempts to yoke ideas about time and money, epitomized by the clock and watch, to their own historical experience, which stressed natural time, a conservative and modern-fearing Weltanschauung, was not unsuccessful.

Historians have always made much of the muchness in American history. David Potter described Americans as a "people of plenty," and others have both fawned and agonized over the excess of democracy both South and North.[115] What historians need to add to this list of plenties is time, both its public and private availability, for one southern constituency at least. For those marginalized from the private ownership of time especially, however, the situation was very different, particularly when white southerners attempted to parlay their clock and watch ownership into a tool of power, specifically in masters' efforts to define the ownership of time and set work against the clock. Before any accommodation or resistance to these demands could take place, however, masters themselves, white southerners generally, had to embrace a mentality commensurate with their ownership of clocks and watches. In short, they had to import along with clocks and watches the capitalist and northern idea that time was money and that clock time could be used to regulate, measure, and exploit labor both free and slave.

II

Taming Time's Pinions, Weaving Time's Web

 Of Times Natural, Sacred, and Secular, 1700–1900

And God called the light Day, and the darkness he called Night.
And the evening and the morning were the first day.
And God made two great lights; the greater light to rule the day,
and the lesser light to rule the night: *he made* the stars also.
—Genesis, 1:5, 1:16

. . . when ruling fate has struck
The unalterable hour; even nature's self
Is deemed to totter on the brink of time.
—James Thomson, "Autumn," 1730

Oh Time!—thy pinions never stay,
Swift o'er the path of life they dance;
And joys, which swell the heart to day,
Melt as to-morrow's hours advance.
—Mary E. Stewart, "The Flight of Time," 1845

The clock is not merely a means of keeping track of the hours,
but of synchronizing the actions of men.
—Lewis Mumford, *Technics and Civilization*

Throughout the eighteenth and nineteenth centuries, God's time, nature's time, and clock time were always coeval in the South.[1] That these various sources of time were juxtaposed does not necessarily mean that they were equally balanced in a constant and stable formula. At the most general level, it may be argued that up until around the 1830s, clock time was the junior partner of sacred and natural time. Thereafter, for a variety of reasons, mechanical time grew in importance in this partnership, never subordinating God or nature completely but making an increasingly urgent and potent bid for primacy in the minds and activities of southerners, planters especially. This chapter explores the presence of what Jacques Le Goff has called a "chronological net" that meshed God, nature, and clock and so constituted what was, for the most part, the enduring fabric of the southern time consciousness.[2] It ends with an analysis of the mercantile conception of time, a conception that was extremely important for the partial secularization and modernization of the South's time sensibility in the middle decades of the antebellum period.

If the long, sweeping rhythms of nature are indeed compatible with the clipped, constant, and regular ticks of the mechanical timepiece, at what point or points in a society's development do the two mesh and how and why is this yoking effected? For plainly, there are points at which various forms of time accommodate one another. There is, after all, no instance in world history when clock time wholly supplanted natural time rhythms. In every postfeudal society, clock time conjoins and mates with natural time. Societies differ in both the degrees to which nature dominates the clock, or, put another way, to what extent the clock suffuses nature and in the rationale, the general historical and social forces behind the marriage, in the first place. What, in short, are the various forces prompting men and women to look to the clock as well as nature to ascertain, appreciate, and evaluate time?

With regard to the splicing of clock and nature in nascent industrial capitalism, we have some answers. Max Weber gave one explanation. Without charging into what C. Vann Woodward has called the "scholarly mêlée" surrounding Weber's Protestant ethic thesis, Weber gave an essentially convincing exposition as to why Protestant, rational asceticism could promote a sense of time thrift generally, the counting of clock hours specifically, in a society that looked to God and nature for much of its understanding of time.[3] Weber argued:

> Waste of time is thus the first and in principle the deadliest of sins. The span
> of human life is infinitely short and precious to make sure of one's own

election. Loss of time through sociability, idle talk, luxury, even more sleep than is necessary for health, six to at most eight hours, is worthy of absolute moral condemnation. It does not yet hold, with Franklin, that time is money, but the proposition is true in a certain spiritual sense. It is infinitely valuable because every hour lost is lost to labour for the glory of God. Thus inactive contemplation is also valueless, or even directly reprehensible if it is at the expense of one's daily work.[4]

Weber's tendency to link predestinarianism ("election") exclusively with Calvinist-Puritan theology notwithstanding (loss of time is a concern to orthodox Christianity generally), the logic of this mentality, so the argument goes, worked itself out under industrial capitalism, most obviously in Britain but also in the American North. Specifically, according to E. P. Thompson at least, this sense of Puritan time thrift, the imperatives surrounding the saving and pietistic application of God's time, were the same imperatives drawn on by industrial capitalists to mold and control their workforces.[5] And because factory work, housed in buildings and fed by artificial sources of light and energy, was relatively independent of nature, the clock quickly became the symbol of profane and religious time thrift. God's imperatives were never quite forgotten, but they readily merged and coexisted with secular, capitalist dictates concerning the proper relationship between time and wage and the legitimacy and necessity of measuring labor power by the clock.[6]

But what of the South? If Weber was correct, the same spirit of rational asceticism should have flourished south of Mason-Dixon's line too. Certainly southerners had the clocks and sometimes the watches with which to embrace industrial capitalism. And certainly, according to Babette M. Levy and Edmund S. Morgan, seventeenth-century settlers in the South were, to one degree or another, of the Calvinist or Puritan ilk. Levy holds that "their presence was felt throughout the colony" of Virginia and that Hugenots in the seventeenth and Scotch-Irish in the eighteenth century assimilated readily to Calvin. Nor were Methodists disruptive to the ethic.[7] Morgan argues in a similar vein. According to Morgan, "the Puritan Ethic," his shorthand for Weber's delineation, embodied "the values that all Americans held," southerners included.[8] But even if southerners were more generally Christian and, less specifically, Puritan, the idea that God's time must be used properly still had currency in the South. As I will argue, slave labor was timed in some manner, and its timing required southerners to entertain a similar understanding of and respect for clock time as northerners. Through the sound of public church time, a general commitment to Christian time thrift, and through the eyes of northern-educated southern, essentially Weberian, women in particular, southerners glimpsed the road to temporal modernity. It was a road that shared much in common with the Protestant route and one that subordinated time not just to God but also to Mammon. And that was the route first pioneered by the medieval mercantile mind. Southern merchants, like northern and British Protestants and Puritans, for reasons secular and sacred, loathed to lose time. For them lost time meant lost money first, incurring His wrath a close second, and it was from these merchants that eighteenth- and nineteenth-century southern slave owners learned their first lessons in equating money with time. In short, the roots, though not the branches, of a modern southern time consciousness that was to reach its apogee in and after the 1830s were born largely of a mentality responsible for the rise of world capitalism: the mind-set and predominantly secular world of the merchant.[9]

The coexistence of sacred, natural, and clock time in societies has been well documented by historians. "The Church calendar," writes Michael O'Malley, "merged the abstract idea of 'Time' with the 'social time' of everyday affairs and seasonal tasks: religion, and not simply natural, seasonal cycles alone, gave time its bite in everyday life."[10] One reason for this intimacy was that all three notions of time embraced both cyclical and linear conceptions of how time moved. Thus God's time in Western culture is, to paraphrase O'Malley, like a hoop rolling along a flat road.[11] Given this duality, the clock and watch, which share both linear and cyclical time, insofar as the hands of the clock go round but whose time is quantified in a linear fashion, fitted readily and easily with the mandates of religious and natural time. Mechanical time, in short, could accommodate to God and nature because all three were simultaneously linear, cyclical, regular, and, in essence, clocklike. Even the watch, a far more private, individualistic item, embodied natural characteristics. It was sometimes compared by southerners to the "pulse of Nature." A "hot and sultry day in summer," it was said, "is like a watch that has not been wound up for thirty six hours."[12]

Father Time, a popular figure in both the antebellum southern and northern literary imagination, for example, though often personified but not subject to human control, was both cyclical and linear:

It is not unnatural, at this season, to think and talk familiarly of old father Time. A sad thing it is that his chariot wheels pass so remorselessly over the earth, crushing so many beautiful flowers of spring-time. . . . Time, much abused old father Time, the revered skeleton whom we dread, is the friend of all; he bequeaths to us parents and ancestors, and the wonders of the elder days. . . . We call upon Time, like fretful children at a play, to unfold his curtain and show us the coming scenes, and chide him because he obeys, and the scenes pass away. Time, after all, though he chafes and rebukes us, is a wise nurse; and what more can we make of him, but that he is the appointed guardian, who soon resigns his keeping of us into the hands of our real parent, Eternity. . . . We moderns, little children by his side, steal close to his chair and pluck his old curiosities blindfold, at random.[13]

Even the cyclical turn of the calendar year accommodated to the time line. As the editors of the *Southern Cultivator* put it in "The Past and Coming Year" in 1860:

Human life is often compared to a journey. The figure is apt. It is, in many senses, a journey which we are all making towards our final resting-place. While travelling a weary road, the mile-stones arrest our attention as we pass; we count the figures upon them and consider how far we have come and how far we have yet to go. The close of the year is one of these mile-stones in the journey of life. Each one of them naturally suggests a review of the past, a consideration of the present, and an anticipation of the future.[14]

And if the source of life's journey was ordained by God, the journey itself was linear. Human life was harried along by "the rapid stream of time," as one writer for the *Southern Planter* put it in 1860.[15]

Southern men of the cloth certainly saw Christian time as having both a cyclical and a linear quality. In his "Narrative of His Own Conversion," Georgia's Rev. John Joice recalled, "I felt myself to be plucked up by the roots; and borne along the stream of time" while simultaneously noting the presence of biblical cyclical time: "In the metaphors of the scriptures the life of man is often compared to the seasons—the spring-time of infancy and youth—the summer of manhood—the autumn of maturer age—and the hoary winter of old-age."[16] Evidently, such time was not wholly divorced from God. Ultimately, for all southerners, some aspects of their time were His. This yoking of and accommodation between religious and profane, natural and artificial, linear and cyclical time were reflected in the very sources of southerners' public time. In an advertisement for sundials, for example, in 1860, the *Southern Cultivator* promoted a dial that was simultaneously contingent on and independent of nature. It was an equatorial dial "for all latitudes," which, "in addition to the hour circle, subdivided to show the true time to minutes, these dials have engraved Equation tables, showing the difference between apparent and true time every day in the year."[17] The reference to true time as opposed to natural and presumably false time was an indication of the growing ascendancy of the clock over nature that had already been prefigured in the late eighteenth and early nineteenth centuries.

Far more obviously, however, church clocks and bells communicated simultaneously religious, natural, and civic time. "Could it be a time machine?" "Is it more than a house of worship?" Recently these questions were asked about the Protestant Episcopal Christ Church near Irvington, Virginia. Built around 1732 and perhaps designed by Sir Christopher Wren, the church, with dimensions and designs not altogether unlike those of Stonehenge, is believed to be simultaneously God's house, a giant sundial, and a temporal compass, with brick dentils, columns, and windows aligned specifically for the purpose of telling clock time, ascertaining equinoxes, as well as housing colonial Virginia's defenders of the faith. Although scholars continue to disagree as to the true function of the church, it is not incredible that the colonial southern mind could have conceived of a church that acted also as a clock and recorder of seasonal patterns.[18]

Sight and sound were the couriers of God's and society's time. The ubiquity of God's time, with the church clock and attendant bells as His visual and aural messengers, is clear from the way southerners described churches. The clock of St. Michael's in Charleston, installed in the 1760s, for example, was depicted as "a strong 30 Hour Clock, to show the Hour Four Ways, to strike the Hour on the largest Bell." In the antebellum period, however, local civil authorities expanded the function of the church's time to include the secular: "It will be noticed that it is 'to show the *Hour* Four Ways,' and this is all it showed till 1840, when, with the consent of the vestry, the City Council added minute hands. The quarters are now struck on three bells, not on four as formerly."[19]

The aural power of church bells should not be underestimated. If the bells of London's St. Mary-le-Bow can be heard over a distance of six miles above ambient late twentieth-century London noise and the tumult of congested city traffic, it may reasonably be assumed that the South's church bells could pierce a less noise-polluted colonial and antebellum soundscape at least as far. During his visit to Charleston in 1837, Henry Summer indicated the geographical area that could be netted by public time and the sound of time: "I had visited the steeple of St. Michael's Church—when I reached the platform, above the hands of the Clock, I ascended no higher but viewed the city. It was spread before me like a map in miniature." The sight and sound of St. Michael's time, communicated through its bells, could delve down into the city and hence the ears and the minds of all who lived there.[20]

God's time and the various civic functions it served, then, punched its way both aurally and visually into the minds and ears of all southerners.[21] Since 1770, for example, the bells in Botetourt County's courthouses and churches had signaled the timing of civic, religious, and social events. During the Revolutionary War, the Episcopal Church bells of Elizabeth City, Virginia, were recruited for the secular purposes of alerting "the surrounding country of the approach of the enemy, and as a signal for relieving [the] guard."[22] Charleston's St. Philip's clock and bells were no different for "truly nothing can be more awe-inspiring than at the silent midnight hour to hear St. Philip's clock with deep funeral knell tolling another day." For this writer at least, it was the clock that was heard. Sound and time were plainly inextricable when it came to communicating public time.[23]

Moravian settlers in Winston-Salem, North Carolina, not only understood that clock time was best communicated through sound but evidently used their church clock and bells for functions, religious and secular, the sources of which were natural and mechanical. Minutes of the town meeting for April 27, 1772, read: "To avoid lagging, hereafter the bell is to be rung at 7 a.m., at 11:30 a.m. and at sunset—in summer at the latest 7 p.m. Br. Koffler is to have charge of this. . . . The bell-ringing shall always be in 2 strokes (back and forth) because the sound is clearer and the bell is more easily rung thus. Before the sermon and other public occasions of worship they shall ring for a longer time, with a pause between." The bell was also used to denote breakfast time and "the close of the day's work."[24]

The sound of public clock time always remained important in the South. As late as 1881, for example, citizens of Rock Hill, South Carolina, complained about its absence: "There is some complaint because the town clock is not kept running. We have been requested to ask the person in charge of it to keep it in such condition that its musical sounds may be heard day and night telling the time."[25] Once destroyed by war and fire, the sound of public clock time, so entrenched in the southern soundscape, was sorely missed. As Emma Le Conte noted in her diary in February 1865 after the leveling of Columbia: "The market [is] a ruined shell supported by crumbling arches, its spire fallen in and with it the old town clock whose familiar stroke we miss so much."[26]

Since its invention, the clock had always proved compatible with natural and religious time. As David Landes puts it: "Few inventions in history have ever made their way with such ease. . . . Even the poets liked the new clocks. That is the most astonishing aspect of these early years of mechanical horology, for no group is by instinct and sensibility so suspicious of technical innovation."[27] Nineteenth-century American poets were no exception. Although Edgar Allan Poe and Nathaniel Hawthorne well understood that the clock could become tyrannical in regulating political and economic life, the idea that the clock, while reified, was nonetheless a part of God and nature remained strong throughout the nineteenth century.[28] For the South's amateur literati the sound of clock time was similarly soothing and in no conflict with nature. "No sound ungrateful to the ear breaks upon the charm of quietness—except the musical chime of the distant bells," waxed eloquent one writer for the *Southern Rose* in 1838, continuing, "as they signal the passing hours."[29]

Nature, broadly construed, was always perceived in both meteorological and clock terms. Early eighteenth-century newspaper reports often noted the timing of nature's forces. "Between 8 and 9 in the Evening," it was reported in Charleston in 1732, "a sudden and very violent Gust of Wind. . . . The Violence of it continued about 8 minutes."[30] The 1740s saw lightning strike ships "at three o'Clock [in the] Afternoon"; the 1750s a hurricane ravaging Charleston at "about 10 minutes after 11 o'clock"; and in 1774 an earth tremor hitting at "about two in the afternoon."[31]

Nor had this tendency evaporated by the early national and antebellum periods. About "an hour before day," noted planter Allard Belin in 1797, "a Tornado happened which killed Mr. Roodes two Negroe Boys," thus at once recording death and weather by time.[32] Similarly, Sumter District, South Carolina, planter John Furman noted in 1839 that "between 1 & 2 OClock PM It rained."[33] Black River, South Carolina, planter William Sparkman also noted nature's time by the clock. "Thermometer at 6 *am 61*," he observed on September 12, 1844. On September 22 of the following year the thermometer stood "at 6 am *47*," and on December 21 the same year it was twenty degrees at "7 am."[34] Planters John and Keating Simons Ball of Charleston District made similar entries in their journals throughout 1849 noting time and temperature and also imposing temporal precision on nature's unexpected: "8 hours 20 minutes P.M. a heavy squall of wind from E.N.E."[35] Dorchester County planter David Gavin on September 4, 1856, recorded, "Hard thunder & rain about 5, O.clock P.M."[36]

Virginia planters were no different. "Rain after midday incessantly until night," noted Middlesex County planter George Llewellyn Nicolson in March 1858, specifying "and still continues as hard as ever up to 7 1/2 P.M. the time at which this note was made."[37] Nature's freaks were similarly reduced to clock-defined measurements in the Old Dominion. In 1819 a "comet of considerable magnitude made its appearance here this Evening, situated nearly N.W. by N. about 10 degrees above the horizon it sets at this time about 45 minutes after 9 Oclock."[38]

One reason for this meshing of natural and clock time was the ubiquity of colonial and antebellum almanacs, which advised planters to plant and harvest according to sacred, natural, and clock time. Some planters took notice of such advice even though the almanac's stress on nature's rhythm could be frenetic at times. As planter Charles Manigault explained to his brother in 1859: "I only wish to call your attention to this year's necessity of *beginning* to plant at the proper time, in advance of the high tides in the Almanac 3, 4, or 5 days previous to the day indicated (the 18th I think)."[39] To coordinate seasonal time with planting and clock time, southern planters were advised to "interleave your almanacs" with their plantation journals.[40] But though such advice was revered by overseers especially, some were becoming increasingly skeptical of almanacs and those who relied on them. "Both my overseers believe that the Almanac will show when there will be rain," noted one planter in 1832. He continued in a somewhat scornful tone: "Often during the drought, they would gravely tell me 'The Almanac maker says ther'll be rain on such & such a day.' "[41] Yet others perpetuated the relationship between clock, nature, and God by following the almanac's advice closely. As Southampton County, Virginia, planter Daniel Cobb wrote in his diary in February 1843: "The Moon to day is 7 days sold [*sic*] Which is the 1st Moon 22 Minuits after 11 in the morning of our Lord 1843."[42]

Although always naturally inspired and God-related, southern communicators of time, whether almanacs, church clocks, or college bells, were also recruited to deal with the secular running of civic and economic affairs. In 1797, for example, the commissioners of Charleston markets contracted out for a "Public Building" with "A Cupola sufficient to hang a Good Bell."[43] Similarly, Augusta, Georgia's, "Bell Tower," called "Big Stephen," was apparently used to signal the times of markets and sound the alarm for fires.[44]

Whether sacred or secular, public clock time as well as privately owned watches, then, could in myriad ways serve the profane function of regulating southern civic life, especially in the region's cities and ports. Much evidence exists indicating that antebellum southerners orchestrated many of their civic, social, and economic affairs by the clock. Early colonial legal statutes even recruited nature's time to promote civic order. A 1719 Charleston statute prohibited foreign ships from unloading their goods at the wharfs "between sunrising and sun-setting," thus suggesting that colonial sailors in particular were subject to civic time.[45] Charleston's market hours were similarly regulated in 1739. All may sell "upon every day of the week except Sundays, from the rising of the sun, all the year long. . . . And if any person or persons whatsoever shall sell . . . provisions in the said market . . . before the ringing [of] the market bell at sun risings in the mornings" they would be fined. But clock time was also part of the provision because "the clerk of the market for the time being is hereby directed and required, to ring, or cause the said market bell to be rung at sun rising, and also at nine of the clock in the morning, on every market day throughout the year."[46]

Colonial urban stores, like physician Andrew Turnbull's of Charleston in 1780, came to be equipped with clocks for customers, thus adding to the sources of public time in colonial southern cities.[47] This is understandable given the importance of civic, public time in the colonial, urban South. In 1751, for example, Charleston's tavern keepers were not permitted to "entertain or employ any seaman or mariner, exceeding one hour in four and twenty," presumably because longer drinking bouts had posed a threat to public order. Likewise with the 1741 statute prohibiting "play at any billiard table after the sun hath been set one hour."[48]

Nor was such temporal regulation limited to colonial ports and towns. In 1740 South Carolina used clock-defined hours to regulate slave labor, the provisions of which were eagerly noted to fend off northern criticism regarding the hours worked by slaves in the 1850s: "The law, as we have shown, protects the slave from the Sabbath, and . . . limits his labor to from 14 to 15 hours per day."[49] This same act also required planters to write a ticket of absence for any slave leaving the plantation. Again, clock time as a regulator of slave behavior specifically, of civic order generally, is clear from the ticket: "Permit this slave to be absent from Charlestown, (or any other town, or if he lives in the country), from Mr. ___ plantation, ___ parish, for ___ days or hours; dated the ___ day of ___ ."[50]

Clock time as monitor of public order appeared in other forms in the colonial and antebellum South. On September 10, 1788, for example, Georgia planter William Gibbons was asked to appear before Savannah's chief justice "at the Court-House . . . at ten o'clock in the morning" for trial proceedings.[51] Courthouse sales of delinquent debtors' goods were advertised "to begin at Eleven OClock" in Georgia in 1797.[52] And by the 1850s, publishers Walker, Evans & Company of Charleston were selling court summonses to the state with appearance times "at ___ o'clock, ___ M.," with spaces for name, date, and time.[53] Voting times were similarly coordinated. Sumter District local elections in 1843, for example, were dependent on the clock: "The polls will be open from 11 O'Clock AM until 3 PM."[54]

In short, in both the colonial and antebellum periods, myriad public and private events and schedules were coordinated by public clocks as well as watches, both because and in spite of clock time's marriage to God and nature. Entries in Mitchell King's 1851 diary speak for the South generally: "Am to send for my carriage today at 5 PM. . . . Call at Capers he has sold the remaining Lots . . . and I am to call & settle with him on Thursday at 10 am. . . . Mitchell & Allen family arrive from Glenroy a little before 2 PM. . . . Am to call Board of Medical College to meet on Saturday 1 PM at Courthouse."[55]

This same meshing of religious, natural, and clock time was also apparent in the personal lives of southerners. Certainly, the priority of God, nature, and clock in the minds of individuals varied according to time. A Virginia eulogy of 1764, for example, had no place for the clock, preferring instead to identify time as a sacred and natural phenomenon: "Prudent is he, who turns early his eyes to Heaven, and surveys the transitory Enjoyments of this world with a philosophic Unconcern. . . . The rising Sun, whose Rays of Gold and Vermillion decorate the Eve of Morning. . . . The annual Circle was yet unfinished . . . when my Lavinia was no more. O my beloved, the breath of thy Life is flown."[56] For the most part, however, clock, God, and nature merged to varying degrees in the minds and actions of colonial and antebellum southerners. Such meshing was especially apparent in attitudes toward both birth and death. According to one 1862 poem, both were part of the mystic but corporeal clock:

There is a little mystic clock,
No human eye has seen,
That beateth on—and beateth on,
From morning until e'en.

The last stanza captured the essence:

Such is the clock that measures life,
Of flesh and spirit blended;
And thus 'twill run within the breast,
'Till that strange life is ended.[57]

Southerners, then, like all moderns generally, attempted to give temporal meaning and a precision to events over which they had no control.[58]

The presence of public clocks and private watches allowed colonial and antebellum southerners to confer clock time on that most natural of events, birth. Stafford County, Virginia's, most famous son, George Mason, paid close attention to birth times of his family members, recording to the hour the births of his sons and daughters in the family Bible throughout the 1750s and 1760s.[59] Antebellum planters too kept note of the time scions were born: "L[achlan] McIntosh born 10 Oclock. Sunday Morning" in July 1807.[60] Such occasions were not always joyous, however. "My beloved Wife," noted John Berkley Grimball in December 1848, "was this evening at 15 minutes past 9 OClock delivered of her ninth child—a boy—still born."[61] Bondpeople, too, were accorded the dubious courtesy of having their time of birth into a world of bondage recorded by clock. "My negro woman Celia," wrote South Carolina

Death, God, and St. Philip's clock, Charleston, South Carolina (© Tina Manley, 1996)

planter David Gavin in 1859, "was taken into labor last night about 10 Oclock was delivered to-day about 3 oclock P.M. about seventeen hours."[62] From cradle to grave, the clock monitored antebellum slave life and labor.

Birth's antithesis was no different. Robert Wetherick's last will and testament, for example, was heard "on Thursday morning last about four a Clock" in September 1700.[63] And late eighteenth-century southern gravestones, like Grace Belcher's of 1793 in Savannah, Georgia's, Colonial Park Cemetery, were engraved with hourglasses.[64] No doubt the unfathomable had meaning when defined in terms of the clock. Planter David Gavin was very precise in the timing of death. In September 1856, he recorded in his diary, "Joseph L. Inabnet . . . died yesterday morning eleven minutes after four Oclock A.M."[65] In 1858 another South Carolina planter noted, "My dear Louis ill from conjestion [*sic*] of Lungs . . . departed this life on Sunday eveng the 17th at 8 o'ck."[66] Sumter and Anderson planter John Durant Ashemore attached temporal significance to his mother's death in 1855: "My mother died last night at 10 minutes before 12 o'clock."[67] Another South Carolina planter in 1849 recorded that "Georgina died Sept. 16 1849 at 8 minutes past One OClock PM."[68] And although the deaths of the anonymous, deliberate or otherwise, were obviously of less personal significance, the timing of public executions was nonetheless noted precisely. As Caroline County, Virginia, planter Timothy Chandler recorded on December 7, 1821: "This day agreeably to the sentence of the Court, John Gillman, was brought to the gallows by the sheriff and at about 3 oclock P.M. was hung [sic] by the neck until he was dead."[69] When it became available, the telegraph added still further precision to the timing of news generally, death included. As one planter wrote in his diary on April 11, 1850: "Received an express informing me of the death of Mrs. H. Harleston, Her Remains were buried at Strawberry [plantation] at 2 P.M. She expired on Wednesday 10th Inst. in Charleston at 1/2 past A.M." In the next breath, his attention turned to nature: "15 minutes to 11 p.m. Raining hard." God's tears had a mechanical tinge to them.[70]

The deaths of slaves, like their births, were also brought within the purview of the clock. Mitchell King's son was informed in 1849 that one of his bondpeople died "about 1 O'clock P.M. on Saturday."[71] And by the late 1850s, the secular activity of burying God's children had been reduced to the clock and, indeed, the time card. In January 1859, Richmond's Hollywood Cemetery introduced the use of "Time Books" to ascertain the wage, to the hour, of its grave diggers.[72]

Although the reason for noting the time of birth and death is not wholly clear, the rationale behind recording life events, sacred and profane, by the watch was hinted at by one South Carolinian in 1881:

> My watch is thirty years old. It is one of those thick silver levers, which some poor wits call "turnips." It has been several times suggested to me that I might exchange it for a thin modern gold watch, which wears easier in the pocket. When I do, you may set me down for a barbarian! Not the best gold and jewelled "Hunter" in existence would tempt me to swap. That watch marked the time when my children were born, and the record is set down in the family Bible; it has ticked in their ears when they could only speak by laughing at it. . . . It has marked the time when the doctor's medicines were to be given. . . . It has made many records that are fast sealed up, to be opened only when another time comes.[73]

The clock gave permanence to life events that would otherwise be forgotten and crushed by the larger march of historical time.[74]

If birth and death involved the clock, so too did the more secular affairs of business and personal meetings. Charleston lawyer Mitchell King, for example, kept a close eye on the watch with visitors. "Call[ed] on Bullerg at 11 precisely. . . . Mr Rudolph Guerrigue occupied me from 3 till 1/2 past 4 PM," he noted in his diary on February 24, 1852. Two months later, "Judge Huger calls on me for 2 hours." Such events were not always gratifying, however, especially when lengthy: "Dr Michel brings the Revd David McEkleran Rector of the Parish of St. Helena Island to see my Library[.] He—the Reverend—spent nearly two mortal hours with me." When time was money, even men of the cloth were not exempt from the charge of wasting secular time.[75]

Prearranged meeting times did not always work out perfectly. Sometimes missed appointments were more the fault of northerners than southerners. As John Berkley Grimball noted in 1836 during a trip to New York following his attempts to contact a northern physician regarding his chest complaints: "Determined to consult Dr Stevens—called at his home—not at home—left on the Slate a request that he wd. visit me tomorrow before 11 OClock—When I came to dinner found that Dr Stevens had been here—am afraid my note was not sufficiently explicit as to the time, and yet when I think it over it seems perfectly so."[76]

Physicians were highly sensitive to the use of clock time because many of their cures and treatments depended on timing.[77] But physicians were not the only ones who concocted and administered these cures. Planter Louis Manigault's prescription book for 1852 included a remedy for cholera to be administered to his slave "every *two hours* beginning from 9 Oclock—gave the last one of these powders at 7 this morning."[78] Another planter's "Cure for the Complaint in the Bowels" involved a concoction of vinegar, salt, and tea. The patient was to "take one Table Spoonful as warm as they can take it—and Repeat every two or three minutes until Relieved."[79] One Virginia cure for an unidentified ailment from the late eighteenth century was distasteful but similarly clock-specific: "Desolve [sic] the Vomit in 6 Spoon fuls of warm water take a spoon, Every 10 or 15 minutes till it works." One would hope the cure was fast-acting.[80]

For wealthy white southerners especially, the involvement of the clock and watch in ostensibly sacred and natural affairs was reinforced through their education. Northern-educated southern scions understood the secular and sacred importance of time and learning. Loss of time in studies was not just a sin but held profane significance. As William Cabell Carrington wrote from Princeton to his father in Virginia in 1841: "That loss of time is, indeed, worthy of consideration,—and, at my time of life, time is to be regarded as more valuable than money." He explained that if he were to attend all the social affairs to which he was invited, "it is obvious that much time will be lost from my studies, and the question is whether I ought to submit to this loss rather than to the alternative of not going into society at all."[81] Student William Burchell Richardson was bombarded with advice about time thrift from secular and religious quarters. In November 1824, his mother wrote to him, "Long very long may you be partaker in the inestimable blessing [of health], I

Timing life—a physician taking the pulse of his patient, ca. 1860s (© Stanley B. Burns, M.D., and the Burns Archive)

humbly ask of God which will enable you to pursue your studies and prevent your losing any time, that you may accomplish in the time allotted to complete your Education." Two years earlier his father gave similar counsel though of a profane sort: "I really regret to hear of this vacation you speak of, you have already lost so much time this year that I am loath that you Should loose [sic] another day." Antebellum southern scions were well versed in the principle and value of time thrift.[82]

The antebellum southern schoolhouse, an institution often associated with ministers, was one of the most potent forces encouraging personal time discipline. Thrift was, after all, a religious and secular virtue and was to be instilled in all Americans worthy of the name. More worrying, perhaps, as Norbert Elias has argued, if a child "does not learn during the first ten years of life" the prevailing social values of time thrift and timekeeping, "it will be very difficult, if not impossible, for such a person to take up the position of an adult in this society."[83] For slaves, who were expected to remain childlike, such a possibility troubled few masters; for custodians of southern boys, however, it spelled disaster. Consequently, vigilance reigned supreme in southern schools and how pupils spent their time was monitored closely. As Louis Manigault wrote to his brother from Charleston in 1844:

> For the last two weeks It has been very cold here which makes every body very lazy, particularly the boys at School, almost every morning half of them are late, One day when the School was called in at 8 1/2 oclock one third of the boys were there, so it made Old Cotes mad, and he said that it would be a fixed rule now in his School that every boy who comes late to School shall bring 6 1/4 cents and give it up to Mr Lesesne every Monday, and he will buy books for the benefit of the School with it.[84]

The College of Charleston's policy on study hours in 1848 read: "The amount of Study, as prescribed by the regular course, is sufficient to employ the most capable Student from three to four hours, in his room at home, each day."[85] Clocklike punctuality was also important at the University of Virginia, whose exam schedule in 1829 was coordinated to within half an hour.[86] Little wonder that *The Teacher and the Parent*, published in the 1850s in New York and used in southern schools, devoted a chapter to punctuality.[87] Rural schools similarly recruited natural and clock time to enforce punctual attendance. The charter of South Carolina's Blackswamp Academy of 1818 required that "the school shall be opened every morning two hours after sun rise, and closed every evening one & half hour before sun set from first of April to first of October with an intermission of two hours, afterwards with an intermission of one hour."[88]

By the late antebellum period, southern children had apparently developed an acute understanding of clock time and its importance for civic coordination. As one South Carolina mother explained in March 1844: "Emma is already talking of packing up her box, as if she had a great deal to carry; this is the day for dancing, and she is coming to me every now and then to know what o'clock it is, if it is time for Harriet to come from school that she might get ready to go to dance."[89] Such clock consciousness is not altogether surprising given the emphases apparent in the informal education of the South's children. Youths' journals ministered much on the secular and religious virtues of time thrift and the appropriate "choice of hours" for performing certain tasks.[90] Again, clock time was intimately linked to nature, sometimes very literally. Like northern children, southern ones were introduced to "flower clocks" and instructed in the possibility of recruiting nature for punctuality: "It is well known that certain flowers open and close at particular hours.—Would it not be an ingenious method of computing time, so as to arrange flowers, that by expanding at regular intervals, an individual would be enabled by mere inspection to ascertain the hour of the day?"[91] Such an idea was lent scientific credibility by savants in London: "The author specifies certain flowers, which might assist in forming the proposed time-piece. Thus, the day-lily, he says, opens at five in the morning, the common dandelion at five or six; the hawk-weed at seven; another of the same genus at eight; the marigold at nine; another which he mentions, at ten or eleven, and the *closing* of these and other flowers in the latter part of the day, offers a similar system of hour-marks."[92] And when children were taught how to tell clock time by their parents, efforts both to integrate and to subordinate natural, life time to the clock were apparent. "When I was a young lad," reported one reader of Charleston's children's journal, the *Rose Bud*, in 1834, "my father one day called me to him, that he might teach me how to know what o'clock it was. He told me the use of the minute-finger and the hour-hand, and described to me figures on the dial-plate, until I was perfect in my part." Having understood time-telling, albeit in anthropomorphic terms, "Humphrey's" father went a step further: " 'Humphrey,' he said, 'I have taught you to know the time of day. I must teach you how to find out the time of your life.' " And here God, nature, and clock merged. "The Bible," the boy was told,

describes the years of man to be threescore and ten, or fourscore years. Now life is very uncertain, and you may not live a single day longer; but if we divide the fourscore years of an old man's life into twelve parts, like the dial of the clock, it will allow almost seven years for every figure. When a boy is seven years old, then it is one o'clock of his life, and this is the case with you. When you arrive at fourteen years it will be two o'clock with you; and when at twenty-one years, it will be three o'clock, should it please God thus to spare your life.

Although God and nature were still important arbiters, the clock held a not insignificant place in southerners' perceptions of life.[93]

God and nature, however, could ultimately be excluded in calculations about how much time southern children should devote to secular activities, as Table 3, which was published in the December 1835 issue of the *Southern Rose*, makes clear. Consequently, Charleston's children were made aware of the secular and pecuniary benefits of early rising: "I love to ride through a city before sun-rise. An observer will detect character then, as at noon-day. . . . The real money-maker is on the alert, throwing open his doors and shutters with a jerk, if he is a bustler, or carefully unlocking them, if he is a plodder." What was considered early? "Charleston at drum-beat."[94]

Such an emphasis on time thrift and punctuality helped promote an internal respect for the clock or a time discipline among white southerners, especially in the antebellum period. "I think it depends much on a man's own Character whether or not time will hang heavily on his hands," opined one South Carolina planter in 1852, recommending "the best plan for one to manage . . . in Summer is to divide his time regularly, as if he were on Ship devoting Certain hours to certain occupations."[95] It was, no doubt, a compliment for one young man, Edward, to be described as "like clock work in his reports about dogs and horses" in 1850.[96]

The watch was to be respected because it regulated personal as well as social, public affairs. One writer, complaining of the South's agricultural societies' tendency toward frivolity rather than serious scientific investigation, made this point indirectly: "As some of them exist at present, it is amusing to behold, how, as the hour for dinner comes on, the countenances which before were heavy and dull, become bright and radiant with expectation. And should some member at this hapless moment arise to protract the meeting; some dozen watches would leap from their fobs to rebuke his trespass upon their unwilling ears."[97] Clearly, the mechanical timepiece could be invoked in an effort to control individual and social behavior.

Ultimately, however, the internalization of clock time, while making southerners aspire to punctuality, actually stole their time and placed temporal, clock-defined strictures on their behavior. As one wit explained in 1829:

My time is not my own,
But this one comes, to try his pow'r
In social confab for an hour,
And thus—the hour is gone.[98]

Table 3. The Recommended Allocation of Time for Southern Children, 1853

Age	Hours of Sleep	Hours of Exercise	Hours of Occupation	Hours of Repose
7	9–10	10	1	4
8	9	9	2	4
9	9	8	3	4
10	8–9	8	4	4
11	8	7	5	4
12	8	6	6	4
13	8	5	7	4
14	7	5	8	4
15	7	4	9	3

Source: "Occupations of Different Ages," *So. Ro.* 4 (Dec. 12, 1835): 62.

The price to pay for well-coordinated public time schedules and the preservation of public order by the clock was the sacrifice of personal freedom from time. It was no small sacrifice to a people accustomed to the habit of mastery themselves.

The balance between secular, sacred, and natural time, the relative weighing of the temporal cocktail, varied among different southern classes and groups. For southern white women, for example, everyday, corporeal clock time was always important, but God's time was their primary focus, as it was for all white American women, North and South. Esther Burr, daughter of Puritan divine Jonathan Edwards, for example, saw her corporeal, household labors in distinctly religious terms: "My time is not my own but God's."[99] This conception of time was to remain with northern women well into the nineteenth century, especially the middle class, who, although as peripheral to direct participation in a wage-labor economy as their southern sisters, black and white, nevertheless came to view time as something to be saved and usefully applied. Catharine Beecher's best-selling 1841 *Treatise on Domestic Economy* stated, as had Burr, that all time was God's time and must be put to good use and, Heaven forbid, not wasted. "Christianity," she advised her female readers, "teaches that for all the time afforded us, we must give account to God; and that we have no right to waste a single hour." The unstinting accountability to God manifested itself in the corporeal world of managing household affairs, which in turn, albeit indirectly, serviced emerging capitalism. Again, according to Beecher, a "woman is under obligations to so arrange the hours and pursuits of her family, as to promote systematic and habitual husbandry; and if, by late break-fasts, irregular hours for meals, and other hindrances of this kind, she inter-feres with, or refrains from promoting regular industry in others, she is ac-countable to God for all the waste of time." Beecher's emphasis on hard work, the "*right apportionment*" of time, and its proper application in the household was rooted firmly in the religious and natural world because "the laws of the natural world, and the constitution of our bodies, alike demand that we rise with the light of day . . . and retire when this light is withdrawn." Clocks could, of course, be used to help the northern housewife in her endeavors, but in the final analysis most time was God's time and rooted in natural, often task-oriented, rhythms. In this way, the northern female mind as well as the north-ern household generally became closely associated with morality, piety, and nature.[100]

This same understanding of time defined the daily and mental activities of eighteenth- and nineteenth-century southern women. God guided the thread and needle of twelve-year-old Catherine Parry of Charleston, for example. In her 1739 sampler, Parry painstakingly inscribed: "Remember Time Will Come When We Must Give / Account To God How We On Earth Did Live."[101] Carolyn Burgwin Clitherall's recollections of time in the late eighteenth cen-tury were similar. She at once reified time and seemed to covet its sacred and secular use: "Oh Time, Time, Thou cruel destroyer of our Live's best treasures, we cannot arrest Thy progress; we cannot recall those precious hours alas, that when in our possession we so little valued."[102]

Henry Manigault's mother preempted Catharine Beecher's sentiments pre-cisely in a letter to her son from Charleston in 1808: "Idleness is the order of the day here. It is melancholy I think to see time wasted in the manner it is here. There is William Heyward, with a fine disposition, & an excellent capacity—lounging away his mornings—smoking & drinking away his afternoons—& his Evenings the only part of his existence which can be said to be employed are passed very unprofitably in company."[103] And what is thought to be a diary of two southern sisters from the 1840s echoes Beecher's northern sentiments exactly. The passage is lengthy but revealing of the intermeshing of sacred and natural time in women's secular duties:

> How easy & practicable would be our duties, exercises & employments be, if we would lay out a regular plan for ourselves—we would then have time for everything; & never seem hurried or embarrassed. Order is the first law of nature, & at nature's God—with out it, a thousand things will be improperly delayed, or wholly neglected. Whilst we are hesitating where to commence, or what to do, hours fly away, insensibly never to return! If everything

knows its place, you will escape the loss of many valuable moments, and the anxiety—of as many unprofitable researches. *Exactness* is, by no means the, *exclusively*, the [*sic*] appendage of an old maid. . . . If you are an early riser you will find time for everything—it is amazing how much is gained by lopping off an hours [*sic*] or two every morning from indulgence. . . . When people think of accounting to God for the talents they have received, they overlook the hours that are lost in the morning. . . . Ought we not to remember for what purposes we are placed here and to whom accountable for such simple waste of time?[104]

Sarah Gayle of Alabama preferred to express her thoughts on the subject of time in verse form in 1827:

> Rise up thou mourner, and give to the earthe,
> All which of her may be taken,
> And look thro' the vista of time to the hour,
> When touched by the breath of Omnipotent Power,
> Thy Mary again shall awaken.[105]

The guilt at not having made good use of God's time in a secular context is implicit in Ann B. Richardson's confessional letter to her children in 1850: "I do not think for the last three weeks I have done as much work as ought to employ me for one day. I get up each morning determined to do better, but by the time breakfast is over & dinner given out, it is too hot to do more than fan ones self."[106]

Other southern women expressed their temporal sins more simply. As Dolly Sumner Burge of Georgia put it bluntly in 1849 after a day of socializing: "Another badly spent day."[107] "How idly and vainly I spend my time!" wailed Martha Crawford of Tuscaloosa, Alabama, in 1850.[108] Should they themselves succumb to this sin, southern mothers were determined to save their children from purgatory. As one Charleston mother counseled: "EARLY RISING.—FOR MY OWN CHILDREN," elaborating: "How unbecoming is it to waste the hours of morning in stupyfying drowsiness, when so large a portion of our fellow men are already engaged in their daily avocations; and how appropriate to join our household with scrupulous punctuality, in the morning aspirations of prayer and praise to the God who spreads out far and around us such signal blessings!"[109] Alicia Middleton of Stono, South Carolina, gave her son identical advice in 1827: "Apply yourself dear child with all your might give not your time to any light or trifling amusements or occupations—take exercise *regularly* & rise very early . . . my dear boy we are not placed in this world to be idle."[110]

When planted firmly in the secular world of business and plantation affairs, southern men preferred to couch what they considered wifely duties in profane terms. But the following advice published in the *Tennessee Farmer* in 1836 no doubt held religious significance to the southern matron: "The true economy of housekeeping is, simply the art of gathering up all the fragments, so that nothing be lost. I mean fragments of time, as well as materials. Nothing should be thrown away so long as it is possible to make any use of it, however trifling it may be."[111] And certainly husbands wanted to know how their spouses spent their time at home. As William Elliott wrote to his wife in 1818, "I must beg . . . that you will give me a particular account of all domestic concerns—Where you have been—. . . . How do you occupy your time?"[112]

Though owing much to God, women's everyday life had, as Catharine Beecher well understood, its purely profane aspects, which owed little to God and more to the task and, increasingly, the clock. To some extent, of course, housework was and still is largely task-, not clock-, oriented and it seems that eighteenth- and nineteenth-century women regulated their domestic and public lives by both clock and task. According to Laurel Thatcher Ulrich, for example, eighteenth-century Maine housewives often reckoned their domestic chores such as spinning in terms of tasks completed. But their public "gadding," as was the case with midwives, required that they measure their work sometimes to the hour.[113] As the changes wrought by the nineteenth century began to usher in separate spheres, however, housework and domestic chores came to acquire a clock-regulated quality that women had sometimes experienced in the public world of eighteenth-century work. In some ways, middle- and working-class northern women were united by a familiarity with either the factory or the domestic clock.[114] But southern women, the mistresses most obviously, did not go to the factory. Instead, the factory and its attendant time discipline came to them, first in the form of the household clock that joined white women's traditional task orientation and, second, in instances when mistresses had to manage household labor, as subsequent chapters demonstrate. Clocks, for example, were important for cooking and recipes. Baked apple pudding had to be cooked "forty minutes," sponge cake baked "fifteen minutes," and the ingredients for "Deborah's Batter Pudding" beaten "fifteen minutes."[115] And William R. Bernard's wife's 1847 recipe for the "Best Yeast Ever Made" required the ingredients to be simmered "slowly 10 or 15 minutes, stirring it all the time."[116] Kitchen clocks alone would suffice here.

This emphasis on southern women as the main proprietors of the Protestant work ethic in the South is not without its problems. Most obviously, one wonders why white southern women felt that their time was God's. Part of the answer to the reason why white southern women's Weltanschauung was more akin to that of northern women than to southern men's devolves on the sticky questions of education, the cult of domesticity, and the extent to which the industrial revolution freed women from such bourgeois, domestic imperatives. Generally, however, it may be argued that although northern and southern women differed over time, place, and class, insofar as they shared a "primary identity as wives and mothers under the protection and domination of their husbands," all white, particularly middle-class women, North and South, were inculcated to an ideology stressing home-based piety and morality. It was a worldview rather different from the secular, more public world of men. Eighteenth- and nineteenth-century American women in general were more aware than were their husbands of God's temporal prescription for a good, honest, and moral life.[117] And though it is certainly true that as "members of a slave society, southern women differed in essential respects from other American women," the similarity between the time conceptions of northern women and southern ladies was so great as to cast into doubt the idea that time and its application and conception was one of those essential differences.[118] If, as Elizabeth Fox-Genovese has argued, "southern society developed its own ideals of womanhood," which were presumably distinct from those fostered in the North by bourgeois domestic economy, the proper application of the southern lady's time was not so different from her northern sister's because "the personal qualities" all American women were required "to muster in the discharge of their . . . responsibilities were fully analogous to those prescribed for male success in the capitalist world: thrift, sobriety, self-discipline, work, rationality."[119] Though perhaps noncapitalist in several respects, the southern household generally, its female heads particularly, nevertheless came under the influence of northern, bourgeois domestic economy and its strictures concerning the proper application of women's time.[120]

The conduit for the northern Protestant ethic to the women of the South was books, which served as both formal and informal sources of their education. As is well known, indigenous literature to the South was scarce because the region boasted few publishers or printers.[121] The editors of *De Bow's Review* complained in an 1852 piece entitled, ironically, "Southern School-Books": "The first thought that enters the mind of the enquirer is, that the school-books of the South *originate* in the North. . . . We do not remember a single text-book of the schools printed or published south of Mason and Dixon's line. . . . The southern booksellers are literally in a state of 'peonage' to the 'barons of Cliff-street' and others of that ilk."[122] As another editorial put it in 1854, "We import our very schoolmasters to teach our children—the primers and Bibles out of which they read."[123] The concern was justified. In 1855 the United States imported $30,224 worth of "articles specially imported for philosophical societies, colleges, and seminaries of learning, schools, &c" from pietistic Europe, many of which made their way south.[124] This predominance of northern-published and foreign-composed literature in the South, in conjunction with the fact that in both formal and informal settings, southern women's education, when they were lucky enough to receive it, was more religiously inclined than men's, helps explain why southern women and not men were the main custodians of God's time in the colonial and antebellum South.[125]

The literature available to women at home and at school, then, was born of northern minds like Catharine Beecher's and Yankee presses. In 1852 *De Bow's Review* published extracts from a northern book, *Woman and Her Needs*, on the proper function of American women, supporting the point that southern women were introduced and inculcated to northern notions of time and piety. The "Woman's sphere," it was argued, was located firmly in the roles of "God-serving . . . self denying labor."[126] Men's education, by contrast, was geared more toward the sciences, arts, and classics with less emphasis on biblical or scriptural instruction.[127]

The net effect of these forces was not only to solidify the sphere of white southern women's existence but to make women's time conceptions more sacred and keep men's time more profane.[128] Evidence suggests that southern women's time was always linked closely to God and nature. The absence of nineteenth-century equivalents of Gallup polls makes it unlikely that we shall ever know precisely the proportion of women and men who turned to the sun and God instead of the clock to reckon time, but a source, albeit from the latter half of the nineteenth-century South, suggests that women's time was more Godly and natural than was men's.

In the 1870s New York publishers Henry Holt and Company produced a book called *Mental Photographs: An Album for Confessions of Tastes, Habits, and Convictions*. The album contained questions for young women to ask their friends. One such question was "Your Favorite . . . Hour in the day?" Between 1876 and 1907, one Sumter, South Carolina, woman, Margaret Carson, asked fifty-seven of her friends, men and women, this question and recorded their answers in her copy of *Mental Photographs*. The answers are revealing. Of the fifty-seven respondents, twenty-two were men, seventeen of whom preferred to describe their "Favorite Hour" in natural or religious time. In October 1880, for example, William Timmons answered, "Sunset." But 29 percent of Carson's male friends preferred to define their favorite time of day in clock time. By contrast, only 6 percent of her female respondents identified their favorite hour of the day by the clock; 94 percent responded in terms of God's or nature's time.

Although hardly scientific, this source suggests that late nineteenth-century southern women were less secular than men in their reckoning of time.[129]

As late as 1882, a mother answered her child's question, "What is an hour Mother?" in distinctly Weberian terms: "A white-winged messenger from our Father in Heaven, sent by him to inquire of you, of me, what we are doing, what we are saying."[130]

Although southern men invested heavily in clock time, this does not mean that they were not religious. Many were. But their religious conviction stopped short of making their secular time beholden wholly to God. Masters that they were, men had to be masters of their own time. Anything less would have made them similar to their bondpeople, whose time was not their own.[131]

Time for masters was largely secular and related most obviously to money and control. The time-money equation was born of and reared by colonial southern merchants. But before merchants could reduce time to money, they had to break free from Christian imperatives stressing that all time belonged to God. This process began, according to Jacques Le Goff, in the Middle Ages, when "among the principal criticisms leveled against the merchants was the charge that their profit implied a mortgage on time, which was supposed to belong to God alone."[132] To rationalize time, merchants used God's time by recruiting newly erected church clocks to coordinate city business life and proclaim, to the public at large, the times of markets and the like. "The same process for the rationalization of time," Le Goff points out, "was responsible also for its secularization."[133] And once this rationalization had taken place and time had been rendered increasingly profane, mercantile activity, while simultaneously "distinct and, at particular points, contingently similar" to His and nature's time, became regulated by the clock.[134]

These essential contours of merchants' time were not much different when these agents of commercial capitalism made their way to the New World.[135] Because of their place in the Atlantic marketplace, southern merchants may well have developed a keen sense that time was money and punctuality in business transactions a virtue and necessity, not only from the exigencies of their own trade but from their dealings with northern and European merchants.[136] Northern merchants throughout the colonial period, for example, coached their southern counterparts in the need for punctuality in business. As Boston merchant Jonathan Johnson advised Edward Telfair's Georgia mercantile firm in 1775, "Let me however request of you to execute this order with the utmost punctuality & Expedition."[137] By 1802, however, the shoe appears to

A country couple, Donald McHood and Frances Hood, ca. 1860, with watch chain (Cased Image Collection, Hargrett Rare Book and Manuscript Library, University of Georgia Libraries)

have been on the other foot. As Charleston merchant Thomas Aiton wrote to his firm's parent company, William Stanley and Company of New York:

> Three mails have arrived since we received yours by Post informing us of your intention to Send us by next Mail 2,000 dollars. We have neither received money nor letter. This appears Strange. Such Conduct may be attended with very serious circumstances if repeated. You know as well as us that the most strict punctuality is necessary in money matters. Suppose for a moment we had bought for Cash last Tuesday Cotton to the Amount of 2,000 Dollars under the full conviction of receiving by next days Mail the promised money. Consider what would have been the consequence of such a disappointment.[138]

If losing time was a sin for southern women, being punctual with credit payments was a point of pride, of virtue, for southern merchants. When George Carter failed to pay the credit on a note written by Landon Carter in 1806, the latter complained that "you [have] done more injury to the respectability of my punctual habits in Fredricksburg than any I have ever had before."[139] The wrath of the mercantile community for the improper and frivolous use of time was almost as great as God's.

Similarly, because they exported goods in sailing ships to Europe, colonial southern merchants were not wholly independent of nature, as Le Goff observed of European merchants of an earlier age. Yet this dependency seems to have made southern merchants even more sensitive to the perils of losing time. This much is clear in a letter from London merchants to South Carolina factor Thomas White in 1759: "With respect to the Indies the Market has fallen at last 6/- pr lb besides from its delay in France we shall have no time to make sales before the [current] crop will be coming to Market."[140]

Though no doubt influenced by the presence of public, church-based time, colonial urban merchants, then, like their medieval forebears, developed their own secularized notion of time, a notion that spliced God, nature, and Mammon. As early as 1747, for example, Charleston merchant Henry Laurens cut short his letter to a client on the grounds that a slew of recent business had left him "now extremely hurry'd to fetch up Lost time." Significantly, Laurens was remembered by antebellum southerners as much for "his extraordinary punctuality" as for his distinguished political career.[141] Merchant Robert Raper similarly complained that the late payment of a bill in 1760 was "so much lost time." So worried about the cost of losing time were other colonial merchants that some seemingly developed nervous disorders, the sort of ailments that George M. Beard was later to attribute to the anxiety caused by losing time and running ragged against the clock in his famous 1886 work, *American Nervous-ness: Its Causes and Consequences.* Quackism or not, the similarities of the disorder outlined by Beard and the complaints of Josiah Smith, colonial Charleston merchant, are striking. For Smith "loosing . . . Time" meant "pay-ing a Heavy price," both fiscally and, apparently, physiologically. Lost time, he opined, exacerbated his "Weak Nerves" and "Nervous Disorders."[142] And even these, for Smith, were reckoned in time. As he explained to merchant John Ray of New Jersey, "Nervous complaints will not permit my setting above an hour or two at one time."[143] Little wonder, then, that colonial southern merchants often signed their business letters, "I am in great haste."[144]

This mercantile notion of making the most of time, scrimping and saving time's moments in the endeavor to save money, continued and intensified during the nineteenth century. As British merchant George Walker wrote to John Ball Sr. of South Carolina in 1811: "Sir, I received your letters on Saturday last but had not time to answer them or call on you till this day."[145] Josiah Smith required payment on his notes "punctually as they shall become due" in 1803.[146] Merchant W. E. Haskell not only dated his letter to John Ball Sr. "June 20th 1829 Saturday 11 OClock" but arranged to pick up his note "at between 10 and 12 OClock on Monday."[147]

The physiological complaints also continued. Certainly Charleston planter-lawyer William Elliott understood well the physiological perils of running ragged against the clock and using time well. He advised his son in 1847 that all work and no play was bad for the nerves: "I commend your resolution of being economical—and that of study—After studying hard—take exercise. It is a good plan to put your mind earnestly to it—when you do study—you acquire more in a short time by that process, and then have time for *exercise* and *relaxation*. This *last* must be attended to—if you would avoid being very ner-vous."[148] The process inaugurated by colonial merchants lasted well into the late nineteenth century, percolating down to society at large. As one observer put it in 1894: "The pure cussedness of inanimate things is exemplified no-where so cantankerously as in clocks that ought to run from Sunday to Sunday, but which, as a rule, make a point of running ahead, or behind, so as to confuse the members of the family, and cause them to reach places behind time, or to strain their nervous systems unnecessarily for fear they are going to be late."[149]

Merchants naturally felt that the agricultural life would be less time disci-plined than their mercantile one. As one South Carolina factor explained to a customer in 1816, "Perhaps you have not yet heard that my Brother and myself have turned our attention to agriculture. . . . Here we are not so confined to hours." In 1816, perhaps they were not. The same would be less true during and after the 1830s.[150] Even those antebellum merchants who did branch into agriculture retained their sense of time thrift and punctuality once on the farm, and they were unforgiving of planters who did not do the same.[151]

In their combined roles of purveyors of timepieces and peddlers of the idea that time was money and its loss was costly, colonial merchants bequeathed an important legacy to the antebellum South. Planters from the 1830s on inherited not only colonial merchants' imported clocks and watches but, perhaps more important, an equation of time with money and an attendant desire for the proper, predominantly secular, application of clock time.

The coexistence of clock, God, and nature in the South made it difficult for foreign observers to discern exactly which form of time was most important to the southern mind. Until the developments of the 1830s elevated the importance of clock time in the South, foreign travelers tended to see the South as a region that appealed primarily to nature in its reckoning of time. Coming from wage-labor, industrializing regions, where working hours were longer (though not necessarily more intensive), these visitors tended to transmute, quite wrongly, southerners' appeal to nonclock time into a cultural and social quirk, which they usually labeled as lazy. German itinerant Johann David Schoepf certainly interpreted the practices of North Carolina's ferrymen in this way in the 1780s. His penchant for exactitude could not be satisfied by one southerner: "When at last on the fourth day the expected boat for ferrying-over the horses arrived, the next morning was fixed for the passage, and everything arranged; but although we now had a right to hope for prompt service for once, we found ourselves deceived again when we came to the water-side at 8 o'clock. The gentleman who kept the ferry was still sleeping quietly in bed. . . . Travellers therefore must have a good supply of interest if they are not to be outdone."[152]

Likewise born in and of an urban industrial society where punctuality, time thrift, and clocks were ubiquitous, British merchant Adam Hodgson could not discern the presence of clock time in a South that meshed many forms of time as late as 1820. Of his journey between Monticello and Richmond, Hodgson noted:

Occasionally we heard a clock, which at first startled me, as I had not seen one since we left Georgia, and very few since we set out from Washington; everything being regulated by the sun. If you ask what time it is, it either wants so many hours of noon, or it is so much before, or so much after *sundown*. Meals are regulated by the sun, even in families where there is a watch, or a timepiece, as it is called; and I have very often heard evening service announced at church, to begin at *early* candle light.

Hodgson's concluding comment, however, is the most revealing: "This want of precision would run away with all the spare hours in our country."[153] And on this point he was right. By the standards of industrial, urban Britain, the pre-1830 rural South was not conspicuously punctual or time conscious. The southern mercantile conception of clock time, by itself, was insufficient to draw the region into time-conscious modernity. But had Hodgson returned to the South a decade or so later, he would have observed not only more clocks and watches but a population more concerned with punctuality, time thrift, and the economic and social application of clock time generally; a society, in other words, more like his own. But at the time, his own prejudice and the South's muffled and as yet immature sense of clock time fooled Hodgson into believing that nature and God ruled exclusively and supremely. Even if this were true, which it was not, the dual monarchy was soon to be demoted though not dethroned.

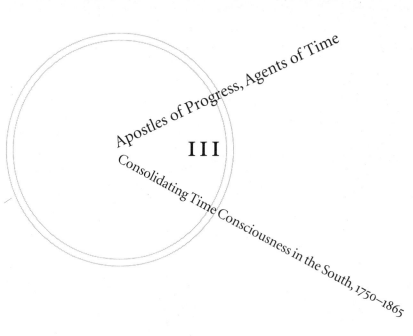

III

Apostles of Progress, Agents of Time

Consolidating Time Consciousness in the South, 1750–1865

To "kill time" was the study and business of all; and in *killing time*, [planters] neglected the management of their affairs, and squandered their estates. The South is now the most prosperous and least skeptical country in the world. Our daily mail (rather unpopular a few years ago, when it was first established) has now become both popular and useful. . . . They hate and oppose modern innovations; yet seem none the worse for it.
—[George Fitzhugh?], "The Valleys of Virginia,"
   De Bow's Review, 1859

The element of time will through all the future be a governing element in transportation.
—[James Henry Hammond], "Letter of Mr. Hammond to
   Assembly Committee," *De Bow's Review*, 1861

The planter is a manufacturer, and as the whole energies of the age are directed to economy of production, he will remain in the rear of mankind until he avails himself of every means of economising his labor and capital, from *smoke*-burners to railroad cars.
—"Rail-Road Influence on Landed Property,"
   De Bow's Review, 1851

Old collaborators though natural, sacred, and mechanical time were in the running of human affairs, the clock began to assert itself more forcefully in this partnership during and after the 1830s in the slave South. Before then, southerners, like their seventeenth-century English forebears, tended to reckon time mainly according to nature's cues and partly through aurally communicated town clocks.[1] In some respects, the groundwork for this temporal reconfiguration had been laid during the colonial period, most obviously by the South's urban merchants. Although there was never any identifiable point at which the clock became ascendant, events coalesced and trends matured in and after the 1830s to urge planters to continue performing what had previously been only sporadic and eccentric experiments with timed slave labor.[2]

The forces behind this heightened time awareness were myriad and were shared by much of the industrializing world. Some, such as the mercantile association of time with money, an inchoate but important familiarity with the principles of time and wage, the punctuality associated with a nascent colonial postal system, and the attendant concern with travel times and urban schedules, had been born in the eighteenth century. These forces gained in potency during the first half of the nineteenth century and were joined by new developments that served to consolidate Americans', including southerners', concern with punctuality and time thrift: the advent of steamboats, railroads, and telegraphs or, collectively, the transport revolution.[3] The yoking of these nineteenth- with eighteenth-century forces, for example the railroad with mail contracts in and after the 1830s, set the stage for southern slaveholders to apply the clock to plantation slave labor. During and after the 1830s the so-called gospel of speed, a credo southerners had always embraced, matured, with the help of these apostles of progress, into a gospel of punctuality.[4]

Because de jure antebellum slavery was born of an ad hoc, de facto colonial slavery first nurtured then slowly consolidated in the seventeenth and eighteenth centuries, there had always been a tradition of occasionally hiring free whites, free blacks, and slaves in the plantation South.[5] Because the legal codification of chattel slavery was gradual, often sporadic, southern planters had always had some experience with the principles of free wage labor and the relationship between time and money that these principles embodied. In other words, planters' dealings with wage laborers in both the colonial and antebellum periods ensured that they would have at least the rudimentary understanding that work could be measured by time.

There are thousands of examples of slaveholders hiring wage labor by the day during the colonial and early national periods.[6] Surveys of hiring practices conducted for every state in the 1790s reported that seasonal and daily, not yet hourly, defined wages were most common.[7] According to studies of eighteenth-century New England time conceptions, the same was true of northern farming communities. "As the century progressed," writes Paul B. Hensley, "records of time spent on work became increasingly more specific in diaries and account books." Hensley notes the case of Abner Sanger, "a farmer of modest means, [who] kept an incredibly detailed log of his daily work routine over the years 1774 to 1794, and he often fractionalized days into increments of hours."[8] Early examples of southern planters similarly fractionalizing the work hours of hired labor can also be found. Charles Pinckney's 1751–52 "Account of Charles and Pompey's Time they Worked for me" contains references to "1/4 day." Such early instances are exceptional, however.[9] But by the last decade of the eighteenth century, things were beginning to change in the South. While the general notion of day labor was common both in cities and on plantations during the colonial period, it was usually on southern plantations like Allard Belin's in the low country of South Carolina that planters had their first taste of wage labor and the timing of work.[10] In 1792, for example, Belin monitored the work time of a slave he had hired, "Mr. Keith's Billey." Obviously the task was an inappropriate measurement for labor hired by the hour. Belin noted in his journal: "Mr. Keith's Billy [sic] came from Laurel Hill this day about 2 o'clock with his Tools," and in 1797 Billey "came here to work at half after two in the afternoon."[11] In December 1773, Chatham County, Georgia, planter William Gibbons Jr. paid one artisan for "29 1/2 days Work" for "repairing a Machine," and one Georgia planter-merchant charged Richard Heather "for a floating punt 1 1/2 days" at three shillings a day in May 1771.[12] Virginia planter William Cabell also reckoned labor time by the half day. "David Dawson began to paint my house & painted one day," he noted in June 1790, explaining, "Am to allow him 6/. for each days work—3 days since above[.] 2 days since above. 3 July 1 day more." Either the house was substantial or the painter agonizingly slow because four years later on the recently inaugurated Independence Day 1794, Cabell again noted: "Gave David Dawson an order for 9/ on Mr R. Rivers, for painting one day & an half @ 6/ p day."[13]

William Chamberlayne of Virginia was a little more precise in his timing of some "7 Sawyers" he employed in 1787. On February 15 the "7 men began to work about 12 OClock" for which he paid them half a day's wages. For February 20, one of the workers, Stephen, went unpaid because "the balance [of the day was] lost by . . . going to see his wife."[14] But whatever the specific amounts of time involved, eighteenth-century planters evidently had some abstract understanding of the relationship between labor power and time. Planter

Robert Johns of Georgia, for example, reminded William Graham that recently hired hands would "come to you for the wages for the time they are employed" and verified that "you know the time allowd. for hands to come up which you must Settle."[15]

This temporal quantification of labor, however imprecise, continued into the antebellum period, when it became more specific. Just like northern farm journals of the period, antebellum plantation journals are replete with hours worked and wages paid to a variety of wage laborers in the South.[16] Three and a quarter days' work, for example, netted laborer James Marsh a little over $7 in 1810, whereas "8 3/4 days Work of White carpenters a[t] $2.00 [per day]" cost planter John Singleton $21.17 in June 1845. Singleton saw nothing wrong with "deducting lost time" for absenteeism.[17] Neither gemeinschaft intimacy nor the Christmas spirit dissuaded antebellum southerners from balancing wages paid with amount of time worked. On December 30, 1810, South Carolina planter Alexander Robert Lawton "had fathers negroes Presten & Martin to work on [the construction of a house]; Christmas carted lumber—They worked in all put together 90 1/2 days at 50 cents per day amt, $45.25."[18] One Chesterfield, South Carolina, planter put the onus of lost time firmly on the shoulders of his hired help. "Daniel Miers" lost "2 1/2 days work" in 1838 and so was paid exactly "66 3/4" cents.[19] Whether owed or to be paid, southerners saw time as representing value. "[Twenty-five cents] Owed [by] Dr. Wm. Parham," noted farmer James Mason in 1842, "By use of horse 1/2 a day at 50 c[ents per day]." A year later he charged G. Nichols one and a half dollars for "3/4 of a days ride."[20]

Planters of the 1850s were similarly sensitive to the value of hired labor, presumably because it was becoming relatively more expensive.[21] When hiring carpenters to shingle a roof on his plantation in 1851, for example, Charles Manigault's overseer, K. Washington Skinner, ordered that the largest shingles be used because "time & labor will be saved as the carpenters can cover the building in half the time that it will take them to cover it with the split ones." Manigault was to receive similar intelligence four years later from his son Louis, who informed him that he had employed a bricklayer on the plantation "up to this morning 16th Inst. 9 Oclock." A bricklayer was also employed by Henry L. Pinckney of Sumter District, South Carolina, in 1864. For "seven & half days at $8.00 per day" Pinckney paid him $60 for miscellaneous plantation repairs.[22] And merchant-planter Stephen Doar of South Carolina apparently applied similar principles to his overseer's labor: "Apr 1 1851: Wages as Overseer from 1st January to 13 Augt. 1851—say 225 days."[23] When hired labor was paid by the day, the duration of the working day was measured by the hour. As Edgefield District, South Carolina, planter John Forsyth Talbert noted in his diary in 1864: "At 3 o'clock in the Evening J. B. Newmans commenced work on Harness &c, worked till Saturday 3 o'clock,=in all 4 days."[24]

Albeit peripheral, the presence of wage labor in the antebellum plantation South alerted planters to the idea that time could be lost. This was especially apparent when slaves hired to work on other masters' plantations did not put in the full time for which they, or more probably their masters, were being paid. A South Carolina planter made this clear to a fellow master who had hired him one of his slaves. "Concerning the time lost by Billy," he wrote to R. B. D. in 1842, "either I make a deduction for the time lost or return him to make it up."[25] It was an idea born of merchants and later bred by planters.

Inevitably, southerners' understanding of the principles and workings of wage labor heightened with the expansion of the market economy and the concomitant tendency toward rationalization in antebellum life generally in and after the 1820s. The increasing complexity of antebellum American social and economic relations, it has been argued, necessitated not only the standardization but also the rationalization of local government and civic institutions. The South was not marginal to this wider trend. As early as 1830, South Carolina's legal scholars acknowledged the confusion created by eighteenth-century statutes' invocation of natural time in foreclosure procedures. Debtors argued that the law's reference to a month meant a lunar month while local sheriffs often interpreted it as calendar. After 1830, the law agreed with the latter and rejected natural time as the proper legal basis for the "computation of time" in South Carolina's legal codes.[26] This rationalization was mirrored by the inner workings of the court system, where recording the amount of time worked by, say, clerks of court became highly specific. By his own watch, clerk of Newberry, South Carolina, County court J. A. Johnson consistently recorded the amount of time he worked. On May 9, 1846, he made a typical entry in his work ledger: "7/8 of this days Recording @ $1 pr. day [equals] 87 1/2 [cents]."[27]

But conscious efforts at bureaucratic rationalization and standardization aside, there were other, larger, and more potent forces at work pushing first colonial and later antebellum southerners toward the adoption of clock time.

In various forms, a postal service had been in existence in North America since the late seventeenth century. Despite attempts to rationalize, systematize, and extend the scope of the mail service during the colonial period, it is widely agreed now, as it was then, that the colonial mail service was rudimentary, irregular, and inefficient. Despite the election of Benjamin Franklin to postmaster general by the Continental Congress in July 1775, it was not until after the Revolution that Franklin's efforts to systematize and expand the service were implemented. But little could be done to deliver the mail to the minute or hour before the railroads were contracted.[28]

Yet early failures to be punctual are not as revealing as the nature of the desire itself. As southerners of the 1840s were perfectly willing to admit, the early postal service was not remarkable for its efficiency. But this was not for want of trying. As early as 1804, southern postmasters published specific delivery schedules. In October 1804, for instance, B. Cenas, the New Orleans postmaster, virtually guaranteed that "the mail for the future will arrive here every Monday, at 5 o'clock, P.M., and will start every Thursday, at 7 o'clock, A.M."[29] By 1835 postmasters were still making contracts with the owners of stagecoach services stipulating precise times for delivery. But it is unlikely that stage owners, like William Smith of Virginia, could have kept to the stringent times demanded by the post office. Inclement weather, shoddy roads, lame horses, and broken spokes probably made Smith absorb the penalty "incurred for each ten minutes delay in the delivery of the mail after the time fixed for its delivery at any post-office specified in the schedule."[30]

Certainly, postmasters always enjoined newly contracted stage carriers to deliver the mail within contract time and tended to dismiss local carriers' excuses for late post. In April 1802, for example, Postmaster General Gideon Granger explained to John Holmes, local postmaster in Bowling Green, Virginia, that tardy passengers on mail stages were not to interfere with the punctual delivery of the post on a new route and, furthermore, insisted that his postal delivery be performed with incredible exactitude:

> I am sensible that the Travellers will not have the same number of hours for Refreshment that many of them might wish, but Sir, you must reflect that no time for rest is allowed from here through the Eastern States. That at this place as is your own are the only resting places on the main post road where the stages travel—that most people from the Eastward will wish to tarry a day or two at the Seat of Government—The evil of having one nights rest infringed upon cannot be great to such persons as travel in the stage.

Surely, hinted Granger, Holmes could emulate the example of other postmasters. "My Arrangements to the Eastward," boasted Granger, "have been in operation for a fortnight, and altho the Mail moves over the rate of 110 miles a day it proceeds with the regularity of a well finished clock—It has in every instance arrived in due season." Or as Abraham Bradley of the general post office put it to stagecoach mail operator John G. Woolfolk of Virginia in 1813, "We shall calculate on your punctually carrying the entire [mail] within the limit of your schedule." But postmasters probably realized the impossibility of precisely timed stage-coordinated mail. As Bradley wrote to Woolfolk later that year, "I hope you will at all events carry on letters and newspapers in the contract time."[31] Hope alone was no guarantee of punctuality, however. In truth, the technology did not yet exist to enable postmasters and mail carriers to approximate their punctual ideals. Only by the standards of the late antebellum period could southerners deservedly scoff at the slowness and inefficiency of the postal service of "Olden Time."[32]

The South's merchants were, not surprisingly, especially aware of the irregularity of the colonial and early national postal system. In 1793 Georgia merchants complained that the late post had disrupted affairs that required punctuality. As Joseph Clay explained to Edward Telfair from Savannah: "By some Accident or neglect the Post has not come in from Augusta this Week as usual, the consequence of [this] is you will not receive mine respecting Mssrs. Roberts & Johnston & Robertsons proposals in time to give an Answer to them." The inefficient post heightened their sensitivity to the fact that "there is not time within the period" to rectify the problem.[33] In some respects, however, late mail always plagued southerners, and it still does. As late as 1829, for example, Columbia, South Carolina, resident, Andrew Johnston wrote to his father: "About 1/2 past 1 oClock the Northern Mail arrived for the first time since Sundays mail which was recd on Monday, instead of Sunday."[34]

Though the reality proved elusive, southerners strove for the ideal of punctuality, of temporal coordination. Sometimes they looked elsewhere for the perfect model. In this context, English mail and stagecoaches were well thought of, as Charleston's children learned from the *Rose Bud*, which published the following account in 1833: "So punctual are many of the coaches in England in arriving at different points along the road, that the country people frequently set their clocks and watches at the moment of time when they see those vehicles, instead of employing the sun as formerly. . . . Only one minute is allowed to change horses, and this operation is often performed in fifty seconds."[35]

In an effort to improve postal efficiency and speed and overland travel, there was some push during the 1840s to make the South's muddy dirt tracks speedy plank roads. Apparently the difference between dirt and plank was considerable. A Georgia "proprietor of the line of stages on this road" in Macon told one inquirer "that a team of horses would perform nine miles an hour, including stops, or ten miles travelling time, with the same ease to themselves that they could perform six miles on a good summer road." The speed attained and time saved on plank roads could be deceptive. "Indeed," continued the reporter, "I heard the remark often, that you never know, or are aware of how fast you are getting forward on a plank road, in consequence of the comparative smoothness of the track and the steady and regular pace of the horse, until examining your watch, you probably find yourself at your journey's end much sooner than you anticipate."[36]

Both physically and intellectually, antebellum southerners were as aware of the post office and the idea of punctuality as were northerners.[37] By June 1851, for example, of the 19,622 post offices in the United States, 7,083, or about 36 percent, were to be found in southern states, roughly the same number in the North, and 5,553, or 28 percent, in the western states and territories.[38] And by the late antebellum period southerners, like their northern brethren, were also aware that the mechanics of delivering the post represented a break in time, a disjuncture with the past, because the "system of posts, as at present in operation, is an invention of modern times." The modernity of the postal system stemmed not only from Franklin's pioneering efforts to systematize delivery schedules in the late eighteenth century but, far more important, was solidified once railroad companies began to secure contracts to carry the nation's mail. Because these contracts demanded minute attention to the clock, because "only seven minutes at the most are allowed for opening and closing the mails," and because "forfeitures of pay, wholly or partial, according to a fixed scale, are to take place when trips are not performed and fines are imposed for arrivals behind time," southerners came to expect, indeed demand, that their mail be delivered on time by that apostle of progress, the iron horse.[39] Woe, then, to mail carriers who chanced to be late, unless good excuses were forthcoming. "This day I wrote a long letter to Miss Coulton [hoping it] might go by todays downward mail," noted Mitchell King in his diary on September 1, 1855, continuing, "but it to my great displeasure past [sic] at 1/2 past 6—3 1/2 hours before its scheduled time." His anger abated when he learned of the cause for such an irregularity: "But I afterwards learned that the Drivers wife was down the road very sick & he had hastened to her, which I consider a valid excuse." Nothing short of sickness permitted clemency for tardiness.[40]

The demand that information generally, mail specifically, be communicated punctually, efficiently, and regularly reached its apogee with the arrival of the telegraph in the South. The first telegraph in the United States, in fact, was laid in the South: the Baltimore-Washington line in 1844. By 1847 lines had been laid along railway tracks from Virginia to Georgia and were soon extended west to Mobile.[41]

The importance of the time-saving telegraph was, predictably, apparent to merchants, whose old penchant for time thrift could now be satisfied and nervous ailments and complaints about tardiness partially, though never wholly, cured. Statements to this effect were common: "Every day affords instances of the advantages which our business men derive from the use of the telegraph. Operations are made in *one day* with its aid, by repeated communi-cations, which could not be done in from two to four weeks by mail—enabling them to make purchases and sales which otherwise would be of no benefit to them, in consequence of length of time consumed in negotiation."[42] And as they did with the mail, southern merchants often used the telegraph to com-municate essential business information to planter-clients. One Georgia mer-chant in a matter of seconds warned his South Carolina client about the potentially deleterious consequences of his son's plantation management prac-tices at "8 o'clock, 23 Minutes, P.M." on January 5, 1858. Similarly, planters came to recruit the telegraph to coordinate plantation affairs when out of town. Via his Georgia merchant, Charles Manigault communicated his "plan-tation rules" to his new overseer in 1859 through the "New-York & New-Orleans Magnetic Telegraph Company." The communication got through and his instructions were carried out accordingly. At other times, planters acted like antebellum brokers ordering their coastal factors, "Dont offer my rice now in Savannah for Sale" by telegraph. The much maligned absentee southern planter was not as divorced from plantation operations as some have been led to believe.[43]

By the 1850s telegraphic communications were widely used to coordinate no small amount of antebellum civic, economic, and social affairs. Politicians, for example, found the wire useful. U.S. senator from North Carolina Willie Person Mangum apparently found the Baltimore-Washington telegraph handy for gathering political intelligence about the 1844 Van Buren and Tyler conventions held in Baltimore. He wrote to his wife, "I have time only to write you a line. This is the day of the Van Buren & Tyler Conventions. By the Miraculous Tele-graph, information of what they are doing at Baltimore, 40 miles off, is commu-nicated in less than ten seconds." In short, the "telegraph and the rail-road, twin sisters," were of immeasurable importance to all, not just merchants.[44]

Although Robert Fulton's *Clermont* had powered its way up the Hudson to Albany in 1807, steamboats did not navigate the South's rivers and coastal waterways in appreciable numbers until the late 1820s, and full steam-powered transatlantic crossings were not common until at least a decade later.[45] Ante-bellum southerners' reliance on sail as opposed to steam continued their close relationship with nature. As William Elliott made clear on a trip to Charleston in 1823: "We were uncommonly fortunate in making our passage. At twelve oclock we were de[ad] calm . . . the wind then springing up we ran to Charles-ton in four hours."[46] But when steam did replace sail, not only was south-erners' reliance on nature lessened and their holy communion weakened, but time itself was contracted, especially on long sea trips. "This morning we passed the Calhoun—which sailed from Charleston on Thursday last," noted John Berkley Grimball on a trip north in 1835, explaining in prose awkward but revealing, "It is in such weather as this that the superiority of Steam is made to appear."[47]

The departure of scheduled steamboats not only affected southerners' mental appreciation of clock time but altered their behavior. Historians sometimes complain about the illegibility of antebellum southerners' handwriting. Henry C. King's hurried note to his father in 1845 from the Charleston docks might explain why: "It now wants 10 minutes of 4 oclock & the Boat is apt to leave me This must be my apology for the looks of this note."[48] The power of steam in transatlantic crossings especially was acknowledged and lauded when the oceanic distance was reduced to between eleven days, four hours, forty-five minutes and thirteen days, eight hours as opposed to actual miles.[49]

But river or oceanic travel, whether by steam or sail, was no match for the railroad, which was faster, more regular, and more independent of nature. In 1847, *De Bow's Review* declared: "At this late day it will not be denied that railroads, from their uniformity of action, speed and certainty, and from the uninterrupted communication which they preserve, not being 'arrested by drought, nor suspended by frost,' have the decided preference in the conveyance of passengers and light goods, over all other methods." Empirical evidence was recruited to support such a claim:

> At a speed of twenty miles per hour, the trip for passengers can be performed from the mouth of the Ohio to Mobile, in twenty-two hours. The trip between Mobile and New Orleans is now made in fourteen to sixteen hours. With the railroad, therefore, the transit could be made between New Orleans and the mouth of the Ohio in from thirty-six to thirty-eight hours. By the river route it is now performed in about seventy-two hours down, and ninety-six hours up, or on an average of eighty-four hours, being a difference in saving of time in favor of the railroad of from forty-six to forty-eight hours in the transit to New Orleans, and from seventy-six to seventy-eight hours to Mobile.[50]

In the same vein were discussions of the New Orleans–New York route:

> The most direct route has always been through Alabama, Georgia, South Carolina, North Carolina, Virginia, and other States on the line of travel. Performed by stages, this was an exceedingly tedious, difficult, and expensive route, and was only used by those to whom time was an object. . . . The time within which the connection is made through to New York, is eight

days; which may be abridged, perhaps to seven, when the one hundred miles of stageing [*sic*] is connected by railroad.[51]

Although more punctual and regular than riparian and oceanic steamboats, railroad time was not wholly independent of nature. Not only was local time defined by the time the sun set and rose, thus making for a multiplicity of times along southern railroad routes, but train timetables often reflected the influence of clock, solar, and seasonal time. The timetable for the Vicksburg and Jackson, Mississippi, railroad, for example, read: "Freights going eastward are received daily, Sunday excepted, at the Vicksburg depot, from 7 A.M. to 5 P.M. in the summer, from 8 A.M. to 4 P.M. in the winter, and freights for Vicksburg at all the other depots from 8 A.M. to sunset."[52] That solar time should merge with clock time on the railroads, however, hardly consigned southern railroads to premodern oblivion. Just as the telegraph complemented the post, so railroads served not only to increase expectations about the punctuality of the mail but the times of travel generally.

Handmaiden to these trends was an increasing concern with punctuality, a concern ushered in primarily by the railroads and the attendant expanded postal service in the 1830s. Historians have been quick, too quick perhaps, to point out how agonizingly cumbersome railroad travel could be in the mid-nineteenth-century South. Indeed, it is perhaps tempting, though mistaken, to impute the slowness and perceived inefficiency of the railroads as much to some putative sense of southern indifference to punctuality as to the technological condition of railroads and their rolling stock.

That antebellum southern railroad travel was tedious and difficult there is no doubt. Historian William Freehling has put the difficulty into appropriate perspective. "A modern jet," writes Freehling, "races over the approximately 650 miles between New Orleans and Charleston in a single easy hour. A modern automobile speeds over the approximately 750 miles of superhighway between the two cities in a single hard day." By contrast, "Mid-nineteenth century trains could meander over the approximately 1000 miles of tracks between the two centers in a long, unforgettable week—if one made connections." And here Freehling hits on an important truth. It was not for the want of a modern time sensibility that southern railroad travel was tedious, arduous, and subject to innumerable stoppages and holdups. Simply put, railroad technology was not as advanced as southerners' railroad mentality. They indeed wanted and tried to be on time. But in a South where myriad local times made it almost an intellectual impossibility to reckon train schedules with any reasonable accuracy, in an age when boilers broke down, driving wheels were "found split & unserviceable," cattle wandered onto open tracks, and railroad engineers were sometimes horribly unqualified to run the engine, delays were inevitable. That all Americans complained, sometimes vehemently, about such delays reveals their concern with being on time. Sometimes their complaints were requited, sometimes not, just as, in fact, modern jet passengers moan about mechanical delays on runways and fret about making their next appointment. The main thing that distinguishes the antebellum southern traveler from his or her late twentieth-century counterpart is not an appreciable difference in time consciousness but merely the technological means enabling and facilitating that same desire for punctuality. The Old South must have been a temporally frustrating place, leaving many people uptight about being late. But the pervasiveness of tardiness did not lessen the desire for punctuality. Rather, it seems to have heightened it.[53]

Of course, railroad travel could never be without its hiccups. Patrons could arrive in time for departures, but the performance of the train might not live up to their expectations. This was made clear by Mitchell King during a trip from Charleston to Greenville in July 1852: "On the morning of thuesday [*sic*] the 20th Inst I left Charleston by the Rail Road for Argyle . . . at 3 PM reach[ed] Cola. in good time for the Newberry train . . . we had got 5 miles from Cola [when we] find ourselves stopped by our own loaded truck that had injured the road and left the track—detained it by 2 hours . . . [did] not reach Newberry until past 8."[54] Ill-equipped southerners, those minus watches, found it similarly hard going to travel by train. Just before embarking on a railroad trip from Colleton to Spartanburg District in 1859, planter David Gavin had the grave misfortune to break "my watch again winding it, this is I think the third time I have broken this watch winding it." Gavin was frustrated because it "is not only annoying but expensive, and I now need it very much as I intend to start to Glenn Springs to-day."[55] And what appears to have been the common practice by railroad companies of frequently changing schedules could hardly have eased an already confused situation. Though they were monthlies, southern agricultural journals did their best to publish these changes ahead of time although one can easily envision planters arriving for a train whose schedule had been changed a day or so before.[56]

Yet the antebellum northern railway network was no more efficient or punctilious. Southerners traveling in the North found it just as grueling as dealing with lackadaisical southern lines. This is clear from one planter's travel diary from the 1830s: "This morning at 6—embarked in the Steam-Boat for South Amboy where we took the Railroad cars. . . . It is 35 miles from Amboy to Bordentown, which we performed in 3 1/2 hours. . . . Reached Philadelphia in time to shave and dress for a 3 OClock dinner. . . . I am certain I have never travelled the distance without much greater fatigue."[57] Even the northern traveler Frederick Law Olmsted, who was bitterly critical of southern trains, conceded a similar point on a trip to Mobile: "I left Savannah for the West, by the Macon road; the train started punctually to a second, at its advertised time; the speed was not great, but regular, and less time was not lost unnecessarily, at way-stations, than usually on our Northern roads."[58]

Predictably, the intermittent nature of railroad travel caused coastal merchants no little inconvenience in their dealings with inland planters. Charleston cotton factor John B. DeSaussure encountered some difficulty in coordinating railroad times when sending his planter client some bagging and rope in 1851. He explained: "I will purchase & forward these articles on Monday so as to leave in the freight train on Tuesday morning." Lest his customer thought him less than punctilious, he went on, "I would send them by Monday's night train, but unfortunately the night train only makes a connection with the Camden train 3 times a week, & Tuesday is one of the intermitted [sic] days; & the passenger train on Monday leaving here at 8 A.M., I could not purchase these articles early enough to be sent to the R.R. for that train." Cotton factoring evidently required a knowledge not just of market prices but also of train schedules.[59]

John Bruce, president of the Winchester and Potomac Railroad Company, recognized that his railroad's unpredictability, tardiness, and inability to transport goods from Harpers Ferry inland on a regular and punctual basis discredited the railroad in the eyes of important customers. "Merchants," he lamented in April 1836, "have lost confidence in the ability of the company to transport." Bruce consequently went to great lengths to make the newly formed railroad run on time by berating his engineers about late departures. By September 1836, his efforts were beginning to pay off: "Tennessee comes in with remarkable regularity—not varying more than five minutes any evening."[60]

But whatever the problems plaguing antebellum railroad time, the prospect of a line replacing a stagecoach route was eminently pleasing to southerners tired of dealing with the toils of preindustrial modes of transportation. As one frustrated visitor to Newberry, South Carolina, in 1840 made clear: "A line of stages conveys you, in a snail's pace, to our far-famed Seat of Government. John Bull, who rattles in the coach from Edinburgh to London at the rate of eleven miles an hour, and grumbles about slow driving, may here read the book of Job, and study patience. These forty miles are accomplished with some exertion in fifteen or sixteen hours, at the rate of two miles and a half an hour, and at an expense, to the impatient traveller, of twelve cents and a half per mile." Such problems, this traveler hoped, would "be mended" when "the railroad is completed."[61]

Like postal officials, southern railroad entrepreneurs took much of their experience from England generally, the various experiments performed during the late 1820s and early 1830s on the Liverpool and Manchester line specifically. As early as 1834, for example, Richmond's *Farmers' Register* reported in detail the "times occupied in descending 278 yards" by various engines in terms of "50 seconds, 40 seconds," and "49 seconds."[62] Southerners also compared the speed of their trains to those in Europe and found their railroads not too far behind their northern and European counterparts, if at all.[63] And if exceptional examples of "railroad rapidity" occurred in the North, southern agricultural periodicals were anxious that their clientele should be made aware of them. When "the Camden Company" managed to run a train from New York to Philadelphia "in less than five hours" the *Farmers' Register* took up the story and was not a little in awe: "This calculation may appear incredible to the public. . . . Ten years ago who would have supposed that in 1834, the distance between New York and this city [Philadelphia] would have been diminished to five hours?" By the 1830s, however, southerners too were in the competition to reduce space to time and with some success.[64]

Inevitably, sectional competition and the fear of falling behind in the national race toward modernity provided much of the impetus for the construction of southern railways and the improvement of their efficiency. Certainly this was the case with one of the South's, and nation's, pioneer steam railways, the Charleston and Hamburg. Fearing that the leveling off of trade with the hinterland that had occurred during the 1820s might continue and so undermine Charleston's economic security in the following decade, president of the South Carolina Canal and Railroad Company Elias Horry explained to the Palmetto State's citizens why it was important for them to complete the Charleston and Hamburg railroad link specifically and pioneer southern tracks generally. In a speech in 1833 he contended:

> By establishing railroads, so located as to pass into the interior of the Several States, every agricultural, commercial, or saleable production, could be brought down from remote parts of the country to these cities and towns; and from them, such returns, as the wants of the inhabitants of the interior required, could be forwarded with great dispatch and economy, thereby forming a perfect system of mercantile exchanges, effected in the shortest possible time, and giving life to a most advantageous commerce.

Horry's concluding remarks proved prophetic. If completed, the Charleston-Hamburg line would, he reckoned, have the following effects: "Space will appear as if diminished. . . . Planters within reach of the railroad will prefer it for sending their crops . . . all in a short space of time, and at a very diminished expense."[65] Space, as Horry predicted, would become reduced to time and such a mastery would not be too long in coming.

Although New England's railroads were the first to standardize their schedule times with the use of the telegraph in 1849, the ideal of achieving such unprecedented temporal coordination appears to have been considered first in the South.[66] Southern railroads, in fact, were perhaps the real pioneers of American railroad building generally.[67] Teething problems aside, the earliest southern railroads of the 1830s at least tried to make their trains run on time, not an insignificant achievement before the introduction of standard time in 1883. By 1834 the 136-mile Charleston-Hamburg railroad in South Carolina, at that time the world's longest railway under single management, had in part achieved its promise to attain "the greatest possible regularity in the time of running Passenger Engines" by strategically placing clocks at six of its most important depots and requiring station agents to send a daily log of arrival and departure times to the railroad's head office in Charleston. The line's chief engineer, northern-born and British-trained Horatio Allen, stipulated fines for drivers arriving early or late: "Regulations have been established fixing the hour of departure . . . as well as that of the earliest time, at which they are permitted under a penalty of five dollars, to arrive at the following [station]." And though Allen readily admitted that "the only difficulty that has been found in carrying this into practice, has arisen from the want of a uniform standard of time at the different points," by 1845 the railroad had nevertheless improved its efficiency enough to persuade the United States postal service that it could deliver the mail on time. Trains failing "to arrive within the contract time" specified by the post office incurred hefty fines.[68] According to one Virginian in 1836, when "the RR is playing the Devil" with the mail, sincere efforts were made to "mark . . . what time the mail [arrives] each way then we can know whose fault it is," and the guilty were fined accordingly.[69]

The yoking of post and rail in the decades after 1830 tells us much about the demands for punctuality from the postal service and the ability of local railroad lines realistically to meet such demands. Railroad companies took advantage of postal provisions allowing private stagecoach companies and ship lines to tender proposals to carry the U.S. mail, but as soon as the iron horse and its tracks were in working order, the companies offered their services to postmasters general. Public altruism, needless to say, was not the motive. Horatio Allen reported to the stockholders of the South Carolina Canal and Railroad Company (SCC&RR) in 1834: "Proposals have been made to carry all the Mails that the Post-Office Department may find expedient or advantageous to send upon the line of road, for the term of four years." Next year's report was nearer the truth. Because railroads could deliver the mail more quickly and with greater regularity, they wanted the post office to up the ante and their own profits. "Upon the estimate for the daily mails," read the report, "we will only remark, that it cannot be less than $10,000, as the mails between Branchville and Columbia, and the great Northern and Southern mails from Aiken to Columbia, from the saving of time . . . , may reasonably be calculated upon, and ought not to be carried for a less sum."[70]

At first, the arrangement worked well and the post office, lured by the prospect of greater speed and punctuality, acquiesced to the SCC&RR's demands. "Lately," reported the company's president in 1839, "a permanent arrangement has been made with the Post-Master General, for a further term of four years, ending the 30th June, 1843, at the above rate of $27,600 per year." They were, it seemed, perfect partners: "Our success with the daily mail has been remarkable,—there was but a single day on which the mail was not delivered in contract time, and was then prevented by the snow storm on the 4th of March."[71]

But it should not be assumed that railroad companies generally, and the SCC&RR specifically, were falling over themselves to procure mail contracts. Contracting with the post office entailed major rescheduling, delaying passenger and, especially, freight trains, and the very real fear that trains could not accommodate the postmaster general's demands that pickup and delivery times be coordinated to the minute. All these points were explained to the SCC&RR's stockholders in mid-1839:

> The Post Master General has solicited proposals . . . for a daily service upon this line, with a view of having the great Eastern and Western mails pass through Wilmington and Charleston to Augusta, Geo.
>
> On the above route there are nine places to deliver and receive mails, each causing a delay of ten minutes, provided only five minutes is allowed the respective Post Masters to put in and take out their letters and packages, as the other five minutes is lost in stopping and starting the engine—not calculating the time occupied in carrying the bags to and from the post-office, as this is about as long as is required to take in wood and water, which is in some instances taken at the mail station. Thus it is shown that the time lost in a trip by the way mails is one and a half hour: long enough to make 30 miles distance.

Slack postal officials, after all, could cost railroads money. The worry that the postal service might not be able to match railroad punctuality and schedules was very real because the post office fined the companies for late arrival and delivery: "In addition to this the petty fines that are imposed for unavoidable delays, or perhaps for some thing that has occurred on some other route, which may not be easily proved not to have been on this, are vexatious." If postmasters would guarantee to make deposits on the trains in "not over *five minutes*" and the compensation was upped to an unspecified amount, the SCC&RR, however, agreed to carry the mail. The rationale behind the railroad company's thinking was simple: the public demanded punctual mail and no one else could deliver the post as quickly or as punctually as the train. Consequently, the SCC&RR could afford to be picky, demand what was deemed fair remuneration, and dictate to the postmaster what times the mail should be ready for pickup. If the postmaster disagreed, the railroads declined the contract, as the SCC&RR threatened to do in January 1839.[72]

As is often the case, it was the average citizen, the businessman especially, who was caught in the middle of debates over contracts and routes between post offices and railroad companies. In 1838, when the postal service threatened to shift its railway mail service going through Raleigh to Augusta in favor of a steamboat service from Wilmington to Charleston, anxious citizens along the original line petitioned the post office not to change the route. Their arguments were compelling and appealed directly to the postmaster general's sense of time. Boats could be delayed more readily by weather, they pointed out, not to mention the ability of the train to save between ten and twenty-two hours, once additional railway lines had been completed.[73]

In the end, however, because money was at stake and because the post office and public alike demanded punctuality, railroads managed to establish fairly punctual schedules and keep to them. Less than a year after its completion, for example, the Winchester and Potomac Railroad Company appears to have satisfied the high standards of its president, John Bruce. By May 15, 1837, Bruce was satisfied that his "passenger train[s were] arriving at each end of the road with great punctuality." The effect of the ability to run trains on time was apparent to Bruce: "Much money received. . . . Passengers much pleased." Revenue was no doubt increased when the line secured a mail contract in 1839.[74]

The net effect of such time-specific forces as the post, steamships, railroads, and telegraphs on the mentalité of antebellum southerners was profound. Not only did these corporeal developments influence southerners' physical behavior, they also altered their intellectual awareness and perception of time. Freneticism, a compulsion to note clock time, be on time, and the tendency to reduce physical, geographical space to time itself are among the most salient but historically overlooked features of the post-1830 South.[75]

The punctuality demanded by the post manifested itself most obviously in southerners' letters, many of which included not just the date but also the time of letter writing. Planter John Ball Jr., for example, dated his latter to "Lucille" in 1832, "5 O'clock Monday afternoon feby 27, 1832."[76] Charleston City Court judge Mitchell King similarly dated one of his letters "2 PM" on June 11, 1855, and another to his merchant clients, "1 PM" two weeks later.[77]

The need to write letters in time for the post office's pickup altered southerners' appreciation of time earlier still. In October 1805, Georgia physician Daniel Turner informed his parents in Rhode Island: "My business from town obliges me to hurry, as I shall not be able to return before the mail closes."[78] Likewise, in April 1809 Ann Simons of Charleston informed her correspondent: "I have only time My Dear Mary to say that I have with pleasure procured the articles of your memorandum, and regret that I could not obtain them in time for the last Post."[79]

Nor were lovers exempt from the push against the clock instigated by the mail. As southerner M. A. J. Washburn wrote to "My darling Fannie" from Saratoga Springs in 1858: "I must say adieu. I could write for an hour longer, but must not delay for fear that I may not mail my letter in time."[80] James Burchell Richardson's letter to his wife in 1829 was also defined by the time the mail departed. He squeezed in what he could: "As the mail does not close before tomorrow 2 OClock, I will retain this letter to the latest period of the mail's departure."[81]

William Jervey of Darlington, South Carolina, felt hurried by the time of the post, too. As he wrote to planter-merchant Josiah Smith of Charleston in 1862, "I have only time before the mail closes to acknowledge receipt of your favor 28th Ult."[82] One southerner's simple introduction to a letter in 1836 disclosed: "My Dear Brother, I have only a few moments before the mail closes to say."[83] South Carolina planter James Burchell Richardson articulated the close relationship between postal time, the household clock, and the punctuality required by the mail in exquisite detail. As early as 1824, Richardson wrote to his son at college, "As this is the day that the Post passes it [this letter] must be hurried to the Office to be in the mail in time." Two pages later, Richardson knew he had to close the letter and get it into the post. "Adieu my Dear William," he closed, noting, "the clock has just announced to me that it is 5 OClock a.m." Simultaneously, "the joyous sound of the Drivers Bugle is rejoicing to summon the workmen to rise to labor; to rouse the drowsy, & stimulate the industrious."[84]

The post was not the only force promoting a heightened time awareness in the antebellum South. Limited though steam travel was, the times of arrival of steamboats nevertheless seem to have been important to southerners, and they arranged their schedules around them. In 1856 Charles Manigault told his son that he was to meet W. B. Pringle, who "will arrive here per Steamer from Georgetown from 2 to 4 oclock this day, with his things, & I will be on the wharf until 3 1/2 for him So that Should he arrive in time I will immediately hurry him off to the Gordon which leaves this [place] at 4 P.M." In this instance, the southerner was more punctual than the boat. In a postscript, Manigault moaned: "3 o.clock P.M. I have just return from Southern Warf looking out sharp for Steamer . . . which is said to be a 'Slow Coach' & when she is first seen entering north chanel [*sic*] near Sullivans Island it *then* takes her 1 1/4 hours to reach the city."[85] And just as the post had rushed Daniel Turner in his letter writing in 1805, the impending departure of a boat north from Savannah rendered another, similarly hurried, letter to his parents in March 1806: "The vessel sails so soon I hardly have time to write." Perhaps the South, even in the early national period, was not as "indolent" or the desert of industry and efficiency that he had fooled himself into believing upon his arrival in Georgia a year earlier.[86]

If mail and steamboat times made southerners frenetic and punctual, railroads only heightened the pace. Train conductors appear to have been merciless when patrons were late. Visitors to Rosanna Law's Greenwood, South Carolina, home in 1853 committed the sin of tardiness and were punished accordingly: "They came to 96 to come in the car, but the Conductor would not wait for them, altho the carriage was in sight, which was certainly very unaccommodating." Law herself did not make the same mistake a couple of months later: "James & I, rose early, & left, before any of the family were up but Ma. We got to the village in time, & came home in the Car."[87] Passengers, of course, blamed the train if they missed it. But the blame may well have rested with their own slovenliness. "This evening the passengers," noted railroad president John Bruce in August 1839, "were left behind to their great mortification. It is generally believed they might have got over in time with their baggage but for their own inattention."[88] Obviously the railroads educated the public as much as the public educated the railroads about timeliness.

The overall impact of railroads on southern notions of progress was considerable. One writer in the 1850s explained how urban characteristics, time presumably included, were transplanted to the rural South by the railroad, thus bringing planters within the purview of a time-conscious modern world: "We may add, truly, that the railroad is the great apostle of progress. . . . It carries out the city into the country and its abundance into the city. It equalizes the value of the products of labor, it gives new life to business, cheapens and expedites transportation, gives it certainty and punctuality . . . and makes travel a delight."[89] Although planters had been in the modern world for some time, now they were of it.[90]

Because of its ability to incorporate far-flung and previously remote southern localities into a national market, entrepreneurs pitching a "rail-road system for New Orleans" stressed the punctuality not just of their railroad route but of the Mississippi and Ohio river barges connecting with their train depots. "The time-telling punctuality of these rail-road boats," it was argued, "will work the trade of those giant rivers into a system of the most perfect business-like economy."[91] Other southern businessmen applauded the saving of time facilitated by railroad travel. "Inasmuch as time is the chief object in transporting food," one southern writer pointed out, "a rail-road travelling at the rate of 15 miles per hour, which is the usual rate for freight trains, will in three hours produce 45 miles, while a wagon will in the same time come but 15 miles. . . . Therefore time and distance must be economized" by freighting by rail.[92]

But as with all progress, there was a price, sometimes mortal, to pay. While people no doubt applauded the iron horse for facilitating visits to relatives and friends that would have been difficult without a reduction of travel time, and although itinerant ministers and businessmen alike probably found the compression of travel time a godsend, too much rushing to meet schedules could be dangerous to more than just the nervous system. As one writer explained in 1853: "But why, we ask, should these frightful rail-road accidents so often occur? We answer, because men are, in these times, and in this country at least, more needful of money than of human life. . . . To save a minute, or a dollar, they are often ready to jeopardize the lives of a whole train of passengers."[93] Sometimes, the price was psychological. More than once, for example, the railroad's claim to precision failed to live up to southerners' expectations. "Delayed at Branchville more than 1 hour for the Charleston & Augusta trains," bemoaned Mitchell King in 1854. More revealing was one planter's chagrin at the laxity of the supposedly punctilious northern railroads. Not only did New York railroad workers lose William Elliott's baggage on his trip north in 1858 but, more seriously, the Albany train "did not come for forty minutes after the regular time."[94] Nervous ailments no doubt followed.

Southerners had good reason to complain about late trains. They had, after all, internalized the need for punctuality instigated by the post and heightened by the train. Lest the joy of leisure should cause them to forget the time of their trains, hotels and restaurants like the Lanier House of Macon, Georgia, began publishing local train schedules in their menus in the 1850s. It is not hard to imagine tremendous indigestion from the boiled "Leg of Mutton" as Lanier

House patrons rushed to meet the "8.50 p.m." to Augusta.[95] In short, in the last three decades of the antebellum period, to be southern was many things and included the desire, and the need, for punctuality.

The residual effects of postal, boat, and wage-labor time combined with the heightened sensitivity to clock time ushered in by the railroads, steamboats, and telegraphs on antebellum southerners profoundly altered the way they viewed the relationship between space and time. For many in the 1830s, for instance, time came to conquer space and the broader impact of these developments was to consolidate and secularize the age-old idea of cyclical time moving along a linear track, figuratively and, in the case of railroads, literally. It was, for example, only because of his familiarity with time and punctuality that Alfred Huger, Charleston postmaster, could philosophize in 1858 that "it is manifest that we *must* go steadily forward, or lose going backward!" It was a reasonable belief because he reasoned, "If there be a 'future,' it can no more be independent of the 'present,' than that 'present' is independent of the 'past'! Are not the periods always in Continuity with Each other?"[96]

Steamboat travel had a similar effect. In 1833 planter John Berkley Grimball preferred to express space in terms of time: "I this morning returned from New York in the Steam Boat 'David Brown'—in the extraordinary space of 86 hours from Wharf to Wharf." Later, in trying to convey where St. Johns Island was in relation to Charleston in 1853, he noted, "The village is from 2 1/2 to 3 hours by water from the City," inadvertently testifying to the role of the steamship in reducing space to time. Public postings boasting the conquering of distance between New Orleans and Natchez were also couched in terms of time, in this case "21hs 18 m."[97] And so in 1839 it was declared: "Already are time and distance half annihilated between this country and Europe by the introduction of steam ships."[98]

In a far more obvious way, railroads also reduced time to space, imposing at the same time a linearity on the country's expanding geography. Ann Elliott's first train ride in 1836, for example, inspired awe not only at the distance covered but at the time it took: "Yesterday and today for the first time in my life I travelled on a *rail road*. We travelled seventeen miles an hour, and for part of the way, at the rate of 25 miles an hour. The velocity is delightful."[99] Public statements on the impact of the railroads were even more illuminating. The 1839 Internal Improvements Convention of North Carolina reported that "the great advantages of the rail-ways, over all other means of conveyance is the saving of time, the annihilation of space. *Time is money*, and the attainment of greater speed and certainty, amounts, in effect, to a reduction of expense."

Railroad cars were conceived as darting "on like a rocket" adding time's linear arrow to its cyclical rhythm.[100] Similarly, James Johnston writing for the *Farmers' Register* in 1838 explained how trains had rendered time linear and annihilated space: "Without rudder or rein . . . this maximum of power in minimum of space—this magic *automaton*, darts forward, on iron pinion, like an arrow from a bow, along its destined course. . . . The steam-carriage nearly annihilates distance between the inhabitants of a state, and thereby converts, as it were, a whole country into a city."[101] Contemplative southerners recognized the changes effected by the train. "When I was a boy, twenty five years ago it was a great thing to have made a trip to Mississippi, it took 20 day[s] then. . . . Now men and women esteem it a small matter, they take the R. Road & stage and perform the trip in 2 or 3 days," mused David Gavin in 1856.[102]

While the railroad compacted American space and time, the telegraph and steamship were technological bedfellows in the quest for global compression. "The steamship is becoming the striking feature of the present century," it was remarked in 1849, "and with these upon the ocean, and the electric telegraph upon land, we are compressing the globe, by the rapid transmission of intelligence, into a thousandth part of its former compass."[103] The telegraph especially was deemed to have tamed nature and, in the process, mastered time. By 1846 "Morse's electro-magnetic telegraph" was vaunted as having an "extraordinary victory over the powers of nature," as seizing "upon the lightning itself," bidding "the terrible slave toil in the enterprise of a master," as having "harnessed the last conquered rebel," and, ultimately as having "no limit. It has no time." Rhetoric aside, the factual description of what the telegraph could accomplish was impressive and sobering: "In illustration of the capacity of the telegraph to convey 'a given amount of information in a given time,' it has been stated, that nearly a whole column of a large newspaper was transmitted in thirty minutes, more rapidly than it could be transcribed by the reporter." It was actually independent of nature because it could function "at every hour of the day or night, irrespective of weather."[104] "This courier," another writer said of the telegraph in 1854, "cleaves space into silence; and, darting from zone to zone, from land to land, commutes, in its volatile flight, all time, by the mere effort of a directing will." Time's pinions had been tamed and threatened to destroy nature in the process.[105]

The ascendancy of telegraph time had the considerable effect of wrenching Americans, southerners included, from local time into world time, telling them, as it were, that they were part of a larger world market where time differences both separated and united localities in a standard temporal universe. This was especially true after the laying of the Atlantic telegraph cable in the late 1850s, which, according to the *Richmond Dispatch*, "has called attention to the difference of time in various cities in different parts of the world. . . . The difference of time between the extreme East and West points of the United States," the author went on to explain, "is 3 hours, 50 minutes."[106] "We may safely say," opined another writer for *De Bow's Review* in 1853 describing the impact of the telegraph, "the acme of human science has been attained, and the phases of time, and the employments of man, totally and eternally changed."[107]

By the 1850s southerners were cognizant of the change that these apostles of progress had wrought on their society and, for the most part, they were pleased. As early as 1835, the *Tennessee Farmer* applauded the salutary effects of the "age of improvement," pointing specifically to the effect of "railroads and canals," travel by which had "been reduced to one half the time." By compounding time and space in this manner, "We almost forget the sun in mid heaven." Almost, certainly, but fully, never.[108]

Not only did southerners relish the compounding of time and space with regard to their own travel needs, but they also saw the saving of time in metahistorical terms. "There has been no period since the commencement of the world in which so many important discoveries, tending to the benefit of mankind, were made as in the last half century," reported the *Southern Planter* in 1851, elaborating:

> Before the year 1800, there was not a single steam boat in existence, and the application of steam to machinery was unknown. Fulton launched the first steam boat in 1807. Now there are three thousand steam boats traversing the waters of America, and the time saved in travel is equal to seventy per cent. . . . The locomotive will now travel in as many hours, a distance which in 1800 required as many days to accomplish. In 1800 it took weeks to convey intelligence between Philadelphia and New Orleans; now it can be accomplished in minutes through the electric telegraph.[109]

Time and space, then, seemed to have been mastered by the technological advances of the first half of the nineteenth century. But as slaveholders came to understand, plantation agriculture was too dependent on nature for the same mastery to take place there. Yet in a world that was increasingly punctual, masters naturally and inevitably both succumbed to and helped initiate efforts to make plantation agriculture more attuned to the larger gravitation toward clock time apparent in the antebellum South. In some respects, the attempt to reconcile the two was deliberate and conscious; in others it was simply part and parcel of the age of improvement. Whatever the case, the last three decades of the antebellum period witnessed masters' attempts to introduce punctuality and temporal efficiency to their plantations. As the *Southern Planter*, which was often critical of planters' perceived sloppiness and haphazard management techniques, reminded its readers: "What should we think of a railroad company that should conduct all their internal arrangements by guesses?" Such complaints about slipshod plantation management had, of course, been voiced before. But for the first time, clock time and precision were proposed as suitable remedies. The machine, as Leo Marx has said in a different context, was slowly coming into the plantation garden, never to dominate it but simply to complement it.[110]

Not all, however, relished the temporal control the railroads in particular, the agents of time consciousness generally, imposed on society. Some older readers of the *Southern Planter* no doubt empathized with the complaints of the "oldest inhabitant" of Massachusetts about the impact of the train in 1859. "What kind o' 'commodation be they? You can't go when you *want* to go; you go when the bell rings, or the noisy whistle blows." Being mastered by railway time was not everyone's cup of tea. But only the oldest knew what it was like not to be so controlled. And what the ignorant knew not, they did not protest.[111]

But such reservations about the effect of modern time were not confined to the North. For once in his life proslavery ideologue of Virginia George Fitzhugh found himself openly agreeing with a Yankee. Characteristically, he went a step further than the Massachusetts rustic and condemned "uniform postage, railroads, telegraphs" for their deleterious effects on the South. These same forces that had compounded American space and time, complained Fitzhugh, had also allowed Yankee fashions to corrupt and weaken the South and let northern "bawdy" sentiments pollute pristine southern thought. Yankee ideas, he lamented, could be more readily communicated and exported to the South through the combined effects of post, rail, and telegraph than in days previous.[112] Fitzhugh failed to realize that at the time of his jeremiad in 1859, Yankee sensibilities about time thrift and clock time, energized by the post, steam-powered travel, and the telegraph, had already percolated and mutated that bastion of southern independence and distinctiveness: the slave plantation. Heaven forbid that masters had a hand in such treachery.

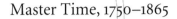

Master Time, 1750–1865

IV

The fact that we now not only call the plantation owners in America capitalists, but that they *are* capitalists, is based on their existence as anomalies within a world market based on free labour.

—Karl Marx, *Grundisse*

After examining carefully what had been defective in its course . . . he drew up rules of regulation, and strictly enjoined their observance upon his people. Thus, he ordained, that the cook should have breakfast at a suitable hour to which the people were to be punctual in attendance. . . . The hour of attendance was to be declared by the sound of the horn, and the time for taking their last meal, was so regulated, that the workers always had ample space for completing their tasks before the call. If any one had not finished at the appointed hour, he was disgraced and went without his dinner for that day.

—Edistonian, "The Successful Planter,"

Southern Agriculturalist, 1832

Who lags for dread of daily work,

And his appointed task would shirk,

Commits a folly and a crime;

A soulless slave—

A paltry knave—

A clog upon the wheel of time.

—"Daily Work," *Southern Planter*, 1860

That natural, sacred, and clock time remained juxtaposed and interdependent well into the nineteenth century should not obscure the growing importance of mechanical time in southern antebellum life. Few historians of the antebellum North, after all, would seriously contend that remnants of natural time rendered Yankee capitalists impotent in their efforts to insinuate timed work schedules in their factories. As Jonathan Prude confidently asserts, echoing E. P. Thompson's findings for industrializing England, "New England mills in the second and third decades of the nineteenth century generally measured labor by time." Or, as David Brody notes in his astute work on the coming of clock time in the industrializing North, "No social process sweeps clean."[1] The South, in particular the planter class, was not marginal either to this northern trend or to the increasing concern with punctuality, clock time, and modernity generally, trends increasingly apparent in their own society.

Perhaps the most potent force pushing the South toward the adoption of clock time in the fields was the rise of scientific agriculture during what one planter called "an age of improvement" in the decades after 1830 and the attendant, inextricably linked desire to embrace progress, to join the burgeoning legion of moderns. As historian Bertram Wyatt-Brown puts it, southerners, in the last three decades of the antebellum period especially, demonstrated a "desire to modernize, to improve the 'home system,' so that its foundations were no less secure, no less progressive than those on which free labor rested." Although certainly influenced by developments outside of the South, the arguments for embracing a more scientific form of plantation agriculture grew from within the ranks of the planter class and both helped fuel and fed off their very real desire to be considered modern, a label that appeared increasingly incongruous with the international rise of the abolition movement in the same period.[2]

As Eugene Genovese has argued, the proslavery arguments of George Fitzhugh, Henry Hughes, James Henley Thornwell, and other major thinkers of the antebellum South articulated a southern dilemma. It was a dilemma faced by a slaveholding society anxious to embrace a qualified notion of progress in a world where progress was increasingly defined by the principles of free wage labor and democratic capitalism. In the end, according to Genovese, the dilemma proved irreconcilable and helped inspire secession.[3] Certainly, Genovese's identification of this dilemma is astute; but he is perhaps less sensitive to some of the methods slaveholders used to try to resolve it. The application of mechanical time to plantation life, it seems, provided planters one possible, though temporary, way out. By appropriating basic tenets of capitalism such as the timing of work, but simultaneously repudiating "the cult of progress" epitomized in northern democratic capitalism, southerners discovered, in Genovese's words, "an alternate route to modernity," a way to garb the South in modern clothes without jeopardizing the integrity of its non-wage-based society. Some important structural impediments to economic growth notwithstanding, the introduction of clock time to plantation labor would, planters hoped, not only improve the intensity, regularity, and efficiency of slave labor but, more critically, empower them to claim the title of modern while simultaneously tightening their grip on class power. Provided masters could import the clock on their own terms, clock time would be eagerly embraced.[4]

In some important respects, the use of the clock to regulate work was potentially of greater benefit to southern masters than to northern or British industrial capitalists. Not only would an appeal to clock-based time give planters a partial claim to progress, but the timing of slave labor might also yield economic benefits. Moreover, and in the most ideal scenario, if the imposition of a respect for the clock among slaves proved successful, then the discipline provided by the lash would be rendered of secondary importance to one governed by the clock. "Negroes," argued one slaveholder, "are like any other ignorant men in a state of subordination." "A little system," he reckoned, "will readily obviate this difficulty." Specifically, the "most exact discipline is as necessary [on the plantation] as in a school or on board a ship." Mutiny on the plantation would be avoided, however, with "a strict observance" to discipline for "punishment will soon be unnecessary, because there will be no disobedience." "The best evidence of the good management of slaves," farmers and planters of Virginia were told in 1834, "is the keeping up good discipline with little or no punishment." "Order," as planters were fond of putting it, after Alexander Pope, "is Heaven's first law." In short, as Marx hinted, the grafting on of carefully selected capitalist management techniques to the slave South would prove of considerable benefit to a society concerned with heightening the dual components of modern political economy: increasing productivity and efficiency and also stabilizing an inherently volatile workforce.[5]

The pace to embrace progress quickened during and after the 1830s. Technological advances by the North and increasingly vitriolic abolitionist attacks against slaveholders combined to encourage a belief that if progress were to be embraced, it must be done in the near future. The responsibility for this rapid but controlled entry into modernity rested with all white southerners. Sometimes the onus was put on overseers as well as planters: "If the overseer desires to become *number one*, he has no time to loose [*sic*]. . . . No, there is no time to lose, if we intend to make ourselves good planters." Significantly, competitions were held for overseers who made "the largest crop per hand of Cotton," with a watch as the prize.[6] For James Henry Hammond's South Carolina overseers, such prizes would have complemented nicely the clocks they already had in their homes.[7] "The *Overseer*," then, "should be a man (to use the language of Solomon) that can 'discern both *time* and judgment,' not only *how* to do, but *when*, as a considerable and important end may be accomplished by thus [*sic*] knowledge, which may have given origin to the well-known maxim, 'A stitch in *time*, saves *nine*.'"[8]

If stubborn older planters could not be forced to change their ways, there was at least hope for the younger generation to whom the cause of progress was often entrusted. "Exhortations to the Young Farmer" included the idea that "time thus lost can never be made up" and advice on how "to produce the greatest amount of combined labor in a given time." Fathers anxious to make their scions modern were told: "Select your finest boy . . . and make a FARMER of him—induct him into the practical details of his business. Teach him, that in no profession is time more precious; learn him to rise with the lark, and remind him that every moment he loses is multiplied by the number of his dependents."[9] Other "maxims for young farmers and overseers" came in the form of sarcasm: "The old adage, that 'time is money,' may do well for the face of a Yankee clock, but is altogether beneath the philosophy of *Young America. Therefore, lie in bed til your breakfast is ready, and be sure to go a fishing every Saturday evening.*"[10] But whether young or old, those planters who appeared to be making headway in the area of systematic plantation management were applauded publicly. The Reverend J. L. Moultrie of Macon County, Alabama, was considered exemplary not only because he enforced "a strict discipline among his negroes" but because the principles of progressive farming were "carried out with the most perfect clock-like precision, to the great benefit of master and servant."[11]

If the public and private demands for a more scientific plantation agriculture characteristic of the decades following 1830 represent planters' general desire to pass through the gates of progress, their use of time-saving plantation machinery and the rigorous application of their slaves' time provided these men with one of the keys with which to enter safely, on their own terms, the august hall of modernity.

Although public ministrations about the value of timing slave labor and establishing plantation order through the clock appeared mainly during and after the 1830s, precedents existed. "Sensible of their own deficiency of knowledge and theory & practice of rural economy" and aiming to nurture "an improved system of Husbandry," farmers in Charlottesville, Virginia, founded the Agricultural Society of Albemarle in 1817. First they looked to time-saving machinery and to the establishment of "Calendars of Work, showing how a given number of labourers & of draught animals are to be employed every day in the year." The society's findings were to be disseminated in the *American Farmer*, their "medium of communicating its proceedings to the public." By 1825, Albemarle farmers had learned much in their experiments with timing agricultural operations and reported their findings accordingly. Farmer Stephen McCormick, it was noted, "opened a cubic space of 76 53/100 cubic inches with a power equal to 400 lbs & broke 1/8th of an acre in furrow of 70 yards long in 15 minutes with two Horses" in 1825. Nicholas H. Lewis plowed a similarly sized field with a lighter plow "& broke 1/8th of an acre in 16 minutes with 3 Horses." Neighboring farmers were less successful. It took John Cravens "17 1/2 minutes with 3 Horses" to break up his eighth of an acre and William Woods "18 1/2 minutes" to do the same. And by 1836 all could marvel at published examples of planters' ability to extract "quick work" from their slaves. Readers of Virginia's *Farmers' Register*, for example, were no doubt impressed by one South Carolina slaveholder's ability to make his bondpeople turn out a bale of cotton "in the unprecedented time of 6 1/2 minutes!"[12] Predictably, manufacturers of labor-saving farm equipment were quick to pick up on planters' anxiety to save time and couched their advertisements accordingly. "Samuelson's rotary digging machine" was heralded as forking five and a half acres "with six horses, in 6 3–4 hours" in 1854, while Hussey's mowing machine was respected because it gave the operation of cutting and hence curing fodder "almost the precision of clock work."[13]

Southern planters were aware of their inefficient farming techniques because, in truth, they were becoming obsolete by northern standards. Certainly, planters never really felt themselves the technological equals of others. As late as 1853, for example, planters still pointed to England, where "farmers are looking to mechanics to furnish them with labor-saving machines of all kinds, so that a hand may accomplish as much on a farm in six days as he now does in twelve." By contrast, this writer lamented, "Our system of rural economy is notoriously defective."[14] But such self-deprecating jeremiads had begun much earlier. Beginning in the 1830s, southern planters testified to their relative backwardness and confessed a desire to ape time-thrifty northern managers. Public pronouncements to this effect littered the South's agricultural and literary journals, which routinely reprinted northern articles concerning the relationship between time and money. Aphorisms from Benjamin Franklin's colonial *Poor Richard's Almanac* were most popular. The *Farmers' Register* in 1838 quoted Franklin as saying, "If time be of all things the most precious, wasting time must be the greatest prodigality." For good measure, the editor added, "lost time is never found again." A reprint from the *Boston Cultivator* in the *Southern Planter* for January 1851 gave similar advice on making the best use of time:

> Are you poor? you will probably forever remain so, if you habitually waste the precious hours of the morning in bed. Who will seek the labor or services of him who sleeps and doses in the morning until seven or eight o'clock? If such a person is poor, he must remain poor. "He that would thrive must rise at five." The poor can ill afford to lose daily two or three hours of the best portion of the day. Economy of time and diligence in business, are virtues peculiarly appropriate to those who depend upon their earnings for the means of subsistence. Allowing twelve working hours to a day, he who by rising at eight instead of five o'clock in the morning, thereby loses three hours' labor daily, parts with one-fourth of his means of supporting himself and family: ten years' labor lost in the course of forty years!

Such advice might help to explain why planter George Kollock of Georgia began recording in his 1837 plantation journal instances of time lost in plantation work. "In [the] last month," noted Kollock in July 1837, "I have lost 24 days work by sickness & 10 by Doll's working away."[15] To those south of the Mason-Dixon line, it did not require a tremendous leap of imagination selectively to apply the homily to their slaves' labor. To those who owned labor for life, "ten years' labor lost" was a more frightening prospect than to those who had the luxury of dismissing free laborers.[16]

Consequently, the ideal planter came to be portrayed in Taylorite terms with a distinctly northern hue. "Above all, our good manager is a great economist in his use of time," crowed Jesse H. Turner in his presidential address to the Henrico Agricultural Society in 1841. Nor was he shy of invoking Franklin: "He believes, with Dr. Franklin, that 'time is money,' and in his estimation it is a coin of inestimable value."[17] Or, as one popular poetic ditty from the 1850s put it:

Let order o'er your time preside,
And method all your business guide.

. . . .

Hire not for what yourselves can do,
And send not when yourselves can go;
Nor till to-morrow's light delay
What might as well be done to-day.[18]

Southern agricultural journals habitually advised planters to agree "with Dr. Franklin, that 'time is money,'" and to save it slaveholders were counseled to avoid "procrastination" by addressing the "business of to-morrow" today. An editorial in the *Tennessee Farmer* asked southern planters, quoting "Poor Richard" directly, "How are the hours to be best improved?" and counseled farmers properly to employ "their time in rainy weather."[19] Such ministrations in turn inspired southerners to proffer advice on, among other things, punctuality, the value of time, and how to save time.[20] Perhaps inevitably, northern farmers were held up as examples to be emulated. Unlike southern planters, argued a writer for *De Bow's Review* in 1854, the capitalist Yankee "has no time for [trifling]. With him life is too short to lose a moment; every hour has its business." "Let us imitate them in all their good and valuable qualities," it was recommended, with, of course, the important proviso that southerners shield their eyes from that northern medusa, abolitionism.[21]

Frederick Law Olmsted encountered firsthand a tangible illustration of this time-money equation during a conversation with an Alabama planter on a riverboat in the 1850s. Olmsted explained that this planter's "impatience to return [to his plantation] was very great, and was constantly aggravated by the frequent and long-continued stoppages of the boat." Indeed, the planter sounded like a latter-day Franklin: "'Time's money, time's money!' he would be constantly saying, while we were taking on cotton, 'time's worth more'n money to me now; a hundred per cent. more.'" Curious as to why time was so important to this master, Olmsted asked him to explain. The planter's answer revealed his assumptions about time and social control: "'Cause I left my niggers all alone, not a dam [*sic*] white man within four mile on 'em. . . . I set em to clairin', but they ain't doin' a dam thing. . . . That's the reason time's an object. I told the capting [*sic*] so wen I came aboard: says I, 'Capting,' says I, 'time is in the objective case with me.'"[22] That this planter was probably better advised to set his slaves at tasks that did not require his physical presence and vigilance just goes to show that planters did make mistakes in their efforts to regulate slave labor by clock time. But such oversights probably did not occur twice for plainly they profiled the very real connection between time and money in a way that only such mistakes could.

Similar sentiments appeared in slave owners' private correspondence, suggesting that public ministrations about time thrift and progress were not simply rhetorical.[23] Some planters evidently acted on published advice. During a trip north in 1828, for example, planter William Elliott told his wife, "I have looked attentively at the machinery of the Great Waltham factory—and think I have secured some hints which may be useful in the preparation of our cotton for market."[24] In 1836 he took a closer look. "I am busily engaged inspecting some of their labor saving machines—with a view to adopt some of the least costly." He was impressed and not a little intimidated: "I have been to Lowell only to wonder at the unsurpassed manufacturing power . . . such is the complication of the machinery, I can hardly hope to understand it to any profit."[25] Elliott was too modest. Not only did he have the wherewithal to understand that "the painstaking of an operative manufacture must be added to the duties of the agriculturalist—or he will reap nothing but disappointment and vexation," but he actively took steps to remedy the fact "that we waste time . . . in the way we cultivate" by introducing threshing equipment to his plantation.[26] As he advised his son Ralph in 1855, it was best to get "a thresher that wd do 500 bushels a day," enjoining that its speed and "*time* should be specified in any contract—or *forfeit.*"[27]

Indeed, Lowell was a well-known model for emulation, especially the factory's use of timed labor. The *Southern Agriculturalist*, for example, published one southerner's account of a visit to Lowell in 1845 and advised "all those who are politically or otherwise unfriendly to the factory system, to read the following article." The visitor, from Kentucky, was particularly impressed that "the very few persons that were occasionally seen at all, hurried to and fro, as if their time was precious," applauded "the most perfect order, system, and regularity . . . everywhere exhibited," and noted the factory's use of time obedience: "At 12 o'clock, M., the factory bells chimed merrily, and the whirl of the spindles, the clatter of the looms, and the hum of the drums and wheels all ceased."[28] Increasing antinorthern political sentiment notwithstanding, by 1845 some denizens of the Old Dominion were proud of their new "Yankee improvements in Virginia" and vaunted the various salutary effects "of Northern enterprise and industry" on their state.[29]

The link between time-saving agricultural machinery and Yankee time thrift became increasingly clear to southerners as the antebellum years wore on. Certainly it was apparent to one planter who wrote a letter of inquiry to the *Southern Cultivator* in 1850: "Although I am a native Georgian, I am a real Yankee as far as all practical labor-saving machines are concerned. . . . Whose corn planter is the best and what is the price?" For others, southern political economy appeared to be gravitating toward the northern model. Nor was this necessarily a bad thing. Another planter, for example, was of the opinion that with regard to the principles of "Farm Economy. . . . We do not inculcate a different doctrine at the North from that taught at the South." If southern planters looked elsewhere for ways to improve their farming efficiency, one Louisiana planter wrote, this was the objective, the raison d'être, of the South's agricultural journals: "Science has industriously collected the fragments of agricultural knowledge, heretofore scattered over this and other countries; and having arranged them with system, we are enabled readily to retain and employ them to our use and benefit." "Neither," he went on, did this application "consume time." By the 1850s, "lovers of system" were ubiquitous, North and South.[30]

The application of labor-saving machinery, the exhortations for system in agriculture, and the increasing notice southerners took of northern advice about time thrift had profound effects. Although it is difficult to say whether these forces produced an empirically verifiable efficient plantation economy, it is certain that they convinced southerners that time was money, that lost time both existed and needed to be prevented, and that, in turn, to save time could be both honorable and was probably, in some unidentifiable but intuitive way, tied to their virtue as participants in the body politic.[31]

Like their mercantile forebears and northern contemporaries, southern agriculturalists, planters and overseers alike, came to appreciate the significance of lost time on their plantations. As early as 1828 even such banal issues as the improper method applied to the "culture of the grape vine" could prompt vehement criticism: "What a loss of labour and money! What a waste of precious *time!*" Louis Manigault's overseer in Georgia was similarly concerned. An unexpected freshet in September 1853, he complained, caused his neighbors trouble, and the damage "we sustained was the loss of time" in cutting the rice. Manigault was apparently one of the lucky ones, however, since "we all know how rare it is to get an industrious, economical overseer,— one who is saving of time, labour, and expense."[32] But Manigault perhaps protested too much. Overseers were apparently just as sensitive as were their employers of the need for plantation time thrift.

While planters' use of time-saving machinery reveals their increasing concern with making the most of time, the failure of this same machinery reveals the extent to which they cherished its fullest use on their plantations. Lured by canny foreign and domestic manufacturers of cotton gins who appealed directly to planters' concern with saving time by boasting gin speeds of "240 revolutions per minute" or rates "of 200 revolutions per minute [which will] clean 400 lbs. [of cotton] each foot in length per day" and of machines that could accomplish "the cleaning of 500 pounds" of cotton "in 31 minutes," planters were understandably chagrined when the devices they bought broke down.[33] It was not that they felt duped. Rather, they, like their colonial mercantile forebears, were loath to lose time, especially to machinery that promised to save it. Charles Manigault's overseer expressed precisely this concern when the rice thresher he had acquired in 1846 experienced operating difficulties. At first, the machine worked well, which, for the overseer, meant cleaning two hundred bushels of rice in a respectable "two hours and a half running time." Further use proved aggravating, however. "The rollers frequently stop when a sheaf of rice has passed about half way through the beater and frequently causes considerable loss of time." Moreover, because this problem occurred "some dozen times an hour," it "cause[d] great loss of time."[34] Similar problems and identical concerns preoccupied Greene County, Alabama, planter William Proctor Gould in 1834. On October 29, Gould noted in his diary: "The Gin has not performed as well as usual today—that is, she drops too much cotton with the motes—She ginned 2000lb in ten minutes less than four hours." Because Gould considered a rate of 8.7 pounds of cotton ginned per minute less than efficient, on November 6 he asked a Mr. Wood to work on the machine. Wood "succeeded at last in making it perform well—." What Gould considered efficient in this context was apparent from his November 7 diary entry: "The Gin picked 100lb [of] Cotton in ten minutes."[35] Ten pounds per minute was clearly preferable to 8.7.

The causes of lost time for planters were myriad, and they did their best to root out the villains. For some planters by the early 1830s, those old guides to agriculture, almanacs, and the people who still used them, had fallen into disrepute, only to be replaced with a newer, scientific "system of Agriculture" which paid attention to the very moments of agricultural time. Instead of appealing to the ancient wisdom of "the almanac maker" and the curious "notions of Farmers" who used them, South Carolina planter John Ewing Colhoun preferred what he considered a "*rational*" "System of Agriculture," which prompted him to devote "every spare moment" to his agricultural operations.[36]

Slovenly agricultural techniques and practices were among the other culprits of perceived southern backwardness and lost time, according to one Tennessee planter. The consequence of ignoring "the science of economy," he warned, "is a lamentable loss of time, of labor, and of money." "There is scarcely an agricultural operation performed in a slovenly, inaccurate and imperfect manner," he went on, "which does not occasion a loss tenfold exceeding the value of all the labor thereby saved; and what is still worse, in many instances, instead of a saving of labor, time, and money, such imperfect operations are not infrequently more laborious, tedious, and expensive."[37]

Solutions to the problem of lost time were not slow in coming. The way to avoid wasting time on the plantation, to stop "procrastination," was to "put off no business till to-morrow which ought and can be done to-day." Specifically, planters asked one another, "How many are in the daily practice of putting off 'business till tomorrow' which should be done to-day; and this, too, rather from habit than indolence." Those who committed the "folly of wasting time" were often the same ones who "are in the daily practice of deferring what could and should be done at once." It was only by establishing "order on the farm," argued another, that "much time may be saved." And there were various ways to accomplish this. Believing that "there is no system; no clock-work regularity maintained" in planters' "yearly routine of labors," one slave owner recommended the keeping of "Plantation Register and Account Books," much like those kept by "the merchant, banker, [and] tradesman" as "a guide for the future" allocation of time and labor. Some "hints and observations" by a Mississippi planter put the matter succinctly: "The old adage, 'a stitch in time,' fully applies to the care of all farm implements and the economy of their use." Given, then, that time could be lost, making the most of it was imperative. "The difference between rising at six and at eight," planters were told, "in the course of forty years, amounts to twenty thousand hours."[38]

In their plantation operations, then, planters strove for "a strict observance of a well timed system of economy."[39] Many took the advice to heart and established a routine of time discipline in their own work. This was especially true of small and yeoman planters whose labor force necessitated the most careful use and allocation of personal time.[40] Yeomen had always owned clocks and watches with which to time labor (see Table 4). Even in the "commonest sort of cabins" among "poor whites of the plantation districts," travelers in the 1850s, like Frederick Law Olmsted, found "a Connecticut clock."[41] "My plan for working," noted one such small planter, "was formed by necessity." He elaborated: "As soon as it was light enough to see, I hitched up and drove briskly until breakfast time—took out and fed while I ate, and for which I only allowed forty-five minutes—worked till one o'clock—rested an hour and a half when cool, two hours when warm."[42] The daily agricultural activities of South Carolina up-country yeoman farmer James F. Sloan show this mentality in action. Not only did Sloan keep a precise account of working time lost to the weather, but he also harbored a heightened sense of his own responsibility for making the most of the time available to him. On occasion, time lost gave rise to guilt:

"Went to Hammetts mill with corn rather idleing time away." On other occasions, lost time was unavoidable because Sloan himself had to work his farm and the injuries he inevitably incurred in the process cost him time. On July 7, 1855, he noted: "Cut my thumb sevearly with the axe—split it open." The price to pay was calculated in terms of time: "Lost 3 days work with my thumb." Presumably, it was this rather precarious existence that led Sloan to pay even closer attention to the everyday timing of his agricultural operations: "Finished ploughing the Cotton about 10 then hauled in some oats," and "Finished running, Lee's land on this sid[e] of the River by 2, o,clock."[43]

Southern plantation mistresses also got in on the act. Cecilia of Virginia advised readers of the *Southern Planter* in 1843: "Never let a servant say to you, 'I forgot it.' That sentence, so often used, is no excuse at all." Instead, she counseled, "let regularity mark every action, and the consequence will be, that every thing will be in its right place and at its right time."[44] God presumably applauded mistresses' efforts to manage slave labor.

But time lost was more than a matter of wasted money. Loss of time also impinged upon southern men's notions of honor and virtue. Although an exhortation to pay the printers of the *Southern Cultivator* on time, the message was clearly designed to appeal to a sense of southern time-based honor, if not republican virtue, and, hopefully, heighten it: "PUNCTUALITY.—Method is the very hinge of business—and there is no method without punctuality. . . . Punctuality gives weight to character. 'Such a man has made an appointment, and I know he will keep it.'" Moreover, punctuality was couched in terms of civic virtue: "This conviction generates punctuality in you; for, like other virtues, it propagates itself. Appointments become debts. I owe you punctuality, if I have made an appointment with you; and have no right to throw away your time, if I do my own. Punctuality in *paying the printer*, is a shining virtue, and is one of the requisites to the character of a good member of the community."[45] Similarly, failed attempts by "Wm H" to sell planter John D. Warren's slaves in Charleston in 1859 were put down to ungentlemanly untimeliness. As Warren's cousin explained to him: "Wm H begs that I would say to you that he finds some difficulties in making the sales of yr. negroes. It is such a busy time with them in Charleston that he can't get purchasers to be punctual as to their arrangements. . . . He . . . got vexed at a disappointment which some of the purchasers caused. They had promised to call at 1/2 past One: the time past & the old man began to &c—tried to pacify him but says the old buck, They gave their word as Gentlemen to be here & they have failed."[46] And what in reality were exceptional instances of timed labor from the eighteenth century were often held up as typical and worthy of emulation during the 1840s. George Washington's instructions to his overseer in 1793 were fre-

Table 4. Small Planters and Yeoman Farmers Owning Clocks and
Watches in Laurens County, South Carolina, 1805–1843

No. of Slaves Owned	Years	No. of Inventories	% with Timepieces
1–5	1805–9	25	16
6–10	1805–9	7	14
1–5	1839–43	34	68
6–10	1839–43	19	95

Source: Data compiled from Appendix, Tables A.20–A.21.

quently reprinted and his "inflexible devotion to order and discipline," his "esteem [of] the most minute details of agriculture," commended. Quoting Washington's directions, "You will recollect that your time is paid for by me, and if I am deprived of it, it is worse even than robbing my purse," no doubt reaffirmed in the minds of many antebellum planters the honor and virtue associated with time thrift.[47] The irony here, of course, was profound and, doubtless, a little disturbing. If honor and virtue were secured by paying the printer on time, then the other ingredient of the republican cocktail, tenacious independence from anything that threatened to hedge freedom, was compromised by the need for punctuality. Although time thrift and clock obedience may have been virtuous, such attributes nevertheless also invited slavery to, and not freedom from, the clock.

Experiments with differently weighted plows, with threshers, with time-saving machinery, and with ways to save that increasingly precious commodity, time, certainly reveal one aspect of slaveholders' increasing time consciousness. Born of trends within the South during the 1830s and of envious, if squinted, glances northward, the application of mechanically defined time to slave labor seemed a logical step. Slaveholders were, of course, aware that timing slave labor was different from the use of the clock under wage labor. "If I employ a labourer to perform a certain quantum of work per day, and I agree to pay him a certain amount for the performance of said work, when he has accomplished it, I of course, have no further claim on him for his time or services. But how different is it with a slave!" rightly observed a contributor to the *Southern Agriculturalist* in 1833. Others drew on their experience with hired labor to explain, often accurately, the relationship between time and money: "The lowest price of any *job, however trifling*, done by a day-labourer in Charleston, generally speaking, is six and a quarter cents. The *fourpence*, as it is termed, is thus the standard of the value of work, which is calculated upwards from it, in proportion of *time*, not of *labour*. An *hour's* work is *twice fourpence*, or twelve and a half cents, no matter what the work is. A day's work is the price of eight hour's time, or one dollar, be the work light or laborious."[48] Virginia senator Robert M. T. Hunter understood perfectly that the purchasing of labor time under both nominally free-wage-labor arrangements or *durante vitae* slavery had much in common: "In practice," he wrote in 1856, "one man may hold property in the services of another for life, as in the law of slavery; for a term of years, as in apprenticeship; or, for months, weeks, days, and hours, in the case of domestics, or mechanics, or lawyers, or doctors."[49] But whatever the similarities between the two systems, there were profound differences, too. Simply put, it was too dangerous and not a little contradictory to the very premise of chattel slavery to allow bondpeople to hire time they technically did not have. When slaves, especially urban ones, were allowed to sell their time, it was considered deleterious to the slave society as a whole. "The evil is," opined one southerner, "he buys control of his own time from his owner," which could serve only to undermine "discipline and control." In a slave society, control of bondpeople's time was of paramount social, moral, and political importance. Hence Christian masters tended to define the essence of their mastery in the following terms: "You command all their time; they labor and rest at your bidding." Though perhaps fanciful, this was an ideal that planters had to approximate if they were to control restive slaves.[50]

Although there were obvious differences between slave and wage labor, these differences did not necessarily mean that the clock or watch should not or could not be applied to plantation labor. Because the ideal for planters was heralded as "the proper application of their [slaves'] time," and because the "plantation might be considered as a piece of machinery, to operate successfully, all of its parts should be uniform and exact, and the impelling force regular and steady," clock time had obvious benefits not only for improving efficiency but for the simple purpose of maintaining plantation order and discipline.[51] Or, as proslavery theorist Henry Hughes argued in his 1854 tract, *Treatise on Sociology*: "The Duties of warrantors or masters, to warrantees [slaves], are economic, political, and hygienic" and included "prescribing the hours, quantity, quality or other accidents of labor."[52]

Nor did importing clocks and watches to the field necessarily conflict with planters' reliance on nature as the engine of plantation routine. Slaveholders were often contemptuous of farmers who attempted to dominate natural forces. "The great error of this system," argued James Hamilton Couper of Georgia in 1833, long considered one of the South's leading scientific planters, "has been, that man, instead of following the golden maxim of Lord Bacon, of conquering nature by obeying her laws, has endeavored, in opposition to those laws, to force her into a subservience to his own views." Or, as one planter put it simply, "In all our attempts at agricultural improvement (to succeed) we must follow the indications of nature." "The Laws of Nature" and the "operation of certain clock-work principles" were, according to one master, in harmony.[53]

All these points were made by one slaveholder, H. B. C., of Walker County, Georgia, in 1853. His communication to the *Southern Cultivator*, "A Word for Progressive Farming," included notions of progress, science, nature, and the need for a hasty but conservative appeal to modernity:

> The farmer in these days of steam and electricity, must not stand still. . . . A science unexplored—vast truths locked up in the arcana of nature, which time and mind alone of the highest order can render available to the common horde. . . . Old mother earth has been sacrificed, skined [*sic*] and bled long enough by ignorance, and the farmer in these days of energy and enterprise, who remains ignorant and makes no effort to avail himself of such means of information as a good agricultural newspaper affords, is decidedly an *old fogy*—not a conservative one either, but a destructive one— neither true to himself, his children, or his country.[54]

Scientific agriculture required planters "to investigate the laws of nature," not subvert them. One Tennessee farmer observed that there was nothing to be gained in "struggling against the laws of nature" because, in the words of a Kentucky planter, "*now* that [planters] have reduced Agriculture to a science, and adapted their operations to Nature's most bountiful provisions . . . no part of the United States can surpass this section."[55]

But if nature should not be subverted, one of her agents, time, was fair game. In 1837 the *Tennessee Farmer* reprinted a "Great Feat in Mowing against Time" from the *Pennsylvania Inquirer*. It was a competition in which "the time was fixed between sunrise and sundown; and Mr. [Benjamin] Asbury accomplished his task within three minutes of the limit." To enslave nature through human agency was improper and impossible; to outrun the sun through an appeal to the clock was legitimate and worthy.[56]

Clock time and nature's round, broadly conceived, however, were never perceived as incompatible by southern planters. "Nature seconds his [man's] efforts, and seems by her compliance, to invite him to prescribe laws to her," it was argued.[57] As J. R. of North Carolina put it: "If we would catch the true spirit of improvement, we must bow at nature's shrine, and consult her oracles. If we would move onward to perfection in agricultural science, we must invoke her aid."[58] Why would clock time and natural time be considered mutually exclusive? In the first place, they had long been partners and, in the second, the "evident indication of nature is, that man should go forth from his sleeping chamber in time to meet the first beams of the rising sun. When all outward nature wakes and commences its diurnal round of activities, man, to be in *harmony* with all nature . . . should wake too, and should be up and doing."[59] Why not, indeed, when nature itself operated on clock time? Even the feeding of plants, one planter convinced himself, was orchestrated by nature around mealtimes: "Another argument in favour of early morning and early evening watering of plants is, that this supply arrives at their meal hours. . . I believe that the Great God of Nature, in his wonderful disposition, has alike, assigned them meal hours; and not only meal hours, but a period of the day for recreation (perhaps too for labour: shooting and bedding their roots, &c) and an other of the night for sleep."[60] And so nature and agricultural science generally, clock time specifically, were in concord on southern plantations. Of "making some progress in the great science of Agriculture," one owner of what was described as "a model southern plantation" apparently did "glean some useful hints from Nature's own volume." With regard to ordering his labor, he followed this advice insinuating clock time within nature's diurnal time. His hands "go to work at day light, stop an hour for breakfast, one hour in winter, and three in summer for dinner, and leave the fields at dark."[61]

That slaveholders should try to yoke natural time to clock time was understandable because the dominion of clock over nature would be inviting too much change for an organically ordered society. Conservatives that they were, planters were loath to revolutionize wholly their productive mode. As one slaveholder put it: "Southern society will continue to improve and progress, but offers no temptation to revolution or organic reconstruction."[62] Instead, the application of clock time to plantation operations could be profitably insinuated within the existing diurnal and seasonal round established by nature and thus be used to reinforce and reconcile southerners' traditional concern with preserving social order with their growing desire to modernize, albeit on their own terms.[63]

Although planters applied mechanical time to plantation labor in varying ways, the evidence is striking inasmuch as it shows that, like southern yeomen, southern planters applied clock time to plantation agriculture in some fashion. Those planters primarily concerned with disciplining or ordering their slaves through the clock and not so concerned about timing the minutiae of their slaves' labor were content merely to regulate work times and breaks. Others attempted to time slaves' rates of work by the clock. Whether on rice or cotton, task or gang plantations, some bondpeople found their work and leisure hedged and defined by mechanically regulated hours. Not that planters considered the regulation of any plantation operation by clock time easy. Even something as simple as the systematic collection of manure "and that which is still more difficult to emulate, *time* also" had its challenges. But that planters attempted to orchestrate both production processes and labor by time is illustrative of their bid for modernity.[64]

Of course, there were always planters like Thomas Cassells Law of South Carolina who felt that though his workers should be ordered according to "plan," the sun alone was an accurate enough arbiter of work and rest hours. His slaves, he reported in 1852, "are required to rise at day break . . . & by half hour by sun, all are ready to commence work & with no excuse to stop until 12 o'clock."[65] But the introduction of clock time to plantation agriculture was actually in concord not just with nature generally but specifically with the frenetic push against time that nature had always engendered. As Michael O'Malley has correctly pointed out, nature can be as frenetic a taskmaster as the clock, pushing time-conscious individuals against both the sun or seasons and the ticking of clock hands.[66] Only because nature can harry individuals in this way can the introduction of clock time in any society be countenanced. If nature were leisurely, no society would have either the inclination or the ability to withstand a shift to mechanically regulated time. In many ways, it was only because southern planters had experience of the inherent temporal push imposed by nature that they could possibly countenance taking that push one step further by introducing the clock to the field.

Certainly, planters had always felt and would always feel nature hurrying them in their planting and harvesting operations. As sea island cotton planter Thomas Spalding observed in 1829: "In most agricultural operations, it is of primary importance to be ahead of time, and of the seasons."[67] Public pronouncements to this effect were rife. For example, "Russell" informed readers of the *Southern Cultivator* in 1848: "When I speak of system . . . I mean that mode of conducting the business which shall have its times and its seasons; which shall mark out and define the time and the manner in which the most important of the operations of farming shall be commenced and ended."[68]

That such concerns were echoed in private plantation journals is hardly surprising. On May 8, 1830, for instance, South Carolina planter Alexander Robert Lawton noted in his journal: "I wish to bear in mind for the future that I commenced plowing this year at least one fortnight too late, & my waggoning of manure too late also by at least the same time." One Georgia overseer also felt the pressure of the seasons: "I have commenced to cut today and find I will not have one idle moment as my second planting will be on me before I can get through with the first."[69] The shortening of days produced similar worries and, sometimes, victories. In "these short days" of January 1837, Charles Izard Manigault's female slaves "all got done by sunset."[70] But sometimes the relentless round of nature and planters' poor preparation produced regret and hurried efforts to recover time lost to nature. As one slaveholder noted on May 31, 1828: "I am greatly behind the mark in forwardness this year. I should have now commenced my third hoing [sic] of cotton instead of the second." More than thirty years later he found himself in a similar position. His overseer wrote to him, "As you remark the planting time is close at hand & all the force is wanted in the fields' [sic] there is not a moment to spare."[71]

Misjudging agricultural, seasonal rhythms could be costly as one McPhersonville, South Carolina, planter discovered in May 1861: "Planted too early for the season, lost time thursd." For others, getting behind the season could cost part of the cotton crop. "The Spring is opening on us very fast," dashed John Berkley Grimball in his journal, lamenting on September 29, 1834: "Cotton has wasted in the field—not having had time to pick it." Planters tried to save time by getting ahead of nature. "We are later in beginning to sow wheat this year than I have ever been before," fretted Virginia planter William Fanning Wickham in 1834. But "by continuing to plough in the cornfield," he reckoned, "we shall be forward in our preparation—& no time shall be lost."[72]

In some respects, because they were harried by the relentless push of nature, because certain operations had a very definite window of time, planters had to make more use of their time than, say, a factory owner who was more independent of seasonal rhythms. One planter made this point: "As our time is limited, there must be none lost."[73] Simply put, if nature so chose, there was little planters could do to prevent it from costing them time. Consequently, when nature seemed favorable, they had to make the most of time.

Planter James Powell Cocke testified to the ultimate control of nature on June 25, 1856: "Lost 1 1/2 days by rain up to this date." And Daniel William Cobb of Southampton County, Virginia, was well aware that both rain and the advancing seasons could cost him time. On August 11, 1843, he made the following entry in his plantation diary: "I have lost by rain 1 days work with my little or few hands. . . . The day passed off without much cloud; The day decreased 1 hour." But what was lost could then be found. By spring the day had "increased 3 hours & 7 Minuits."[74] More often, however, time could not be made up if nature so decided. "I lack about a days work—to finish planting corn," moaned William Haynie Hatchett in May 1853, and he blamed nature's seasonal round: "Spring is very backward."[75] Only the most precise planning and preparation for nature's unpredictable vagaries like that conducted by

Prince George County, Virginia, planter Charles Friend could avoid the loss of time. For Friend to "not loose [sic] but one hours work" to unexpected drought was no small feat.[76] It was, in short, the freneticism of nature's round in conjunction with acquiring the virtue of punctuality and the title of modern that made southern planters so sensitive about making hay while the sun shone and performing the business of today, today.[77]

Several solutions were available to planters to make the most of the time that was available to them. One was to systematize planting and harvesting times. Although it is certainly true, as Eugene Genovese has pointed out, that planters had to work within nature's diurnal round and could hardly appoint the times of harvest and planting, they could operate within these seasonal constraints, assigning specific days for specific tasks.[78] James Hamilton Couper of the Georgia low country was but one of many who attempted to routinize his agricultural practices within nature's seasonal rhythms. "The 12th of March," for instance, Couper singled out as the best time to begin planting cotton. "The first of August" signified the end of cotton hoeing, while "the 20th of November" was the beginning of the harvest. Couper believed this "systematic" husbandry, underpinned by "regularity and precision," to be eminently efficient.[79] Nor was Couper alone in such practices. North of Couper's Georgia estate was Thomas Miliken's South Carolina rice plantation. Like Couper, Miliken preferred to perform certain tasks on particular days of the year. In his journal entry for Monday, February 16, 1857, for example, he noted that his male hands were plowing number eight rice field. Exactly one year earlier on Saturday, February 16, 1856, he made the same entry: "Men ploughing in number eight rice field." On Friday, February 16, 1855, Miliken recorded that plows were working in number eight rice field. And a year earlier still, on February 16, 1854, Miliken noted that number eight rice field was under plow. Many other entries recording the same or similar activities can also be found, if not always to the day then usually with a four- to five-day variance.[80] Identifying certain key days within the broader agricultural rhythm was certainly one way planters tried to keep a check on nature's temporal round and ensure that she did not overtake them. But this broader effort to control the pace of nature worked on a seasonal, not daily, basis. For the daily regulation of plantation affairs planters had to recruit an ally more minute in reckoning time, the clock or watch.

Most often, planters introduced clock time into seasonal and diurnal rhythms for the purpose of regulating labor and establishing plantation order.

Public statements to this effect were commonplace. An Alabama slaveholder informed readers of *De Bow's Review* at some length in 1852 that he required his slaves to

> rise in time to be at their labor by light. Their breakfast hour is eight o'clock. At this meal they have bread, a small portion of meat, a cup of coffee, and butter-milk, which requires fifteen minutes. At dinner, at twelve o'clock, I repeat the meat and bread. . . . In the winter they have one hour, and summer three to rest, in the heat of the day. . . . I require them to retire at nine o'clock precisely. The foreman calls the roll at that hour, and two or three times during the night, to see that all are at their places.

"By pursuing this plan with my servants," he concluded, "they become attached to me, and have respect for my orders."[81] These public pronouncements in agricultural journals were duplicated in the gritty, thumbed pages of plantation journals. Richard Eppes of Hopewell, Virginia, for example, issued instructions to his slaves in 1857 that clearly articulated the question of plantation times: "Three quarters of an hour will be allowed you to breakfast and one hour and a quarter to dine from the month of October until April. One hour to breakfast and three quarters to dine from April until October."[82] James Henry Hammond's up-country South Carolina plantation manual for 1844 contained the following instructions: "The first morning horn is blown an hour before day in the morning. . . . The second horn is blown just at good day. . . . The plow hands leave their houses for the stables at the summons of the plough drivers 15 minutes before. . . . At 11 1/2 A.M. the plow gang knock off & repair to the nearest feeding house."[83]

But how, precisely, were planters to make slaves obey and understand that certain hours denoted certain tasks' beginnings and ends? Planters who, for various reasons, owned only a clock, not a watch, but who wanted to introduce mechanical time to the field obviously encountered the problem of how to communicate time. Housebound as was the plantation clock, some planters were forced to appeal to the old urban tradition of communicating time through sound. Not only did such a practice have very real pecuniary and disciplinary benefits, but planters felt comfortable in their appeal to a past tradition that promised to safeguard their future. Planter and proslavery thinker James Henry Hammond considered that the safest way for slaveholding southerners to embrace progress was to ascertain the "best criterion of the future" by examining "the past." Thus planters tended to invoke a conservative past to embrace a potentially disruptive future. "To reveal from the past, the deep hidden secrets of the future. . . . To recall from the past, valuable lessons for the future," was the aim of another planter concerned about future agricultural improvements. "Time, after all, though he chafes and rebukes us, is a wise nurse; and what more can we make of him, but that he is the appointed guardian, who soon resigns his keeping of us into the hands of our real parent, Eternity."[84] Appealing to a past with which they were familiar to guarantee an unknown future provided masters no little solace.[85] But old as was the sound of clock time, it was also being recruited, in the North especially, for the modern purpose of regulating factory work hours. Modernity and tradition were thus merged in the mind of the master class.[86]

By verifying the time with the plantation's housebound clock, some slave-holders translated house time into field time by ringing bells and blowing horns and thereby attempted to regulate at least work times, if not work rates. In a revealingly titled tract of the 1850s, "Plantation Management—Police," one Virginia planter explained in detail his use of the clock-regulated plantation horn in scheduling plantation affairs. The first point in his list of instructions to his overseer read: "It is strictly required of the manager that he rise at the dawn of day every morning; that he blow a horn for the assembling of the hands; require all hands to repair to a certain and fixed place in ten minutes after the blowing of the horn, and there himself see that all are present, or notice absentees." The sixth point explained: "There will be stated hours for the negroes to breakfast and dine, and those hours must be regularly observed. Breakfast will be at eight o'clock, and dinner at one o'clock." The thirteenth point: "A horn will be sounded every night at nine o'clock, after every negro will be required to be at his quarters."[87] To coordinate labor with the sound of clock time, another planter had advice for small and large slaveholders alike: "A large-sized cow bell could be heard two miles, and would not cost more than three or four dollars, would serve not only as a signal for bed time, but also for getting up of a morning, for ceasing work at noon and resuming it after dinner. Where the distance to be heard is not great, a common bar of cast steel hung up by passing a wire through one end, may be struck with a ham-mer, and will answer in place of a bell."[88]

Testimony by former slaves interviewed during the 1930s verifies that the practice of communicating housebound clock time to the fields through sound was common. Former Mississippi slave Laura Montgomery told her interviewer that in the plantation house, "De clock sot on top of de mantle an' Marse Bill had to stan' up in a cheer to win[d] dat clock." When it was time for her to go to the field, "Marse would blow [his horn] dat hour every mornin' an' we had to git out right now and start dat work." Former slave Prince Johnson's testimony echoed Montgomery's: "Every morning about four o'clock we could hear that horn blow for us to get up and go to the field." Likewise, Anderson Williams and Sam Anderson said, respectively: "At 3:00 O'clock in de mornin'

Overseer's house and bell, Hampton Plantation, Maryland (Photograph by E. H. Pickering, 1936, Historic American Buildings Survey, Library of Congress)

de bell was rung . . . an' at 4:00 o'clock every nigger must be ready to go to the field" and "De overseer had a darky ring bell or blow horn at four o'clock to get up by mornings."[89]

Planters evidently believed that slaves comprehended the meaning of sound-regulated time. One planter who arranged for inspection at nine o'clock on Sunday mornings thought that "every negro distinctly understands, that at this hour he will be reviewed. An hour or so previous to the review, I make it the business of the driver to sound the horn." Apparently, it worked. According to one traveler in Mississippi, "At a certain signal upon the cook-house bell, the young gang came up in fine order to the yard for their dinner."[90]

Paternalism, racial stereotypes, and economic efficiency were part and parcel of another planter's decision to regulate his slaves' "Hours of rest" by clock and diurnal time. None too modestly one planter, Foby, sent his system "for the management of plantation servants" to the *Southern Cultivator* in 1853. "The fundamental principles upon which the system is based," explained Foby, "are simply these: that all living on the plantation, whether colored or not, are members of the same family." Foby considered himself "the patriarch (not the tyrant)" and insisted that all his orders "must be obeyed." If overweening paternalism was one ingredient of his system, racism was another: "Plantation negroes are much more ignorant than most persons suppose. . . . They require

Plantation bell at Thornhill, Alabama (Photograph by Alex Bush, 1934, Historic American Buildings Survey, Library of Congress)

a guardian, and although willing to work, they will work to no advantage, they will do nothing properly unless directed." With such notions of paternal stewardship in mind, Foby turned to the clock, in part at least, to regulate his bondpeople's "hours of rest" and, indirectly, their work times: "The bugle sounds at 9 o'clock, P.M., and every servant is required to return to his own cabin. . . . At noon, they of course rest and take their dinners. The time allowed must be regulated by circumstances, say from one to two and a half hours during the long hot days of summer. If the condition of the crop will admit of it, they should rest two and a half hours."[91]

If work was defined by the clock, then so, too, was leisure, which, when regulated by the sound of clock time, seemed less like leisure and more like the end of work. Slaves on one Sumter, South Carolina, plantation, for example, were required "to disperse at . . . Nine O'Clock at night" after weekend prayer meetings. And rule five of another slaveholder's "Rules for the Plantation" stated: "The horn must be blown in winter at 8, in summer at 9 o'clock, after which no negro must be seen out of his house."[92]

For planters to embrace clock-regulated plantation time, they needed certain information. Occasionally, such masters sought advice from the editors of

Barn at Bremo Plantation, Fluvanna County, Virginia (Photograph by C. O. Greene, 1940, Historic American Buildings Survey, Library of Congress)

southern agricultural periodicals. In July 1855, S. H. C., for example, wrote to the editors of Georgia's *Southern Cultivator*. "Permit me," he asked, "through the medium of your valuable paper, to inquire whether or not, there is such a thing as a plantation Clock?" He went on to describe his needs and the justification for such an inquiry: "It often happens on a plantation, that the overseer or driver, is not at his post just at the proper time in the morning to start all hands promptly, thereby causing confusion and disorder, rarely restored during the day." Preamble over, he got to the point of his communication: "Now, what I want, is, an alarm clock, of sufficient size and capacity to ring, or put in motion, a 50 or 60 pound bell, so arranged as to alarm at any hour desired. If there is such a thing in use, where can it be had? If there is nothing of the sort known, who will make one, or suggest the best plan?" S. H. C.'s question was not as unusual as he perhaps thought. The editor's answer was brief, matter-of-fact, and to the point, suggesting that such inquiries were commonplace: "If your overseer *sleeps at home*, a common alarm clock ought to be sufficient to awake him, at any hour desired. If you wish a clock large enough to wake up every person on the plantation, you can have it made at a cost, probably at $30 or $40, by addressing C[hauncey] Jerome, Clock Manufacturer, New Haven, Conn."[93] As recent work on the architecture of plantation slavery has shown, Cuban sugar planters who routinely had a "clock steeple, with clock and bell," built on their plantations were hardly more time conscious than their southern cousins.[94]

By the eve of the Civil War, planters had found clock time to be the ideal plantation regulatory and disciplinary device. And they cherished it, believing it fair, economical, and modern. Even when defending themselves against the onslaught of abolitionist attacks in 1860, for example, southern planters portrayed the supposedly leisurely hours of slavery, as opposed to free wage labor, not in terms of a romanticized solar time but by the putatively more stringent clock time. The southern slave, argued one master, "is not overworked. . . . He goes out when it is light enough to work, at 8 o'clock takes his breakfast, at 12 o'clock his dinner, at 2 o'clock goes to his work again . . . and about 9 or 10 o'clock goes to bed." That they chose to defend the supposed comfort of slavery in such terms suggests that southern planters were convinced of the fairness and efficiency of clock-regulated plantation work hours.[95]

Yet as with most of southern history, there was no small irony in such defenses. The same system that slaveholders loved to excoriate, free wage labor, maintained virtually identical working hours. Ignoring references to place, the following account hardly differs from those of southern slaveholders during and after the 1830s: "The following were the hours of labor imposed upon the children employed in a Factory at Leeds the summer before last. On Monday morning work commenced at six o'clock; at nine, half an hour for breakfast; from half past nine till twelve, work. Dinner, one hour; from five till eight, work; rest for half an hour. From half past eight till twelve, (midnight,) work; an hour's rest."[96] As it had for all moderns who peddled the equity of time-wage relations, it plainly took a little dose of hypocrisy to embrace progress. But by the same token, it took either a fanciful spirit or an active denial of reality for northerners to dismiss the presence of clock-regulated slavery in the antebellum South. When Harriet Beecher Stowe had St. Clare give Miss Ophelia the following description of the peculiar institution in *Uncle Tom's Cabin*, she was writing fiction most deserving of the name: " 'My dear Vermont, you natives up by the North Pole set an extravagant value on time! What on earth is the use of time to a fellow who has twice as much of it as he knows what to do with? As to order and system, where there is nothing to be done but to lounge on the sofa and read, an hour sooner or later in breakfast or dinner is n't of much account.' "[97] Rarely have truth and fiction been so far apart.

The most modern planters, those presumably most devoted to the cause of progress, mimicked northern factory-owning moderns to the extreme. This most progressive planter could be a user of the task or gang system; to him it was the timing of work rates that mattered. In short, these were planters who did not want simply to order the times of plantation work but aimed to regulate the productivity of labor as well.

Because antebellum "laborlords," as Gavin Wright has called southern planters, sought to maximize output per hand rather than yield per acre, the saving and manipulation of labor time was of great importance to them.[98] Although, as John F. Olson has argued, slaves worked fewer clock time hours per year than free laborers, North and South, slaves nevertheless "worked more intensively per hour" because their masters were able to regulate their slaves' labor by the clock. According to Olson, "Slaves on plantations using the gang system worked 94 per cent more (harder) each hour than did free men."[99] Planters were able to achieve this intensity for two reasons. First, many manipulated nature's rhythms and reallocated labor around unpredictable events. Some planters, says Olson, "who were inclined to give either a half-day or a full day off on Saturdays, appeared to have substituted rainy days for such holidays. This had the effect of shifting the burden of the limited opportunities during inclement weather to slaves."[100] When all time was the master's, such reallocations were accomplished more often than not. The second reason why slaveholders were able to increase the intensity of their slaves' labor is revealed in one slave owner's views on the management of slaves published in 1854. According to Robert Collins of Macon, Georgia, slave labor was most efficient if regulated by the clock in the context of the season and the amount and type of work that needed to be completed. "In the winter time," Collins argued, his hands worked "until twelve o'clock; then one hour for dinner, then work until night." "In the spring and summer," when Collins needed labor the most to cultivate precious staples, he appears to have been, paradoxically, more generous with his time. In these seasons, his hands would "work until 12 o'clock, and two hours for dinner, and work from 2 o'clock till night."[101] The apparent paradox is resolved, however, when we consider the varying lengths of the day in winter, spring, and summer. The average winter day in the South, according to Olson, lasted 10.4 hours. In Collins's case, this was reduced to 9.4 hours because he allowed one hour, by the clock, for lunch. The spring day lasted 13 hours, the summer day, 13.9 hours. Even though Collins allowed 2 hours for rest in spring and summer, his working days in these busy seasons were 11 and 11.9 hours respectively (1.6 and 2.5 hours more than in the winter). Thus when Collins needed labor the most, he gave longer breaks to allow his sun-baked slaves more time to recuperate. Such a strategy was eminently sensible because the longer working day and hotter weather no doubt enervated bondpeople. To maintain their productivity, Collins allowed longer breaks while squeezing, with the help of nature, longer actual working hours out of his hands. As Olson puts it: "The apparently long breaks for meals and rest, especially during summer . . . ought not to be attributed to the philanthropic instincts of the planters. They were conditions for achieving a desired level of intensity. The intense pace of work required rest not only for the slaves, but also for the draft animals, and planters gave explicit recognition of the value of rest breaks."[102]

This level of intensity was, it seems, achieved because slaveholders recognized that work and leisure regulated by clock time would increase and maintain the intensity of slaves' labor. Although planters were often shy to confess it (presumably because doing so would be to concede that they had failed to instill a respect for the clock among bondpeople), the greater efficiency of slave labor that Olson identifies was likely a product not of the clock per se but of the clock *coupled* with the whip. Since both southern slaves and northern workers were timed by the clock, the greater efficiency of slave labor serves as testimony to the superiority of planters' association of the clock and whip over northern managers' coupling of the clock and wage docking. Hence James Thomas, Hancock County, Georgia, planter, gave his bondpeople a five-minute break after every thirty minutes of labor because he found that such respites increased the amount of work his slaves did by 15 percent.[103] The whip, no doubt, lurked quietly in the background for those failing to return from breaks on time.[104] Whatever the plantation activity, then, time for such planters could always be saved, their slaves' labor abstracted, then translated and commodified into clock time: "To make one negro cook for all is a saving of time. If there be but ten hands, and these are allowed two hours at noon, one of which is employed in cooking their dinners, for all the purposes of rest, that hour had as well be spent in ploughing or hoeing, and would be equal to ten hours work of one hand; whereas the fourth of that time would be sufficient for one to cook for all."[105]

Even the physically delicate, such as pregnant slave women, found their work measured against the clock rather than by volume. In some respects, this makes sense because the clock encouraged steady labor rather than spurts of physical exertion, which might injure the human capital such women were bearing. South Carolina planter Andrew Flinn made this point precisely in his 1840 "Plantation Rules." The fourteenth point of his rules ordained: "The children must be very particularly attended to, for rearing children is not only a duty, but also the most profitable part of plantation business." To safeguard this profit from the beginning, the clock was used to ensure steady, not strenuous, work from profit-bearing slave mothers. The fifteenth point of Flinn's rules mandated: "Pregnant women & sucklers must be treated with great tenderness, worked near home & lightly. Pregnant women should not plough or lift, but must be kept at moderate work until the last hour if possible." Flinn's "last hour" was "in Summer, at 9 & in winter at 8 O'clock."[106]

Other planters devised and in turn propounded various formulas to "ascertain the actual cost of any specific work," when "the time it occupies being known." Examples were given: "The *daily labor of a team* must necessarily be regulated by the manner in which it is employed, as well as by its strength. In some of the southern and midland counties, the carters who generally sleep in the house, rise at four in the morning, feed, clean, and harness the horses, get breakfast, and are ready to go a-field at six-'clock, or after seven in the winter, when they work till two, thus making at the utmost a yoking of eight hours."[107] Such mental gymnastics could be born only of a mind concerned to the extreme with regulating labor time.

These abstractions were realized in that most corporeal of settings, the plantation field. Some masters kept a close eye on average hours worked. "The [dam] work was finished at 12 M[idday] on Saturday 22nd," noted planter John Ball in December 1849, adding, "The hands all worked cheerfully and well [and] at the end average[d] 11 hours work per day." The benefit of standardizing the length of workdays within seasonal rhythms was obvious to those slaveholders concerned about losing time. Only by having a workday of standard duration could a Virginia planter claim with satisfaction in 1858: "Last night we had sown 588 bushels of wheat. . . . We have not lost an hour's work."[108]

In some cases, masters' use of the clock is implicit in plantation records. Sumter District, South Carolina, planter Samuel Porcher Gaillard appears to have kept track of the finishing times of his slave laborers, and the precision of his journal entries suggests that he used a watch to do so: "25 Hands planting in the Grass field and finished it by half past 3 P.M." But Gaillard also used clock time to measure the duration of specific work. In 1847, he noted: "Robert Joe & Paris working in the new corn house, they were two hours employed in carrying the dry fodder in the loft."[109] Members of the southern literati also kept track of time. Writer-planter William Gilmore Simms noted in his plantation journal in May 1847 that his slaves commenced plowing his forty-acre field "this morning 10 oClock [and] finished Monday at 10 oClock [=] 2 days." And David Wyatt Aiken applied the clock to cotton picking. In 1856 his hands picked "640 lbs of cotton. Hauled one load of 1530 to Pa's gin, that amount having been picked this week up to 2 PM this afternoon."[110]

Other masters took the watch to the field and were explicit about its use. As one South Carolina planter noted in the back of his plantation journal under entries headed "Work timed by watch" for August 1843:

Summer House field. It takes exactly 5 minutes to run a furrow from one end of the cotton rows to the other that is to say *from the S. H. thicket [d]own to the Bay.*

From S. House thicket down to Jackson Branch, next [to] Charleston road = 15 minutes.

Planted the *Alligator* [field] in Corn 6 by 4, 1 hand to drop & 2 hoes to cover—in 3 days—commencing on the 1st day about 8 o'clock.

Alligator. Time taken to run round a row with shovel 14 minutes this allows for stopping, turning. &c.[111]

Until low-country planters managed to reduce the task system to clock time, slaves were bound to declare in favor against such clock-regulated work. "Negroes thus employed," observed one planter, "that is, working by time, it is well known move much more tardily than when tasked."[112]

If not labor itself then productive processes could be timed and some, obviously, more than others. This was especially the case with sugar production, as the published journal of one such planter revealed to readers of the *Southern Agriculturalist* in 1830: "Dec. 10th [1830]: Extracted with my mill and one pony, 65 gallons of juice in 28 minutes, added one gill of lime as before, boiled 4 hours and 45 minutes. . . . Dec. 16. . . . Boiled 4 hours and 26 minutes. . . . Dec. 28. . . . Measured one gallon of juice which I reduced to sugar in 64 minutes."[113] Although indigo operations had always been subject to fairly close timing, the influence of the age of improvement was apparent in the manufacturing of indigo dye by the late 1820s. New methods and equipment meant that "an operation which formerly required much experience and many days of labour, is now performed in less than twelve hours. . . . And the fermentation [formerly] of twenty or thirty hours . . . *is now reduced to a simple infusion of two hours.*" The conclusion was revealing: "It is the watch that now guides the series of operations."[114]

Others invoked the watch to add credibility to their findings, no matter how trivial the observation. Planter M. W. Philips of Mississippi believed that "Negroes cannot, or will not—they do not—eat in as short time as whites; I can, and do eat my meals in from ten to fifteen minutes; they will eat thirty by the watch, and oft-times forty-five; I have timed them, and know it to be a fact." That Philips should have timed the eating habits of his slaves, however, was perhaps not surprising. After all, this was the same planter who regulated plantation labor by the clock: "My hands go out at 5 o'clock, the call is at 11, and they return to the field at 2, they knock off at say quarter past 7, working eleven and a quarter hours." Sometimes plantation watch time bordered on the absurd. One East Tennessee planter recommended that slaves' feet be bathed "for about 8 minutes, night and morning" and none too convincingly linked this practice to the better "management of Negroes."[115]

For the most part, however, the plantation clock and watch were recruited to deal with the serious matter of running a business and controlling the labor of what were believed to be undisciplined bondpeople. Some slaveholders like Ben Sparkman used time simply to record progress in planting: "Memorandum of Planting for 1858, Commenced to plant 7 Acre ridge today Wednesday 14th [April] about Ten Oclock but did not finish [until] Thursday 15 about Eleven Oclock." He also set future agricultural work against the clock: "Memorandum of Planting for 1859. . . . Tuesday 28th June[:] will have up Potatos about 10 Oclock." Others used time to keep an eye on the speed of slaves' work: "Cut our Sorghum this morning—the blades were stripped and the seeds cut off yesterday. . . . It took Josey & Adam about 1/2 hour to cut down, with hatchets about 1/4 acre—which was the quantity planted."[116]

The application of watch time to slaves' work was not limited to the gang system. Although the task system, used primarily in the rice-growing regions of the South, has been subject to much inquiry, historians have yet to ascertain precisely how a task was defined by planters. On the surface, it would appear that the task system, with its built-in incentives for slaves to finish their work or predetermined day's task and then claim the rest of the day as their own, would obviate the need for the timing of work by watch. In one sense, this is true. Slaves established an almost inviolable (if sometimes exaggerated) right to work at their task at their own pace; those who worked quickly finished early.[117] But what remains unclear is exactly how planters defined a day's work or task. Obviously, the nature of the task changed depending on the type of work. But even so, how and against what standard was a task defined? Former slave John Brown of Georgia shed light on this issue in his antebellum autobiography. Brown's master was a firm believer in the watch as the best measure of task work. Explained Brown: "My old master . . . would pick out two or more of the strongest [hands], and excite them to race at hoeing or picking. . . . He would stand with his watch in his hand, observing their movements, whilst they hoed or picked. . . . Whatever [the winner] did, within a given time, would be multiplied by a certain rule, for the day's work, and every man's task would be staked out accordingly."[118] Brown's labor may have been task-oriented, but beyond the domain of the watch it was not. Though cryptic to a point, one planter testified to conducting a similar practice: "The tasks given are calculated to require so much labour." And South Carolina planter Alexander Robert Lawton seems to have conducted experiments similar to those of Brown's master. On April 10, 1832, "I gave the hands 6 tasks, but by requiring a little less unnecessary work, (such as bedding between the hills of corn where the plows had already bedded) they could have done two acres. The hands were done 6 tasks by 12 Oclock." Or, as one planter put it simply in 1857: "A task is as much work as the meanest full hand can do in nine hours."[119]

Nor was slaves' free time, the essential component behind recent analyses of the slaves' economy, entirely free from the strictures of the planter's clock. Although, as historian James Walvin has argued, slaves lived their lives within the broader rhythms of the Christian calendar, students of slaves' off times and the slave economy have been less sensitive to the fact that such off time was itself often regulated and defined by the clock.[120] Although it was in the master's interest to allow slaves time to cultivate crops and gardens of their own, planters nevertheless placed carefully considered temporal parameters around when slaves were permitted to commence their free time and how long it lasted. Because the boundaries of plantation work time were clock regulated, so too was the beginning of slaves' off time and some of the things they were allowed to do in it. Furthermore, because this was the case, because the actual, absolute ownership of time was nonnegotiable, masters and slaves came to accept and realize that all time on the plantation, whether work or leisure, was ultimately the master's to bestow, manipulate, and define. In other words, although it is important to examine the features and contours of the slave economy, it is equally critical to acknowledge the way in which this additional form of slave work was temporally defined and regulated. This regulation of off time suggests that the antebellum South was moving toward an ostensibly industrial system in which respite from work was contingent not solely on the whim of masters but also on the dictates of the slaveholders' clock. Leisure, because it was defined by clock-wielding masters, could be as regular and delineated as plantation work itself. And here, masters of the Old South seemed to be groping for an idea that would later become codified by that most time-conscious of industrial thinkers, Frederick Taylor. "As Taylor has so convincingly demonstrated," remarks a recent theorist, "only those of a brutish nature who are 'mentally sluggish,' such as his model pig-iron handler, 'Schmidt,' can excell as industrial laborers. It becomes imperative . . . to extend the time-discipline of industrial capitalism beyond the walls of the factory to encompass the home and the hearth. . . . What was true for labour-time or the work-space soon came to be true for leisure-time or the domestic space." Preclassical masters that they were, antebellum planters thought it only sensible that their putatively sluggish Schmidts should have their time, on and off, regulated for them.[121]

Former bondpeople who were interviewed during the 1930s made this point themselves in a variety of ways. Many acknowledged that there was no such thing as slaves' time. Martha Colquitt of Georgia, for example, equated the absence of slave garden plots with the monopoly of time by her master: "Dey won't no separate gyardens. Dey didn't have no time to work no gyardens of dey own."[122] William McWhorter, also of Georgia, agreed: "No, mam, slaves never had no gardens of deir own; dey never had no time of deir own to wuk no garden."[123] For Austin Grant of Texas, all plantation time was master's time: "We didn' have no little garden, we never had no time to work no garden. When you could see to work, you was workin' for him."[124]

There is an unmistakable sense that even when gardens and the time to work them were permitted, bondpeople knew this time was bestowed by the master; that it was his time to give, not theirs, in the first instance, to take. Aunt Laura expressed her master's apparent magnanimity in such terms: "He give us enough ter eat an' plenty of time ter weave clothes for us to wear."[125] Laura Thornton echoed these sentiments when describing how her enslaved father was allowed to grow cotton, enabling him to buy his own house: "He belonged to his white folks but he had his house and lot right next to theirs. They would give him time you know."[126] Anne Bell of South Carolina put it more simply still: "They give us a half Saturday, to do as we like."[127] Benevolent masters were those who did not necessarily recognize the customary rights of slaves' time. Rather, they were those who generously bestowed it in the first place. "Me first Moster," recalled Sam Anderson, "I liked him best, as he would give Saturday evenings."[128] Hannah Scott agreed: "I heard some white folks treat dey slaves good and give dem time off, but Marse Bat don't."[129]

Clock and master defined not only the temporal boundary of the slaves' off time. The clock and masters' preoccupation with order and discipline extended beyond work and into play. "We could do whatsoever we pleased," recalled former slave Mark Oliver, "just so [long as] we got to bed by nine o'clock."[130] Isabella Dorroh was more specific: "Marse Fair let his niggers have dances and frolics on his plantation, and on Saturdays dey danced till 12 o'clock mid-night. . . . But Marse wouldn't let his slaves dance atter 12 o'clock."[131] Cyrus Bellus of Mississippi explained that slaves on his former master's plantation "were allowed to get out and have their fun and play and 'musement for so many hours." But "outside of those hours, they had to be found in their houses."[132] Small kindnesses to slave children were also clock regulated. Nancy Rogers Bean's former mistress gave her a doll to play with but placed strictures on its use: "She allowed me one hour every day to play with it."[133] Little wonder, then, that the clock itself figured prominently in slave children's games. Explained Madison Bruin of Texas:

> Us boys have good time playin'. Us draw de line and some git on one side and some on de other. Den one sing out

"Chickama, Chickama, craney crow,
Went to de well to wash my toe;
When I git back my chicken was gone,
What time, old witch?"
De somebody holler out, "One o'clock" or "Two o'clock" or any time, and
den one side try to cotch dem on de other side.[134]

Masters, in short, ensured that clock time not only regulated work but also
defined the parameters of the slaves' economy, free time generally, and reinforced the notion that all time was ultimately master's time. Slaves' free time,
then, was anything but. Because it was governed by the master's clock, free
time was as calculated and controlled as work itself.

For all their manipulation of slaves' time, the commitment to plantation clock
time ultimately took its toll on masters. Some, for example, succumbed to
nostalgia by appealing to a past that had never really existed: "Oh for a Snug
little farm where I could indulge my fondness for the Country & for Agriculture," mused James Henry Hammond in 1846. In maudlin and romantic terms
he wished he could abandon a society that "depends on having every screw
tight & the whole machinery moving on clock work principles." It was not only
the time consumed by finding a new overseer and buying his slaves' clothes but
also the very concept of time ownership and the inroads made by clock-
regulated slavery on his own time that William Elliott loathed. He told his
mother in December 1857: "I regret that I cannot fix a time for visiting you. I
am the slave of circumstances, some of them not free from vexation, which
does not allow me to call my time my own."[135] Echoes of colonial merchants
rang loudly.

For others the heightened sense of punctuality instilled in plantation households by time obedience proved too much. " 'Order is Heaven's first law' and a
good thing in any family," agreed one planter's guest in 1859. But the clockwork
punctuality demanded by the plantation owners was, in his opinion, excessive
and threatened his very freedom: "Then the terrible punctuality which made
slaves of all of us, and kept me always looking at my watch, and always afraid of
being late for something, as, indeed, I was once for dinner, in spite of all my
precaution—four minutes and a half exactly. Shall I ever forget it?" Allies
against the tyrant time and his enforcer, the plantation mistress, were found in
the children, however, "they conveying to me private warnings as to how soon
the prayer bell would ring in the morning, and furnishing me with much
valuable secret intelligence as to the enemy's weak points."[136]

Time could be a cruel master for planters whose misapplication of it had led them into debt. For such unfortunate souls, time was merciless: "He has chalked out to himself a hard lot, and voluntarily enters on a state of servitude worse than Egyptian bondage. His work is never accomplished. He toils at all hours, and yet is never ahead of his work. . . . With him, there are no pleasant associations with the *past*; the *present* is full of anxiety, care, and hard labor, and a dark cloud rests upon the *future*." This writer concluded his warning with a doggerel that made all too clear the precarious balance slaveholders had to maintain between being masters of or slaves to their own temporal dictates:

Work—work—work!
From weary chime to chime;
Work—work—work!
As prisoners work for crime.[137]

Once they had created time the tyrant, masters could not depose him. Democratic in his sources Father Time may have been, totalitarian in his rule he nonetheless was.

Embracing modernity in the form of clock time, then, had a hefty price tag for southerners. It was a cost that capitalist Yankees could and had learned to live with partly because they had to in a free-wage-labor economy dependent on the regulation of time by work and partly because, unlike their southern brethren, liberty was a notion independent of ideas about absolute mastery over all, time included.[138] But slaveholders, like up-country South Carolina yeomen and Georgia black belt populists, increasingly found themselves trapped by a mental and actual world capitalist market which they had periodically entered but found they could not escape.[139] For southern slave owners, clock time, even though married to nature and the past and once a panacea and a ticket to the modern world, was also a fetter. Once they had come to rely on clock time to regulate slave behavior and plantation affairs, they, like all moderns, found that they could not do without it. More worrying still, while they managed to master their bondpeople's time, time came to master them in turn. But there was room for only one tyrant in the South, and no white man, because he was white, could ever be anything less than free. Finding themselves slaves to a time they had created, with the help, albeit indirect, of increasingly despised Yankees, was a bitter pill for masters to swallow. And so while the South and the North began, in the period from 1830 to 1860, to move apart politically, southerners found themselves moving, sometimes uncomfortably, toward the so-called Yankee ideal of time thrift: a simultaneous economic and cultural rapprochement between two regions politically at odds.[140] And such was the nature of clock time that it became increasingly difficult to distinguish northern from southern clock time. The South had to adapt to much in the bourgeois nineteenth century and in no other field, perhaps, was it more successful in its adoption of bourgeois practices (though not norms) than in its qualified embrace of clock-regulated labor. Janus-faced and paradoxical though it was, master time, by 1860, could hardly be differentiated from Yankees' or, in some senses, slaves' time.

Time in African American Work and Culture

V

There remains the hope that, in the period of world history which is now beginning, the period of docile masses governed by clocks, some men can still be found to offer resistance.
—Max Horkheimer, *Critique of Instrumental Reason*

Three full moons shone and disappeared. . . . The peace of the fifth night after the fourth full moon's appearance was shattered by noises louder than any we had ever heard. . . . The white men want us to obliterate our remembrance of our way, the way, and in its place to follow their road, road of destruction.
—Kwei Armah, *Two Thousand Seasons*

The first object that engaged my attention was a watch which hung on the chimney, and was going. I was quite surprised at the noise it made, and was afraid it would tell the gentleman anything I might do amiss.
—*The Life of Olaudah Equiano or Gustavas Vassa the African Written by Himself*, ca. 1750, Virginia

One reason why African Americans have been described as "more than an ethnic group, less than a nation," why, in other words, they have remained marginal to white, bourgeois, American society, is because they both accommodated and resisted their masters' attempts to inculcate a modern, clock-based time sensibility during slavery.[1] American whites and blacks are both united and separated by their sometimes competing, sometimes complementary notions of time. African Americans can adjust to white time sensibilities, which stress punctuality and are future oriented, but they can also reject these same sensibilities as a form of protest against democratic capitalism generally, white bourgeois sensibilities specifically, by eschewing the authority of the clock and adopting presentist and naturally defined notions of time, a tendency that sociologists and the public alike have come to call Colored Peoples' Time, or CPT.[2] Of course, this emphasis on race as the sole arbiter of time consciousness simplifies a very complicated relationship. White, northern, and European nineteenth-century workers, for example, enlisted strategies similar to CPT in an effort to resist the imposition of clock time by their managers, thus suggesting that slaves resisted not simply as African Americans but also as a class of workers.[3] But used to identify a form of resistance to clock time in the particular context of the nineteenth-century South and divested of its pejorative connotations, CPT is a useful shorthand to describe how African Americans as a class of laborers resisted planter-defined time during and after slavery. CPT was an intuitive intellectual and social construct serving to repudiate the demands of time-conscious southern agrarian capitalists, old and new. Because masters could not force slaves to internalize time, slaves helped open a window of resistance to planter-defined time, and it was a window which they used when they could. Whether this resistance took the form of an appeal to the sun, a presentist time orientation, or the use of the clock itself, it stayed with them after freedom came. Yet as other nineteenth-century workers found, this resistance was by no means wholly successful. In fact, many of the strategies of resistance African Americans employed during and after slavery became increasingly redundant and unsuited to combating a modern conception of time whose very vocabulary, idea, and legitimacy black workers had already gone some way toward accepting during slavery. In other words, by 1865, African American time sensibilities, minor differences notwithstanding, were more akin to those of white working- and middle-class Americans than they were to those of black, pre-twentieth-century and preindustrial West Africans.

Because few if any clocks or watches were present in pre-twentieth-century West Africa and because West African cultures and economies had little need for minutely measured, regular time, it is difficult to entertain the idea that slaves newly arrived in the colonial American South would have harbored anything but a task-oriented, natural time sensibility.[4] Although the trading activities of New England merchants in West Africa could have imparted an appreciation that time was money as well as for timepieces themselves, this seems not to have been the case. Philadelphia merchant Samuel Swain, for example, complained in 1810 that his African counterpart "is not remarkable for his punctuality as a merchant." And Rhode Island merchant John Howeland's efforts to sell watches there in 1823 met with failure: "I sold my rum and trinkets to good advantage on the coast. . . . My watches I lost on." Even when West Africans did begin to buy mechanical timepieces in some quantity in the late nineteenth century, it was for reasons other than temporal accuracy. Unapologetically racist though it is, the following account from *Scribner's Magazine* in 1897 is revealing:

> One clock manufacturer of Waterbury, Conn., found that a certain rival was doing a large trade in cheap clocks sent out to the wilds of Africa. He got hold of a sample clock, and finding that there was a heavy profit in the enterprise, invested a large sum of money in making a still better clock, thousands of which were shipped to the same market. Strange to say, sales were very slow, while his rival, turning out a cheaper and far less accurate time piece, was selling all he could make. Finally the explanation came. Savages like noise. The clocks made by the original exporter had a particularly loud and aggressive tick.

Certainly, the impact of European colonization on West African time sensibilities and its influence on Africans before their enslavement and transportation to the American South are difficult to determine. Eighteenth- and nineteenth-century sources suggest that the British military practice of firing fort guns on the hour may have helped insinuate at least a vague idea of clock time, albeit confined to coastal regions, in West Africa.[5] But, like Australian aborigines and Natal Zulus and, in fact, like all preindustrial peoples whose culture and economy does not require coordination by the clock, West African peoples did not harbor, nor did they need, a sense or appreciation of clock time.[6]

On balance, then, mechanical timepieces were rare in West Africa, and without them African time sensibilities not only fell necessarily within the general rhythm of natural phenomena and task orientation but also tended to compound all time, past and future especially, into what Kenyan scholar John Mbiti calls "No-time." The net effect of this time orientation, argues Mbiti, is that the "linear concept of time in Western thought, with an indefinite past, present and infinite future, is practically foreign to African thinking."[7] And since "time is a language, and since people from different cultures 'speak' it differently," the stage had long been set for a conflict between both a cyclical and linear philosophy and the increasingly capitalistic and mechanical application of Western time and a more presentist, task-oriented, natural West African time sensibility.[8] Consequently, if slaves did succumb to time obedience and planter-defined time generally, one would expect to see a change not only in the way southern bondpeople appreciated clock-defined time but also an alteration in their philosophy of time with their concept of an immediate present being supplemented by a sharper notion of linear time, past and future.[9]

Certainly, work on African time sensibilities supports Mbiti's general conclusion, and the impressions of eighteenth- and nineteenth-century European travelers in West Africa serve to reaffirm the belief that mechanically regulated time was alien to these societies.[10] "The Yoruba worships the objects of nature above him," observed one late nineteenth-century missionary, adding: "The moon is one of them." Nor was this method of timekeeping inaccurate for Yoruban purposes: "He is a good calculator. He tells his age by the number of moons he has seen." Hugh Crow made similar observations following a trip to West Africa in 1830: "The Bonnians compute time by observing the moon, and it is surprising with what accuracy they will calculate the ebbing and flowing of the tides." Other travelers in the region stated similar findings more simply still. "The natives [of Asante]," said John Beecham in 1841, "reckon time by moons," an observation echoed by another traveler, John Duncan: "All reckoning here is done by the moon." Such observations too easily fed European stereotypes about slothful Africans. During his stay in Gambia in 1795–96, Mungo Park made an association between naturally reckoned time and indolence that was to fuel stereotypes about Colored Peoples' Time in the nineteenth and twentieth centuries. Said Park: "Loss of time is an object of no great importance in the eyes of the Negro. If he has anything of consequence to perform, it is a matter of indifference to him whether he does it to-day or to-morrow, or a month or two hence; so long as he can spend the present moment with any degree of comfort, he gives himself very little concern about the future."[11] More than thirty years later, southern slaveholders hardly bothered to reformulate Park's observation, their diatribes sounding like well-rehearsed mantras: "A negro has no idea of providing for the future. . . . His thoughts are limited to the present—he never thinks of to-morrow." After all, this master mused, what else could one expect from "incompetent Africans"?[12] And so, planters came to believe, it was the master's paternal duty to regulate time for bondpeople because, left to their own devices, slaves would revert to their putatively natural state of sloth and, possibly, recklessness.[13] Classical economists' putatively benign view of workers laboring to improve themselves had little room to grow in a society so tightly hedged by profoundly skeptical assumptions about the proclivities of the laboring class, especially if it happened to be black.

As long as southern slaveholders were committed to natural time, recently arrived African slaves were unlikely to find their time sensibilities attacked. Certainly, evidence from the eighteenth-century South suggests that slaves kept their commitment to naturally defined time intact.[14] Runaways in Virginia in the 1760s, for example, told their white captors: "They say they have been ten Moons from home," as did South Carolina slaves from the mid-eighteenth century: "Says . . . that he has made two crops for his master, and has been absent from his service two moons." When pushed to provide more specific estimates of time, slaves from the colonial period turned to the sun. "Sun about one or two hours high," recalled George Nichols, a slave implicated in a 1748 South Carolina conspiracy.[15] For the colonial slave, at least, African definitions of time, especially its source, remained largely unmolested partly because of the strength of the collective African American memory but, perhaps more important, because such definitions had as yet to come under attack from slaveholders.[16]

It would be grossly misleading to say that an African time consciousness, broadly construed, crumbled as soon as slaveholders introduced clock time to the plantation. Evidence suggests that naturally defined time remained important to African Americans even after the Civil War.[17] But this should be of little surprise. After all, as E. P. Thompson rightly pointed out, the ascendancy of mechanically defined time over natural time is an ongoing process which occurs in degrees, not absolutes.[18] But there were several other important reasons why southern slaves, even after the 1830s, were sometimes able to reject and ignore masters' use of plantation clock time.

The nature of the South's timepiece manufacturing industry in conjunction with masters' understandable reluctance to make timepieces available to bondpeople ensured that slaves had to turn to the sun or moon if they were to estimate time at all. Masters seemed to have guarded both the secret of time telling and the instruments themselves, reserving the use of a clock or watch for the few slaves whose plantation duties necessitated reading and understanding mechanically defined time. But even in these instances, the secret was not always forthcoming. The ability to tell clock time, requiring some formal training as it did with white children, was guarded jealously by whites lest it should be used against them in, say, the planning of escapes or insurrections.[19]

Generally, though, house servants, cooks especially, needed to know the time so they could serve meals punctually and hence they were one of the few groups privy to the secret of the clock. As former Georgia slave James Bolton revealed: "Mistess done larned the cook to count the clock, but none of the rest of our niggers could count the clock." Cooks could, however, recruit the sun for accuracy if occasion demanded. Explained former slave Sina Banks: "My sister done all the cooking and as they were short handed in the field she had to help in the field, too. She would put the meat for the vegetables on to boil and she would mark on the floor to show me where the sun would be when it was ten o'clock and I would put the vegetables in to boil with the meat. . . . It was a lonesome job just sitting there waiting for the sun to tell me it was ten o'clock."[20] It is also likely that slave nurses and "sucklers," required as they were to measure time to the minute, had access to a timepiece, at least on a temporary basis. Charged to help raise human capital that would have to remain healthy and profitable, the black women entrusted as nurses were required to be very sensitive to timing. According to James Henry Hammond's section on "Sucklers" in his 1857–58 plantation book,

> Sucklers are not required to leave their houses until sun-rise, when they leave their children at the children's house before going to field. . . . Their work lies always within 1/2 a mile of the quarter. They are required to be cool before commencing to suckle—to wait 15 minutes, at least, in summer, after reaching the children's house before nursing. It is the duty of the nurse to see that none are heated when nursing, as well as of the Overseer & his Wife occasionally to do so. They are allowed 45 minutes at each nursing to be with their children.[21]

Charlotte Beverly was one such nurse: "I blow d'horn fo' d'mudders 'r' d' little babies t' come in from d' fiel's 'n' nuss 'em, in d' mawnin' 'n' atternoon."[22] Slave women, then, because of their central role in household work and the maintenance of the future labor force, may well have been more exposed to the rigors of the clock than any other group of slaves, with, perhaps, the exception of black slave drivers. In other words, if plantation mistresses and northern working- and middle-class women had aspects of their lives regulated by clock time, so too did some slave women.

The vast majority of slaves, however, did not own or have access to clocks or watches although it is, of course, difficult to say so authoritatively because, as chattel, any possessions slaves might have accumulated were not recorded in probate inventories. There are few reliable sources that even hint at the extent to which slaves may have owned timepieces. One is the *Records of the Committee of Claims (Southern Claims Commission)*, which recorded the claims made by southern freedpeople and whites for property lost to Union troops during the Civil War, although even this source is hardly representative. Between 1871 and 1880, 22,298 claims were filed, only 17 of which were for watches lost by freedpeople during the war. And of the more than two thousand slave narratives in George P. Rawick's *American Slave: A Composite Autobiography*, only one mentions actual clock ownership during slavery. Clearly, a clock- or watch-owning slave was a rarity. Erstwhile bondman Tob Davis of Texas spoke for the majority of slaves: "Dey don't have de watches dem deys fo' de nigger so dey can't tell de time."[23]

Without access to the timepiece, slaves sometimes drew on their African heritage to determine and define time and so, in part at least, kept alive a cultural tradition and defined time by their own standards.[24] Missouri slave Jane Simpson described just such a process. "We didn't own no clocks dem days," she recalled, explaining: "We just told de time by de sun in de day and de stars at night. If it was clouded we didn't know what time it was." As to why this was the case, she was explicit: "De white folks didn't want to let de slaves have no time for der self." Marginalized from mechanical sources of time, slaves like Jane Simpson attempted to carve out their own definitions of time using their West African heritage. Sometimes such efforts were successful: "De old folks used to let us chillun run and play at night, while de white folks sleep and dey watch de stars to tell what time to call us in and put us to bed, 'fore de white folks know we was out." Even in the late antebellum period, some slaves apparently retained the ability to reckon natural time and still insisted on natural cues to guide aspects of their lives. "I had to get up in the morning, around four o'clock—I guessed the time by the stars," recalled one former slave. Another explained how a medicinal root used during slavery "had to be used only at a certain time ob de moon." But even the cultural significance and divinity of the sun came to be polluted and overshadowed by the regimen imposed by slavery: "We hated to see the sun rise in slavery time, 'cause it meant another hard day."[25]

If slave owners' inability and reluctance to share mechanical timekeeping knowledge and instruments with the majority of slaves, and if slaves' collective memories of African, preindustrial time sensibilities explains why, even by the late antebellum period, some bondpeople still looked to natural cues as representing legitimate time, then, to this list, we must recall one other explanation. Put simply, slave owners neither wanted nor were able to eschew altogether natural time rhythms themselves. Predicated on seasonal rhythms, plantation agriculture was necessarily dependent to no small degree on nature's temporal parameters. Rather than engage in fruitless combat with nature, slave owners worked within its seasonal and daily constraints, insinuating mechanically defined time, where appropriate. The result was a plantation routine that looked to natural as well as artificial, mechanical cues, a routine that relied as much on the rising of the sun as it did on the ticking of the clock.

This admixture was especially apparent in planters' efforts to communicate household clock time to the fields. Former Texas slaves Lee McGillery and Jack Harrison described this juxtaposition of natural and mechanical time precisely. Recalled Harrison of his master: "He gets up every morning about 3:30 o'clock [and] we always out in the field waiting for it to get light so we could see how to work. We worked every day just as long as we could see." The practice of preempting sunrise with the clock and thus enabling masters to get their slaves to the field in time for dawn's light was described by McGillery: "Master always wake the slaves his self about four o'clock every morning, so's we would be in the field waiting for daylight to come then." Harriet Jones revealed not only the irritating power of the clock-regulated horn to intrude on sleep (the sound of time was, like today's alarm clock, difficult to ignore) but her master's attempts to beat the rooster: "Ole Massa had a horn he blow fer de niggers ter git up by, long 'bout four o'clock hit begin ter blow, yer be sleepin so good dat w'en dat horn start blowin yer just turn ober an tries ter take 'nuther nap, den hit goes argin' b—l—o—w, how loud dat ole horn do blow' jes as well wake up fer taint no use ter try ter sleep nohow. . . . W'en de breakfus ober dey all starts fer de fiel as dey go dey sing ter wake dem up, got ter be in de fiel by time hits light, so w'en de rooster crow's hit time ter start ter de fiel." Sometimes only one part of the working day would be defined by the clock. According to Lucendy Griffen, "Master he would wake the slave on work days about 4:40 every morning and we worked jest as long as we could see." Plantation clock time could also be partly diurnal. Most frequently, clock time was invoked when masters needed slaves to labor most intensively: during the harvest of treasured staples. For Amelia Barnett, for example, only "durin' de cotton pickin' time a big bell was rung to git us up about four o'clock in de mawnin."[26] This meshing of mechanical and natural time and the room for maneuver that it provided explain slaves' limited ability to appeal to and retain an African, preindustrial time sensibility. But as with all forms of slave resistance, there were identifiable, sometimes impenetrable, limits.

Although a natural time awareness persisted well into the nineteenth century, this hardly distinguished the slave South from either Britain or the North.[27] Everywhere, natural and mechanical time vied for primacy in the minds and actions of managers and workers. And simply because slaveholders were unwilling and unable to instill a time discipline among their workforce does not mean that slaves escaped altogether the rigors of clock-regulated labor. In truth, they did not.[28] Willing as they were to work in tandem with nature but simply unable to inculcate a time discipline among their workforce through conventional means, planters appealed to their own past in an effort to embrace and safeguard their future. Although watchless slaves could hardly be expected to develop a northern, internalized respect for time, they could be forced to obey time. Well aware of the regulating power of the sound of the church clock and the punctuality demanded by the railroads and the mail, planters looked to making slaves obey mechanical time mostly, though not exclusively, through the sounding of bells and horns in accordance either with what one slave called the plantation clock-defined "nigger bell" or their own watches.[29] And if the regularity of the sound of scheduled times failed to inspire time obedience, then the lash would. Of course, contradictions emerged, and planters, in the process of solving one dilemma, found themselves in another. Because instilling an internal time discipline among slaves would have involved giving them watches and because such an act on anything but the smallest scale was anathema (time-owning slaves would, after all, readily become like free, time-negotiating northern workers), planters' only feasible solution was to try to inspire an obedience to the sound of their clock time with the whip. The whip and the watch, both literally and figuratively, were, after all, closely related. As Charles Ball showed, masters could recruit the watch to time the whip: "After a delay of ten minutes, by the watch, I received another dozen lashes." Conversely, whipping slaves detracted from the amount of time they could work, as Ball's master realized: "My master Ned was in favour of giving me a dozen lashes every morning for a month, with the whip; but my old master said, this would be attended with too much trouble, and besides, it would keep me from my work, at least half an hour every morning." In any event, splicing clock with whip was a compromise with which planters were willing to live, even if it did subject them to the tyranny of the clock.[30]

If their recollections are to be believed, slaves who were timed in the field by their master's watch felt the pressure of time hurrying them in their labor.[31] Mose Smith, former Louisiana bondman, attested: "When I growed up they give me so many rows of cotton to hoe or pick. I work my own rows and they timed me so I had to hurry to get the work done, and when they send me off the farm to do a chore they time me on that." So too with Calvin Moye: "When dey all goes to work dey would work till 11:30 and den takes off and eats dinner and go back to work at 1 o'clock by Maser Ingram's watch." For some slaves, the hours of slavery seemed little different from the perspective of the 1930s.

"Quitting time was five o'clock," mused James Southall, "just about union hours nowadays." And it was "dis wuck time," slaves came to realize, that "is in de push of de wuck."[32]

Pushing slaves against the clock seems to have made them more punctual and sensitive to being on time. "One mornin'," remembered a former Alabama slave, "I had started to the 'field an' on the way, I los' my piece o' bread." Having found it, he felt compelled to "hurry to make up for los' time." If his master was anything like Lue Bradford's Texas owner, his compulsion was understandable. Explained Bradford: "They would have to work until the horn sounded before they could stop for noon. In the morning the field boss would have the record book and each person was supposed to report before starting for work and all were punished who were late." The rationale for such a practice was clear to her: "This encouraged punctuality." Still others tended, like their masters, to conceive work in units of time. As Henry Huce Smith noted, during slavery "it was good work to put out about one bale every hour." The point that certain tasks had a clock-defined value was noted by Ed Domino, former Texas slave: "Us go down d' row [in] 'bout t'ree minutes." When the master got his arithmetic wrong and assigned "a task which was impossible for me to complete in the few hours allotted it," there was little, if any, appellate process available. Even factory slaves (indeed, free industrial workers) had a scarcely more developed sense of clock time. Compare, for example, the foregoing accounts with that of John Washington, who, in 1860, went to work in a Virginia tobacco factory. "We began Work at 7. Oclock in the Morning," explained Washington, elaborating, "Stopped from 1. to 2. O,clock for dinner. Stoped Work at 6 P.M. If we chose to make Extra Work We began at any hour Before 7. and worked some times till 9. P.M."[33]

Even without being physically timed in the field, slaves were perhaps doomed to succumb to the punctuality required by mechanical time. Sometimes this occurred simply because slaves, too, lived in an increasingly punctilious and hectoring society and so ended up sharing their masters' concerns about precision. "Oh! Lord yes," recalled North Carolina former slave Sarah Louise Augustus, "I remember the stage coach. As many times as I run to carry the mail to them when they come by! They blew a horn before they got there and you had to be on time 'cause they could not wait." If the master was somehow a participant in the wider market revolution, then so too were his slaves. Minnie Davis of Georgia recalled: "Marse John didn't have many slaves and they had to get up and get going early every morning. Marse John was post-master of Athens and had to be in his office by eight o'clock every morning so he ordered that his breakfast be served regularly at seven-thirty." Nor were urban slaves immune to the regulatory power of the town clock, a device masters appear to have recruited in their efforts to order behavior even during town slaves' supposed off times. "In Augusta [Georgia] you had to have a pass to go from house to house. You couldn't go out at night in Augusta after 9 o'clock. They had a bell at the old market down yonder, and it would strike every hour and half hour," remembered Aunt Adeline. Emma Knight of Hannibal, Missouri, revealed the regulatory power of the town bell with still greater precision: "We never was 'lowed on the street after nine o'clock. We sure run for home when the church bell done rung on de hill at nine o'clock." Similarly, master-arranged courtship meetings between slaves were regulated by the clock. "Young man was allowed to stay only 3/4 hours," recalled Mildred Graves of Virginia.[34] Even without the clock, however, some slaves, like John Washington of Virginia, recalled that during the 1850s if he "had any desire to go out again in a reasonable time," the time specified by his master on his "permission" slip enabling him to leave the plantation "must be punctually obeyed." According to Lu Lee of Texas, most often it was: "That nigger would get a pass and come over and stay with he gal and then he would say, 'I am sorry but it is that certain time and I got to go.'"[35]

From their own experience with public, urban time, planters realized the power of communicating time through sound and so attempted to regulate plantation operations with clock-governed bells, horns, and improvised carillons. The sound of clock time was potent, and its memory stuck in the minds of many quondam slaves, sometimes keenly. "Bells and horns! Bells for this and horns for that! All we knowed was go and come by the bells and horns," smarted Charley Williams. Dave Walker, former Mississippi slave, elaborated: "We wuz trained to live by signals of a ole cow horn. Us knowed whut each blow meant. All through de day de ole horn wuz blowed, to git up in de mo'nings, to go to de big kitchen out in Mars' back yard ter eat, to go to de fields, an' to come in an' on lak dat all day."[36] Cole Thomas of Texas revealed at some length the presence of a clock-regulated bugle on his plantation and the method his master used to ensure that it would be heard:

We has ter git up early every day in de year, rain or shine. De slaves was woke up every mornin at four thirty by a slave blowin a horn it was his job ter gits up and blow a bugle and den he would go ter work in de fiels wid de rest of de slaves. Dar was no danger of you not wakin up when de bugle blowed cause he blows it long and loud. He allus gits up of a mornin and gits his bugle down and comes out and climbs up on a platform wintah and summah and blows his bugle. Dis platform was about eight or ten feet tall.[37]

Cora Carroll of Mississippi remembered: "All the stock men worked in the field also—so many hours." These men "had a bell for them to go to work in the morning, a bell for them to get up by, and another one for noon, and another in the evening when they would knock off for dark."[38] Because well-rested workers labored best, bedtime was early and regular. Louis Cain recalled that his master made his hands "put out the light and go to bed at 9 o'clock. He would walk to his back door and hit a piece of steel and every negro would scamper off to bed and get quiet cause he knew the next day was work day."[39] The constant reinforcement of time through sound gave slaves a keen understanding of what time, precisely, plantation affairs occurred: "[At] half-past eleven they would send the older children with food to the workers in the field," recalled one South Carolina slave, and Betty Cofer testified that this time awareness hurried slaves in their labor: "On one plantation the field hands had to hustle to get to the end of the row at eleven o'clock dinnertime, because when the cooks brought their dinner, they had to stop just where they was and eat, and the sun was mighty hot out in those fields."[40] Staggered bell times figured prominently, too. According to Harrison Cole, "W'en four o'clock in de mornin's cum de bell from de big house rings, an' dis means dat everybody dat is able to work has to get up an' eat his breakfast an' be ready for de nex' bell dat rings at five o'clock to go to de fields."[41]

Many former slaves testified to the freneticism that the sound of the bell engendered. "Wuk started on place in mawnins 'bout fo' 'clock," noted Robert Young. "Overseer would ring a bell an' I member hearin' feets hit de flo' one right atter 'nother when de bell would ring. All de darkies got out to field as fast as they could." "The hands was woke up in the morning with a big bell," remembered former slave Susan Merrit. "When Master pulled that bell rope," she said, "the Negroes fell out of them bunks like rain falling."[42] Obedience to the sound of time was paired with harried behavior. "There was a big dinner bell in the yard," recalled an erstwhile Oklahoma slave, explaining: "When meal-time come, someone ring that bell, and all the slaves know it's time to eat and stop their work. . . . We had our time to go to bed and our time to get up in the morning." "We was woke by a bell and called to eat by a bell and put to bed by that bell," explained another former slave, adding, "and if that bell ring outta time you'd see the niggers jumpin' rail fences and cotton rows like deers or something, gettin' to that house, 'cause that mean something bad wrong at massa's house." Bugles blown "outta time" were prominent in J. C. Alexander's memory, too. "I heard someone blowin' de bugle at de 'big house,'" Alexander told his interviewer, explaining, "I knowed it wasn't time to go to dinah. At fus' it was a big blowin' . . . den dah toot-toot—two times—and dat meant fo' us to hurry to de 'big house.'" So intrusive, so commanding was the sound of plantation time that "at twelve o'clock de cooks would blow a horn [and] Even de hosses an' de mules knowed dat horn an' dey wouldn't go a step further."

Only the master, so it seemed, was immune to the dictates of the clock-regulated horn: "When de horn blowed fo' tuh stop wuk at noon dey was still abeatin' him."[43]

Slaves' compulsion to obey the sound of plantation time was a product not simply of the inherently despotic quality of the bell but of the way masters ensured obedience to their sounding of the times. Although some slaves, like Bill Colins, felt that the "large plantation bell which rang every morning at four o'clock" had a despotic quality because "the bell called and said, get up I'm coming to get you," he nevertheless understood that if slaves "did not answer the call the overseer would whip them."[44] With their monopoly over both the tools of time and of violence and playing as much on the fear as the reality of physical punishment, planters were none too shy in compelling bondpeople's obedience to the sound of time with the whip. According to William Byrd, former Texas slave: "Master, he had great iron piece hanging just out side his door and he hit that every morning at 3:30. The negroes they come tumbling out of their beds. If they didn't master he come round in about thirty minutes with that cat-o-nine tails and begins to let negro have that and when he got through they knew what that bell was the next morning." Other slaves got a second chance. Abram Sells's Texas overseer "might not whip him fo' bein' late de fus' time but dat nigger better not fo'git de secon' time 'n' be late." More often, however, demands for punctuality and violence went hand in hand. The responsibility for enforcing this association was often the overseer's. As Austin Seward noted of work on his master's plantation: "It was the rule for the slaves to rise and be ready for their task by sun-rise, on the blowing of a horn or conch-shell; and woe be to the unfortunate, who was not in the field at the time appointed, which was in thirty minutes from the first sounding of the horn. I have heard the poor creatures beg for their lives, of the inhuman overseer, to desist from his cruel punishment." As well known as they are, historians appear to have overlooked the significance of Frederick Douglass's observations on this subject. According to Douglass, slaves "sleep till they are summoned to the field by the driver's horn. At the sound of this, all must rise, and be off to the field. There must be no halting." Moreover, "if they are not awakened by the sense of hearing, they are by the sense of feeling" because the overseer was always "ready to whip any one who was so unfortunate as not to hear . . . the sound of the horn." "The overseer giv' them fifteen minutes to eat dinner," recalled another former slave, explaining, "He didn't tell us when the time to go back to work, but when he started cuffing some of them over the head we knowed it was time to go back to work."[45] Of course, there was some room to maneuver but, as William Coleman explained, cuffings, like wage-labor fines for tardiness, took their toll: "Maser woke us up every morning about 4:30 o'clock with a great large bell that hung just outside of his bed-[room]. Son I'se dressed several times, out behind my quarters cause if we did not get right up when Maser rung that bell, here he come with a rawhide whip and gun buckled on him, and he would whip us all the time we were trying to dress."[46]

Nor were house hands immune to slaveholders' efforts to enforce time obedience through violence and cruelty. House servant Harriet Jacobs well knew the meaning of punctuality. "If dinner was not served at the exact time," noted Jacobs, her mistress "would station herself in the kitchen, and wait till it was dished, and then spit in all the kettles and pans that had been used for cooking."[47] And although it was in their interest to be "exceedingly punctual in their attendance" of planned frivolities like plantation balls, the fact that slaves sometimes turned up on time for off-time festivities also alerted planters to the likelihood that tardiness at work was probably deliberate and must not be forgiven.[48] When frivolity and relief beckoned, the mask of ignorance dropped and exposed the time obedience of otherwise dilatory bondpeople. But if slaves' harried, prompt, at times feverish responses to the clock-defined plantation bell is reminiscent of time discipline, it should be remembered that their "respect" for the clock was born more of fear and less of an internalized Protestant work ethic. Take away the whip and most slaves would have undoubtedly resisted more stridently, more successfully.

Faced with masters willing and able to whip for tardiness and having plantation rhythms constantly reaffirmed through clocks via bells and horns, slaves' ability to reckon time according to nature's rhythms must have provided little, if any, solace. To believe otherwise would be to underestimate the power of the clock-regulated bell or the sound of time in shaping slaves' behavior, to entertain an overly romantic view of the putative leisurely quality of natural time, and to demand, quite unreasonably, Herculean resistance by the enslaved. Few nineteenth-century waged labor workers, it should be remembered, managed to eschew wholly the authority of the clock. Most, in fact, came to accept its legitimacy.[49]

This is not to say that attempts to resist did not occur; they did, depending largely on the occupation of the slave. House servants, those most likely to be trained in mechanical time-telling and "more capable of defining their working hours," seemingly feigned ignorance of clock time with plantation visitors who knew no better. Harriet Martineau encountered what may have been subtle and perhaps gendered attempts at resistance by female house servants in 1838. "The waking in the morning is accomplished by two or three black women staring at you from the bedposts," she noted, complaining, "Then it is five minutes' work to get them out of the room. Perhaps, before you are half dressed, you are summoned to breakfast. You look at your watch, and listen whether it has stopped, for it seems not to be seven o'clock yet. . . . The young people drop in when the meal is half done, and then it is discovered that breakfast has been served an hour too early, because the clock stopped, and the cook has ordered affairs to her own conjectures." Mealtimes were also at the discretion of the servants at Milbank plantation, Virginia. According to one British visitor in 1862: "Dinner . . . is dependent entirely on the arrangements, or rather accidents of the negroes. . . . The Milbank servants were very irregular. We never knew until the dinner-bell rang, whether it would be before twelve, or after three, or any intermediate hour." Similarly, Frederick Law Olmsted characterized Virginia hotel servants as "without being very exactly punctual." Given what we know about the subtle dynamics of planter paternalism and slave resistance, what these observers probably construed as typical black indifference to clock time may well have been a clever ploy by southern house servants to manipulate white time definitions and racial stereotypes by feigning ignorance and causing, for want of a better phrase, temporal inconveniences.[50] By playing on whites' assumptions about black sloth, house servants may well have forged one of the few tools with which to resist the clock. The value of this resistance is, of course, difficult to evaluate, but at best it probably represented only a minor inconvenience to the master or mistress and gave domestic slaves only fleeting satisfaction and respite. Ultimately, of course, such resistance serves as testimony to the extent to which house slaves, female ones especially, were drawn into the temporal, clock-defined matrix of the white household. Moreover, masters were wise to feigning when they encountered it. Slaves could get away with duping northern and foreign visitors, but southern slaveholders well understood that the "most general defect in the character of the negro, is hypocrisy; and this hypocrisy frequently makes him pretend to more ignorance than he possesses." Racist though their explanation may have been, masters nonetheless recognized that this "is a very convenient trait, as it frequently serves as an apology for awkwardness and neglect of duty."[51]

Resistance in the field was possible, though more dangerous. Historians have, for example, provided ample documentation demonstrating that slaves were sometimes able to control and define the pace of their labor and thus, in a very practical sense, regulate the rate of their work.[52] But such efforts were not without their dangers. "For killing time" in this way, recalled a former slave, "you got 25 licks." Even if slaves completed their tasks but did not devote the remainder of their time to plantation work they could receive what South Carolina planter John Edwin Fripp liked to call "a poping." Starvation was another punishment "because the overseer thought he hadn't done enough work in a given time." Alternatively, accomplishing "much work in a little time" could stay punishment for other, unrelated misdemeanors. Black slave drivers in particular were able to detect slackers in the field, presumably because they themselves had experience of how much work could be done in a certain time. For this reason, perhaps, some planters made favored slaves temporary custodians of their time, thus creating an elite cadre of black time arbiters. This sometimes meant buying them watches. South Carolina planter Edward Thomas Heriot, for example, "paid . . . E. H. Shackelford for repairs to two watches for Driver" in 1854.[53] Other slaves regulated starting and finishing times for their master. Asked what her father did on the plantation, for example, Mary Jane of Georgia testified to the presence of such time custodians when she answered, "My father was timekeeper." Green Cumby's "gradfather, Tater Cumby, wuz de cullud overseer fo' forty slaves. He called us at four o'clock in de mornin.'" Likewise, Charles Coates was one of a small group of privileged slaves who "rung [the bell] at 5:30 a.m." to get his fellow laborers to work on time. And as George Skipworth, a slave entrusted to run his absentee master's Alabama plantation, informed his owner in 1847: "When I come to them [the field hands] at twelve o clocke, they had cut me nineteen rows, and it would not take them more than ten minits to cut one roe." Skipworth meted out punishment accordingly.[54]

But the plantation timekeeper could be punished for perceived slovenliness and, in the bargain, make the situation bad for everyone. "Since the illness of Master," recalled slave Mattie Griffiths, "things had not gone on with the same precision as before. There was a few minutes difference in the blowing of the horn; and for offenses like these, Master had sworn deeply that 'every nigger's hide' should be striped, as soon as he was able to preside at the 'post.'" A watchful plantation mistress could, however, obviate the need for slave time custodians: "Missus would go upstairs and watch out of the window at the slaves working and if she seen one that wasn't working for a minute she would tell the master when he come in and he would sure catch the dickens."[55] Resistance to clock time was risky for all concerned.

It is, however, more than a little ironic that the few instances when slaves did manage to acquire the skills denied them by the slaveholders' regime sometimes involved the mastery of clock time. Efforts by a slave woman in Natchez, to teach slaves to read and write, for example, were successful only because she had mastered an understanding of how to tell time and so was able to run a " 'midnight school,' teaching her people between the hours of eleven to two." That teacher and pupils managed to turn master's time into a weapon of their own reveals not only the danger planters faced with time-telling slaves but the accommodation to clock time that slaves had to make to stand some chance of acquiring a smattering of human dignity.[56] And here we hit upon a central

A black slave driver with a
watch chain, 1829 (Eleanor S.
Brockenbrough Library, Museum
of the Confederacy, Richmond,
Virginia)

irony in slaveholders' efforts to reduce plantation labor rhythms to clock-based regularity. The drive for precision and regularity in plantation schedules was an important reason for planters' use of clock time; if slaves were made time obedient, efficiency and order would follow. But the very essence of plantation regularity—predictability—could be recruited by slaves to resist overbearing masters. If slaves learned that, for instance, plantation checks were held at nine o'clock every night, they simply organized their off time around this temporal requirement and so recruited the regularity and predictability of the plantation routine for their own ends. While masters often cottoned on to such practices, they also recognized that to avoid being defeated at their own game, they would have to relinquish or at least manipulate certain aspects of the plantation schedule. This is clear from James Henry Hammond's advice to his overseers in 1857–58. Hammond's overseers were issued the following instructions: "The overseer must see that all the negroes leave their houses promptly after horn blow in the morning. Once, or more, a week he must visit every house after horn blow at night to see that all are in." But Hammond realized the dangers inherent in this regular and, to the slaves, predictable regimen. Hence he was forced to make the regular irregular: "*Remarks.—*He should not fall into a regular day or hour for his night visit, but should go so often and at such times that he may be expected anytime." The effect of this strategy was no doubt suffocating to Hammond's slaves. He had, after all, formalized the tacit idea that all plantation time was under his control even though it might be enforced in different ways. Hammond's terminology on this point is revealing: "*Church.—*All are priveleged & encouraged to go to church on Sundays, but no religious meeting is allowed on the plantation beyond singing & praying, & at such times as will not conflict with the plantation hours."[57] In short, if clock time provided a window of resistance for slaves because of its predictability, it was a window quickly closed by masters who realized that simple plantation regularity was not as effective as carefully manipulated plantation clock time.

Masters' need to whip in order to enforce slaves' obedience to the clock demonstrates that most slaves were far from internalizing a time discipline, and the constant reinforcement through lash and bell of clock-coordinated plantation schedules, combined with the risks of resistance, had a profound impact on slaves' cultural assumptions and values about mechanically defined time. To be sure, slaves' tendency to view time as a naturally defined phenomenon did not die out completely. But by the late nineteenth century, the continuous obedience to clock time required during slavery had taken its toll on African American attitudes toward the mechanical representatives and symbols of time, the clock and watch. In their songs and riddles, in their attitudes toward death and God, even in their definitions of freedom, African American behavioral patterns and value systems were littered with the images of the clock and watch. Some freedpeople even came to find comfort in being near public clocks. Although freedom gave him geographical mobility, Jack Dodson of Texas told his wife: " 'I wouldn't never go out of sound of dat city clock in town, de clock on de old city market.' "[58] Although emancipation presumably meant the end of master-enforced time obedience, the symbols most closely associated with plantation time lasted well after slavery had ended, percolating in myriad ways through African American folklore and culture.

Most commonly, the symbol of the clock surfaced in late nineteenth-century African Americans' ideas about death. As former slave George Womble ex-

African American grave with clock, Sea Islands, South Carolina, 1933 (Library of Congress)

pressed it, "If the clocks in a house are not stopped on the death of one of the members it will soon stop of its own accord and will never run again." Former slave Elizabeth Bunts explained why: "I would not stay in a house that would not stop the clock the minute the person dies, for every minute that clock runs takes the soul that much longer to cross the valley of the shadow of death alone, and if the clock is stopped he makes the crossing swiftly and unafraid." Presumably to expedite the deceased's journey to safety, clocks were, up until quite recently, placed on African American burial grounds. Photographic evidence from the South shows the practice to be not uncommon. Interestingly, the clocks are "broken deliberately," probably for the same reasons that the clocks were stopped at the time of death.[59] That the twentieth-century Dahome of West Africa also came to place "clocks, vases, porcelains, and so forth" on the markers of their dead is perhaps the ultimate testimony of the symbolic power of the clock not only in African American but also in African culture.[60]

The image of the clock is also found in African American Christianity. "Jesus called my attention to a clock," recalled a former slave, recounting her conversion experience. She explained: "I was at the church one night and there was a fellow who preached a sermon comparing a man with a clock, that is, a clock will run and run and stop then you will carry it to the jewelry shop and have it repaired from time to time; then after a while you will take the clock and throw it in the trash basket. The same with a sinner." That the Son of God should proselytize through the symbol of the clock, or what some slaves referred to as "that mystic clock," was hardly surprising when the Lord himself was as punctual as freedpeople's erstwhile masters. "But the God I serve is a time God," professed a former slave. "He don't come before time, He don't come after time. He come just on time."[61] The splicing of punctuality and African American Christianity was witnessed by a northern teacher, Abby Munro, in Mt. Pleasant, South Carolina, in 1891. In a semisacred, semiprofane rite ushering in the New Year, both the watch and a keen sense of the exact time were present and, apparently, of considerable importance. "The little 'ten cent' church," wrote Munro, "was literally packed. Nevertheless room was made for 'de buckra." So rarely seen by whites was this ceremony that Munro's description of it warrants full disclosure. "At the close of the sermon," noted Munro,

> the congregation fell upon their knees, and there was weeping and wailing all over the house, at the fast approaching death of the Old Year. Amidst it all Brudder Dunkin led in prayer, after which the congregation arose, seated themselves, and there was a general silence followed by a kind of stirring about we did not quite understand—One of the "locust preachers" came down from the pulpit, open watch in hand, and knelt down within the chanel. There four of the brethren after considerable whispering and moving around, stationed themselves at different points around the room. The lights were turned partially down, and the deepest silence pervaded the house.

At this point, God's time and clock time joined in a holy matrimony. Munro went on:

> The minister broke this silence, by asking, slowly and solemnly, "Watchman, what time is it?["] Whereupon the kneeling man answered, in the same deep, solemn tone, "ten minutes of twelve. Time mos' gone." Then came the echo from the brethren stationed around the room, "time mos' gone." Then came another silence, and the room was still further darkened. Again the question was asked, and again the watchman replied by saying "*five* minutes of twelve, time mos' gone" and again the echo was sounded[.] And this silence, total darkness prevailing: The third and last time, the watchman was required of, in the same words, and this time came the final response "twelve o'clock, time gone." The whole congregation took up the refrain, and "time gone" "time gone," was wailed forth, all over the house. Suddenly the lamps were re-lighted and the mourning for the death of the Old Year, was turned into rejoicing for the birth of the New; and certainly their joy knew no bounds.[62]

Although the real significance of this ceremony is unclear and although it seems to yoke superstition with the sacred, the point that the Lord's house was often host to, and perhaps co-opting of, exact clock time is beyond dispute. "Christ," after all, according to one former slave, "he done hung on d' cross fo' 160 minnits fo' our sins."[63]

If the Christian God was punctilious, however, so were the spirits of the netherworld. Carolina Hunter, for example, told her interviewer: "I never will forget when I was a little girl an' my young missus was sick." She continued, "At three o'clock one day a raven flew over de house an' moaned. Mamma came runnin' to me an' said, 'It ain' goin' be long now fo' our young missus is goin' leave us!' Do you know, honey, bout four o'clock she died." Former Mississippi slave Mattie Logan explained how the spirits were recruited to deal with a cruel overseer, apparently demanding clocklike punctuality. "One of the slaves told how to cure him," she recalled. "Get a snake and put the snake in the overseer's cabin. Slip the snake in about, no, not about, but just exactly nine o'clock at night." But time and failing memory shrouded the rationale: "Seems like the time was important, why so, I don't remember now."[64] No doubt, however, the punctuality demanded by the spirit was an effort to fight fire with fire against overseers who gave slaves but "fifteen minutes to git dinner" and who whipped them for "losin' time."[65]

References to time gods, however, reveal more than just the African American accommodation to white-defined clock time. They also demonstrate the extent to which linear notions of time, rooted firmly in the basic tenets of Christianity and reinforced by the tendency of clock and watch to marry cyclical to linear time, affected an ostensibly present-oriented, preindustrial African time conception. That slaves came to develop linear conceptions of time, however, is clear: "Negroes are generally fatalists, and believe that every one has his time appointed to die, and if it be 'come' they expect to die," argued one southerner in 1858.[66] But former slaves, too, testified to having adopted an understanding of linear time. Sometimes this understanding was a product of, and rooted in, the corporeal world of work. Timed work apparently rendered Ellen Betts insensible to the idea that the earth was spherical but simultaneously persuaded her that not only was time linear but work by the hour tedious and fatiguing: "To dem dat work cuttin' de cane, it don't seem lak much, but to dem dat work hour in hour out dem sugar fields sho stretch from one end of de earth to de other."[67]

More often, however, slaves' abandonment of presentist time in favor of linear time which embraced an identifiable future time was a product of Christianity. In the words of Michael Mullin, "Christianization introduced Africans to a sense of history moving linearly."[68] Sometimes cyclical and linear time were yoked, as is clear from the following slave song: "Isiah mounted on de wheel ob time / Spoke ter God A-mighty 'way done de line."[69] But the presence of a purely linear time conception is also apparent in African American culture and religion. According to Mattie Griffiths, for example, "Time sped on (as it will always do), and brought the end of the week." The influence of Christian eschatology was also important in promoting a linear time consciousness. "God looked down through the scope of time and saw every generation, even down to this day," recalled one former slave. This idea was echoed by another, although more cryptically: "In the very beginning every race and every creature was in the mind of God and we are here, not ahead of time, not behind time, but just on time."[70] And as historians have long known but neglected to relate to slaves' time conceptions, the hope that freedom would come often took on a distinctly millennial and quasi-linear coloring. "Time— the great developer of all things,—will in the future," predicted the eloquent bondman George Teamoh, "roll up to the surface, in fixed view to the unwilling gaze of falsely inspired man, wringing from him the reluctant recognition that Jehovah, [demanded] equal justice shewed to all."[71]

If the profane and religious values of late nineteenth-century African Americans were imbued with images of the clock and laden with notions concerning punctuality, then their most poignant nineteenth-century collective experience, emancipation from bondage, was little different. Surprising numbers of former slaves recalled, almost to the minute, what time freedom came. For Mary Anderson, for example, freedom dawned at "nine o'clock" on her North Carolina plantation, while for Steve Jones of Texas, the "day we is sot free it was bout 8 o'clock in the morning." Such a formal measuring of time, as Daniel Kaiser and Peyton Engel have pointed out, is indicative of a modern time sensibility.[72] In short, slaves remembered what their masters told them. Other slaves defined freedom as independence from the clock-regulated plantation bell, a rejection of time obedience, as it were. For Katie Rowe of Oklahoma, for example, freedom meant that "dey ain't no more horn after dat dey." And Jennie Bowen of Alabama interpreted her freedom similarly: "No bell ringing fa' me, I'se a free nigger!"[73]

But freedom involved more than just a recollection of the exact time it came and an abandonment of the way plantation time was communicated. As Eric Foner and others have pointed out, former slaves tended to interpret their freedom in terms of having the right to regulate and define their own work and rest hours, in other words, to lay incontrovertible claim to their own nonnegotiable time.[74] But former slaves also tended to define the meaning of freedom in terms of clock and watch ownership, which, in a most literal sense, enabled freedpeople to claim real, tangible ownership of time by acquiring mechanical timepieces themselves. Tentative though this finding may be, it is given credence by John Thompson, former Texas slave, who recalled: "De ole Marster, he had a great big clock an' it 'ud ting instead oh strikin' an' Mammy she'd allus say: 'Lissun, dat's shore strange, it tings at twelve an' strikes ebery odder time.'" He continued: "De day 'fore Freedom, she said an' Ize heard her tell it many, many a-time sence, she says 'Gwine er somethin' mighty strange gwine er be,['] an' she say dis ebery day long 'bout time fer de clock at de big house to ting. De day ob Freedom, Mammy say 'Son, let's go home. Ma'll soon have a clock fer her ownself dat will ting for her.'" Although cryptic up to a point, Thompson's mother seemingly associated the chiming and acquisition of her own clock with the arrival of her freedom. And there is other evidence, both empirical and anecdotal, to suggest that the South's freedpeople began to acquire clocks and watches in some numbers after freedom came. Probate evidence, for example, reveals that by the 1880s between 73 and 83 percent of all southerners, including blacks, owned a clock, a watch, or both. Apocryphal evidence, though less reliable, is also suggestive. Former slave Herndon Bogan inadvertently noted his possession of a watch in the early postbellum years: "One night I kills a white hobo who am tryin' ter rob me o' my gol' watch an' chain." And Dock Owen, describing a race riot in the spring of 1865 at Laurens, South Carolina, did the same, again unwittingly: "Some one shot at their [freedmen's] clock through a window and demolished it." Even in the poorest black cabins, observed Booker T. Washington during his sweep around the South in 1881, "I often found . . . showy clocks for which the occupants of the cabins had paid twelve or fourteen dollars." It took clock ownership to give full, glorious voice to Gabriel's horn after all.[75] The reason may be straightforward. Denied access to the clock under slavery, bondpeople had few ways to ascertain the accuracy of the work times sounded by their masters. Freedom, however, gave them, like workers in wage-labor societies, the means and the need to debate time and to establish the true length of the working day. Just as New England antebellum mill workers had campaigned for the erection of public clocks in their effort "to counter the millowners' monopoly of public time" and to "directly challenge the millowners' power to define" public and work time, so freedpeople adopted a similar strategy. Freedom meant the long-awaited extension of the temporal franchise to include black people even if this did entail debating clock time on its own terms.[76]

Perhaps most evocative, however, is an African American riddle from the late nineteenth century which suggests that masters experienced some success in enforcing and instilling an obedience to the clock among slaves. Because of their experience during slavery, southern freedpeople came to realize that time was no longer the exclusive domain of nature, that it now demanded not a sun-based guess but rather a precision instrument for its accurate representation and reckoning:

> Round as a biscuit, busy as a bee,
> You can guess every riddle but you can't guess me.
> Answer. A watch.[77]

In other words, celestial Heaven, sun, stars, and all, as George Washington Cable so eloquently described at a later date, were denuded and replaced with "the clock in the sky."[78]

With natural time polluted, linear time ascendant, and the sound of clock time regulating work, it is little wonder that some slaves believed freedom would mean a repudiation of master's time, broadly construed. Charlie Davenport of Natchez, Mississippi, defined what freedom meant to him: "Aint no marster gwine a-say to you, 'Charlie, you's got to be back when de clock strikes nine.'" Or as Sarah Wooden Johnson said of freedom: "Dis here is new time. Let dat be."[79] But Charlie and Sarah were in many ways wrong. Both the forces promoting freedom and the experience of slavery colluded after the Civil War further to undermine natural time and consolidate the trend toward clock-regulated plantation labor.

New South, Old Time

VI

When everything harasses him, why should man have such
unbroken attachment for this world? The question is easily
answered—the dread of a mysterious future.
—David Wyatt Aiken, South Carolina planter,
    September 28, 1856

The future can only be judged by light drawn from the history
of the past.
—J. C. Nott, "The Problem of the Black Races,"
    De Bow's Review, 1866

We are apt to think the present times
Are sadly out of joint,
To sigh and then toward ages past—
The reverent finger point!
Of model husbands, model wives,
Said we, there was no lack,
Of manners, morals, pride and worth,
A generation back.

.   .   .   .

And thus it is from age to age,
And thus 'twill ever be;

The scenes enacted years ago,

With partial eyes we see.

Our offspring, in the years to come,

Will tread the beaten track,

And praise the conduct of their sires

A generation back.

—"A Generation Back," *Southern Planter and Farmer*,

January 1872

That the end of the Civil War ushered in a new era of capitalist social relations in the postbellum South and that the attendant changes in the region's society, economy, and polity were both profound and unprecedented seem beyond dispute.[1] But as profound as the freeing of some four million bondpeople may have been and as new as the postbellum South was, one crucial continuity existed between the old slave and new free American South.[2] That continuity was in the way white southerners viewed, appreciated, and applied time.[3] If, as one historian has argued, "A culture's sense of time is the key to its nature," and if changes in a society's appreciation and application of time, or its time consciousness, are both a reflection and a product of fundamental social and economic change, then surely the tumult of the Civil War and the profundity of emancipation would also have revealed the presence of a new time consciousness if, in fact, one existed.[4] But that cataclysmic change in the South's understanding and use of time did not occur, not because the war was not profound or because the postbellum South was not new, for the change was profound indeed and the postbellum South was, in many respects, new.[5] There was no new time consciousness simply because southerners had already developed an understanding of time both compatible with and complementary to the type of time essential to the new bourgeois social and economic order demanded by emancipation. In short, to borrow Julie Saville's words, "in the wake of Sherman's march, it required a fine eye to distinguish the twilight of slavery from the dawn of freedom."[6]

Planters' immediate concern in 1865 focused not so much on the retention of their lands to which emancipation in the South, unlike the coming of freedom in other slave societies, posed no real threat, but rather on maintaining or reasserting control over what they believed would be and, if their antebellum jeremiads are to be believed, had always been, an indolent and volatile work-force.[7] Abraham Lincoln's Emancipation Proclamation provoked just such a response from a Louisiana sugar planter in 1863: "Free labor, as it is so called, will inevitably prove a failure in the South. The negroes are naturally a low, lazy set. They are not influenced by any desire or gain, as are all the members of the white race. When they have earned a dollar, they will do nothing until it is gone, and starvation compels them to work again. I have lived among them twenty years, and I know them to be a dependent race."[8] For some, such fears seemed prophetic. "One difficulty is to get the Labor done. It now requires from two to three hands to do per Diem what one hand used to do for a day's work in former years," lamented one South Carolina planter in 1870.[9]

Yet in truth, planters were better equipped to deal with freedom and to control freed laborers than some of them were willing to believe or admit. For the most part, planters' worries about controlling freedpeople and making them into what they considered to be efficient and diligent workers were rooted in antebellum, and probably colonial, racist assumptions about blacks' putative inability to work hard and assiduously and, just as important, in the reports planters had read about emancipation and its seemingly disastrous consequences in the British West Indies and elsewhere. On blacks' supposed innate, incurable indolence, antebellum southern planters had deliberated much and come to the conclusion that only a firm, disciplined, and regular system of plantation management could compel black people to work regularly. Recall, for example, *Dysaethesia Aethiopica*: a pseudo-scientific theory advanced in the 1850s explaining slaves' apparent "natural indolence" caused by "a hebetude of the intellectual faculties." The stereotype was shared by northerners and southerners, as one Massachusetts visitor to the South in 1865 demonstrated: "Lynchburg, Va., August 12, 1865. . . . Occasionally a Negro Man or woman is met . . . wishing a 'Good morning' if the time is earlier than one o'clock in the day, and, if it is later, always saying 'Good evening, sir.' " This same visitor felt no obligation to comment on occasions when southern blacks demonstrated temporal accuracy, however: " 'I suppose you couldn't get me a dinner ma'm?' " he inquired of a freedwoman. " 'Hed our dinner at half-past eleven.' " The reply elicited no comment.[10] One openly racist if rather obscure postbellum newspaper made the same point even more precisely. Under the leader "White Outrage" written in 1865, the white editor, parading as a freedman, "Pluto Jumbo," reported that "a cupple ob de colored ladies pushed a white gal off de sidewalk, when de purpusperous white wench gib sass to dem two epectable colored ladies, and told dem dey ought to be ashamed!" According to the writer, the event took place "yesterday arternoon, in de ebening, about thirteen o'clock[.]"[11]

The perceived impact of emancipation on the working habits of laborers in the West Indies added credence to such nonsense, at least in the minds of antebellum planters. Of the effects of emancipation in Jamaica, for example, they were told: "The negroes in some districts will only work the first four days of the week. . . . Hardly in any case will the *people* work more than five days in the week; in several districts they refuse to work more than four days in the week; and the average time of field labor is from five to six hours daily. The labor is not only inadequate in quantity, but generally ill performed. . . . The negroes are incurably indolent and pathetic."[12] Consequently, when slavery was abolished in the American South, planters, in the short term at least, tended to view the event with trepidation and couched their concerns in terms of race and class and pointed to what they perceived as the failed emancipation experiments of other slave societies.[13]

Such expressed fears served to heighten southern planters' larger concern of how to maintain an obedient and efficient workforce after emancipation. A thoughtful northern observer recognized the crux of planters' angst: "The planter is looking at his own interest simply, when he argues this point; and, when he talks of the slave's laziness and imbecility, he means, simply, that he will, through freedom, get beyond his reach,—nothing more."[14] By 1866, many planters had come to express this concern openly and, in the process, testified to the role time played in maintaining order and efficiency on New South plantations. If work hours under freedom could be enforced as they had under slavery, many reasoned, the plantation would retain its essential economic and social integrity. Such was the gist of one planter's letter to *De Bow's Review* in 1866:

How to make them work more is well worthy of consideration. . . . Mr. Carlyle has most humorously shown that the laws of demand and supply have no more influence on the conduct and industrial habits of the free and improvident negroes of the West Indies than such laws have on wild horses in a summer pasture. Political economy stands baffled and perplexed in presence of the negro. . . . How to make him work ten hours a day whose every present want can be supplied by laboring three hours a day? . . . The negro slave worked eight or nine hours a day; the negro freedmen will not average three hours a day.[15]

Much of the remainder of the nineteenth century was devoted to trying to resolve these issues. Myriad though the various solutions posited by planters were and dangerous though sweeping generalizations are, what is apparent is that virtually all such answers, like other capitalist solutions for regulating production and maintaining a healthy level of exploitation, focused on how to regulate freedpeople's work time.[16]

Sometimes instructions on how to control freedpeople's labor through the application of time came from other postemancipation societies. "Believing that the experience gained in other regions, where slavery has existed and emancipation has taken place, will be of interest and use in considering and effecting the reorganization of industry in the Southern States of the Union," one West Indian planter suggested that southerners look to St. Croix, specifically to the provisions of the 1849 act regulating the labor of freedpeople issued by the Danish government. The need to regulate work hours so as to establish an efficient and orderly rural landless proletariat was obvious from the provisions: "PARA. 6. . . . The ordinary work of estates is to commence at sunrise and to be finished at sunset every day, leaving one hour for breakfast and two hours at noon, from twelve to two o'clock. . . . The laborers shall be present in due time at the place where they are to work." And the punishment for tardiness and absenteeism also merged at the time-wage nexus: "Laborers abstaining from work half a day, or breaking off from work before being dismissed, to forfeit their wages for one day. Laborers not coming to work in due time to forfeit half a day's wages."[17]

Still other counsel on how to regulate freedmen and women by time came from transplanted northerners, who, complacent in their opinion that they were the sole custodians of America's modern time sensibility and just as contemptuous as southern planters of blacks' supposed ignorance of clock time, ministered, quite unnecessarily, to former masters on the subject. Ordinarily, this advice came in the form of "compensated labor contracts" issued either by occupying federal forces during the war or by the Freedmen's Bureau after it. General Orders No. 23 issued by the "Commander of the Department of the Gulf" in New Orleans on February 3, 1864, for example, required all plantation laborers, whether "public or private," to be subject to a workday of "*ten* hours in summer, and *nine* hours in winter." Publicly posted "Regulations by the Superintendent of Plantations in the Treasury Department 5th Special Agency" in New Orleans in 1864 gave the following advice "To Govern Hands":

1st. All hands to be in the field of within one half hour after bell rings.
2d. Each hand two hours late in the field, without proper excuse, shall be docked one half day's labor for each two hours so absent. . . .
4th. Half hour shall be allowed for breakfast each day, and two hours each day for dinner.

5th. No hand shall be allowed to roam at will over plantations in the night, and any hand found out of his or her quarters after 9 o'clock, each night, without proper excuse, shall be fined one half day's work.

Superintendent of plantations in New Orleans H. Styles presumably thought he was acting as the guiding light of modernity and revealing some secret known only to bourgeois Yankees when he confided the strategy of running a plantation in the postbellum South: "I would first establish a regular time for labor,—say ten hours a day,—as making a day's work."[18] If Styles's intended audience was southern planters he was, emphatically, preaching to the choir.

Instead of taking their lessons on how to deal with freedom from transplanted northerners and rather than look outside their geographic borders to societies whose peculiar conditions may not have approximated their own, planters more often appealed to their own pasts to safeguard their plantations of the future. "A recurrence to only recent history," advised a former master in 1887, "will convince us that whatever improvements we of to-day have made upon the methods of *ante-bellum* days is due more to the growth of the ideas of our predecessors than to our own boasted probity and enterprise." He had no doubt that "most of our wisdom is inherited."[19] A good illustration of how this may have worked in practice is provided by two proclamations, one issued in 1827, the other in 1865, by Alabama planters William and Robert Jemison respectively. In 1827, William Jemison, Robert's father, issued a proclamation to his slaves which, though liberal for its time, placed the issue of lost time at work squarely on the shoulders of his bondpeople. "I have this day," Jemison told his slaves on January 1, "placed you under Richard Coal as your overseer for the present year, 1827." He continued: "Now, provided you will strictly obey him, be honest, careful, industrious you shall have two thirds of the corn and cotton made on the plantation. . . . When your crop is gathered, one third is to be set aside for me. You are then to pay your overseer his part and pay me what I furnish. . . . You are to be no expense to me. . . . There will be an account of all lost time kept and those that earn most shall have most. What comes off the lazy shall be added to the industrious." Although perhaps remarkable as a quasi-sharecropping system under slavery, the real significance of this 1827 proclamation is disclosed when it is placed beside the 1865 pronouncement issued by Robert Jemison Jr. a generation later, apparently on the same plantation. Having informed his former slaves that "each of you who wish to go to the Yankees may do so," Jemison set out the terms of employment for those who remained in the form of shares of plantation crops and livestock. But just as in 1827, apparent equity and actual productivity were to be regulated and established by time: "That the amount of services of each may be known, the overseer will keep an account of all lost time and the manner that each does his work, and of his general conduct, all of which shall be taken into consideration in the division amongst you."[20] Time under slavery had much to recommend it to planters grappling with the implications of ostensibly free labor. It was, in short, southerners' familiarity with time past that helped shape the contours of a battle between erstwhile masters and former slaves in time present and future.

The dual concerns of maximizing production and preserving plantation order and discipline that had been partially resolved through the introduction of clock time on antebellum plantations were the same concerns facing postbellum planters and were also resolved through an appeal to clock time. There were, of course, new issues to be confronted, issues that planters under slavery had not encountered. One concerned the type of labor system to be employed, which basically came down to a choice between paying former slaves wages, which in turn permitted planters to use time to measure that labor power, or paying laborers with a portion of the year's crop, an arrangement later known as sharecropping.[21] An associated and far more problematic issue for the planters concerned the demands of the freedpeople themselves.[22] Like planters, former slaves drew on their experience under slavery when confronting the ostensibly new choices bestowed by freedom. And just like planters, who remembered clearly the benefits of timed labor under slavery, erstwhile slaves recalled all too clearly the tyranny of planter-defined time under unfreedom. It was only because they had experience of and knew too well the insidious control timed work could effect that they could resist its imposition in the form of wage labor after freedom came. Not surprisingly, then, the postbellum South saw a renewed battle over the ownership and control of time, a battle that devolved on the sharecropping system supported by former slaves and the wage system advocated by former masters and, from freedpeople's point of view, planters' newfound northern allies.[23] Without the presence or use of plantation clock time under slavery, no such battle could have taken place under freedom. In some very real senses, however, the battle was moot and centered more on accepting the specifics of clock time than on its wholesale eschewal. In a world where battles fought over the precise amount of time to be worked took precedence over a battle against the legitimacy of clock time itself, both former slave and planter were co-opted by the tyranny and language of clock time, no matter what specific accommodations they reached among themselves.[24]

In the immediate postbellum years, however, planters and freedpeople alike considered the debate over the competing labor systems to be of utmost importance. Scarce though ready cash was in the postbellum South, planters overwhelmingly opted for the wage system.[25] Although procuring currency to pay workers made this system onerous, postbellum planters thought the benefits of a wage-labor arrangement, with all the control mechanisms that the attendant use of timed work provided, was worth the bother not only of procuring cash but also of keeping accurate time logs for each worker.[26]

In planters' numerous debates concerning the relative advantages of wage over share, the question of time and its contingent benefits stood at the forefront. One planter, G. A. W. of Brazos County, Texas, advised readers of the *Southern Cultivator* in 1868: "I notice that your correspondents are discussing the best plan to work negroes. The usual custom in this country, is to work on shares, and failure has universally followed." Alternatively, paying freedpeople by time worked or wages enabled this planter to dismiss workers for failure to get to work on time. The benefit of such a practice was that "the others took warning."[27] Freedpeople as laborers, counseled another planter, "are too fickle, too ready to assert their entire independence, too lazy and too well satisfied to live for the present, and to let the future take care of itself, to ever make what may be considered first-class farm hands." He went on, "Many have tried giving them a share of the crop—others have tried renting them the land. But in our experience, altogether the best way is to pay them the cash at the end of the day or week or month, as their term of labor may be."[28] W. H. Evans, president of the Pomological and Farmer's Club of Society Hill, South Carolina, systematically compared the relative merits of the share and wage systems and testified to the disciplinary and pecuniary advantages the time-wage system held for planters. Among the disadvantages of the share system he listed: "1st. The difficulty of discharging hands when they become inefficient or refractory. . . . 2nd. . . . The tendency of the share system, has been to drift insensibly into the mere system of cropping—that most pernicious of all systems under which the labor of a country has ever been employed—a system which leads to idleness on the part of the laborer for a large part of the year, to indolence and indifference on the part of the farm owner." Alternatively, the advantages of contract wages included "1st. It gives the farmer control over his labor, by enabling him to discharge his hands when they become inefficient. Control over labor is essential. . . . 3d. It leads to economy in labor. When the farmer pays a specific money equivalent for labor, he naturally seeks to reduce the amount employed." And although the disadvantages of this system were that "it involves far greater labour in supervising and protecting the crop," most planters seemed willing to spend the extra time counting freedpeople's time. To Evans, the logic seemed ineluctable, and he recommended that "the wages system should be adopted," with the proviso that "if hands are employed for wages and then left to take care of themselves, it is obviously the worst of all contracts. The very essence of the system lies in constant and active supervision."[29]

As their antebellum experience with time had taught them, there were many ways to effect the proper application and use of time on postbellum plantations aside from attempts to regulate former slaves' work by the clock. Certainly, as one New South planter noted, emancipation had heightened everyone's sense of time and its pecuniary value. "The free labor movement here produces exactly the same effects as elsewhere," he pointed out, concluding, "It makes all persons economical of money and time."[30] But the devices postbellum planters used to save time in agricultural operations were virtually the same ones to which they had turned during and after the 1830s. Because "labor at the South is at present very dear—apparently cheap enough when expressed in form of so many dollars per month, per hand—but really dear, when measured in terms of so much work, done in a given time," there was general agreement, as there had been more than thirty years earlier, that "work done by machinery is always cheaper than that done by hand" and that planters could lessen their dependency on free labor by investing in time-saving agricultural machinery.[31] Similar concerns were voiced in the *Southern Planter and Farmer*. "Every year renders unskilled labor less valuable to the farmer. . . . We therefore need men who understand the principles of mechanics to superintend farm operations, and the laborer must at least become an expert in the use of machinery before he can be useful." The article ended on an optimistic note: "We think the day is not far off when it will be practicable to perform all necessary labor on the farm during eight hours daily, and perhaps six."[32]

Some postbellum planters reminded their brethren that the concept of time, especially its equation with money, must first be properly understood and then practically applied to the day-to-day operations of the plantation. "Labor is money, or the equal of money, and we should exercise as much economy in its expenditure as we would on the expenditure of our dollars and cents," explained South-Sider to readers of Richmond's *Southern Planter and Farmer* in 1872. His ministrations concerning the proper application of time echoed those of the 1830s and 1840s exactly: "Time is the next item in the account of economy, which I propose to notice here. Time, also, is money, or the equivalent. Ah! it is a vast deal more valuable and important. It is so precious, indeed, that our beneficent Creator has given us but one moment of it at a time. How important, then, to 'husband the time' and 'count the moments as they fly.' " But South-Sider also gave practical advice, albeit lengthy, on how to implement these rather abstract and ethereal recommendations:

> In order to [establish?] a proper economy of time and labor, the practical farmer should establish order and system on his farm. . . . Early rising is another requisite for the proper economy of time. . . . Much time and labor may be saved by the proper location of the buildings, farm-pens and the roads of the farm. The farmer who locates his buildings at one end of his farm, will lose an immense amount of time and labor in hauling and passing to and from his daily work. . . . The great objection to negroes as laborers is their slothfulness, and their great propensity to waste time. . . . With many of them this is a habit, which might be corrected, and the employer would do well to take the trouble of training them into habits of greater activity and quickness in the dispatch of light work especially. On many farms a great deal of time is lost in hunting up tools that have been misplaced. No suitable place is provided for keeping them, and when the hands happen to stop using them, they are carelessly thrown aside, and when they are again needed very often half a day is lost in hunting them up.[33]

Poor management, as much as refractory workers and badly organized plantations, could also cost time, and planters needed to adopt rigorous management systems. "Labor is money or its equivalent, and should be so considered on the farm as well as in the workshops," noted one farmer, explaining, "If an hour is lost, it should be counted at its value. When we say an hour lost, we do not mean by absence or idleness alone, but have reference to any occasion. . . . If ten hours are consumed in performing the work of eight for lack of system, or by mismanagement, a loss of twenty per cent is experienced."[34] Occasionally, the real onus for saving time was placed firmly on the shoulders of postbellum planters:

> Rules for Farmers.
>
> 1. The farmer ought to rise early to see that others do so, and that both his example be followed and his order obeyed. . . .
>
> 3. In a considerable farm it is of the utmost consequence to have hands especially appropriated for each of the most important departments of labor, for there is often a great loss of time where persons are frequently changing their employments.[35]

Time thrift was revived in the postbellum plantation household, where it encountered former plantation mistresses already familiar with the use of the clock to regulate household affairs. The refrain was familiar, as were the remedies proposed:

I hear daily complaints of inefficient servants—triflers. My greatest assistant in having work done orderly and in time has been the kitchen clock. Allot so much time for a specified work; take the trouble to overlook personally for a few days. When a servant finds out that you know how long it takes to accomplish certain work you will be astonished to find out how much more rapidly your domestic matters will be arranged. . . . The clock helps wonderfully in these arrangements, as you will soon find out.[36]

These, of course, were rhetorical ideals—ideals once embraced by Old South planters and now again coveted by often these same people in a postemancipation society. In the antebellum South, the ideal of time thrift, because it occurred in a context where time and its ownership was monopolized by planters was, on the whole, implemented successfully. But emancipation imposed a new reality. Freedpeople, now custodians of their own time and well versed in the liturgy of time obedience, were better able to resist planters' efforts to regulate their labor by time even though, ironically, free wage labor and timed work were inextricably linked.[37] Even if appreciable numbers of freedmen and women failed to acquire clocks and watches immediately after the Civil War (and this is by no means certain), they nonetheless had the intellectual wherewithal, nurtured during slavery, to understand that to agree to wage-labor contracts would again involve them in a conflict over the ownership and definition of time with their erstwhile masters. And lest they had forgotten these lessons, pious, capitalistic northerners sought to remind them through the combination newspaper-textbooks like the *Freedman* and the *Torchlight* which routinely carried simple, patronizing homilies preaching the importance of doing "every thing in its time," making "the most we can of every day and hour," counseling how not to "lose an hour or a half-hour" through "lazy dozing," and recommending that the "alarm-clock" be "*promptly obeyed.*"[38] But the South's emancipated slaves needed little if any coaching in this department. The great mistake of emancipators, of course, was that their racial stereotypes persuaded them that former bondpeople required training in the appreciation of clock time. Freedpeople's northern teachers often mistook blacks' attitudes toward time as indicative of an indelible racial flaw and so helped perpetuate the CPT stereotype. As northerner Abby D. Munro, principal of the freedmen's Laing Normal and Industrial School in Mt. Pleasant, South Carolina, wrote to the school's northern sponsors in 1891: "And, then, you must remember, we live in a country where no note is taken of time. 'Shortly' and 'directly' common expressions, may mean an hour, a day, or a week hence. One is as satisfactory as the other. Attending a public service may mean being on hand five minutes before the opening of the exercise, or five minutes before the close. It seems to be one and the same thing to these people." Convinced by her own logic that black people had no sense of time, she continued, "The only place where *we* can reach or influence them, is in school attendance; and here we insist on punctuality; and lock the gates at the hour for opening school. It is seldom that a pupil is locked out, even those that live farthest." But when southern freedpeople did demonstrate obedience to and cognizance of the clock, Munro chose to ignore such instances and tended simply to report them and let her stereotyping go unaffected. Five years before she made the above observation, for example, she had testified, albeit unwittingly, to a well-developed time consciousness among her students. In January 1886, she wrote: "Now, you must know, Ida rings the rising bell, at the alarm of the clock, and so impressed is she with her duty in that direction that without fail, at first sound of the alarm, or, at the appointed time, even if the alarm fails, asleep or awake her hand clutches that bell, whose peals break the stillness of the early morning hour."[39]

But freedpeople coveted their freedom and tended to define it in their own terms. As both Marx and freedpeople well understood, to be hired out for wages would be tantamount to selling a part of one's time, a part of oneself, and, in the process, would allow alienation to undermine freedom.[40] But by insisting on what one historian has called share wages (as opposed to cash wages), freedpeople were "offered the discrete prospect of immediate gain; it meant to blacks that they were partners with the landowners in the enterprise of planting, harvesting, and marketing the crop, and that meant the opportunity for independence and control over the disposition of their labor power."[41] In other words, from the perspective of time, because share wages could not, theoretically at least, be reduced to units of time, and because cash wages could, freedpeople opted for the former because this system would give them control and discretion over their labor and hence the allocation of their time. Again, without the experience of slavery and all the demands for punctuality and time obedience it entailed, it is highly unlikely that, given what we know about the gradual evolution of a modern time consciousness in industrial capitalist societies, freedpeople and, indeed, planters, could have embraced such an advanced understanding of time and its meaning for their labor within just a few years of freedom. Although the South was exceptional in many ways, it was not so different that it could accomplish in the space of a few years what the North and Britain had taken over half a century to do.[42]

Forearmed, then, with an understanding of what timed labor meant and reluctant to have their newfound freedom undermined by this old foe, freedpeople, when faced with planters insistent on wage contracts, resisted. Sociologist John Horton, although talking about the late twentieth century, captures well the sort of battle over time and its ownership and application that took place in both the Old and New South. "The diversity of time perspectives can be understood intellectually—but it is rarely tolerated socially," argues Horton, explaining, "A dominant group reifies and objectifies its time; it views all other conceptions of time as subversive—as indeed they are."[43] These were precisely the contours of the debate over time that took place in the postbellum South. Freedpeople resisted planters' renewed efforts to reimpose notions of time thrift on their work which threatened, from their point of view, to compromise their freedom and return them to a state of de facto servitude. Their resistance differed from that during slavery in that freedpeople now had many more ways to protest and more power to negotiate. Freedpeople understood these options and used them without hesitation. "They are very rapidly learning their own power and worth," noted an observer of freedpeople in Louisiana in 1863. "In every contest between the master and his slaves [freedmen], the latter invariably win the day. They have a mine of strategy, to which the planter sooner or later yields." In some ways, of course, freedpeople's forms of resistance to planter-defined time were, as they had been during slavery, reminiscent of preindustrial forms of protest. Rather than accept the premise from which planters operated and engage in negotiations about the length of time to be worked and thereby accept the legitimacy of clock-defined labor, freedpeople often refused outright even to debate the merits of planters' definitions of fair compensation for their labor power. Instead, the careful withdrawal and rationing of their labor power (what planters described as lethargy) was the preferred means of protest: "Already he begins to exhibit his indifference; and, in order to get the same amount of work out of him, the overseer, since the whip has been prohibited, is compelled to offer all kinds of inducements. The moment he gets into a passion, and, forgetting that it is '63, and not '61, strikes the black man, down go the hoes and shovels of a dozen men."[44] And when confronted with unveiled efforts to time their labor, former slaves sometimes got the upper hand. Despite, or perhaps because of, his best efforts to reduce his laborers' work to a "Book's [sic] of Times," Virginia planter Daniel Cobb encountered tenacious resistance. Cobb's time log for February 23, 1872, for example, makes the battle over time and the victors in this particular case quite clear: "Jan 1st 1872 Book's of Times[.] 23 Feb 1872: Our farm going on tolerable well only I cant get hands to work sooner than from 1/2 to [h]our by sun which is deducted." Nor did docking wages for lost time seem to work in this case: "25 March 1872: I cant tell what will be done for honest & working men[.] The idlers are stealing generally . . . plundering & stealing there [sic] days labour & sleep in the day."[45] According to his South Carolina employer, J. G. McKim, former slave John Watt fought a similar battle, albeit a lonely one. Explained McKim: "He paid no regard to his contract; and told me repeatedly that he did not care a *damn* for it; would not work, was insolent; would leave his work and visit the adjoining plantation during work hours, would frequently come home one hour by Sun in the morning . . . and get to work 2 hours by sun when he was required by the Contract to go to work by Sun rise. And tell me he was free now and would go when he pleased and return when he pleased."[46] Northern plantation lessees in Mississippi encountered similar problems: "Our experience shews that the same amt. of labor cannot be obtained under a free, as under a compulsory system of labor, this must be apparent to any person conversant with the working of the two systems, under the old regime, they were aroused at dawn. in the field before sunrise & did not leave it until after dark. . . . Now they never go to the field until after sunrise, have two hours for dinner & leave the field at sunset. . . ." The net effect of such resistance from this planter's point of view was considerable: "There is one third less time labored & full one third less daily labor performed now."[47]

So frustrated were some planters by such resistance that they gradually adjusted to freedpeople's preferred pace of work, substituting fairness for freneticism and, in effect, surrendering their own predilection for squeezing the very most out of labor time. If they were to get labor at all, some planters realized, they would have to employ that labor on its own terms. As Z explained to readers of the *Southern Planter and Farmer* in 1873:

> One class of employers know how to treat a man as a human being. . . . He goes to the field with his hands, and returns with them at the proper hour for meals. . . . At noon ample time is given for rest and recuperation of the system. "Rest time," as it is called, is often enlivened by music, song, and cheerful conversation. . . . Often, the employer, satisfied with the day's work, stops before the sun has gone down, saying, "Boys, we have done enough." . . . Such a man can always get help, and the very best.
>
> On the other hand, there are employers who are never satisfied with their work, never make as much as they want. . . . They eat in a hurry and go immediately back to their work. . . . In short, this class make their days as long as they can. . . . As might be expected, they never have anything well done, and their help is of the most worthless and shiftless kind.[48]

Whatever strategies of resistance to wage-labor time freedpeople may have adopted, however, planters refused, insofar as they were able, to relinquish wholly their insistence on time-regulated work. The reasons for this refusal were many, the most salient of which rested first on planters' inability to eschew, even if they had wanted to, a habit and a way of equating time, money, and work that had been with them for nigh on fifty years, and second, on their conviction that the tools of mastery were not wholly redundant and meaningless in a society where profit maximization and labor control were still paramount considerations.[49] In several respects, in fact, the demise of their slave regime may well have freed planters themselves when it came to the obvious and unapologetic application of the capitalist watch to free labor. Even though planters were still convinced of their workers' inherent sloth, provided they could retain social and political control over freedpeople and define the terms on which labor power was bought, many New South planters no doubt felt that they could freely embrace progress without fear of contradiction. And as it turned out, postbellum owners of capital found the clock as congenial to their plans as had antebellum owners of capitalized labor.

Strategies of the past informed the needs of the present, sometimes to an absurd degree. Even when freedpeople's demands had forced planters to abandon their commitment to a purely cash-wage labor system in favor of a hybrid cash/share-wage arrangement, they nevertheless managed, albeit awkwardly, to reduce both wage and share to quantifiable units of time. How they did so, precisely, is not altogether clear, at least not from the numerous published labor contracts that appeared in southern agricultural periodicals after the war. South Carolina planter Samuel Porcher Gaillard hinted at the existence of what must have been at times an arbitrary and localized equation of how long it took to complete a certain amount of work when he noted in 1868: "Put Mustapha to cut a cord of wood, one of his 1/2 cords is only 3 feet high so charged him 1/8 day lost."[50] Presumably, however, planters themselves would have understood the nuances of the following contract published in *De Bow's Review* in 1867, which, though vague in its practical implementation, makes clear planters' efforts to splice both wage and share with time. "The following form of contract has been adopted very generally in Virginia as possessing much to recommend it to the planters generally," it was noted. The first part of the contract was evidently an effort to accommodate the demands of former slaves: "The said parties of the second part are to be employed shall receive the *one-fourth* part of all crops raised." The remainder, however, demonstrates the importance planters placed on timed work in their efforts to define and control both the relations and means of production:

No laborer shall lose any unnecessary time from his or her work, and if any one shall be absent from his business without the knowledge or consent of the proprietor or manager, he shall forfeit one dollar for each day so lost and proportionally less for a shorter time: and the amount so forfeited shall be deducted from his share and divided among the other hands. . . . Time lost by sickness or leave of absence shall be accounted for as follows: first class hands, forty cents a day and seventeen cents for rations; second class hands, thirty two cents a day and seventeen cents for rations, and third class hands sixteen cents a day and thirteen cents for rations. Entries will be made by the proprietor or manager at the end of each week, of all lost time.

That the time was part sidereal, part diurnal, and part clock hardly lessened the control that planters' time imposed on the workers: "Labor shall commence at sunrise and end at sunset. Half an hour in the morning will be allowed for breakfast and one hour and a half at mid-day for dinner during the months of October, November, December, January, February, March, and April, and three-fourths of an hour for breakfast and two hours for dinner during the other months of the year."[51] Even in the South's rice-growing districts, where the task was necessary to the crop's cultivation, planters managed to insinuate timed labor where they could, as was made clear in a reprint of a published labor contract from the *Charleston Daily News* for a sea island planter. Of this contract the editor of the *Southern Cultivator* remarked: "Fines also for bad work are especially necessary, and deductions must be made not only for days lost, but for the fractional parts of days, and regular hours for commencing and closing the day's labor prescribed," even though the contract also promised one-third of the crop to the hands. The "Articles of Agreement" read: "Article 2. . . . In all cases where the task cannot be assigned, they agree to labor diligently ten hours per day. Article 3. The said freedmen agree to forfeit for every day's absence from labor 50 cents per day. If absent voluntarily and without leave, two dollars per day. If absent more than one day without leave, to be dismissed from the plantation, and forfeit their share of the crop."[52]

The advice contained in these published labor contracts did not fall on deaf ears for two reasons. First, the agencies entrusted to ensure fairness in such contracts, initially the occupying Union army and later the Freedmen's Bureau, apparently felt comfortable with the provisions for timed labor within these contracts and often encouraged them. As early as November 1862, for example, Benjamin F. Butler, commander of the Department of the Gulf, recommended that part of the "Memorandum of Contract" for Louisiana parishes include the following provision: "Ten hours each day shall be a day's labor, and any extra hours during which the laborer may be called by the necessities of the occasion to work shall be reckoned as so much towards another days labor, Twenty six days of ten hours each shall be deemed a month's labor except in the month of December, when twenty shall make a month's labor, It shall be the duty of the overseer to keep a true and exact account of the time of labor of each person."[53] Union commanders and Freedmen's Bureau officers were, after all, time-thrifty Yankees anxious to see bourgeois relations of production imposed on a prostrate South.[54] And, second, the architects of these contracts, the protests of freedpeople either notwithstanding or nominally accommodated, were often planters themselves. Given these factors, it is hardly surprising to encounter sincere efforts by planters to regulate their New South plantations often to the letter of these contracts.

The "Articles of Agreement" made between Alexander R. Lawton of Beaufort, South Carolina, and his workers in January 1866, for example, barely deviated from the published ideals. The second article of the contract explicitly tied Lawton's freedpeople's work, cash or share, to time: "We also agree to forfeit fifty cents for each unauthorized days absence from labor (except in case of sickness), and if any of us shall remain absent from labor without permission for more than two days it shall be optional with the said Alexr Lawton of the First Part to discharge us without any pay or portion of the crop for the time previously worked."[55] Similar strictures are apparent in the labor contract between up-country planter P. B. Bacot, owner of Mars Bluff plantation in Darlington District, South Carolina, and his freedpeople in 1866:

> The said servants agree to hire their time as laborers on the plantation of P. B. Bacot from 1st January 1866, to 1st January 1867. . . . The said servants agree to perform the daily tasks hitherto usually allotted on said plantation; to wit: 125 to 150 rails; cutting grain, 3 to 6 acres. . . . In all cases where tasks cannot be assigned, they agree to labor diligently ten hours a day.
>
> For every days labor lost by absence, refusal or neglect to perform the daily task said servants shall forfeit fifty (50cts) cents. . . . If absent more than one day without leave, to be subject to dismissal from the plantation & forfeiture of his or her share in the crop. . . . The employer or his agent shall keep a book in which shall be entered all advances made by him, & fines & forfeitures for lost time, or any cause which book shall be received as evidence in same manner as merchants books are now received in courts of justice. . . . The laborers shall commence work at sunrise, & be allowed from one to three hours a day for their meals according to the season of the year.[56]

For many planters the logic of timed labor proved delicious and gave way to what was nothing short of a tyrannical compulsion to resurrect the clock as the ultimate arbiter of plantation work and order. Frightened by the prospect of unruly, independent former slaves, some planters went to the extreme when regulating plantation affairs by the clock, tenaciously clinging to the past in a concerted bid to guarantee the future. "The greatest means of successful farming is a mild but rigid discipline among the operatives. . . . Now, I follow the business as a profession. . . . I try to improve upon any system I work after," professed one North Carolina planter in 1871. His appeal to the clock rendered his discipline anything but mild: "1st. I require every hand on my farm to be at his work at 7 o'clock in the morning, and if one fails, I simply charge him one fourth of a day; five minutes behind time loses him just as much as if he were to come at half past nine." To effect this system, antebellum precedents were invoked:

> At twelve o'clock my bugle sounds for dinner. I allow one hour for eating from 1st January to 1st March, one hour and a half from 1st March to 15th May, two hours from 15th May to 15th August. I am particular that no one transgresses these rules more than five minutes. I demand of each hand 10 hours labor a day. I pay him for it when he performs it. I do not pay him for 10 hours when he does not perform it. . . .
>
> My hands expect to comply with my rules. I suffer no manager to scold at his hands. If a hand persistently fails to make time I simply pay him off and discharge him.

This planter's justification for his constant appeal to the clock would have warmed the cockles of many a northern factory owner's heart: "This rule throws all losses of time where it properly belongs, to those who lose it. Suppose I work fifty hands and each of these hands loses twelve minutes during the day. You see I lose a whole day or the work of one hand. But, you may ask, how can you keep up such strict discipline? A great deal easier than not to keep it up."[57]

Given these various incentives encouraging planters to regulate free labor by time, it is hardly surprising to find their postbellum journals, accounts, and day books littered with notes recording "time lost" by their laborers. Echoing the antebellum practice of timing hired labor, postbellum planters usually counted lost time in units of half or whole days. This tendency is clear from Charles Craddock Wimbish's account books kept in Mecklenburg County, Virginia, 1865–70. The following entries are typical: "[1867] Harry Hutcheson. . . . Jan. 19th to loss of work one half days .75 [cents]. . . . Sandy Bowers. . . . 1869 June 21st lost 1/2 the day (in harvest) .50 [cents]."[58] Some South Carolina planters also apparently reckoned lost time by the day and half day. On September 24, "Philis . . . lost two days," while Bob was "out on 6th [September], lost 1 day" at John Blount Miller's Sumter plantation in 1866. The "Work account for Elick Roberson" at Eugene Dabbs's neighboring plantation read similarly: "Elick Commenced work on the first of Jan [1884] at Seven Dollars per month.... Oct 20 [1884] To 1 day lost 40 [cents].... Nov 1 [1884] To 1/2 day lost time 25 [cents].... Nov 29 [1884] To 1/2 day lost time 25 [cents]."[59] Others, however, were a little more specific. Planter-lawyer Henry Laurens Pinckney, also of Sumter District, South Carolina, kept a "Memorandum of Lost Time" that, among other things, recorded time lost to the nearest quarter of a day: "[June 28 1865] Charles (Emma's) sick 3/4 day[.] [June 30 1865] Andrew—gone to Stateburg—1/2 day[.] Isaac—sick from 8th to 12th [July 1865] 5 days."[60] James Henry Hammond, the up-country South Carolina planter who, during the antebellum period, imposed strict time obedience on his plantation, recruited similar strategies to deal with his freed workforce. As early as 1866, Hammond began computing "Charges for lost time, Extra Rations, &C." For May of that year, he noted: "Sarah out the 11th but unable to go far from house & 2/3 time lost." October's report was similar: "Otelia & Winston as last month. Toward the latter part of the month loss of time at meals &c—say 1/2 an hour daily = 1 [day]." And for December 1866, Hammond's entry read like a factory manager's log book: "Ned & family getting slower every day—often 10 o'clock before getting to work.... About 4 days each by hour losses.... Summary.... 10 hours to the laboring day."[61] Fearful of relinquishing economic, social, and, ultimately, political control over their newly freed workers, these men quickly adapted the rules of capitalist time discipline by resurrecting antebellum time obedience in a free-wage context to guard their admittedly uncertain future.

Low-country planters were little different. Paul Fitzsimmons Hammond kept the following accounts for time worked at his Cathwood plantation for April 15, 1884, demonstrating that more than one type of agricultural labor was reducible to time:

Paid Jim   for 3 1/4 days work at saw mill @ 65 c[ents] 2.10
 "   Fred   "   2 3/4 "   "   at saw mill @ 60 c[ents] 1.60
 "   Amos   "   1 1/4 "   "   cotton planting @ 50 c[ents] [equals] 85
[cents][62]

Many planters, then, conducted their New South plantations like northern factories, counting the time lost by freedpeople to the hour, often to the minute. "Lucinda," for example, put in on Lewis Edmunds Mason's Virginia plantation "3 days & 3 hours work . . . May 9th 1867."[63] And John Forsyth Talbert of South Carolina could hardly have been more precise had he insisted on the use of time cards. For virtually every one of his thirty or so hands that he employed in 1866–68, Talbert kept incredibly precise "Loss Time" records. The following is the "Account of Elbert's Loss Time for 1868," one of Talbert's shorter time logs:

	days	hrs	mins
March 15th Elbert lost by taking *Brandy*	0	8	0
May 4th " lost in repairing shoes	"	6	0
. . .			
August 21st, 22nd, & 24th. . . .	"	2	6
[Sept.] 8 " Lost in getting home	"	1	0

Sometimes Talbert would construct "Loss Time" accounts for families of workers while detailing the amount of time to be deducted individually. In his "Account of loss Time of Phill, his wife Susan and his son Pierce, for the year 1867" all three were identified as taking time off from work and thereby reducing the collective wage. On January 18, for example, "Susan lost 4 hours this day" through sickness, while on March 23 "Pierce [lost] 10 minutes walking from fields to the house on his own business and in violation of orders." And both Phill and Pierce "got to work too late each one lost 15 minutes" on September 27, 1867.[64] If working as a family was a litmus test of freedom for freedpeople, then it surely came at a price: collective responsibility for managing time.

While time was central to what one historian has called antebellum masters' status of "laborlords," planters, always conscious of the need for social, political, as well as economic control, now recruited the clock to prevail over freedpeople's noneconomic affairs or nonwork time as well.[65] Again, however, antebellum precedents abounded, most obviously in masters' regulation of slaves' off time by the clock. After the Civil War, new, nonphysical punishments were recruited to control such time. This was achieved primarily through punishing workers who took the time, literally, to, say, take care of their family or, very often, exercise their right to vote. Such efforts are apparent in the plantation time books of one postwar Virginia planter who docked time for virtually anything, profane or sacred:

> [1867] George Simmons. . . . July 12th to one day lost(to register) .50 [cents]. . . . Oct 15th To loss of time (sick) .50 [cents]. . . . [1867] Patrick Hutcherson. . . . Feb 16th to loss of time, (go down home) 1/2 day .25 [cents]. . . . July 16th To 1/2 the day lost (toothache) .25 [cents]. . . . July 24th To 1/2 the day lost (funeral). . . . Adam Towns. . . . 1869 . . . July 12th To 1 day lost (see his mammy) .50 [cents]. . . . July 24th To 1/2 the day lost (funeral) .25 [cents]. . . . Aug 30th To 1 day lost (cousin died) .50 [cents][66]

Lewis Edmunds Mason of Southampton County, Virginia, followed an almost identical practice with his workers: "Account with Eldridge Heath for 1867. . . . [Oct] 22 1 day lost at Election 43 [cents]. Account with Randall Broadnax

1867. . . . Oct 9 Day lost in going to Henry [town]—Except 1 1/2 hours in morning. . . . Cherry for 1865. . . . time lost in attending to it [her child] [$]4.00."[67] Likewise, Samuel Porcher Gaillard docked one of his workers, Jimmy, for having the gall to "[lose] 2 1/2 hours of time to go for the Dr."[68] Predictably, that consummate Taylorite John Forsyth Talbert of Sumter, South Carolina, followed suit. Not only were Charly "& wife Susan" docked two hours "Lost in coming home from the election" on November 18, 1867, but Charly was forced to suffer an ignominious deduction when Talbert docked him one and a half day's pay for time "Lost from dog Bite" on May 6 earlier that year.[69]

Obviously, the South's freedpeople were, when occasion demanded, willing to absorb the very pecuniary cost of lost time. That they took time off at all was, in all probability, a very tangible way some chose to exercise and, indeed, protect their freedom. Ultimately, however, planters succeeded in paying such close scrutiny to workers' lost time and thereby making the taking off of time potentially costly that the right to one's own time became almost specious. And freedpeople well recognized this fact. According to John Mosley of Texas, when freedom came, "We asked Maser for a job and he finally gave us a crop with him on the halves and that is the way we worked for several years." Mosley's concluding remarks are revealing: "We could not tell much difference on that from slavery as Maser bossed everything, the only difference was us negroes could go and come when we wanted to except on work days as Maser would not let us go in work time."[70] In other words, if freedom meant the right to take time off, it also imposed an obligation that stood at the crux of bourgeois political economy and was enforced by planters: an obligation to make time up.

What was truly tragic is that freedpeople, like all free laborers, came to accept the legitimacy upon which these demands were premised, even if it that acceptance was grudging. Even if freedpeople did occasionally appeal to that older, comparatively fairer but almost as frenetic arbiter of time, the sun, they nevertheless came to accept the idea that time lost was time to be made up and that this time in turn was defined by the clock. John Forsyth Talbert's freedpeople, for example, came to accept and so legitimize his method of measuring their labor by making up for time they may have taken off: "[April] 17th [1868] Chisly worked 5 hours this Saturday evening—his own time to pay loss time."[71] So too with Samuel Porcher Gaillard's Sumter District freedpeople in 1868: "All hands to day except Waley who beat rice—Tommy also beat rice to make up one of the days he lost and Hector did also, to make up for a day he worked on his crop in my time."[72] Another planter, Ivey Foreman Lewis of Alabama, went a step further and managed to include some of his freed workers in the process of defining and punishing the loss of time. Part four of his 1874 "Articles of Agreement" stated: "To deduct from this each share one Dollar per day for wilful loss of time, and in case of disobedience or Violation of this contract to be dismissed and to forfeit his or their share of the crops: this to be decided by Ivey F. Lewis & three freedmen."[73] Still others felt aggrieved, justifiably, when they had stuck to a planter's time schedule but were punished nevertheless. As one hired hand complained to a Freedmen's Bureau officer after a seemingly gratuitous beating: "Boss, I been working all de time; ask any nigger on de plantashn ef I'se ever lazy nigger."[74] In truth, of course, New South planters, because slavery was forever lost, could never be satisfied with freed labor, even when the principle of timed work had been accommodated by their workers.[75] But the following complaint by a South Carolina sea island planter barely a year after the war's end says more about freedpeople's entry into the capitalist world of time-wage negotiations and their attendant capitulation to the clock than it does about planters' intransigence: "By-and-by picking comes, and there's so much a pound for all the cotton picked; everything as easy and regular as clock work. But if he's wanted to do a quarter of an hour's work at any time, he expects pay for that."[76] Similarly, former slaves in Alabama demonstrated for "an advance of 23¢ per hour for their services" in 1867.[77] As E. P. Thompson remarked of an earlier generation of English factory workers: "They had accepted the categories of their employers and learned to fight back within them. They had learned their lesson, that time is money, only too well."[78]

And so, once freedpeople had accepted the logic of timed labor, albeit reluctantly, they effectively joined the ranks of a burgeoning international proletariat whose only commonality with the concomitant burgeoning bourgeoisie was that they all understood the value and nature of time, its marriage to money, its insidious, ubiquitous tyranny, and that its ownership stood at the fulcrum of class relations.

Marx, perhaps intuitively, called southern capitalism a sporadic phenomenon that grafted itself onto the slave society.[79] And engrafted and sporadic it seems to have been. In the process of importing northern definitions of time discipline to the South, important elements of this idea were either filtered out or forced to adapt to local circumstances, so producing time obedience. It was not so much the resistance by slaves and the stifling web of paternalism described by Eugene Genovese that stopped planters from duplicating time discipline but rather masters' own monopoly of time and their grave reservations about taking the conventional route to modernity that made their society sporadically capitalist. According to Genovese, although paternalism afforded slaves protection from excessive economic exploitation, it had a long-term disadvantage which "lay in its encouragement of a way of life that, however admirable intrinsically, ill prepared black people to compete in the economic world into which they would be catapulted by emancipation."[80] But the evidence presented in this book suggests that this interpretation needs qualifying. Slaves and freedpeople, though to varying degrees, learned only too well the lessons of the clock, even if it was backed by the whip. If paternalism really was so debilitating, the remarks of former slave Mattie Mooreman in the 1930s suggest that its effects were hardly enduring. Mooreman was black, but she plainly did not share in the black work ethic noted by Genovese: "I asked a man when I was on the way [to work the other day] and it was 25 minutes until 5. Besides, my clock had stopped and I couldn't tell what time it was."[81] In other words, black peoples' failure to compete in the economic world after emancipation was not simply a result of their putative inability to learn the rules of the capitalist game. Rather, that failure was the result of African Americans' forceful exclusion from access to the means of production and genuine, enduring political power. It was an exclusion bolstered by a worldview, couched in terms of race as well as class, in which workers, black ones in particular, were deemed incapable of assiduous, independent labor.

It was, then, the presence of a muted, garbled, bastard capitalism in the South that produced time obedience and in the process made this highly derivative southern version of time discipline just as deadly to beleaguered, time-obedient southern bondpeople as it was to E. P. Thompson's time-disciplined British proletariat.[82] In the process of trying to resolve their dilemma and ambivalent view of progress, slaveholders mimicked northern and European capitalists to such an extent that although they were plainly born in the Atlantic capitalist marketplace, by the end of the antebellum period they might as well have been of it. Certainly, slave owners, if they were to safeguard their slave society, had to use the clock in ways different from those of their northern counterparts. But that masters managed to rely on aural time obedience, backed by the whip, instead of watch-owning, time-negotiating workers to regulate labor by the clock; that they introduced probably the most capitalist tool of economic exploitation and social control without rupturing their organic society and without importing the mobocratic, time-negotiating ethos with which northern factory managers had to contend is sure, if unpalatable, testimony to the dynamism of the late antebellum slaveholders' regime. In their bid to safeguard their future, slaveholders scoured time and space. They found partial answers in the modernizing North and partial solutions in the past. By combining the old, even revered practice of aural time obedience, the trusty whip, and the clock-backed efficiency drives of northern capitalists, slaveholders to a considerable extent modernized their society on their own terms. Southern masters used the clock and watch so much like their northern counterparts that the real differences between the slave and free-labor modes of production at the everyday level of social interaction, and not at the larger level of historical abstraction, were of ever-lessening importance to the slaves and masters themselves than has often been assumed. Yet both the presence and the significance of these similarities were often lost to people at the time, especially, it seems, to northerners traveling South. Even though he witnessed the watch regulating slave labor, Frederick Law Olmsted, for example, complained bitterly while in Virginia in the 1850s, "You notice in all cases, vagueness in ideas of cost and value." Olmsted thought he was illustrating his point when he noted: "For instance, I noticed a rivet loose in my umbrella, as I was going out from my hotel during a shower, and stepped into an adjoining shop to have it repaired. 'I can't do it in less than half an hour, sir, and it will be worth a quarter,' said the locksmith, replying to inquiries." Appalled at what he perceived as slovenliness, Olmsted returned to his hotel "and with the fire-poker did the work myself, in less than a minute, . . . saving half an hour and quarter of a dollar, like a 'Yankee.'" But it apparently escaped Olmsted that this southern slacker shared his language of time and its equation with work. Their differences were over degrees of time, not absolutes, and, in the final analysis, these differences were, historically at least, minimal.[83]

Of course, important differences remained: slave owners were a distinct and dying political class. But as an economic class, they had gravitated so far toward the capitalist application of clock time that by the eve of the Civil War they had essentially abandoned the title of premodern. For all their reluctance to join nineteenth-century moderns, masters had simply been too good at aping them to avoid joining their ranks.

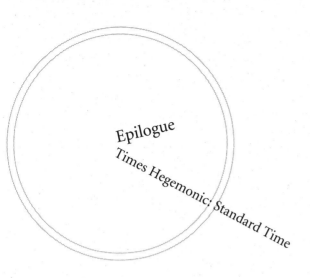

Epilogue
Times Hegemonic; Standard Time

We confess that it has always been to us an almost
incomprehensible matter that all our times are referable, not to
any one actually-existing heavenly body, but to an ideal one. . . .
The changes rung on time in this country are endless,
confounding and annoying. Not only do we hear and read of
Philadelphia time, of Altoona, Pittsburg, Collumbus [*sic*] and
Chicago times, on our railroad time-tables, but each village,
town and city has its own, till "confusion worse confounded"
must be an inevitable result.

—"Uniformity in Railroad Time," *De Bow's Review*, 1870

At noon on November 18, 1883, standard time was imposed on the United States. American cities, towns, and villages abandoned approximately forty-nine local or sun-regulated times in favor of four scientific, clock-defined time zones. This new time was regulated not only by Greenwich mean time but by the Gilded Age marriage between money-grubbing telegraph companies and scientific, astronomical observatories.[1] The telegraph, not the sun, now communicated time to a temporally unified nation and, in the process, helped pave the way for the globalization of abstracted, decontextualized, world time.[2]

Because some places were ahead of clock-defined, "true" noon, the introduction of standard time on November 18 has been called the "day of two noons."[3] It might also be called the day of one nation. For more than Lincoln's conscription fiat during the Civil War, more than the standardization of American currency during and after the war, more than the Civil War itself, the standardization of time in America represented the temporal destruction of sectionalism based on the North-South axis, replacing it with, if not a wholly homogenized America, at least an America where the differences between East and West were greater, by about three hours, than the time difference between North and South.[4] In short, by the end of 1883, there was no longer any such thing as local or southern time or, indeed, a southern time consciousness. Nor, for that matter, was there a northern, eastern, or western one. In both a literal and figurative sense, the longitudinal time zones now bracing the nation had replaced the sectional, political, latitudinal lines that had served to separate the country during a previous generation. Charleston shared the same time as New York, literally. The northernization of southern time which became apparent in and after the 1830s had reached its apogee in 1883: southern time was not just northernized, it was now Americanized. The clock ruled supreme over all Americans and had begun, in earnest, its dominion over God and nature.

Because the question of time is peripheral to Richard Bensel's *Yankee Leviathan*, covering 1859 to 1877, he rightly argues that "the modern state's inheritance from the antebellum period was nil."[5] From the perspective of time and time awareness, however, this is clearly not the case. It was only because all Americans, southerners included, had, for over one hundred years before the introduction of standard time, nurtured a familiarity with the imperatives of mechanical time that the railways could even countenance substituting national for local time in 1883.

Although historians disagree on who exactly was responsible for the introduction of standard time, it is clear that both the scientific community and railroad interests had long considered the need for a system of uniform and standard time in their vast and sprawling country.[6] The idea of a standard, albeit localized, time was considered as early as 1834 by the engineer of the South Carolina Canal and Railroad Company.[7] Between 1840 and the 1870s, various New England railroads either introduced standard times on their lines or at least toyed with the idea.[8] In addition, as Ian Bartky has shown, "astronomers, many of whose observatories provided time to the railroads," via telegraph signals, also "began to write about uniform time in the early 1870s."[9] The combined forces of the need for a uniform time system in the fields of geophysics, surveying, and, especially after the completion of the transcontinental railroad in 1869, railroading, slowly pushed the United States toward the adoption of standard time in 1883.[10]

Although instigated by a variety of figures, the implementation of standard time was effected by William F. Allen, a lifelong employee of the Camden and Amboy Railroad and its former president. Allen was also the first secretary of the General Time Convention, which, after months of preparation for the shift to uniform time, met in Chicago on October 11 to finalize arrangements for the changeover. Circulars were sent to virtually every railroad terminus in the country explaining what the new time would be for each station.[11]

The new standard time map divided the country into four time zones. Allen, drawing on several previous plans, adopted a map dividing the zones into four parts, each exactly fifteen degrees of longitude, or one hour, apart. This division ignored state geopolitical boundaries and the existing time divisions established by individual railroad companies. "Practicality," as Michael O'Malley writes, "ruled the minds of railroaders, and they felt no sentimental or patriotic attachment to the time of one particular city. . . . What they wanted most was a plan that altered existing division breaks, and the accustomed day to day operations of the roads, as little as possible."[12]

To this end, Allen unveiled a map at the meeting of the General and Southern Railway Time Conventions in April 1883, displaying each of the four zones in a different color, copies of which quickly made their way into the press.[13] With no little arrogance, Allen proclaimed that the "railroad trains are the great educators and monitors of the people in teaching and maintaining time" and argued that "with the standards cities or governments may adopt . . . we should have nothing to do."[14] Once railways had been informed of and agreed to the new zoning, virtually all American railroads implemented the time of the zone assigned them at noon on November 18.

It was a coup of no small proportions. From atop the Western Union Building in New York City, Allen observed the changeover with justified pride: "Standing on the roof of that building . . . I heard the bells of St. Paul's strike on the old time. Four minutes later, obedient to the electrical signal from the Naval Observatory . . . the time-ball made its rapid descent, the chimes of old Trinity rang twelve measured strokes, and local time was abandoned, probably forever."[15]

At its simplest, the new time required railroads and, by implication, everyone who used the train, to advance or retard their clocks and watches so many minutes, according to the zone in which their locality lay. Those in New York City stopped their clocks for four minutes; those in the nation's capital advanced their clocks eight minutes; Chicagoans retarded theirs nine minutes. The zoning required denizens of New Orleans, Denver, and Philadelphia to do nothing. What amounted to a revolution in time was, for most people, a matter of adjusting clocks and watches a few minutes. Jewelers, train station and post office clocks, and public town clocks, once local, civic authorities had assented to the change, quickly adopted the new time and provided the source for people to set their watches to standard time.[16]

Of course, the introduction of standard time zones did not obliterate local or natural time completely or instantaneously, primarily because the initiative of the railroad companies in 1883 was not federally endorsed or mandated. Standard time, in fact, was one of the few private, non-government-instigated forces promoting the formation of the American nation-state. Trends toward a standard currency, toward free wage labor, and other factors promoting the nation-state in the last half of the nineteenth century were mostly initiated or actualized by the federal government. It was not until 1918 that the federal leviathan began to legislate civil time. Indeed, the option for communities to adhere to local time continued until 1967, when federal legislation finally preempted all civil time statutes. "Even today," as one historian has pointed out, "the United States' civil-time system is not uniform: About 3 percent of the population lives in areas that do not observe daylight saving time."[17] Revealingly, Washington, D.C., was one of the last places legally to adopt, by an act of Congress, standard time. The capital's attorney general, Benjamin Brewster, was unsure of the constitutionality of standard time in the District and so ordered government offices not to adopt the new time until Congress authorized them to do so. It did so in March 1884. In some instances, leviathan was slow to catch up in the march toward progress.[18]

But it was not just the absence of a federal mandate that encouraged no small number of Americans still to appeal to local, sun time even after November 18, 1883. Some clergymen, for example, argued that their local time was immune to molestation by private, Mammon-worshiping railroad interests because their time was God's. Still others resisted the new time precisely because they thought it was introduced by the railroads. As the *Indianapolis Daily Sentinel* put it three days after the introduction of the new time, "The sun is no longer to boss the job. People . . . must eat, sleep and work . . . by railroad time. . . . People will have to marry by railroad time." In an age distrustful of railroad conglomerates, railroad time lacked the legitimacy that local time and all its affiliations with God and nature bestowed.[19]

Yet such objections were peculiar and exceptional. After all, ministers in New York, Philadelphia, and Chicago embraced, or least did not denounce, the new time. And outside of Indiana, where distrust of the railroads was similarly strong, few public complaints against the new "railroad time" were made.[20] Nor did opposition to the new time devolve on a rural-urban or a North-South axis. While the very largest cities like Chicago and New York made the transition to standardized clock time smoothly, there was considerable resistance to the abandonment of sidereal time in such urban centers as Boston, especially from the working poor, and in Savannah, Georgia. Nor did the shift elicit different responses from black and white. The African American *Cleveland Gazette* demonstrated the same ambivalence to standard time that white newspapers reflected. On November 3, the newspaper simply alerted readers to the upcoming change, and on November 24, a week or so after the new time came into effect, it posted the specifics with regard to railroad schedules. The December 1 issue contained the only complaint, which read, simply, "The new time is a nuisance." On the whole, however, the shift went smoothly and, quiet grumbles aside, Cleveland's black community adjusted to the change as readily as did the rest of the nation.[21]

Reaction in the South was also ambivalent. While the *Atlanta Constitution* applauded "the utter contempt into which the sun and moon have fallen," thus allowing Atlanta to "progress into the future," southern "country folks continued to set their clocks by the sun" and insisted on sidereal time to "estimate the time with uncanny accuracy." But citizens in Bangor, Maine, Detroit, Michigan, and throughout Ohio also refused to accept the new time.[22]

Instead, opposition was strongest and most enduring in those localities concentrated in the eastern regions of the two most eastern time zones. Although Allen had predicted that the standardization of time would cause a variation between local and standard time of no more than thirty minutes, the new eastern zone's standard time actually caused a discrepancy between the old, local time and the new national time ranging from thirty-two minutes on the zone's eastern edge to thirty-eight minutes on its western. Similarly, in the adjacent central time zone, the discrepancy between standard and local time ranged between forty-five and sixty-six minutes. The net effect for people at the extreme of these zones was a perceived and real change, either a reduction or increase in the amount of sunlight. As one historian explains it:

> Consider Savannah. Allen's plan assigned it, like all of Georgia, to the central zone. If central time were adopted, Savannah's sun would set over thirty minutes earlier than people there were used to. . . . Citizens tried the new time but then rejected it. People in Maine cities like Bangor and Bath perceived similar early sunsets in mid-November 1883. Citizens in Ohio balked at the change. Detroit and Port Huron, Michigan, residents denounced the new system and stayed with local time.[23]

Augusta, Georgia, which lay on the border of two zones, did not adopt eastern time until 1888. And even then some demurred. "The only people," proclaimed one city official, "that want standard time are the railroads. . . . The city doesn't want it, the laboring people don't want it . . . nine tenths of the population of the city are opposed to it." As for "the ladies," he noted, "why, they have always been opposed to it."[24] But Ohio was little different. Cincinnati, on the central time zone border, refused to put the city clocks back twenty-two minutes, as did Dayton, Ohio, Detroit, Michigan, and several other states and cities located along the zones' borders. Between 1883 and 1915 standard time came to trial before the supreme courts of various states at least fifteen times. Supreme courts in Nebraska (1890) and Kentucky (1905) and the Texas Circuit Court in 1895 all ruled that although the uniform time had been adopted in many places, local time still ruled legally.[25]

Conversely, places that had to adjust their times by only a few minutes, those not on the borders of time zones, accepted the change quietly. New Orleans, for example, was barely affected by the changeover and so proved quite accommodating. As the *Daily Picayune* noted on November 17, 1883: "We say New Orleans time, because that is very nearly 90° standard. We are about six hours and twenty seconds behind Greenwich time, and consequently ought to set our timepieces 20 seconds ahead, but so small a divergence will not be noticed by the people at large."[26] Likewise, the *Atlanta Constitution* took some satisfaction that "it is remarkable how quickly things have become accommodated to the new time. Atlanta is one of the promptest cities to secure it general use."[27] Little Rock's *Arkansas Weekly Mansion* explained in sober and practical terms the reasons for the change and the impact it would have and gave its readers a copy of Allen's map.[28]

So too with some of Tennessee's small towns, even though their time adjustment was sometimes substantial. Rugby's *Plateau Gazette and East Tennessee News* simply informed its readers: "Last Sunday the time on all the railroads were [sic] changed to the new 'Standard Time,' which will make our time 22 minutes slower." The relatively substantial loss elicited little comment.[29] And Louisville's *Courier-Journal* similarly argued that "the adoption of the new railway standard in this country can be accomplished without much difficulty by all communities; otherwise there will be misunderstanding about local and standard time which will continue to befog travellers." To facilitate the changeover and avoid public confusion, Louisville's mayor "made arrangements to have the City Hall clock turned back eighteen minutes." So that public and personal time could be adjusted precisely, he explained: "The fire bells will ring punctually at 12 o'clock by the new standard, so that people will be able to set their time-pieces accordingly." But even the best-laid plans have a habit of going awry, and the mayor was doubtless surprised to learn that his arrangements were temporarily foiled by one of the city's railroad companies. Explained the *Courier-Journal*:

> The Walnut-Street Railroad Company will not adopt the new standard time, because it involves the necessity of making new time cards. This will prove disadvantageous to people who wish to take a certain car to Riverside or on the Beargrass roads. As it is now, those cars leave Fourth and Main streets on the hour or half hour, so the person who wishes to take a car at say noon, must be governed by the company's arbitrary time, and not by the city time which will be the standard recognized by all citizens. The position assumed by the company will prove of great inconvenience to the thousands of people who patronize their several roads, and it is one from which, sooner or later, the managers will be compelled to recede.[30]

Because the time change was not considerable for most of South Carolina's towns and cities, the leader of secession a couple of decades earlier acquiesced to the changes. The state's most rural newspapers reported what the new time meant in matter-of-fact terms. The *Abbeville Press and Banner* stated simply: "The train now comes in at half past five o'clock by the new time, which is eight minutes faster than Washington time," while the *Newberry Herald* was almost fawning in its endorsement of Allen's tinkering: "The Change is a good thing and will be a great convenience to the travelling public."[31] The *Orangeburg Times and Democrat*'s support was lukewarm, however, because it realized that "it seems that we will all have to make our time pieces conform to the above to prevent confusion."[32] Yet on the whole, if the newspapers are to be believed, the changeover went smoothly with little opposition.[33] Of course, there were always the temporally challenged whose understanding of the importance of the change was less than acute. Twelve days after the introduction of the new time, a man in Columbia "stopped yesterday on Main street and set his watch by a wooden sign clock that hung in front of a jeweler's store. He had heard of the new time and wanted the latest."[34]

In sum, resistance to the new time depended mainly on the extent of the discrepancy between old time and new in certain localities.[35] Whether rural or urban, North or South, the defining factor in resistance was whether the locality was on the border of the new zones. If the imposition of standard time had fueled a renewed secession movement, the partners would have been very different than they were in 1860. South Carolina and New York would have been steadfast Unionists; Georgia, Maine, and Ohio, die-hard secessionists— all this just twenty-three years after that real and very bloody secession.

APPENDIX

REFERENCES TO timepiece "makers" in Tables A.1–A.10, as Chapter 1 shows, should not be taken literally. Those who advertised themselves as makers either in newspapers or to census takers were more probably timepiece repairers. When considering the data contained in Tables A.11–A.25, it should be borne in mind that the estimates for personal, inventoried wealth are based on material wealth only. Because many of the inventories often fail to note the value of invisible capital (for example, bonds and notes) at the individual's time of death and because it is often impossible to determine from the records whether the deceased was a debtor or creditor, invisible capital was excluded from these calculations. In all likelihood, individuals were wealthier than is suggested herein. Second, the estimates for clock and watch costs are based solely on what the person conducting the inventory considered the timepieces to be worth and thus do not reflect actual market value. In the absence of price indexes for these commodities, these estimates are the best that we have available.

Table A.1. Distribution of Timepiece Makers by Time and Region in South Carolina, North Carolina, Virginia, and Georgia, 1666–1881 (percent)

	S.C.	N.C.	Va.	Ga.	Total
1666–1750	64	0	33	3	4
1751–1800	26	12	50	12	40
1801–81	21	14	49	16	56
Totals	25	13	48	14	100

Source: *Index of Early Southern Artists and Artisans*, MESDA.
Note: Those makers who changed partnerships, relocated, or whose working life bridges two time cohorts have been counted twice.

Table A.2. Geographical Mobility among Southern Timepiece Makers by Number
of Separate Working Establishments during Working Life, 1666–1881

Number of establishments at which individual worked	South Carolina			North Carolina		
	1	2	3+	1	2	3+
1666–1750						
Number	14	4	0	0	0	0
Percent	78	22	0	0	0	0
1751–1800						
Number	70	13	1	26	7	3
Percent	83	15	1	72	19	8
1801–81						
Number	91	4	4	43	14	3
Percent	92	4	4	72	23	5
Number of establishments at which individual worked	Virginia			Georgia		
	1	2	3+	1	2	3+
1666–1750						
Number	8	3	0	0	0	0
Percent	73	27	0	0	0	0
1751–1800						
Number	115	19	6	33	4	2
Percent	82	14	4	85	10	5
1801–81						
Number	173	27	5	48	8	6
Percent	84	13	2	77	13	10

Source: *Index of Early Southern Artists and Artisans*, MESDA.
Note: Those individuals whose working life bridges two time cohorts have been counted twice.

Table A.3. Regional and National Origins of Timepiece Makers Working in
South Carolina, North Carolina, Virginia, and Georgia, Combined, 1666–1881

Origins	1666–1750	1751–1800	1801–81
Europe[1]	n = 10 (30%)	n = 71 (21%) (London, n = 34)	n = 50 (10.5%) (Swiss, n = 7) (French, n=8)
North[2]	n = 0 (0%)	n = 10 (3%)	n = 23 (5%) (NYC, n = 7)
Native to South[3]	n = 23 (70%)	n = 259 (76%)	n = 402 (84%)
Other[4]	n = 0 (0%)	n = 0 (0%)	n = 1 (0.5%)

Source: *Index of Early Southern Artists and Artisans*, MESDA.
Note: Data assessed according to date when individual first started working in the South.
[1]Specific origins: Austria, England (London, Birmingham, Liverpool, Plymouth); France (Paris); Germany (Hanover, Cologne); Holland; Ireland (Dublin); Prussia (Thuringia); Russia; Scotland (Edinburgh); Switzerland.
[2]Specific origins: Connecticut; Massachusetts (Boston); New Jersey; New York (New York City); Pennsylvania (Philadelphia, Pittsburgh).
[3]Specific origins: Georgia (Augusta, Savannah); Maryland (Baltimore, Annapolis); South Carolina (Charleston); Virginia (Alexandria, Lynchburg, Norfolk, Petersburg, Williamsburg).
[4]Specific origin: Bermuda.

Table A.4. Emigration of Timepiece Makers from South Carolina,
North Carolina, Virginia, and Georgia, Combined, 1666–1881

Destination	1666–1750	1751–1800	1801–81
Europe[1]	n = 0 (0%)	n = 11 (4%)	n = 8 (2%)
North[2]	n = 0 (0%)	n = 8 (3%)	n = 13 (3%)
Remaining in South[3]	n = 32 (97%)	n = 317 (92%)	n = 453 (94%)
Other[4]	n = 1 (3%)	n = 4 (1%)	n = 2 (1%)

Source: *Index of Early Southern Artists and Artisans*, MESDA.
[1]Specific destinations: Austria, England, France, Germany, Holland, Ireland, Prussia, Russia, Scotland, Switzerland.
[2]Specific destinations: Connecticut, Massachusetts, New Jersey, New York, Pennsylvania.
[3]Specific destinations: Georgia, Maryland, South Carolina, Virginia.
[4]Specific destinations: Africa, West Indies.

Table A.5. Specialization among Timepiece Makers in South Carolina,
North Carolina, Virginia, Georgia, and Combined, 1666–1881 (percent)

	Highly Specialized[1]	Specialized[2]	Unspecialized[3]	Totals
South Carolina				
1666–1750	81	9.5	9.5	100
1751–1800	72	22	6	100
1801–81	68	28	4	100
North Carolina				
1666–1750	0	0	0	0
1751–1800	32	55	13	100
1801–81	24	63	13	100
Virginia				
1666–1750	75	25	0	100
1751–1800	56	36	8	100
1801–81	37	56	7	100
Georgia				
1666–1750	0	100	0	100
1751–1800	54	39	7	100
1801–81	32	60	8	100
Combined				
1666–1750	76	18	6	100
1751–1800	57	35	8	100
1801–81	41	51	7	100

Source: *Index of Early Southern Artists and Artisans*, MESDA.

Note: Those makers who changed partnerships, relocated, or whose working life bridges
two time cohorts have been counted twice.

[1]Highly specialized: solely clock and/or watch makers.

[2]Specialized: clock and watch makers who were also silversmiths, jewelers, engravers, and
instrument makers.

[3]Unspecialized: includes the above who were also enamelers, painters, brickmakers,
gunsmiths, coppersmiths, tinsmiths, shipwrights, and other miscellaneous occupations.

Table A.6. Division of Labor in Timepiece-Making Establishments
in Southern Colonies and States, 1666–1881

State	1666–1750	1751–1800	1801–81
South Carolina			
In partnership without apprentice or journeyman	0 (0%)	10 (12%)	15 (15%)
Journeyman employed	0 (0%)	5 (6%)	5 (5%)
Apprentice employed	0 (0%)	3 (3%)	6 (6%)
In partnership employing apprentice and/or journeyman	0 (0%)	5 (6%)	6 (6%)
One-man establishment	21 (100%)	64 (73%)	69 (68%)
Totals	21 (100%)	87 (100%)	101 (100%)
North Carolina			
In partnership without apprentice or journeyman	0 (0%)	4 (10%)	16 (24%)
Journeyman employed	0 (0%)	3 (7%)	0 (0%)
Apprentice employed	0 (0%)	7 (17%)	13 (19%)
In partnership employing apprentice and/or journeyman	0 (0%)	4 (10%)	4 (6%)
One-man establishment	0 (0%)	23 (56%)	35 (51%)
Totals	0 (0%)	41 (100%)	68 (100%)
Virginia			
In partnership without apprentice or journeyman	0 (0%)	16 (9%)	28 (12%)
Journeyman employed	1 (8%)	7 (4%)	11 (5%)
Apprentice employed	0 (0%)	22 (13%)	22 (9%)
In partnership employing apprentice and/or journeyman	0 (0%)	18 (11%)	42 (18%)
One-man establishment	11 (92%)	109 (63%)	129 (56%)
Totals	12 (100%)	172 (100%)	232 (100%)
Georgia			
In partnership without apprentice or journeyman	0 (0%)	6 (15%)	22 (29%)
Journeyman employed	0 (0%)	3 (7%)	2 (3%)
Apprentice employed	0 (0%)	6 (15%)	3 (4%)
In partnership employing apprentice and/or journeyman	0 (0%)	3 (7%)	8 (11%)
One-man establishment	1 (100%)	23 (56%)	40 (53%)
Totals	1 (100%)	41 (100%)	75 (100%)
South			
In partnership without apprentice or journeyman	0 (0%)	36 (11%)	81 (17%)
Journeyman employed	1 (3%)	18 (5%)	18 (4%)
Apprentice employed	0 (0%)	38 (11%)	44 (9%)
In partnership employing apprentice and/or journeyman	0 (0%)	30 (9%)	60 (13%)
One-man establishment	33 (97%)	219 (64%)	273 (57%)
Totals	34 (100%)	341 (100%)	476 (100%)

Source: *Index of Early Southern Artists and Artisans*, MESDA.

Table A.7. Clock and Watch Manufacturing in Southern States, 1810–1870

	Md.	Va.	Ky.	N.C.	Tenn.	S.C.	Ga.	La.	Miss.	Ala.	Tex.	Ark.	Fla.	Total
1810														
No. clock/watch makers	9	—	—	—	—	—	—	20	—	—	—	—	—	29
Value clocks/watches made ($)	3,880	7,027	—	—	—	—	—	—	—	—	—	—	—	10,907
1850														
No. watchmakers	93	69	55	17	42	36	31	155	26	14	22	4	6	570
No. clockmakers	22	8	9	5	3	6	6	7	1	34	0	0	0	101
1860														
Watchmaking:														
Establishments	—	—	—	—	—	—	—	—	—	—	—	—	—	5
Av. no. hands employed in each	—	—	—	—	—	—	—	—	—	—	—	—	—	1.2
Annual value of products ($)	—	—	—	—	—	—	—	—	—	—	—	—	—	5,650

Watch repairing:

Establishments	—	5	3	1	6	5	2	5	1	3	—	—	31
Av. no. hands employed in each	—	1.4	1	1	1.6	1.2	1	2	1	1.3	—	—	1.5
Annual value of products ($)	—	7,275	1,550	1,000	12,500	5,650	1,700	30,000	800	3,900	—	—	64,375

1870

No. clockmakers	14	11	74	4	13	—	4	3	—	4	—	—	127
No. clock/watch repairing establishments	40	31	19	7	24	5	22	16	15	6	13	5	203
Av. no. hands employed in each establishment	2.1	1.5	1.5	1.4	1.4	1	1.4	1.6	1.3	2.6	1.2	1.6	1.6
Annual value of products repaired ($)	66,485	41,125	26,600	7,000	33,550	3,600	37,420	16,900	22,250	10,000	21,857	8,800	295,587

Source: Compiled from *A Statement of the Arts and Manufactures of the United States of America for the Year 1810; The Seventh Census of the United States: 1850; Manufactures of the United States in 1860; Ninth Census,* vol. 3.

Table A.8. Clock and Watch Manufacturing in Northern and Middle States, 1810–1870

	Me.	Mass.	N.H.	Vt.	R.I.	Conn.	N.Y.	N.J.	Penn.	Del.	Total
1810											
No. of clock and watch makers	—	—	—	—	—	—	—	—	—	—	—
Value of clocks and watches made ($)	—	46,185	350	—	—	—	—	—	—	—	46,535
1850											
No. of watchmakers	45	213	37	10	41	28	708	122	712	3	1,919
No. of clockmakers	16	59	22	10	6	582	173	15	105	0	988
1860											
Watchmaking and repairing:											
No. establishments	—	—	—	—	—	—	—	—	—	—	15
Average no. hands employed in each establishment	—	—	—	—	—	—	—	—	—	—	8.6
Annual value of products ($)	—	—	—	—	—	—	—	—	—	—	1,009,200

Clock making:											
No. establishments	—	—	—	—	—	—	—	—	—	—	24
Average no. hands employed in each establishment	—	—	—	—	—	—	—	—	—	—	40
Annual value of products ($)	—	—	—	—	—	—	—	—	—	—	1,233,150
1870											
No. of clockmakers	7	84	10	3	2	1,153	172	29	80	0	1,540
No. of clock and watch repairing establishments	15	98	10	13	11	15	128	22	142	1	455
Average no. hands employed in each establishment	1.5	2	1.9	3	1.7	1.8	2.2	1.6	1.9	1	2
Annual value of products repaired ($)	19,600	258,195	12,000	17,300	14,400	22,150	311,601	26,700	227,127	800	909,873

Source: Compiled from *A Statement of the Arts and Manufactures of the United States of America for the Year 1810; The Seventh Census of the United States: 1850; Manufactures of the United States in 1860; Ninth Census,* vol. 3.

Table A.9. Number of Timepiece Repairers, Importers, Makers, and Those in Partnerships in South Carolina, 1699–1901

	1699–1750					1751–1800					1801–1901				
	1	2	3	4	T	1	2	3	4	T	1	2	3	4	T
Abbeville	0	0	0	0	0	0	0	0	0	0	3	0	2	1	6
Anderson	0	0	0	0	0	0	0	0	0	0	0	0	2	0	2
Beaufort	0	0	0	0	0	0	0	0	0	0	0	0	0	0	0
Bennetsville	0	0	0	0	0	0	0	0	0	0	0	0	0	0	0
Camden	0	0	0	0	0	1	0	0	0	1	3	1	3	0	7
Charleston	1	2	3	0	6	2	7	16	2	27	4	8	24	2	38
Cheraw	0	0	0	0	0	0	0	0	0	0	0	1	1	0	2
Chester	0	0	0	0	0	0	0	0	0	0	0	0	2	0	2
Columbia	0	0	0	0	0	0	0	0	0	0	3	6	2	15	26
Darlington	0	0	0	0	0	0	0	0	0	0	0	0	0	0	0
Edgefield	0	0	0	0	0	0	0	0	0	0	0	0	2	1	3
Georgetown	0	0	0	0	0	0	1	0	0	1	2	0	3	0	5
Greenville	0	0	0	0	0	0	0	0	0	0	5	2	2	0	9
Lancaster	0	0	0	0	0	0	0	0	0	0	0	0	1	0	1
Laurens	0	0	0	0	0	0	0	0	0	0	5	1	1	0	7
Marion	0	0	0	0	0	0	0	0	0	0	0	0	0	0	0
Marlborough	0	0	0	0	0	0	0	0	0	0	0	0	0	0	0
Newberry	0	0	0	0	0	0	0	0	0	0	1	0	0	0	1
Orangeburg	0	0	0	0	0	0	0	0	0	0	1	1	0	0	2
Pendleton	0	0	0	0	0	0	0	0	0	0	0	0	3	0	3
Spartanburg	0	0	0	0	0	0	0	0	0	0	0	0	2	0	2
Sumter	0	0	0	0	0	0	0	0	0	0	2	3	1	0	6
Walhalla	0	0	0	0	0	0	0	0	0	0	0	1	1	0	2
Winnsboro	0	0	0	0	0	0	0	0	0	0	0	0	1	0	1
York	0	0	0	0	0	0	0	0	0	0	2	0	0	0	2
Total	1	2	3	0	6	3	8	16	2	29	31	24	53	19	127

Legend:
1 = Number of clock and watch repairers
2 = Number of clock and watch importers
3 = Number of clock and watch makers and repairers
4 = Number of clock and watch makers, importers, and/or repairers in partnerships
T = Total

Source: Compiled from Burton, *South Carolina Silversmiths*; *Manufactures of the United States in 1860*.
Note: Combined annual value of watch repairing for the state = $5,650. The manufacturing census returns have no record of timepiece makers working in the state.

Table A.10. American Clock Makers by Region, 1650–1860s

	1650–1750	1751–1800	1801–1860s	Total
North/Middle	98 (79%)	796 (82%)	2,002 (85%)	2,896
South	26 (21%)	177 (18%)	190 (8%)	393
West/Midwest	0 (0%)	0 (0%)	162 (7%)	162
Total	124 (100%)	973 (100%)	2,354 (100%)	3,451

Source: Compiled from Dreppard, *American Clocks and Clockmakers*, 197–293.

Table A.11. Wealth Levels and Timepiece Ownership among Slaveholders and Nonslaveholders, Charleston District, 1739–1744

	Number of Slaves Owned[1]					
	0a	1–5b	6–10c	11–20d	21+e	Total
Wealth by group (£)						
Total wealth	16,240	30,558	51,817	91,590	472,145	662,350
	(2%)	(5%)	(8%)	(14%)	(71%)	(100%)
Average wealth	464	954	1,850	3,392	10,731	
Average wealth of non-timepiece owners	495	762	1,634	3,151	8,205	
Average wealth of timepiece owners	343	1,533	2,641	4,776	14,869	
Ownership by group						
% owning timepieces	20	14	21	15	36	23
As % of all groups	20	25	20	16	19	100
Total cost of timepieces	155	112	159	153	742	1,321
Average cost of timepieces	17	16	26	30	46	
% of timepiece owners' wealth devoted to timepiece ownership	6.4	0.9	1.0	0.8	0.3	

Source: Compiled from Charleston District Inventories, 1739–44, vol. KK, SCDAH.
Note: Base data: n = 166; % of timepiece owners of n = 23; % of slaveholders who are timepiece owners = 19.
[1]a: n = 35 (21%); b: n = 32 (19%); c: n = 28 (17%); d: n = 27 (16.4%); e: n = 44 (26.6%).

Table A.12. Wealth Levels and Timepiece Ownership among Slaveholders and Nonslaveholders, Charleston District, 1763–1767

| | Number of Slaves Owned[1] | | | | | |
	0a	1–5b	6–10c	11–20d	21+e	Total
Wealth by group (£)						
Total wealth	64,559	178,320	179,240	279,521	1,718,263	2,419,903
	(3%)	(7%)	(7%)	(12%)	(71%)	(100%)
Average wealth	935	1,682	2,716	4,904	18,279	
Average wealth of non-timepiece owners	942	1,197	2,283	4,560	12,145	
Average wealth of timepiece owners	917	3,032	3,473	5,494	22,261	
Ownership by group						
% owning timepieces	27.5	26	36	37	61	38
As % of all groups	13	19	16	14	38	100
Total cost of timepieces	424	635	769	729	2,329	4,886
Average cost of timepieces	22	23	32	35	41	
% of timepiece owners' wealth devoted to timepiece ownership	2.4	0.7	0.9	0.6	0.2	

Source: Compiled from Charleston District Inventories, 1763–67, vol. W, SCDAH.

Note: Base data: n = 392; % of timepiece owners of n = 38; % of slaveholders who are timepiece owners = 33.

[1]a: n = 69 (18%); b: n = 106 (27%); c: n = 66 (17%); d: n = 57 (14%); e: n = 94 (24%).

Table A.13. Wealth Levels and Timepiece Ownership among Slaveholders and Nonslaveholders, Charleston District, 1783–1787

	Number of Slaves Owned[1]					
	0a	1–5b	6–10c	11–20d	21+e	Total
Wealth by group (£)						
Total wealth	68,531	106,339	109,302	141,452	3,235,487	3,661,111
	(2%)	(3%)	(3%)	(4%)	(88%)	(100%)
Average wealth	1,038	714	1,438	1,790	23,277	
Average wealth of non-timepiece owners	1,608	937	683	1,917	5,756	
Average wealth of timepiece owners	265	245	3,775	1,481	44,413	
Ownership by group						
% owning timepieces	42	32	26	29	45	36
As % of all groups	15	26.5	10.5	13	35	100
Total cost of timepieces	76	275	239	217	1,227	2,034
Average cost of timepieces	3	6	13	9	19	
% of timepiece owners' wealth devoted to timepiece ownership	1.0	2.3	0.3	0.6	0.04	

Source: Compiled from Charleston District Inventories, 1783–87, vol. A, SCDAH.
Note: Base data: n = 509; % of timepiece owners of n = 36; % of slaveholders who are timepiece owners = 34.
[1]a: n = 66 (13%); b: n = 149 (29%); c: n = 76 (15%); d: n = 79 (15.5%); e: n = 39 (27.5%).

Table A.14. Wealth Levels and Timepiece Ownership among Slaveholders and Nonslaveholders, Charleston District, 1805–1810

	Number of Slaves Owned[1]					
	0a	1–5b	6–10c	11–20d	21+e	Total
Wealth by group ($)						
Total wealth	81,876	167,008	275,414	168,059	1,494,237	2,186,594
	(4%)	(8%)	(12%)	(8%)	(68%)	(100%)
Average wealth	635	1,606	4,832	4,668	21,974	
Average wealth of non-timepiece owners	457	1,556	3,210	4,383	23,780	
Average wealth of timepiece owners	804	1,679	6,511	5,067	20,461	
Ownership by group						
% owning timepieces	51	40	49	42	54	48
As % of all groups	35	22	15	8	20	100
Total cost of timepieces	1,761	1,192	916	460	1,356	5,685
Average cost of timepieces	27	28	33	31	37	
% of timepiece owners' wealth devoted to timepiece ownership	3.3	1.7	0.5	0.6	0.2	

Source: Compiled from Charleston District Inventories, 1805–10, vol. D, 1800–1810, pp. 313–536, SCDAH.

Note: Base data: n = 394; % of timepiece owners of n = 48; % of slaveholders who are timepiece owners = 46.

[1]a: n = 129 (33%); b: n = 104 (26%); c: n = 57 (15%); d: n = 36 (9%); e: n = 68 (17%).

Table A.15. Wealth Levels and Timepiece Ownership among Slaveholders and Nonslaveholders, Charleston District, 1839–1844

	Number of Slaves Owned[1]					
	0a	1–5b	6–10c	11–20d	21+e	Total
Wealth by group ($)						
Total wealth	26,137	74,635	92,346	83,032	984,326	1,260,476
	(2%)	(6%)	(8%)	(7%)	(77%)	(100%)
Average wealth	622	2,574	6,596	9,226	75,717	
Average wealth of non-timepiece owners	532	2,343	4,390	5,435	82,261	
Average wealth of timepiece owners	713	2,761	8,803	13,965	70,108	
Ownership by group						
% owning timepieces	50	55	50	44	54	51
As % of all groups	38	29	13	7	13	100
Total cost of timepieces	446	420	297	201	250	1,614
Average cost of timepieces	21	26	42	50	36	
% of timepiece owners' wealth devoted to timepiece ownership	3.0	1.0	0.5	0.4	0.05	

Source: Compiled from Charleston District Inventories, 1839–44, vol. H, pp. 371–512, SCDAH.

Note: Base data: n = 107; % of timepiece owners of n = 51; % of slaveholders who are timepiece owners = 52.

[1]a: n = 42 (39%); b: n = 29 (27%); c: n = 14 (13%); d: n = 9 (8%); e: n = 3 (13%).

Table A.16. Wealth Levels and Timepiece Ownership among Slaveholders and
Nonslaveholders, Charleston District, 1863–December 31, 1865

	Number of Slaves Owned[1]					
	0a	1–5b	6–10c	11–20d	21+e	Total
Wealth by group ($)						
Total wealth	92,846	59,563	53,968	7,178	39,186	252,741
	(37%)	(24%)	(21%)	(3%)	(15%)	(100%)
Average wealth	2,211	9,927	17,989	3,589	13,062	
Average wealth of non-timepiece owners	1,721	10,972	4,884	3,183	15,300	
Average wealth of timepiece owners	2,430	4,703	24,542	3,995	11,943	
Ownership by group						
% owning timepieces	69	17	67	50	67	63
As % of all groups	82	3	6	3	6	100
Total cost of timepieces	842	48	150	1	130	1,171
Average cost of timepieces	29	48	75	1	43	
% of timepiece owners' wealth devoted to timepiece ownership	1.2	1.0	0.3	0.02	0.5	

Source: Compiled from Charleston District Inventories, Appraisements, and Sales, 1863–67
(1863–December 31, 1865), vol. G, SCDAH.
Note: Base data: n = 56; % of timepiece owners of n = 66; % of slaveholders who are
timepiece owners = 43.
[1]a: n = 42 (75%); b: n = 6 (11%); c: n = 3 (5%); d: n = 2 (4%); e: n = 3 (5%).

Table A.17. Wealth Levels and Timepiece Ownership, Charleston District, January 1, 1866–1867

	Wealth Cohort ($)[1]					
	0–500a	501–2,000b	2,001–5,000c	5,001–10,000d	10,000+e	Total
Wealth by group ($)						
Total wealth	10,415	45,009	38,210	40,216	208,798	342,648
	(3%)	(13%)	(11%)	(12%)	(61%)	(100%)
Average wealth	289	1,000	3,474	6,703	29,828	
Average wealth of non-timepiece owners	262	948	2,966	7,108	24,272	
Average wealth of timepiece owners	306	1,054	3,664	6,297	37,236	
Ownership by group						
% owning timepieces	61	49	73	50	43	55
As % of all groups	38	38	14	5	5	100
Total cost of timepieces	893	1,341	313	154	263	2,964
Average cost of timepieces	41	61	39	51	88	
% of timepiece owners' wealth devoted to timepiece ownership	13.25	6	1.1	0.8	0.2	

Source: Compiled from Charleston District Inventories, Appraisements, and Sales, 1863–67 (January 1, 1866–67), vol. G, SCDAH.
Note: Base data: n = 105; % of timepiece owners of n = 55.
[1]a: n = 36 (34%); b: n = 45 (43%); c: n = 11 (10%); d: n = 6 (6%); e: n = 7 (7%).

Table A.18. Wealth Levels and Timepiece Ownership, Charleston District, 1883–1886

	Wealth Cohort ($)[1]					
	0–500a	501–2,000b	2,001–5,000c	5,001–10,000d	10,000+e	Total
Wealth by group ($)						
Total wealth	5,176	5,475	13,116	6,265	11,175	41,207
	(13%)	(13%)	(32%)	(15%)	(27%)	(100%)
Average wealth	157	1,095	3,279	6,265	11,175	
Average wealth of non-timepiece owners	87	0	4,209	6,265	0	
Average wealth of timepiece owners	187	1,095	2,969	0	11,175	
Ownership by group						
% owning timepieces	70	100	75	0	100	73
As % of all groups	72	16	9	0	3	100
Total cost of timepieces	242	133	83	0	5	463
Average cost of timepieces	10.5	27	28	0	5	
% of timepiece owners' wealth devoted to timepiece ownership	6.0	2.4	0.9	0	0.04	

Source: Compiled from Charleston District Estate Files, microfilm rolls PR-EF 053-PR-EF 057, Charleston County Courthouse, Probate Office, North Charleston, S.C.
Note: Base data: n = 44; % of timepiece owners of n = 73.
[1]a: n = 33 (75%); b: n = 5 (12%); c: n = 4 (9%); d: n = 1 (2%); e: n = 1 (2%).

Table A.19. Wealth Levels and Timepiece Ownership among Slaveholders and Nonslaveholders, Laurens County, South Carolina, 1788–1796

	Number of Slaves Owned[1]					
	0a	1–5b	6–10c	11–20d	21+e	Total
Wealth by group (£)						
Total wealth	3,467	3,901	1,124	618	22,185	31,295
	(11%)	(12%)	(4%)	(2%)	(71%)	(100%)
Average wealth	87	217	562	618	22,185	
Average wealth of non-timepiece owners	87	226	624	309	22,185	
Average wealth of timepiece owners	84	139	500	0	0	
Ownership by group						
% owning timepieces	7.5	11	50	0	0	10
As % of all groups	50	33	17	0	0	100
Total cost of timepieces	5	2	0.5	0	0	7.5
Average cost of timepieces	1.6	0.8	0.5	0	0	
% of timepiece owners' wealth devoted to timepiece ownership	1.9	0.6	0.1	0	0	

Source: Compiled from Laurens County Appraisals and Inventories, WPA Typescript, book no. 597, 1788–1802 (1788–96), SCDAH.

Note: Base data: n = 62; % of timepiece owners of n = 10; % of slaveholders who are timepiece owners = 5.

[1]a: n = 40 (64%); b: n = 18 (29%); c: n = 2 (3%); d: n = 1 (2%); e: n = 1 (2%).

Table A.20. Wealth Levels and Timepiece Ownership among Slaveholders and Nonslaveholders, Laurens County, South Carolina, 1805–1809

	Number of Slaves Owned[1]					
	0a	1–5b	6–10c	11–20d	21+e	Total
Wealth by group ($)						
Total wealth	13,096	39,282	21,481	7,062	—	80,921
	(16%)	(48.5%)	(26.5%)	(9%)		(100%)
Average wealth	327	1,571	3,069	7,062	—	
Average wealth of non-timepiece owners	313	1,487	3,138	7,062	—	
Average wealth of timepiece owners	428	2,013	2,655	0	—	
Ownership by group						
% owning timepieces	12.5	16	14	0	—	14
As % of all groups	50	40	10	0	—	100
Total cost of timepieces	40	67	20	0	—	127
Average cost of timepieces	8	17	20	0	—	
% of timepiece owners' wealth devoted to timepiece ownership	0.4	0.8	0.7	0	—	

Source: Compiled from Laurens County, Inventories and Appraisements, 1802–9 (1805–9), WPA Typescript, book no. 598, SCDAH.
Note: Base data: n = 73; % of timepiece owners of n = 14; % of slaveholders who are timepiece owners = 15.
[1]a: n = 40 (55%); b: n = 25 (34%); c: n = 7 (10%); d: n = 1 (1%); e: n = 0 (0%).

Table A.21. Wealth Levels and Timepiece Ownership among Slaveholders and Nonslaveholders, Laurens County, South Carolina, 1839–1843

	Number of Slaves Owned[1]					
	0a	1–5b	6–10c	11–20d	21+e	Total
Wealth by group ($)						
Total wealth	16,018	42,989	107,830	205,378	186,693	558,908
	(3%)	(8%)	(19%)	(37%)	(33%)	(100%)
Average wealth	400	1,264	5,675	12,081	16,972	
Average wealth of non-timepiece owners	308	1,844	3,515	8,529	11,122	
Average wealth of timepiece owners	539	987	5,795	12,842	17,557	
Ownership by group						
% owning timepieces	40	68	95	82	91	67
As % of all groups	20	28	22	17	13	100
Total cost of timepieces	118	445	299	142	582	1,586
Average cost of timepieces	7	19	17	10	58	
% of timepiece owners' wealth devoted to timepiece ownership	1.4	1.9	0.3	0.1	0.3	

Source: Compiled from Laurens County, Inventories, Appraisements, and Sales, 1837–39, 1840–43 (1839–43), SCDAH.

Note: Base data: n = 121; % of timepiece owners of n = 67; % of slaveholders who are timepiece owners = 80.

[1]a: n = 40 (33%); b: n = 34 (28%); c: n = 19 (16%); d: n = 17 (14%); e: n = 11 (9%).

Table A.22. Wealth Levels and Timepiece Ownership among Slaveholders and Nonslaveholders, Laurens County, South Carolina, 1863–December 31, 1865

	Number of Slaves Owned[1]					
	0a	1–5b	6–10c	11–20d	21+e	Total
Wealth by group ($)						
Total wealth	127,705	227,889	139,444	214,718	411,718	1,121,474
	(11%)	(20%)	(12%)	(19%)	(38%)	(100%)
Average wealth	1,616	8,440	17,430	30,674	102,929	
Average wealth of non-timepiece owners	1,661	9,882	21,858	50,351	123,747	
Average wealth of timepiece owners	1,596	8,028	15,955	22,811	95,990	
Ownership by group						
% owning timepieces	68	78	75	71	75	71
As % of all groups	61	23	7	6	3	100
Total cost of timepieces	1,439	2,062	122	134	1,342	5,099
Average cost of timepieces	27	98	20	27	447	
% of timepiece owners' wealth devoted to timepiece ownership	1.7	1.2	0.1	0.1	0.5	

Source: Compiled from Laurens County, Inventories, Appraisements, and Sales, 1862–68 (1863–December 31, 1865), SCDAH.

Note: Base data: n = 125; % of timepiece owners of n = 71; % of slaveholders who are timepiece owners = 76.

[1]a: n = 79 (63%); b: n = 27 (22%); c: n = 8 (6%); d: n = 7 (6%); e: n = 4 (3%).

Table A.23. Wealth Levels and Timepiece Ownership, Laurens County, South Carolina, January 1, 1866–December 31, 1867

	Wealth cohort ($)[1]					
	0–500a	501–2,000b	2,001–5,000c	5,001–10,000d	10,000+e	Total
Wealth by group ($)						
Total wealth	6,184	21,763	23,921	5,020	68,497	125,385
	(5%)	(17%)	(19%)	(4%)	(55%)	(100%)
Average wealth	213	946	2,990	5,020	22,832	
Average wealth of non-timepiece owners	148	532	4,418	0	10,254	
Average wealth of timepiece owners	251	986	2,786	5,020	29,121	
Ownership by group						
% owning timepieces	62	91	87	100	67	76
As % of all groups	37	43	14	2	4	100
Total cost of timepieces	114	220	59	20	162	575
Average cost of timepieces	6	10	8	20	81	
% of timepiece owners' wealth devoted to timepiece ownership	2.5	1.0	0.3	0.4	0.3	

Source: Compiled from Laurens County, Inventories, Appraisements, and Sales, 1862–68 (January 1, 1866–67), SCDAH.

Note: Base data: n = 64; % of timepiece owners of n = 76.

[1]a: n = 29 (45%); b: n = 23 (36%); c: n = 8 (12%); d: n = 1 (2%); e: n = 3 (5%).

Table A.24. Wealth Levels and Timepiece Ownership, Laurens County, South Carolina, 1880–1889

	Wealth Cohort ($)[1]					
	0–500a	501–2,000b	2,001–5,000c	5,001–10,000d	10,000+e	Total
Wealth by group						
Total wealth	5,369	13,337	11,374	10,020	—	40,100
	(13%)	(33%)	(28%)	(26%)		(100%)
Average wealth	244	953	2,843	5,010	—	
Average wealth of non-timepiece owners	153	1,149	2,513	0	—	
Average wealth of timepiece owners	258	874	2,954	5,010	—	
Ownership by group						
% owning timepieces	86	71	75	100	—	83
As % of all groups	54	29	11	6	—	100
Total cost of timepieces	133	25	52	57	—	267
Average cost of timepieces	7	2.5	17	28.5	—	
% of timepiece owners' wealth devoted to timepiece ownership	2.7	0.3	0.6	0.6	—	

Source: Compiled from Laurens County, Inventories, Appraisements, and Sales, 1875–89 (1880–89, pp. 391–509), SCDAH.
Note: Base data: n = 42; % of timepiece owners of n = 83.
[1]a: n = 22 (52%); b: n = 14 (33%); c: n = 4 (10%); d: n = 2 (5%); e: n = 0 (0%).

Table A.25. Clock and Watch Ownership and Average Values of Both in Charleston District, 1866–1886, and Laurens County, South Carolina, 1866–1889

	Type of Timepiece Owned (%)			Average Values ($)	
	Watch(es) Only	Clock(s) Only	Clock(s) and Watch(es)	Ws	Cs
Charleston					
1866–67	42	51	7	88	24
1883–86	35	59	6	36	4
Laurens					
1866–67	2	92	6	15	12
1880–89	15	73	12	14	7

Source: Compiled from Charleston District Inventories, 1866–67, and Laurens County Appraisals and Inventories, 1866–89, SCDAH; Charleston District Estate Files, 1883–86, Charleston County Courthouse, Probate Office, North Charleston, S.C.

Note: All values derived from the assessor's estimate of the timepiece's monetary worth at the time of death of the owner.

NOTES

ABBREVIATIONS

Am. Sl.   *The American Slave: A Composite Autobiography*. Edited by George P. Rawick, 1st and 2d series, 19 vols., continuously numbered (Westport, Conn.: Greenwood Press, 1972); 1st supplement series, 12 vols. (Westport, Conn.: Greenwood Press, 1977); 2d supplement series, 10 vols. (Westport, Conn.: Greenwood Press, 1979).

AWD   *American Women's Diaries (Southern Women)* (New Canaan, Conn.: Readex Film Products, 1993)

DBR   *De Bow's Review*

DU   Duke University, William R. Perkins Library, Manuscript Department, Durham, N.C.

FR   *Farmers' Register*

LC   Library of Congress, Manuscript Division, Washington, D.C.

MESDA   Museum of Early Southern Decorative Arts, Research Center, Winston-Salem, N.C.

RASP   Kenneth M. Stampp, ed. *Records of Ante-Bellum Southern Plantations from the Revolution through the Civil War*. Part 1 (15 microfilm reels); series A, part 2 (26 microfilm reels); series F, part 2 (16 microfilm reels); series J, part 2 (41 microfilm reels), (Frederick and Bethesda, Md.: University Publications of America, 1985).

RB   *Rose Bud, or Youth's Gazette*

SCDAH   South Carolina Department of Archives and History, Columbia, S.C.

SCHS   South Carolina Historical Society, Charleston, S.C.

SCL   South Caroliniana Library, University of South Carolina, Columbia, S.C.

SHC   Southern Historical Collection, Manuscript Department, Wilson Library, University of North Carolina at Chapel Hill, N.C.

So. Ag.   *Southern Agriculturalist, and Register of Rural Affairs*

So. Cab.   *Southern Cabinet*

So. Cult.   *Southern Cultivator*

So. Pl.   *Southern Planter*

So. Ro.   *Southern Rose/ Southern Rosebud*

SPF   *Southern Planter and Farmer*

TF   *Tennessee Farmer*

VHS   Virginia Historical Society, Richmond, Va.

INTRODUCTION

1. Olmsted, *Cotton Kingdom*, 158, 190. The specifics of his latter observation are not without foundation. About eighty years later, former slave

Martha Spence Bunton recalled, "About twelb o'clock de men would unhitch de mules, and wait fo' us." See *Am. Sl.*, supp. ser. 2, vol. 2, Texas narrs., pt. 1, 521.

2. Thrift, "Owners' Time and Own Time," 57. On the evolution of an industrial-urban nineteenth-century time consciousness in these countries see Thompson, "Time, Work-Discipline"; Behagg, "Controlling the Product"; Gutman, "Work, Culture, and Society"; Hensley, "Time, Work, and Social Context in New England"; Davison, *Unforgiving Minute*; Atkins, *The Moon Is Dead!*; and her "'Kafir Time.'"

3. Although he does not make the comparative point, Martin Bruegel notes a rural time consciousness in the Hudson Valley after the 1830s especially. See his "'Time That Can Be Relied Upon.'" For the comparative analysis see Mark M. Smith, "Old South Time in Comparative Perspective." Whether rural British laborers remained impervious to clock time is unclear. It appears that as long as the indigenous peoples of Natal and Australia remained in their rural environment, an environment where cultural values about time dictated that they appeal to naturally defined time, they were able to resist the efforts of European colonizers to convert them to time discipline and clock-defined time. See, too, Hall, *Dance of Life*, 3–4; Atkins, *The Moon Is Dead!*, 95; Davison, *Unforgiving Minute*, 8–9, 27–31.

4. See, for example, the perceptive remarks in Adam, *Timewatch*, esp. 86–91. For an excellent review of how Karl Marx, Max Weber, Werner Sombart, Gustav Bilfinger, Lewis Mumford, Marc Bloch, and Yves Renouard, among others, have variously dealt with clock consciousness and its relationship to modernity, see Dohrn-van Rossum, *History of the Hour*, 8–15.

5. Consult esp. Le Goff, "Merchant's Time and Church's Time in the Middle Ages"; Thrift, "Owners' Time and Own Time."

6. Landes, *Revolution in Time*. See also the discussion in Rezsoházy, "Concept of Social Time," esp. 31–32.

7. See, for example, Genovese and Fox-Genovese, *Fruits of Merchant Capital*; Genovese, *Roll, Jordan, Roll*.

8. See esp., Oakes, *Ruling Race*. The main positions in the debate, at least by the mid-1970s, are usefully reviewed in Wallerstein, "American Slavery and the Capitalist World Economy." A broader and more recent review is Merrill, "Putting 'Capitalism' in Its Place."

9. This position is best stated in Fogel and Engerman, *Time on the Cross*.

10. As wonderfully argued in Genovese, *Slaveholders' Dilemma*.

11. Ibid.

12. See Nyland, "Capitalism and the History of Worktime Thought," 516. See, too, the summary by Lane, "Meanings of Capitalism." For a historian who conflates the premodern with the preclassical arguments of George Fitzhugh, for example, see Wenzel, "Pre-Modern Concepts." Genovese himself has written that "no one would argue that a strong dose of capitalism did not exist in the South. The argument turns on the proportions and their significance." A modern time consciousness was both preponderant and significant in the Old South. Quotation from Genovese, "Marxian Interpretations of the Slave South," 119. Much has been written on the relationship of slavery to capitalism. Useful theoretical statements may be found in Miles, *Capitalism and Unfree Labour*; Padgug, "Problems in the Theory of Slavery"; and, more generally, Danilova, "Controversial Problems of the Theory of Precapitalist Societies." Of the more useful attempts to characterize southern planters, one is by Shearer Davis Bowman, who, borrowing Jürgen Kocka's distinction, suggests that planters were capitalists but not modern industrial ones. With regard to clock time in the South, however, the formulation breaks down not least because industrial time and southern agricultural time were more similar than they were distinct. For further details see Bowman, *Masters and Lords*, 95–96, 100. See, too, Post, "American Road to Capitalism." In

many respects, it might be more useful to follow through with Bowman's formulation of describing various capitalisms and conceive of the Old South as embracing what I have elsewhere termed plantation capitalism. See Mark M. Smith, "Time, Slavery and Plantation Capitalism."

13. On sympathetic views of the laborer and his acquisitive nature before 1750 as well as for vestiges of mercantilist views after, see Coates, *On the History of Economic Thought*, 1:63–85, 159–85. Also useful, if not altogether in agreement with Coates, is the classic by Furniss, *Position of the Laborer*. For a detailed examination of the American context, see Crowley, *This Sheba, Self*. Thomas R. Dew and Thomas Cooper, especially, ranked among the qualified fans of Smithian political economy. The more representative views of George Fitzhugh, however, remained steadfastly opposed. See Shore, *Southern Capitalists*, esp. 24–29.

14. On incentives under slavery see, generally, Fogel and Engerman, *Time on the Cross*. More recent work by econometricians suggests that the whip was masters' preferred tool to induce labor. See Crawford, "Punishments and Rewards." For arguments that the two systems of incentive and coercion were not mutually exclusive, however, see Fogel, "Moral Aspects." I do not wish to minimize the racial aspect of southern slavery but merely aim to highlight how inextricable race and class were to southern planters. While masters often deemed blacks to be incapable of hard, independent work, they also shared the pre-Smithian conviction that all workers were slothful. I can think of no better short illustration of this than the observations of one South Carolina planter whose assessment of emancipation was typical of the general distrust of all laboring classes. In 1866 he wrote: "I determined that negroes like white people would work only from necessity." Quoted in Foner, *Nothing but Freedom*, 83, and esp. 15. Generally, consult the wise words in Fields, "Slavery, Race and Ideology."

15. Quoted in Nguyen, "Spatialization of Metric Time," 36; McKendrick, "Josiah Wedgewood and Factory Discipline."

16. Brody, "Time and Work," esp. 38–39.

17. On various discipline and incentive systems in an industrial context, see Gregory Clark, "Factory Discipline," esp. 128–37. That the northern wage fine for tardiness had its rough equivalent in the southern whip, see Mark M. Smith, "Old South Time in Comparative Perspective." For parallel developments involving race and class see the trenchant essay by Cooper, "Colonizing Time," esp. 210, 222, 229, 238–40.

18. On the shared class interests of both groups, see Lynd, "On Turner, Beard, and Slavery"; and the evidence in Sinha, "Counter-Revolution of Slavery," 421–24.

19. Quoted in Brody, "Time and Work," 14. See the discussion in Crowley, *This Sheba, Self*, esp. 83–91.

20. Northern workers did not always find the transition to wage labor palatable. For many, it seemed to encroach on their freedom. On this, much has been written, but see, especially, Wilentz, *Chants Democratic*.

21. Generally, see Thompson, "Time, Work-Discipline"; and Brody, "Time and Work," esp. 43–46.

22. Quotations from Thompson, "Time, Work-Discipline," 86. Edmund Ruffin of Virginia seemed to suggest that slaves were best spared the responsibility of wage negotiations lest they slip into the moral degradation that he thought accompanied such discussions. See Shore, *Southern Capitalists*, esp. 17–21.

23. Thompson, *Making of the English Working Class*, esp. 8–14.

24. Genovese, *Roll, Jordan, Roll*, 286, 309, 729. He quotes two pieces of slave testimony and very little supporting evidence to justify this rather sweeping conclusion. Of course, any summary of Genovese's rich and complex work risks oversimplification, and one is best off consulting Genovese himself rather than his interpreters. Recommended in this context are

his "Marxian Interpretations of the Slave South"; *Political Economy of Slavery*; and with Fox-Genovese, *Fruits of Merchant Capital*. The South-as-precapitalist argument is stated most forcefully in Luraghi, *Rise and Fall of the Plantation South*. Among those historians stressing the capitalist, modern nature of the slave South, the position is stated most clearly by Fogel and Engerman, *Time on the Cross*, esp. 1:202–9, and Oakes, *Ruling Race*. The classic statement is by Elkins, *Slavery*, esp. 37–80. On the notion that white southerners lack a disciplined understanding of, and commitment to, time see Bertelson, *Lazy South*. These issues are discussed briefly in Kolchin, *American Slavery*, 106–7. Historians who have examined southern time sensibilities in some detail have done so for the colonial period only where they correctly discern a natural time awareness among black and white southerners. See Sobel, *World They Made Together*, 15–64; Isaac, *Transformation of Virginia*, 77–78, 84–85; and, more comparatively, Fischer, *Albion's Seed*, 158–66, 368–73, 560–66, 743–47.

25. American historians have usually focused on northern timekeeping practices. See O'Malley, *Keeping Watch*; Roediger and Foner, *Our Own Time*, esp. xi; Hensley, "Time, Work, and Social Context in New England"; Bruegel, " 'Time That Can Be Relied Upon.' " On the burgeoning scholarship for the study of time and time consciousness for other countries, see, for example, Cross, *Quest for Time*; Cross, *Time and Money*; Davison, *Unforgiving Minute*; Atkins, *The Moon Is Dead!*; Mark M. Smith, "Old South Time in Comparative Perspective." For a historian who sensibly sees the evolution of clock consciousness in Europe as best measured in degrees over a period stretching from the Middle Ages to the nineteenth century, see Dohrn-van Rossum, *History of the Hour*, esp. 271.

26. Genovese, *Roll, Jordan, Roll*, 291.

27. Ibid., 286.

28. Ibid., 297, 308.

29. On the essay's enormous influence in American historiography, see O'Malley, "Time, Work and Task Orientation"; Gutman, "Work, Culture, and Society"; Prude, *Coming of Industrial Order*. Genovese's indebtedness to Thompson's essay is obvious. See his *Roll, Jordan, Roll*, 289–94, 729, n. 15. Sobel also relies on Genovese and Thompson. See *World They Made Together*, 250, n. 3, 251, nn. 20, 22, 26. For a thoughtful critique of Thompson's essay and its limitations as applied to Tokugawa Japan, see Thomas C. Smith, "Peasant Time and Factory Time in Japan." Also in this context see Mark M. Smith, "Time, Slavery and Plantation Capitalism." For the northern situation see Roediger and Foner, "Time, Republicanism, and Merchant Capitalism"; Paul E. Johnson, *Shopkeepers' Millennium*, esp. 42; Hensley, "Time, Work, and Social Context in New England," esp. 531–33.

30. Thompson, "Time, Work-Discipline," 57.

31. Genovese, *Roll, Jordan, Roll*, 291–92. See Thompson, "Time, Work-Discipline"; Cross, *Quest for Time*, 2. The most convincing statements about southerners' lack of a Protestant-inspired work ethic and their aversion to Puritanism are by Woodward, "The Southern Ethic in a Puritan World," and Peacock, "The Southern Protestant Ethic Disease." For a different interpretation, see Edmund S. Morgan, "The Puritan Ethic and the American Revolution."

32. Booth, "Economies of Time," esp. 9; Dohrn-van Rossum, *History of the Hour*, 7–8.

33. Booth, "Economies of Time," 19–20; Schwartz, "Labor, Politics, and Time in the Thought of Karl Marx," esp. 130–37. Regarding the relationship between clock time and capitalism see Adam, *Timewatch*, chap. 4. On the decline of the clock's hegemony under postmodernity, see Paolucci, "Changing Dynamics of Working Time."

34. Sobel, *World They Made Together*, 1–52; Isaac, *Transformation of Virginia*, 77–78, 84–85; Breen, "Of Time and Nature."

35. O'Malley, "Time, Work and Task Orientation." See also O'Malley, *Keeping Watch*, 1–54. Indeed, many modern industries, though capitalist, necessarily rely on natural and seasonal time. The construction and oil industries are cases in point. For work that stresses

this interdependency of seasonal time and capitalism, see Gareth Stedman Jones, *Outcast London*, 33–51; Cooper, "Colonizing Time," esp. 220.

36. Richard D. Brown, *Modernization*, 33. For a more nuanced account consult Hensley, "Time, Work, and Social Context in New England," esp. 531–39.

37. See, for example, Atkins, "'Kafir Time'"; Thompson, "Time, Work-Discipline"; Roediger and Foner, *Our Own Time*, 1–18; Adam, *Timewatch*, 86–88; Hensley, "Time, Work, and Social Context in New England"; Bruegel, "'Time That Can Be Relied Upon'"; Mark M. Smith, "Old South Time in Comparative Perspective."

38. Thompson, "Time, Work-Discipline." Generally see Pollard, "Factory Discipline in the Industrial Revolution"; Keith Thomas, "Work and Leisure"; Rodgers, *Work Ethic in Industrial America*. See also Bowman, *Masters and Lords*, 95.

39. Thompson, "Time, Work-Discipline," 61, 66–70; Thrift, "Owners' Time and Own Time."

40. See Mayr and Stephens, *American Clocks*, 3–5; Rifkin, *Time Wars*, 86–87, 173–79; Neustadter, "Beat the Clock." One must judge Norman Mailer's assessment a little one-sided. Writes Mailer: "With the clock, certain kinds of time have to be measured in numbers so great that man is run off the stage" ("Political Economy of Time," 321).

41. Lukács, *History and Class Consciousness*, 89–90. Similarly, Daniel Defoe said that the English were the most "diligent lazy" people on earth. See Landes, "Debate," 196. Masters' clock-regulated pursuit of the good life, it seems, has all too often been misconstrued as testimony to their supposed laziness.

42. See Jordan, *White over Black*; Marx, *Capital*, 944, 76, 1027–28; Current, *Northernizing the South*, 15, 35; Barrington Moore, "The American Civil War," esp. 114–17.

43. David S. Landes argues that the watch facilitated time discipline while the clock was limited to making individuals obedient to time. For, as he says, "Punctuality comes from within, not from without." See *Revolution in Time*, 7. Quotation from Schafer, *Tuning of the World*, 56. Also useful is Leppert, *Sight of Sound*, 19–23. For extensive evidence pointing to clock consciousness, timed labor, and public time obedience during the medieval and early modern periods, see Dohrn-van Rossum, *History of the Hour*.

44. The epistemological premise of this study has been influenced by the arguments propounded by Norbert Elias's book, *Time*. It begins from the premise that time is first and foremost a social and historical construct. That is, time, as conceived here, is not an a priori of human nature, nor is it an immanent force independent of human interaction—as the natural sciences conceive of it. Rather, the historical study of social, cultural, and economic time makes sense only if we conceive of it as a product of human creation, both real and symbolic. How men and women use time, how they evaluate it, and to what ends and in which forms they apply and appreciate it is the only historically verifiable way of understanding time. This study, then, is as much an intellectual history of the southern time consciousness as it is about how this consciousness in turn was allied, at the everyday level of interaction, to the gritty reality of the South's social and economic relations. Given this emphasis, and because time in all its forms suffuses everyday life in myriad ways, this study does not pretend to be catholic. Much more research needs to be carried out on, for example, the increasing clock consciousness in colonial and antebellum sports (horse racing, in particular) and on Native Americans' time consciousness, to name but two areas of many. For leads on the latter subject, see Mark M. Smith, "Old South Time in Comparative Perspective," 1468–69.

45. Bruegel, "'Time That Can Be Relied Upon.'" That rural Britain, Australia, and South Africa did not develop a clock consciousness, see Mark M. Smith, "Old South Time in Comparative Perspective."

46. See Oakes, *Ruling Race*, and his *Slavery and Freedom*.

1. Freehling, *Road to Disunion*, 1:25–26; Herskovits, *Myth of the Negro Past*, 153; Joyner, *Down by the Riverside*, 43–45; Blassingame, *Slave Community*, 250–51; Genovese, *Political Economy of Slavery*, 48–54; Stampp, *Peculiar Institution*, 44–46.

2. Fogel, *Without Consent or Contract*, 78–79; Fogel and Engerman, *Time on the Cross*, 1:202–9; Oakes, *Ruling Race*.

3. Generally see Burlingame, "Technology as Cause in History." On the watchmaker as harbinger of the modern age, see Mitman, "Watchmakers and Inventors."

4. This chapter draws from Mark M. Smith, "Counting Clocks, Owning Time." On recent interest in this topic see O'Malley, *Keeping Watch*, and Shackel, *Personal Discipline*. According to an unpublished study by Margaret Bohn Alexander ("'Apprize the People of the Time': Clocks and Watches in Preindustrial America") there were thirty thousand clocks and forty-two thousand watches in the entire United States by the Revolution. This is noted in Roediger and Foner, *Our Own Time*, 282, n. 12. See, too, the discussion of extensive watch ownership in antebellum New York in Stott, *Workers in the Metropolis*, 175. The most thorough research on clock and watch ownership in the antebellum North based on an analysis of 198 probate inventories is by Bruegel, "'Time That Can Be Relied Upon,'" esp. 551. On task orientation versus time discipline see O'Malley's trenchant analysis of recent literature, "Time, Work and Task Orientation." See also Hindle and Lubar, *Engines of Change*, 219–21.

5. On public clocks in American history generally see Mayr and Stephens, *American Clocks*, 4–5.

6. "First Things in the United States," *Southern Christian Advocate* 68 (Aug. 11, 1904): 12.

7. Hitt, *Some Colonial Churches*, 2–4, 37–38, 65, 70, 75. Estimate compiled from the pen and ink drawings in Hazel Crowson Sellers, *Old South Carolina Churches*.

8. Typescript by Dr. Arthur L. Rawlings, p. 4, Folger Collection, 1953, LC; "A Famous Old Clock," *Rock Hill [S.C.] Herald*, Mar. 17, 1894, 1.

9. Jacoby, *Churches of Charleston and the Lowcountry*, 27. See newspaper clipping in Colhoun Papers, ser. 4, in *RASP*, ser. J, SHC, pt. 3, r. 29, fr. 582; "Public Improvements of Charleston—Part 2," *DBR* 7 (Nov. 1849): 401.

10. See Fouché, "St. Philip's Episcopal Church," 1–29, 43, 49, 56–58, 66, 78–79. A picture of the church from the *Gentleman's Magazine* may be found in Marion B. Smith, "South Carolina and *The Gentleman's Magazine*," 111, and in Hooker, *Carolina Backcountry*, 70.

11. MESDA file, "Architecture, South Carolina, Charleston, Independent Congregational Church construction, 1777–1806."

12. See Estill Curtis Pennington, *Look Away*, 157; Bilodeau and Tobias, *Art in South Carolina*, 177.

13. See, for example, Sidney Thomas, *Historical Account of the Protestant Episcopal Church*, 805.

14. See the photographic evidence in Julien and Hollis, *Look to the Rock*, 17, 30, 75, 77, 84, 93, 105, 107.

15. The First Scots Presbyterian of Charleston donated its bells for Confederate cannon in 1862, as did the Holy City's St. John's Lutheran. Estimates compiled from Bolick, *Laurens County Sketchbook*; [Laurens County Historical Society], *Scrapbook*; Jacoby, *Churches of Charleston and the Lowcountry*, 39, 49.

16. MESDA file, "Sundial," 1709, "Goldsmith Chandlee"; advertisement for a sundial in *So. Cult.* 18 (June 1860): [109]; MESDA file, "Sundial," 1858. Although an equatorial sundial can be used at any latitude, the more common horizontal one cannot. As one authority puts it: "If a sundial is to tell the time accurately it must ordinarily be designed for the particular latitude in which it is to be used." The relative scarcity of sundials in probate inventories

may be partly explained by the widespread use of noon marks in farmhouses. These marks were handmade (marks to which the modern eye is often oblivious) and scored into wooden floors and porches. See Waugh, *Sundials*, 18, 29, 35, 37.

17. MESDA file, *Charleston Courier*, July 12, 1806, 3.

18. Compiled from Scrapbook, 1942, compiled for the Pocahontas and Chanco chapters by May Adelia Jones, Daughters of the American Colonists, Virginia, Pocahontas Chapter, bd. vol. of newspaper clippings, VHS; Adams, *Courthouses in Virginia Counties*.

19. MESDA file, "Clock Movements, British."

20. Charles Dimmock, Superintendent of Public Buildings, Richmond, Virginia, to Joseph Johnson, Governor of Virginia, Mar. 11, 1852, Robinson Family Papers, sec. 23, p. 1, VHS.

21. For a different interpretation, see Rogers, "Changes in Taste in the Eighteenth Century." But also see Pease, "A Note on Patterns of Conspicuous Consumption among Seaboard Planters." Some interesting ideas on this subject are in Bruegel, " 'Time That Can Be Relied Upon,' " although I suspect that his distinction between the social value of timepieces and the need for accurate clocks and watches is too rigid. See also Pessen, "How Different from Each Other Were the Antebellum North and South?," esp. 1135.

22. Quotation from Cowan, *Time and Its Measurement*, 76. For examples of the clock as a mechanical curiosity during the Middle Ages, see Aveni, *Empires of Time*; Landes, *Revolution in Time*. On the colonial and antebellum clock and watch as precision instruments, see N. Hudson Moore, *Old Clock Book*; Hoke, *Ingenious Yankees*. On the duality of aluminum watches in the late nineteenth century, see "Aluminum Watches," *Rock Hill [S.C.] Herald*, Aug. 15, 1894, 4.

23. See *South Carolina Gazette*, Feb. 22, Aug. 10, 1752. On the value colonial Americans placed on European culture, see Bushman, "American High-Style and Vernacular Cultures."

24. Thomas Slater, London, to John Ball Sr., Charleston, Mar. 30, 1812, John Ball Sr. and John Ball Jr. Papers, in *RASP*, ser. F, DU, pt. 2: S.C. and Ga., r. 2, fr. 573, p. 2.

25. *South Carolina Gazette*, Jan. 21, June 4, Nov. 5, 1772.

26. Alexander Hamilton to Robert Morris, Albany, N.Y., Oct. 5, 1782, in Catanzariti and Ferguson, *Papers of Robert Morris*, 6:505; John Rhea of Tennessee, to his constituents, Washington, D.C., Feb. 27, 1815, in Cunningham, *Circular Letters of Congressmen*, 2:923.

27. *South Carolina City Gazette*, Aug. 21, Sept. 13, 1806, Feb. 9, Mar. 20, 1820, May 12, 1832.

28. Cowan, *Time and Its Measurement*, 82–85; Chamberlain, *It's about Time*, 19–241.

29. See, for example, John Tobler's *South Carolina Almanac for 1756* (n.p.), 2.

30. *South Carolina Gazette*, June 6, 1743.

31. *South Carolina Gazette*, Jan. 10, Apr. 20, Aug. 10, 1752.

32. *South Carolina Gazette*, Jan. 9–16, 23–30, June 12–19, 1762.

33. Farish, *Journal and Letters of Philip Vickers Fithian*, 84; William Ancrum to Parker Quinn, Mar. 10, 1777, Ancrum Letterbook, SCL.

34. [Advertisement by Robbins & Appleton of New York], "The Watch Question. American vs. Foreign Watches," *DBR* 27 (Oct. 1859): n.p. See also *South Carolina Gazette*, May 12, June 11, 1832; [Advertisement], "Watches," *DBR* 12 (June 1852): 3; N. P. Willis, "Visit to the Watch Factory of the American Watch Company," *So. Pl.* 20 (July 1860): 415–16.

35. *South Carolina Gazette*, Jan. 24, 31, 1743.

36. Account Book, Aug. 20–Oct. 24, July 30, 1864, Aug. 20–Oct. 24, 1770, Chatham Co., Ga., William Gibbons and Joseph Gibbons corresp., Gibbons Papers, in *RASP*, DU, ser. F, pt. 2, r. 1, fr. 189, 470.

37. Josiah Smith, Charleston, S.C., to James Poyas, London, Oct. 4, 1774, Josiah Smith Jr. Letter Book, in *RASP*, ser. J, SHC, pt. 3, r. 10, fr. 304, p. 274.

38. John Ball Sr. Account Book, June 27, 1796, John Ball Sr. and John Ball Jr. Papers, Charleston District, in *RASP*, ser. F, DU, pt. 2, r. 2, fr. 54.

39. MESDA file, *Republican Advocate*, Aug. 5, 1803, 3.

40. Barentine Ledger, Dec. 18, 1852, p. 111, uncertain provenance records, Marlboro Co., S.C., SCDAH. Similarly see Allen and Johnston (Charleston Factors), Journal, July 1835, p. 72, uncertain provenance records, Charleston District, S.C., SCDAH.

41. John Rodgers, General Merchant, Account Book, March 27, Apr. 3, 18, 26, May 21, Aug. 29, Dec. 1, 24, 1817, uncertain provenance records (contained in Master Sales Book, 1823–34), Union Co., S.C., SCDAH.

42. G. D. Smith General Store Ledger, pp. 1–440, uncertain provenance records, Newberry Co., S.C., SCDAH. See also Atherton, *Southern Country Store*, 34–67.

43. Eppes Diary, Dec. 6, 1851, VHS. See Dusinberre, *Them Dark Days*, 25.

44. Wright, *Hawkers and Walkers*, 77–85, 58; Train, *Story of Everyday Things*, 158–59; *Rock Hill [S.C.] Herald*, Feb. 16, 1882, 3. See also Jaffee, "Peddlers of Progress."

45. MESDA file, *Raleigh Minerva*, Feb. 3, 1815, n.p. For similar taxes elsewhere see the *Richmond Enquirer*, Dec. 24, 1814, 3; the Charles Town, West Virginia, *Farmers' Repository*, Jan. 5, 1815, 2, 3; Norfolk, Virginia's *American Beacon and Commercial Diary*, Feb. 27, 1816, 2; Virginia's *Lynchburg Press*, Apr. 27, 1815, 4; and Frederick, Maryland's *Political Examiner and Public Advertiser*, Apr. 5, 1820, 2, all in MESDA files.

46. [Ed.], "United States Imports for 1845," *DBR* 1 (Mar. 1846): 281. On the British watchmaking industry, see Berg, *Age of Manufactures*, esp. 272–73. On its earlier years, see C. Octavious S. Morgan, *List of Members of the Clockmakers' Company*.

47. [Ed.], "The New Revenue, Sub-Treasury, and Ware-Housing Bills," *DBR* 2 (Sept. 1846): 195.

48. [Ed.], "United States Commerce," *DBR* 3 (Feb. 1847): 172, 175.

49. [Ed.], "Trade with Great Britain and France," *DBR* 13 (Oct. 1852): 405.

50. [Ed.], "Manufactures of United States," *DBR* 17 (Dec. 1854): 631–33; "The American Manufacture of Watch Movements"; Waldo, "Mechanical Art of American Watchmaking"; E. Howard, "American Watches and Clocks"; Townsend, *Almost Everything You Wanted to Know*, 3–63; Robert A. Howard, "Interchangeable Parts Reexamined."

51. [Ed.], "Commerce of the United States," *DBR* 20 (Apr. 1856): 436; "American Watches," *Rock Hill [S.C.] Herald*, Sept. 9, 1880, 1.

52. For an author who has taken the advertisements of clock and watch makers at their word and who does not seem to doubt that the South had its fair share of actual makers, see Gibbs, *Dixie Clockmakers*. Philip Whitney has not made this mistake. His explanation of the problem, though lengthy, deserves quoting: "Sometimes the term clockmaker means different things to different people. Technically the term means the metalworker who fabricates only the movements—the works—of a clock. . . . Often a clock repairer called himself a clockmaker, and sometimes a casemaker called himself a clockmaker. Silversmiths advertised themselves as clockmakers in local newspapers or on 'watch papers,' small round pieces of paper that they put in the watches they sold, and these have contributed to the confusion. Two Winchester [Virginia] silversmiths, for instance, advertised on their watch papers that they were 'watch and clock makers.' Yet no watch or clock made by either has been found" (Whitney, "Shenandoah Valley Clockmakers," 13–14). As jewelers well knew, "A common trick of clock makers and repairers of years ago, when the craze for antique 'Grandfather' clocks first showed itself, was to alter the names and dates of the original makers on such of these clocks as came to them. This trick has made it difficult to . . . learn the name of the real maker" (*Jewelers' Circular Weekly* quoted in *Tampa Morning Tribune*, July 28, 1901, 3). On the situation in the North and Britain, see Richard D. Brown, "Modernization and the Modern Personality," 220; Hindle and Lubar, *Engines of Change*, 219–21; Church, "Nineteenth-Century Clock Technology."

53. See, for example, Prown, Hurst, and Priddy, "Fredericksburg Clock Cases"; Jane Webb Smith, "'A Large and Elegant Assortment.'" These estimates are based on those who adver-

tised themselves in colonial and antebellum newspapers as clock and/or watch makers but who conceded that, in fact, they could only repair or clean them and are contained in the exhaustive list in the *Index of Early Southern Artists and Artisans* held at MESDA.

54. See Benjamin Barton, "Autobiography," 1837, and Benjamin Barton Letterbook, 1853–56, both in Barton Papers, VHS. The same was true of early eighteenth-century makers. The journal of Nicholas De Longuemare, 1703–11, shows that he never fabricated a timepiece. See Stoney, "Nicholas De Longuemare."

55. John D. Smith Watchmaker's Daybook, uncertain provenance records, Fairfield Co., S.C., SCDAH.

56. P. A. Gardener Watchmaker and Jeweller's Cashbook, uncertain provenance records, Spartanburg, S.C., SCDAH.

57. See, for example, Albright, *Johann Ludwig Eberhardt and His Salem Clocks.*

58. Whitney, "Shenandoah Valley Clockmakers," 14; Laura Clark, "Williams and Victor," 2.

59. [Advertisement by Wm. Steffins], *DBR* 21 (Nov. 1856): n.p.

60. *Records of the 1820 Census of Manufactures,* r. 19, record no. 7.

61. "Virginia Watch Papers."

62. MESDA files, "John Fessler," photograph numbers S-9682 a–g, S-9268.

63. MESDA files, *Richmond Enquirer,* Oct. 5, 1813, 1, photograph number S-14,936. According to Brad Rauschenberg, curator at MESDA, the practice of applying labels to foreign and northern-made clocks in the South was common and misleads many historians into thinking that the South had a thriving clock-making industry. My thanks for his help in this matter.

64. MESDA files, "John McKee," photograph numbers S-433, S-14,637.

65. Compiled from *Seventh Census of the United States: 1850*; *Manufactures of the United States in 1860*; *Ninth Census,* vol. 3. Complete data are in Appendix, Tables A.7, A.8.

66. See Appendix, Table A.10.

67. Appendix, Table A.1. See Bailey, *Two Hundred Years of American Clocks and Watches,* 73–79.

68. Appendix, Table A.9. In 1849 Charleston made a belated bid to expand its flagging watch- and clock-making industry by offering Gold Medals for the best improved watch and clock at the city's Mechanics' Institute fair. See "Public Improvements in Charleston—Part 1," *DBR* 7 (Oct. 1849): 347.

69. See Appendix, Table A.2.

70. See Appendix, Table A.3.

71. MESDA file, *South Carolina Gazette, and Public Advertiser,* Jan. 26, 1785, 1.

72. Appendix, Table A.4. This is consistent with the more general findings concerning northern immigration to southern cities in 1860. See Berlin and Gutman, "Natives and Immigrants," esp. 1177–83. See also Sokoloff, "Inventive Activity in Early Industrial America."

73. Appendix, Table A.5. See Burton, *South Carolina Silversmiths*; Cutten, *Silversmiths of Virginia*; Hollan, "John Gaither, Silversmith."

74. Appendix, Table A.6.

75. Jacks's advertisement in *South Carolina Gazette,* Aug. 19, 1791. Crawford's activities are detailed in Crawford Daybook, May 8, 20, Oct. 28, 1790, SCHS.

76. Cabell Commonplace Book, June 15, 1773, VHS. See also Strodtbeck and Sussman, "Of Time, the City, and the 'One-Year Guaranty.'"

77. Hatchett Diary, Jan. 23, 1854, VHS.

78. Gould Diary, June 14, 1852, p. 31, SHC.

79. James Ritchie Sparkman Books, Birdfield Plantation Ledger, 1844–63, Georgetown District, S.C., in *RASP,* ser. J, SHC, pt. 3, r. 1, fr. 163–237, pp. 6–79; Gavin Diary, vol. 3, in *RASP,* ser. J, SHC, pt. 3, r. 11, fr. 34–66, pp. 301–32.

80. Unidentified to Mitchell King, Charleston, S.C., June 1856, King Papers, ser. 1, subser. 1.3: 1845–57, in *RASP*, ser. J, SHC, pt. 3, r. 4, fr. 27–28, pp. 1–2.

81. Grimball Diary, ser. 2, vol. 2, folder 19, June 26, 1847, in *RASP*, ser. J, SHC, pt. 3, r. 15, fr. 927, p. 23.

82. In order see Phillips, "The Slave Labor Problem in the Charleston District"; Ford, *Origins of Southern Radicalism*; Freehling, *Prelude to Civil War*; Peter H. Wood, *Black Majority*, 35–62; Coclanis, *Shadow of a Dream*, 13–27; Norrece T. Jones Jr., *Born a Child of Freedom*, 5–6.

83. Coclanis, *Shadow of a Dream*, 13–26; Ford, *Origins of Southern Radicalism*, 244–50.

84. De Bow, *Seventh Census of the United States*, 340.

85. On this point see Michael P. Johnson, "Planters and Patriarchy." In 1860, the city of Charleston had a total population of forty-one thousand, 58 percent of whom were white, 34 percent slave, and 8 percent free black. See Berlin and Gutman, "Natives and Immigrants," 1177.

86. Michael P. Johnson, "Planters and Patriarchy"; Wade, *Slavery in the Cities*, 325; Rogers, *Charleston in the Age of the Pinckneys*; Radford, "Charleston Planters in 1860."

87. Ford, *Origins of Southern Radicalism*, 44–96.

88. Klein, *Unification of a Slave State*, 256.

89. De Bow, *Seventh Census of the United States*, 340.

90. For example, see Carr and Walsh, "Inventories and the Analysis of Wealth."

91. There are some limitations to the historical use of such records. As Joyce Chaplin has noted, probate records tend "to make a population look wealthier than it actually was" because the destitute, slaves, and the very poor were rarely inventoried. Conversely, the affluent are overrepresented because people "tend to die when they are in later years, which is also when they tend to have more property than the population average." Historians have pointed to other biases inherent in such records. Yet for all their limitations, a good body of probate records provides the historian with excellent data for making comparisons over time and place, for glimpsing what ordinary people chose or could afford to purchase, and for hinting at some of the cultural assumptions undergirding the socioeconomic system of which they were a part. See Chaplin, *Anxious Pursuit*, 367–68; Main, "Probate Records as a Source for Early American History," esp. 96; Carr and Walsh, "Inventories and the Analysis of Wealth," 81–104; Leone, "Georgian Order."

92. The following analysis is based on a sample of 2,005 probate inventories for Charleston District, 1739–1865, and Laurens County, 1788–1865. The Charleston records cover a longer period because the district was settled earlier. Also the Charleston inventories were generally better recorded (it was the seat of government for South Carolina until 1808; see Wallace, *South Carolina*, 358–59) and they are more numerous, a reflection of the district's denser, quasi-urban population. The number of clocks and/or watches in each inventory list was counted for three- to five- (on one occasion for thirteen-) year blocks, depending on the number of separate inventories recorded, at roughly twenty-year intervals. The erratic nature of the records prevented the devising of more equal cohorts. All tables are based on probate inventory records for Charleston District, 1739–1865, and Laurens County, 1783–1865, SCDAH. All figures are rounded to the nearest whole number. Consult Appendix, Tables A.11–A.25, for the statistical breakdown of the data.

93. All percentages refer to percentage *point gains* as opposed to percent increases.

94. Burton, *South Carolina Silversmiths*, xx.

95. Manigault Letterbook, Apr. 18, 1767, p. 50, SCHS; Henry Laurens, Charleston, to James Habersham, Sept. 5, 1767, in Rogers and Chesnutt, *Papers of Henry Laurens*, 5:293.

96. See Abbott, *Watch Factories of America*, 10–13; Church, "Nineteenth-Century Clock Technology," 616–30; Jerome, *History of the American Clock Business*, 7, 15–17; Murphy,

"Entrepreneurship in the Establishment of the American Clock Industry"; E. Howard, "American Clocks and Watches."

97. Of course, the definition of nonslaveholders in this context is potentially problematic. Ministers, lawyers, teachers, and the like who were most likely to have timepieces may well have been from slaveholding families that provided them with slaves. Alternatively, such classes may have rented bondpeople on a temporary basis.

98. Burton, *South Carolina Silversmiths*, xx–xxi.

99. Wallace, *South Carolina*, 548–55.

100. See Appendix, Tables A.11–A.25.

101. The same was apparently true for rural and urban eighteenth-century Maryland clock owners. See Shackel, *Personal Discipline*, 171, 180.

102. Soltow, *Distribution of Wealth and Income*, 42.

103. Leone, "Georgian Order," 240–42; Hindle and Lubar, *Engines of Change*, 219.

104. Landes, *Revolution in Time*, 182–87; Jerome, *History of the American Clock Business*, 20–23.

105. Klein, *Unification of a Slave State*, 256. Similar conclusions for eighteenth-century Maryland are reached by Shackel, *Personal Discipline*, 171, 180.

106. Church, "Nineteenth-Century Clock Technology"; Gitelman, "The Labor Force at Waltham Watch Factory"; Waldo, "Mechanical Art of American Watchmaking."

107. Ford, *Origins of Southern Radicalism*, 260.

108. Leone, "Georgian Order," 241–42.

109. Bruegel, "'Time That Can Be Relied Upon.'" See also Shackel, *Personal Discipline*.

110. O'Malley, *Keeping Watch*, 33–44.

111. Mark M. Smith, "Counting Clocks, Owning Time," 253–54.

112. Gen. C. T. James, "Southern Cotton Mills," *DBR* 10 (June 1851): 681.

113. "The Marvels of Invention," *DBR* 28 (Feb. 1859): 236–37; [Ed.], "What We Pay New England to Support Her John Browns," ibid., 223.

114. Gavin Diary, vol. 1, Colleton District, S.C., Jan. 26, 1861, in *RASP*, ser. J, SHC, pt. 3, r. 10, fr. 1042, p. 226.

115. Potter, *People of Plenty*; Donald, *Excess of Democracy*.

CHAPTER TWO

1. See, for example, Breen, "Of Time and Nature"; Charles A. Miller, *Jefferson and Nature*, 50–51, 104–5, 266–73. Generally see Eliade, *The Sacred and the Profane*, esp. 68–113.

2. Le Goff, "Labor Time in the 'Crisis' of the Fourteenth Century," 48.

3. Woodward, "The Southern Ethic in a Puritan World," 27.

4. Weber, *The Protestant Ethic and the Spirit of Capitalism*, 157–58. Challenges to Weber's thesis are numerous. The best include Kolko, "Max Weber on America"; the essays in Robert W. Green, *Protestantism and Capitalism*; and Eisenstadt, *The Protestant Ethic and Modernization*. Useful discussions of Weber's thesis as applied to the South and North are by Woodward, "The Southern Ethic in a Puritan World"; and Edmund S. Morgan, "The Puritan Ethic and the American Revolution." See also Breen, "Of Time and Nature"; Walsh, "Holy Time and Sacred Space in Puritan New England."

5. Thompson, "Time, Work-Discipline." See Rodgers, *Work Ethic in Industrial America*, esp. 8–25; Adam, *Timewatch*, esp. chap. 4; and Innes, *Creating the Commonwealth*.

6. According to most authorities, similar if not the same forces informed the impetus behind industrialization in the American North. Imbued with a Puritan ethic apparently even more condemning of spontaneous and frivolous leisure than the Protestant variety, the conjoining of clock time with nature in the pursuit of industrial capitalism in the late

eighteenth and early nineteenth centuries was a sometimes confused but largely straightforward marriage. See Hensley, "Time, Work, and Social Context in New England"; Prude, *Coming of Industrial Order*; Gutman, *Work, Culture, and Society*; O'Malley, *Keeping Watch*, esp. 1–54, 145–99.

7. Levy, "Early Puritanism in the Southern and Island Colonies," esp. 86, 119, 308. On the southern clergy and Calvinism see Holifield, *Gentlemen Theologians*, 187–98.

8. Edmund S. Morgan, "Puritan Ethic," 4. No less of a scholar than Perry Miller concurs: "However much Virginia and New England differed in ecclesiastical polities, they were both recruited from the same type of Englishmen, pious, hard-working, middle-class, accepting literally and solemnly the tenets of Puritanism." See Miller, *Errand into the Wilderness*, 108, 138. See also Bonomi, *Under the Cope of Heaven*. For the antebellum period, consult Mathews, *Religion in the Old South*, esp. 42–65, 110–43.

9. See, for example, Bloch, *Feudal Society*, 1:72–75; Braudel, *Mediterranean*, esp. 1:611–15; Le Goff, "Merchant's Time and Church's Time"; Thrift, "Owners' Time and Own Time," esp. 57–59.

10. O'Malley, "Time, Work and Task Orientation," 347. Also see Zerubavel, *Seven Day Circle*.

11. Although Jonathan Z. Smith has questioned the idea that linear or teleological time is peculiar to the Judaic-Christian tradition on the grounds that such an argument has served simply "to protect the Bible from the enterprise of comparison," there is a sense in which Christian time is linear. But it is not just linear. Rather, Judaic-Christian time is both cyclical (the Resurrection) and, simultaneously, linear (Armageddon) and so bound to nature. See Jonathan Z. Smith, "A Slip in Time Saves Nine," 70. On God's time in Western culture, see O'Malley, "Time, Work and Task Orientation," 346–47; O'Malley, *Keeping Watch*, 13; Gould, *Time's Arrow, Time's Cycle*, esp. 10–16. For a different emphasis consult Boman, *Hebrew Thought Compared with Greek*. Some useful if brief remarks on the concept of time in Judaic and Christian thought are in Brandon, "Deification of Time," esp. 380–81.

12. "Critical Notes, &c.," *Southern Literary Gazette* 1 (July 1829): 74. Natural time by itself, as Norbert Elias points out, does not have a readily identifiable linear quality to it, however (*Time*, 79–80).

13. Evert A. Duyckinck, "The Hystorie of Hamblet [*sic*]," *Southern and Western Monthly Magazine and Review* 1 (Jan. 1845): 61–62. See also Gifford, "Space and Time as Religious Symbols in Ante-Bellum America," 1–29, 42–51, 73–105.

14. [Ed.], "The Past and Coming Year," *So. Cult.* 18 (Jan. 1860): 9. See also "Thoughts for the First of the Year 1839," *TF* 4 (Jan. 1839): 16.

15. "The Voyage of Life," *So. Pl.* 20 (Jan. 1860): 64.

16. Rev. John Joice, "Narrative of His Own Conversion," in John Joice, Darien, Ga., to "My dear Uncle and friend," May 16, 1824, Middleton Papers, in *RASP*, ser. J, SHC, pt. 3, r. 8, fr. 821, 837. See also Thomas Rivers Dunn, [Cloversdale, Va.?] to "My dear son," [William Melville Dunn], Buffalow Gap, Va., June 22, 1855, p. 2, Dunn Family Papers, VHS.

17. [Advertisement by W. W. Wilson, agent], "New and Highly Improved (Patented) Metallic Sun Dials," *So. Cult.* 18 (Mar. 1860): [109]. Relatedly, see Faust's discussion of proslavery theorists' conception of historical time in *Sacred Circle*, esp. 73–80; and, more generally and suggestively, Genovese, *Southern Tradition*.

18. See the various newspaper clippings in the Christ Church (Protestant Episcopal) Papers, Lancaster Co., Va., VHS.

19. Unidentified newspaper clipping, ser. 3.2: Misc. Items, Undated, Colhoun Papers, in *RASP*, ser. J, SHC, pt. 3, r. 29, fr. 582. A picture of the four-faced clock may be found in Simons and Lapham, *Early Architecture of Charleston*, 25. Generally consult Conser, *God and the Natural World*, esp. 10–36.

20. "Cockneys' Bow Bells Peal to a Wider Audience," *Manchester Weekly Telegraph*, Apr.

6–12, 1994, 29. My thanks to Nelson D. Lankford of the Virginia Historical Society for bringing this article to my attention. See Summer Journal, Feb. 4, 1837, SCL. Generally, also see Pred, "Production, Family, and Free-Time Projects." On the technological and historical significance of bells, striking clocks, and aural time generally, see Dohrn-van Rossum, *History of the Hour*, 108–13.

21. Schafer, *Tuning of the World*; Tyack, *Book about Bells*. Southerners were aware of the history of bells and their secular and religious significance. See B., "Superstitions Connected with Bells," *Virginia Literary Museum and Journal of Belles, Lettres, Arts, Sciences, &c* 1 (Mar. 10, 1829): 613–15.

22. Carla White, "Bells of Fincastle"; U.S. Congress, House, Committee of Claims, *Churchwardens—Elizabeth City Parish, Virginia*, n.p.

23. "St. Philip's Church," *Southern Literary Gazette* 1 (Nov. 1828): 173.

24. Quotations in MESDA files, Helpers Conference Minutes, Apr. 27, 1773, Aufseher Collegium Minutes, May 3, 1775, Sept. 19, 1797, Moravian Archives, MESDA. When the familiar sound of time malfunctioned, whether its source was college bells, courthouse clocks, or church bells, it was immediately apparent. In February 1751, Virginian John Blair, for example, noted: "Last Night the College Bell tolled they say abt. an hour, very slow & regular, till some [one] went up & stopt it, who saw nobody." See Blair Diary, Feb. 2, 1751, diary interlaced with the *Virginia Almanac for 1851*, VHS.

25. *Rock Hill [S.C.] Herald*, Oct. 6, 1881, 3.

26. Miers, *When the World Ended*, 62.

27. Landes, *Revolution in Time*, 83; Neustadter, "Beat the Clock," esp. 380; Macey, *Clocks and the Cosmos*, 123–66; F. W. Walker, *Romance of Church Bells*.

28. O'Malley, *Keeping Watch*, 44–50.

29. A., "Idle Hours—No. 1. Twilight," *So. Ro.* 7 (Dec. 22, 1838): 135.

30. *South Carolina Gazette*, Mar. 25–Apr. 1, 1732. Generally see the entries in Woodfin, *Another Secret Diary of William Byrd*; Benson, *America of 1750*, 2:738–69. For the northern situation see Hensley, "Time, Work, and Social Context in New England," 541.

31. *South Carolina Gazette*, Jan. 10, 1743, Sept. 19, 1752; Betts, *Thomas Jefferson's Garden Book*, 57.

32. Belin Plantation Journals, vol. 2, Aug. 18, 1797, SCHS.

33. John Blount Miller and John H. Furman, Cornhill Plantation Book, Dec. 27, 1839, McDonald Furman Papers, in *RASP*, ser. F, DU, pt. 2, r. 9, fr. 77, p. 66.

34. Entries in William Ervine Sparkman Plantation Journal, Georgetown and Williamsburg Districts, S.C., in *RASP*, ser. J, SHC, pt. 3, r. 1, fr. 529, 548, 553, pp. 30, 49, 50.

35. See John Ball and Keating Simons Ball Books, ser. 1: Plantation Record Books, folder 5a, vol. 5, in *RASP*, ser. J, SHC, pt. 3, r. 2, fr. 10–44, 22.

36. Gavin Diary, Colleton District, S.C., Sept. 3, 1856, in *RASP*, ser. J, SHC, pt. 3, r. 10, fr. 867, p. 54.

37. Nicolson Diary, Mar. 8, 1858, VHS.

38. Chandler Commonplace Book, July 4, 1819, in Grigsby Family Papers, VHS.

39. Charles Manigault, Charleston, to "Mon Cher Louis," Mar. 12, 1859, in Louis Manigault Papers, in *RASP*, ser. F, DU, pt. 2, r. 6, fr. 186, p. 1. For the eighteenth century see Stowell, *Early American Almanacs*, 219–21; O'Malley, *Keeping Watch*, chap. 1. On the religious significance of colonial American almanacs, see Butler, *Awash in a Sea of Faith*, 80–89.

40. "Interleave Your Almanacs," *So. Pl.* 8 (June 1848): 165.

41. Plantation Journal, Aug. 1, 1832, Colhoun Papers, in *RASP*, ser. J, SHC, pt. 3, fr. 516–17.

42. Cobb Diary, Feb. 6, 1843, VHS. See Crofts, "Southampton County Diarists in the Civil War Era."

43. MESDA file, "Architecture, South Carolina, Charleston, Market, 1797," in *City Gazette Daily Advertiser*, Aug. 19, 1797, 3.

44. Brother Peterson, "Augusta," *So. Cult.* 20 (July and Aug. 1862): 147. On the regulatory power of the town clock in antebellum New England, see Kulik, Parks, and Penn, *New England Mill Village*, 265; Hensley, "Time, Work, and Social Context in New England," 534–38; Bruegel, "'Time That Can Be Relied Upon,'" 553–54. For an interesting parallel with Britain see Harrison, "Ordering of the Urban Environment."

45. In Cooper, *Statutes at Large of South Carolina*, 3:61.

46. In McCord, *Statutes at Large of South Carolina*, 9:692–93. On the tentative and modest beginnings of market time in fourteenth-century Europe, see Dohrn-van Rossum, *History of the Hour*, 245–51.

47. Simons and Lapham, *Early Architecture of Charleston*, 168.

48. In Cooper, *Statutes at Large of South Carolina*, 3:735, 585.

49. [Ed.], "Laws Affecting American Slaves and British Subjects," *DBR* 15 (Mar. 1853): 271. See also Catterall, *Judicial Cases Concerning American Slavery*, 2:565.

50. McCord, *Statutes at Large of South Carolina*, 7:398.

51. William Gibbons Jr. and the Estate of Mrs. Sarah Gibbons, Sept. 10, 1788, in Gibbons Papers, Chatham Co., Ga., in *RASP*, ser. F, DU, pt. 2, r. 1, fr. 727. See the various statutes regulating antebellum market times, the times of the watch, and bell ringings in Ward, *Ordinances of the City Council of Charleston*; Walker, *Ordinances of the City of Charleston*; Horsey, *Ordinances of the City of Charleston*.

52. Edward Telfair, Savannah, to George Jones, June 6, 1797, Telfair Papers, in *RASP*, ser. F, DU, pt. 2, r. 11, fr. 647, p. 1.

53. Summons, June 24, 1859, Richardson Papers, in *RASP*, ser. F, DU, pt. 2, r. 15, fr. 516.

54. Alex B. Brailsford to Capt. W H B Richardson, Feb. 18, 1843, Richardson Papers, in *RASP*, ser. F, DU, pt. 2, r. 14, fr. 298.

55. King Diaries, ser. 3, Apr. 15, Nov. 2, Dec. 28, 1851, King Papers, in *RASP*, ser. J, SHC, pt. 3, r. 6, fr. 351, 368, 372, pp. 164, 199, 207.

56. "Funeral Oration to the memory of Mrs Mary Bolling—humbly inscribed to her Father William Burton Esqr of Northampton in Virginia," May 15, 1764, by Robert Bolling, Bolling Commonplace Book, Powhatan and Richmond, Va., pp. 39–41, VHS.

57. From the German, "The Life-Clock," *So. Cult.* 20 (July and Aug. 1862): 146.

58. See Kaiser and Engel, "Time- and Age-Awareness in Early Modern Russia"; Fischer, *Growing Old in America*, esp. 82–84. On the image of death and the importance of time in New England, see Ludwig, *Graven Images*.

59. Rutland, *Papers of George Mason*, 1:480–81.

60. McIntosh Memorandum Book, July 25, 1807, McIntosh Papers, Georgia Historical Society, Savannah, Ga. Similarly see Gramling Plantation and Account Book, Orangeburg District, Mar. 15, 1846, Jan. 4, 1847, May 13, 1849, SCL.

61. Grimball Diary, Dec. 8, 1848, ser. 2, vol. 3, in *RASP*, ser. J, SHC, pt. 3, r. 16, fr. 12, p. 8.

62. Gavin Diary, July 10, 1859, in *RASP*, ser. J, SHC, pt. 3, r. 10, fr. 985, p. 70.

63. Misc. Records, Wills, and Inventories, Charleston Co., vol. 52, r. 1, SCDAH.

64. MESDA files, "Colonial Park Cemetery."

65. Gavin Diary, Colleton District, S.C., Sept. 3, 1856, in *RASP*, ser. J, SHC, pt. 3, r. 10, fr. 866, p. 53.

66. DeSaussure Journal, Oct. 9–17, 1858, in *RASP*, ser. J, SHC, pt. 2, r. 17, fr. 983, p. 37.

67. Ashemore Plantation Journal, Aug. 13, 1855, in *RASP*, ser. F, DU, pt. 3, r. 27, fr. 613, p. 111.

68. Anon., Misc. Planting Records, 1849, n.p., SCL. See also Aiken Diary, Mar. 4, July 24, 1855, SCL.

69. Chandler Commonplace Book, Dec. 7, 1821, Grigsby Family Papers, VHS.

70. Plantation Record Books, folder 5a, vol. 5, Apr. 11, 1850, John Ball and Keating Simons Ball Books, in *RASP*, ser. J, SHC, pt. 3, r. 2, fr. 59, p. 53.

71. McMillan King to Mitchell King, Savannah, July 23, 1849, ser. 1, subser. 1.3, folder 22, King Papers, in *RASP*, ser. J, SHC, pt. 3, r. 3, fr. 894, p. 2. On the timing of slaves' deaths, see Touchstone, "Planters and Slave Religion in the Deep South," esp. 125.

72. Time Book, Jan. 31, 1859–Nov. 30, 1869, Hollywood Cemetery Co., Richmond, Va., Records, VHS.

73. *Christian Neighbor* [Columbia, S.C.], Nov. 3, 1881, 176.

74. See Earle, *Child-Life in Colonial Days*, esp. 5–6.

75. King Diaries, ser. 3, Feb. 25, Apr. 28, 1852, Feb. 13, 1854, King Papers, in *RASP*, ser. J, SHC, pt. 3, r. 6, fr. 469, 475, 529, pp. 6, 18, 127.

76. Grimball Diary, vol. 5, July 22, 1836, ser. 2, in *RASP*, ser. J, SHC, pt. 3, r. 15, fr. 691, p. 3.

77. Especially with their professionalization in the antebellum period. See Steven M. Stowe, "Seeing Themselves at Work," 52–53.

78. Louis Manigault, Prescription Book, 1852, Louis Manigault Papers, in *RASP*, ser. F, DU, pt. 2, r. 6, fr. 946. A similar cure for cholera administered by the clock may be found in Blow Commonplace Book, July 31, 1832, VHS.

79. Folder 69, Recipes, ca. 1802, Grimball Family Papers, Colleton and Charleston Districts, S.C., in *RASP*, ser. F, DU, pt. 3, r. 13, fr. 341. For a cure for dysentery with similar time specifications, see Cocke Diary, Woodland Plantation, Amelia Co., Va., Nov. 1, 1854, Cocke Family Papers, VHS.

80. White Commonplace Book, ca. 1784, VHS.

81. William Cabell Carrington, Princeton, to "My dear Father," [Henry Carrington], Charlotte Court House, Va., Oct. 22, Jan. 26, 1841, corresp. of Henry Carrington, folder 1, Carrington Family Papers, VHS.

82. Ann G. Richardson, Sand Hills, Sumter, S.C., to "My dear my beloved William," Nov. 10, 1824, p. 1; James B. Richardson, James Ville, Sumter, S.C., to "My Dear William," Apr. 18, 1822, pp. 1–2, Richardson Papers, in *RASP*, ser. F, DU, pt. 2, r. 14, fr. 43, 13–14. For an example of the English origins of time thrift in education and how it influenced a mid-eighteenth-century southerner, see "Advice to a Young Student," 1733/4, p. 2, Alexander Commonplace Book, Georgetown, S.C., SCL.

83. A rough equivalent may be found in the seventeenth-century northern idea of competency. See Vickers, "Competency and Competition." Quotation from Elias, *Time*, 11.

84. Louis Manigault, Charleston, to Charles H. Manigault, Long Island (College Point), N.Y., Feb. 10, 1844, in Louis Manigault Papers, in *RASP*, ser. F, DU, pt. 2, r. 4, fr. 1055, p. 1. The same was true for schoolhouses outside the South. See Turner, *Lewis Miller*, 41. On education as a key to instilling time thrift and discipline, see Thrift, "Owners' Time and Own Time," 65–67; Foucault, *Discipline and Punish*, 150; Davison, *Unforgiving Minute*, esp. 16, 24–28, 82–89; Adam, *Timewatch*, 59–83. Generally, see Cohen, *Calculating People*, esp. 116–49.

85. College of Charleston's Monthly Abstract of the Journal of the Faculty, for the Sophomore Class, from the 1st of Dec. to the 15th of Dec. 1848, Middleton Papers, in *RASP*, ser. J, SHC, pt. 3, r. 8, fr. 862. On European origins of school times in the fifteenth century, see Dohrn-van Rossum, *History of the Hour*, 251–60.

86. [Ed.], "Scheme of the Approaching Examinations," *Virginia Literary Museum and Journal of Belles Lettres, Arts, Sciences, &c* 1 (July 8, 1829): 63.

87. Advertisement, "The School Teacher's Library: Seven Volumes," *DBR* 26 (Apr. 1859): n.p.

88. Folder 64, Record of the Proceedings of the Trustees of Blackswamp Academy, 1818, Lawton Papers, in *RASP*, ser. J, SHC, pt. 3, r. 27, fr. 7, p. 5.

89. E. H. Manigault, Charleston, S.C., to Charles Manigault, Long Island (College Point), N.Y., Mar. 21, 1844, in Louis Manigault Papers, in *RASP*, ser. F, DU, pt. 2, r. 4, fr. 1065, p. 3.

90. C. G., "The Choice of Hours," *RB* 1 (Aug. 11, 1832): 64.

91. "Flower Clocks," *RB* 1 (June 8, 1833): 163.

92. Watchman, "Flower Clocks," *RB* 1 (June 15, 1833): 167.

93. Selections from *Christian Advocate*, "Observations of Old Humphrey on Time," *So. Ro.* 2 (Aug. 2, 1834): 195. The importance of widespread numeracy should not be underestimated here because the clock obviously required a familiarity with numbers. On the extent of this familiarity, see Cohen, *Calculating People*.

94. "Charleston at Drum-Beat," *So. Ro.* 3 (May 2, 1835): 141.

95. Dr. Inlano de Tal to "My Dear Cousin Harry," Oct. 24, 1853, Louis Manigault Papers, in *RASP*, ser. F, pt. 2, r. 5, fr. 390, p. 1.

96. Anon., from Burch Hill, Sumter, S.C., to unidentified, Jan. 16, 1850, Richardson Papers, in *RASP*, ser. F, DU, pt. 2, r. 14, fr. 438, p. 4.

97. Colleton, "On Agricultural Societies," *So. Ag.* 8 (Mar. 1835): 114.

98. "My Time," *Southern Literary Gazette* 1 (Aug. 1829): 160.

99. Quoted in O'Malley, *Keeping Watch*, 11; Ulrich, *Good Wives*, esp. 78.

100. O'Malley, *Keeping Watch*, 50–51. See also Hareven, "Synchronizing Individual Time."

101. MESDA file, "Catherine Parry," photograph S-9658.

102. Clitherall Diary, vol. 2, "Reminiscences," ca. 1800, p. 6, r. 1, in *AWD*, SHC.

103. "Mother," Charleston, S.C., to [Gabriel Henry] Manigault, Philadelphia, Dec. 6, 1808, in Louis Manigault Papers, in *RASP*, ser. F, DU, pt. 2, r. 4, fr. 689, p. 1.

104. "Diary Entries of Two Sisters, 1843, 1849, and undated," Aug. 23, 1843, ser. 4, Ravenel Family Papers, in *RASP*, ser. J, SHC, pt. 3, r. 9, fr. 942, pp. 2–3.

105. Gayle Diaries, June 15, 1827, p. 23, r. 1, *AWD*, W. Stanley Hoole Special Collections, University of Alabama Library, Tuscaloosa, Ala.

106. [Ann B. Richardson] to "My Beloved Children," Aug. 11, 1850, Richardson Papers, in *RASP*, ser. F, DU, pt. 2, r. 14, fr. 505, p. 1.

107. Burge Dairies, Mar. 24, 1849, *AWD*, Woodruff Library, Emory University, Atlanta, Ga.

108. Crawford Diaries, vol. 1, Feb. 10, 1850, in *AWD*, DU.

109. "Early Rising—For My Own Children," *So. Ro.* 4 (Oct. 27, 1835): 27.

110. Alicia Middleton, Stono, S.C., to Nathaniel Russell Middleton, Geneva, N.Y., Apr. 30, 1827, ser. 1.2, Middleton Papers, Charleston District, in *RASP*, ser. J, SHC, pt. 3, r. 7, fr. 308, p. 1.

111. Anon., untitled, *TF* 17 (Apr. 1836): 260.

112. William Elliott, Columbia, S.C., to "My dear Wife," Nov. 23, 1818, Elliott and Gonzales Family Papers, Beaufort and Colleton Districts, S.C., in *RASP*, ser. J, SHC, pt. 3, r. 18, fr. 215, p. 2.

113. Ulrich, "Housewife and Gadder."

114. See the remarks in Kerber, "Separate Spheres," esp. 16–17.

115. From the *Farmer and Planter*, "Domestic Economy, Recipes, &c.," *So. Pl.* 20 (Sept. 1860): 572–73; Earle, *Home Life in Colonial Days*, 64–65.

116. Bernard Commonplace Book, Mount Gray Plantation, Caroline Co., Va., ca. 1847, VHS. See the hundreds of recipes in Randolph, *Virginia House-Wife*.

117. Quotation from Fox-Genovese, *Within the Plantation Household*, 61. The literature on American women is vast and sophisticated. On differences based on class, region, and context among American women see the excellent review essay by Hewitt, "Beyond the Search for Sisterhood." On the pre-nineteenth-century situation primarily in the North, consult Norton, "Evolution of White Women's Experience." On the cult of female domesticity, see Catherine Hall, "Early Formation of Victorian Domestic Ideology"; Barbara J. Harris, *Beyond Her Sphere*, esp. 38–41. And on women's infiltration of the public sphere through political action and work, see Lerner, "The Lady and the Mill Girl"; Ryan, *Women in Public*; Spruill, *Women's Life and Work*.

118. Quotation from Fox-Genovese, *Within the Plantation Household*, 39. See also McMillen, *Southern Women*, esp. 64–85.

119. See the trenchant essay, Genovese and Fox-Genovese, "Ideological Bases of Domestic Economy," 303. On northern women's understanding and appreciation of clock time, see the important discussion in Cott, *Bonds of Womanhood*, 58–62. Also useful is Dublin, *Farm to Factory*, esp. 6–15.

120. As evidence in Chapter 5 of this book suggests, even female slaves, especially those who worked in the southern household, were drawn into the matrix of clock time and household relations.

121. Generally see Kett and McClung, "Book Culture in Post-Revolutionary Virginia."

122. [Ed.], "Southern School-Books," *DBR* 13 (Sept. 1852): 258–59.

123. [Ed.], "The North and the South," *DBR* 17 (Oct. 1854): 366.

124. [Ed.], "Commerce of the United States," *DBR* 20 (Apr. 1856): 434; Elson, *Guardians of Tradition*, esp. 304–11.

125. A useful study on southern women's education and its emphasis on Scripture, as opposed to men's more humanistic, secular education, is Griffin, *Less Time for Meddling*, esp. 4–5, 86–87, 98–99. See also the important essay by Fletcher M. Green, "Higher Education of Women."

126. Mrs. E. Oakes Smith, "Woman and Her Needs," *DBR* 13 (Sept. 1852): 276.

127. See Censer, *North Carolina Planters and Their Children*, esp. 50–55; Clinton, "Equally Their Due"; Steven M. Stowe, "The Not-So-Cloistered Academy."

128. Friedman, *Enclosed Garden*, esp. 21–37; Anne Firor Scott, *Southern Lady*, 1–80.

129. Compiled from Margaret Carson, Mental Photographs Album, SCL; Saxton, *Mental Photographs*. For the rise of a secular clock consciousness in the late nineteenth-century Home Economics Association, see Kessler-Harris, *Out to Work*, esp. 118.

130. *Christian Neighbor*, Mar. 23, 1882, 45.

131. Generally see Greenberg, *Masters and Statesmen*; Edmund S. Morgan, *American Slavery, American Freedom*.

132. Le Goff, "Merchant's Time and Church's Time," 29. God, however, was not the only impediment to secular, commercial time. Le Goff explains: "Like the peasant, the merchant was at first subjected by his professional activity to the dominion of meteorological time, to the cycle of seasons and the unpredictability of storms and natural cataclysms. He long had no choice but to submit to the natural order and no means to act other than prayer and superstitious practice" (ibid., 34–36). See also Borst, *Ordering of Time*, chap. 6; Moran, "Conception of Time in Early Modern France," esp. 4–5, 8, 14–15. For a stiff challenge to Le Goff's interpretation, which argues that monarchs and princes were more responsible than merchants for introducing clocks into towns, see Dohrn-van Rossum, *History of the Hour*, esp. 12–13.

133. Le Goff, "Merchant's Time and Church's Time," 34–36. On northern merchants' conflict with Puritan authority, see Bailyn, *New England Merchants*, esp. 105–11.

134. Le Goff, "Merchant's Time and Church's Time," 38. See also Nguyen, "Spatialization of Metric Time," esp. 29–30; Moran, "Conception of Time in Early Modern France."

135. As Toby Ditz has pointed out, the notion of time thrift and saving time was important to eighteenth-century Philadelphia merchants. But the thrift was profane, not religious, so much so, in fact, that these merchants attempted to distance themselves from the more religiously inspired, Puritan notion of time associated with women by attaching secular and very masculine traits to their own business activities, including the use of their time. Philadelphia merchants assured themselves in 1757, for example, that despite their wives' miscarriages, "We have not lost any Time" in their business transactions. See Ditz, "Shipwrecked," 77.

136. Generally see Doerflinger, *Vigorous Spirit of Enterprise*, 6–7, 136–39, 345–49; Bailyn, *New England Merchants*, esp. 105–11. In some respects, of course, merchants' ship-bound trade and, indeed, the systematic peopling of the North American continent, were in some

ways contingent on the widespread use of the nautical clock introduced by John Harrison in the 1760s. But these clocks, not widely used until the last quarter of the eighteenth century, were used for navigating and could hardly instill a time discipline. In many respects, both literal and metaphoric, the nautical clock remained on board the ship after eighteenth-century passengers had disembarked. Useful accounts of Harrison's clock may be found in Landes, *Revolution in Time*, esp. 146–52, and, more generally, in Boorstin, *Discoverers*, 25–78. That eighteenth-century ship life was disciplined but not by the clock see Rediker, *Between the Devil and the Deep Blue Sea*, esp. 200–201, 113. For the various theoretical positions historians have taken on the relative importance of merchant capitalism in the rise of capitalism, see the useful summary by Woodman, "Foreword," in Fox-Genovese and Genovese, *Fruits of Merchant Capital*, xv–xx. A less explicit notion of time, which focused on interest payments on debts, was apparent throughout colonial America. See, for example, Rothenberg, "Emergence of a Capital Market in Rural Massachusetts."

137. Jonathan Johnson, Boston, Mass., to [Edward Telfair], Oct. 21, 1774, Telfair Papers, in *RASP*, ser. F, DU, pt. 2, r. 10, fr. 537, p. 2. Generally see Gras, *Business History of the United States*, 1–77; Coakley, "Virginia Commerce during the American Revolution," 297–314. Generally, see Breen, *Tobacco Culture*, esp. 106–23.

138. Thomas Aiton & Co., Charleston, S.C., to William Stanley & Co., N.Y., Feb. 18, 1802, Aiton & Co. Letterbook, SCL.

139. Landon Carter to George Carter, Oatslands, nr. Leesburg, Va., Sept. 29, 1806, sec. 52, corresp. of George Carter, folder 1, Carter Family Papers, VHS.

140. Bird, Savage, & Bird, London, to Thomas White, Nov. 19, 1759, Smith Papers, in *RASP*, ser. F, DU, pt. 2, r. 12, fr. 629, p. 1. Although see, too, the points made in Cole, "Tempo of Mercantile Life."

141. Henry Laurens to David Bellegarde, Charles Town, S.C., Dec. 19, 1747, in Hamer, *Papers of Henry Laurens*, 1:91, 158; "Henry Laurens," *Hunt's Merchants Magazine*, (Nov. 1844): esp. 439.

142. Robert Raper to Sarah Holmes, Charlestown, S.C., July 10, 1760, Raper Letterbook, SCHS; Josiah Smith to Thomas Stoddard & Co., Boston, Mar. 26, 1779; to James Poyas, London, June 15, 1771; to George Austin, London, June 17, 1771; to Dr. Joseph Kenson, Bermuda, Dec. 28, 1771, in Josiah Smith Lettercopy Book, Charleston & Georgetown, S.C., in *RASP*, ser. J, SHC, pt. 3, r. 10, fr. 40–44, 71–72; George M. Beard, "Causes of Nervousness."

143. Josiah Smith to John Ray, N.J., Mar. 7, 1778, in Josiah Smith Lettercopy Book, in *RASP*, ser. J, SHC, pt. 3, r. 10, fr. 380, p. 348.

144. For example, see J. Guerard, Hilton Head, to Edward Telfair & Co., Oct. 7, 1775, Telfair Papers, in *RASP*, ser. F, DU, pt. 2, r. 10, fr. 704, p. 1. Telfair told clients that to pay bills "at about 3 OClock in the afternoon will be the most convenient time." See Edward Telfair to J. Wright, Apr. 25, 1775, ibid., r. 10, fr. 290. Or, as John Chesnutt of Camden, South Carolina, wrote to fellow merchant William Ancrum in 1794, "Not having time to get the Exon at your Suit renewed, I was under the necessity of sending to the Sheriff to postpone the Sale." See John Chesnutt, Camden, S.C., to William Ancrum, Apr. 12, 1794, Chesnutt Letterbook, LC.

145. George Walker, Westminster, to John Ball Sr., Jan. 29, 1811, in John Ball Sr. and John Ball Jr. Papers, Charleston District, in *RASP*, ser. F, DU, pt. 2, r. 2, fr. 540, p. 1. On the mercantile impetus behind nineteenth-century American capitalism, see Charles Sellers, *Market Revolution*, esp. 20–25.

146. Anonymous agreement with Josiah Smith, Charleston, Oct. 1, 1803, Smith Papers, in *RASP*, ser. F, DU, pt. 2, r. 12, fr. 814.

147. W. E. Haskell to John Ball Jr., June 20, 1829, in John Ball Jr. and John Ball Sr. Papers, Charleston District, in *RASP*, ser. F, DU, pt. 2, r. 3, fr. 318.

148. William Elliott, N.Y., to William Elliott Jr., Cambridge, Mass., Oct. 12, 1847, subser. 1.5, Elliott and Gonzales Family Papers, in *RASP*, ser. J, SHC, pt. 3, r. 19, fr. 372, p. 2.

149. "Faithless Clocks," *Outlook* 49 (Mar. 31, 1894): 603.

150. Dan Cannon Reid, Fisher Hill, Union, S.C., to William Moultrie Reid, Charleston, June 4, 1816, subser. 1.3, Colhoun Papers, in *RASP*, ser. J, SHC, pt. 3, r. 29, fr. 213, p. 3.

151. S., "Industry, Promptness and Punctuality, Crowned with Success," *FR* 6 (Dec. 1838): 739.

152. Schoepf, *Travels in the Confederation*, 2:118–19. On the intensity and lengths of the northern and southern work years, see Olson, "Clock Time versus Real Time," esp. 234–35.

153. Hodgson, *Letters from North America*, 1:306–7.

CHAPTER THREE

1. Sobel, *World They Made Together*, 21–22; Breen, "Of Time and Nature." This was true of northerners too. See O'Malley, *Keeping Watch*, chap. 1.

2. Thomas Jefferson, for instance, experimented with timing his slaves' labor. In 1769 he noted, "Four good fellows . . . in 8 1/2 hours dug in my cellar a mountain of clay a place 3 f. deep, 8 f. wide and 16 1/2 f. long . . . I think a mid[d]ling hand in 12. hours (including his breakfast) could dig & haul away the earth of 4 cubical yards, in the same soil" (Betts, *Thomas Jefferson's Garden Book*, 16–17). See also Edmund S. Morgan, *American Slavery, American Freedom*, 309.

3. Generally see Larson, " 'Bind the Republic Together.' "

4. See Stephens, " 'The Most Reliable Time,' " esp. 22; John, "Postal System," unpaginated and revised copies of this paper entitled "Completing the Network," and "The Imagined Community" in author's possession. My thanks to Professor John for kindly sharing this work. Generally see Brown, *Modernization*, esp. 13–16. For an analysis of the same forces behind Britain's heightening time consciousness see Thrift, "Owners' Time and Own Time," esp. 69–75; for New Zealand, consult Pawson, "Local Times and Standard Time in New Zealand."

5. On the sporadic legal codification of southern slavery and the colonial origins of the hiring-out system, see Higginbotham, *In the Matter of Color*, esp. 174. For the importance of the indentured servant system to this evolution, see Warren B. Smith, *White Servitude in Colonial South Carolina*; and Daniels, " 'Without Any Limitacon of Time.' " And for the employment of free blacks in the antebellum period, see the excellent study by Berlin, *Slaves without Masters*.

6. Early eighteenth-century examples may be found in Gundersen, "Double Bonds of Race and Sex"; and Daniels, "Gresham's Laws," esp. 222–29.

7. See William Strickland, "Observations on the United States of America [1796]," *FR* 3 (Aug. 1835): 209. For a Georgia planter who hired black labor by the day throughout the eighteenth century, see C. M. Corty to William Gibbons Jr.[?], [July 30, 1757]; Account with Jonathan Bryann, Mar. 19, 1768; Account with Philip Allman, [May 25, 1773], in Gibbons Papers, Chatham Co., Ga., in *RASP*, ser. F, DU, pt. 2, r. 1, fr. 30, 300, 535.

8. Hensley, "Time, Work, and Social Context in New England," 550. See also Bruegel, " 'Time That Can Be Relied Upon' "; Brody, "Time and Work," 10.

9. Charles Pinckney Accounts, June 28, 1752, July 4–Aug. 27, 1752, SCL. According to a detailed study by Mary Allison Carll-White, the vast majority of contracts issued to Charleston's colonial black artisans were yearly and monthly and sometimes daily ("Role of the Black Artisan," esp. 67–70).

10. See Chaplin, *Anxious Pursuit*, esp. 23–64; and Crawford, "Problems in the Quantitative Analysis," 347. On the urban practice in the antebellum period consult Wade, *Slavery in the Cities*.

11. Belin Plantation Journals, vol. 1, May 2, 3, 24, 1792, vol. 2, Apr. 26, 1797, SCHS. Planter Joseph Palmer, also of the South Carolina low country, began to fractionalize at roughly the

same time. See John [*sic*] Palmer Ledger, Sept. 16, 1787, p. 14, SCL. See also the related examples noted in McCurry, *Masters of Small Worlds*, 58.

12. [Memorandum], Dec. 1774, Gibbons Papers, in *RASP*, ser. F, DU, pt. 2, r. 1, fr. 475; Accounts, May 24, 1771, in Telfair Papers, Savannah, Augusta, and Burke Co., Ga., ibid., r. 10, fr. 299. See also Alexander Diary, Aug. 15, 1804, VHS.

13. Cabell Commonplace Book, Colleton and Union Hill Plantations, Nelson Co., Va., vol. 1, June 18, 1790, vol. 2, July 4, 1794, VHS.

14. Chamberlayne Account Book, Kent Co., Va., LC.

15. Robert Johns to Wm. Graham, Savannah, Ga., June 10, 1786, Telfair Papers, in *RASP*, ser. F, DU, pt. 2, r. 11, fr. 195, p. 1. For a good case study of hiring slave labor in a mixed farming economy, see Medford, " 'There was so many degrees in slavery,' " esp. 39–41; and in the naval stores industry, Outland, "Slavery, Work and the Geography of the North Carolina Naval Stores," esp. 46–49.

16. Hensley, "Time, Work, and Social Context in New England"; Bruegel, " 'Time That Can Be Relied Upon.' " In the South, the hiring of slaves was probably more common in urban regions. According to two econometricians, "In 1860 half of all Richmond slaves were rented out, compared to only 6 percent of slaves in rural Virginia" (Friedman and Manning, "The Rent and Hire of Slaves," 77).

17. Singleton Financial Papers, Oct. 23, 1810, June 12, 1845, Sept. 7, 1850, in *RASP*, ser. J, SHC, pt. 3, r. 40, fr. 647; r. 37, fr. 623; r. 35, fr. 217. For similar examples from Virginia, see Chandler Commonplace Book, Broomfield Plantation, Caroline Co., Va., Mar. 16, 1823, in Grigsby Family Papers, VHS. Generally see Glickstein, *Concepts of Free Labor*.

18. Lawton Plantation Journal, in *RASP*, ser. J, SHC, pt. 3, r. 26, fr. 600.

19. Anon., Ledger, July 22, 1838, uncertain provenance records, Chesterfield Co., S.C., SCDAH.

20. Mason Farm Accounts, uncertain provenance records, Spartanburg, S.C., July 7, 1842, Mar. 17, 1843, SCDAH. See also Smith Account Books, vol. 1, Mar. 6, 1833, VHS; Cosby Account Book, VHS.

21. See Gavin Wright, *Political Economy of the Cotton South*, esp. 45–46.

22. K. Washington Skinner, Hermitage [plantation], to Charles Manigault, Charleston, June 14, 1851; Louis Manigault, Gowrie Plantation, to Charles Manigault, Feb. 16, 1855, Louis Manigault Papers, Charleston District, S.C., and Chatham Co., Ga., in *RASP*, ser. F, DU, pt. 2, r. 5, fr. 236, 460; Pinckney Plantation Journal, Dec. 29, 1864, ibid., r. 9, fr. 413.

23. Doar Account Books, vol. 1, "The Estate of E. M. Doar deceased, in account with Stephen D. Doar, Administrator," Apr. 1, 1851, p. 2, LC.

24. Talbert Plantation Journals, vol. 4, Sept. 20, 1864, in *RASP*, ser. A, SCL, pt. 2, r. 2, fr. 893.

25. William Mellett to R.B.D., "Near Statesburg," S.C., Oct. 11, 1842, Deveaux Papers, in *RASP*, ser. F, DU, pt. 2, r. 13, fr. 608, p. 1. Similarly, see D. B. M. Samin, Wateree, S.C., to W. H. B. Richardson, July 17, 1854, Richardson Papers, ibid., r. 14, fr. 771.

26. [Edgefield, Spring Term—1830. Before Judge Gantt. John Williamson vs. Susanna Farrow], "Computation of Time," *Carolina Law Journal* 1 (Oct. 1830): 184–94. On antebellum rationalization, see Charles Sellers, *Market Revolution*; Novak, "Public Economy and the Well-Ordered Market"; and Rose, *Voices of the Marketplace*, esp. 60–62.

27. Johnson Ledger, May 9, 1846, uncertain provenance records, Newberry Co., S.C., SCDAH.

28. Scheele, *Short History of the Mail Service*, 47–56, 64–70; Ranft, "Colonial Post Office"; William Smith, "The Colonial Post-Office." On Virginia's colonial mail system, see Gaines, "Nerve Center of the Colonial Mails"; Murden, "Post and Post-Roads in Colonial Virginia," 1941, VHS. Generally see Pelzer, "Pioneer Stage-Coach Travel." On an eighteenth-century interest in minimizing the time in transit of information, see Weir, "Role of the Newspaper Press in the Southern Colonies."

29. [From the *Louisiana Gazette*], "The Early Times in New Orleans," *DBR* 18 (Feb. 1855): 160.

30. Postal Contract between the Postmaster General of the United States and William Smith, July 7, 1835, Pleck, Wellford & Co. Papers, sec. 3, VHS. Also useful in this context is the Pleck, Wellford & Co. Letterbook, in the Pleck, Wellford & Co., Fredericksburg, Va., Papers, VHS.

31. In order see Gideon Granger, General P.O., Wash. D.C., to John Holmes [Postmaster] Bowling Green, Va., Apr. 23, 1802, pp. 1–2; Abraham Bradley, Gen. P.O., Wash. D.C., to J. G. Woolfolk, Bowling Green, Nov. 10, Dec. 28, 1813, in Woolfolk Family Papers, sec. 2, VHS. Bradley was born in Connecticut and, according to Richard John, was "widely respected as a leading authority on the scheduling arrangements that the general post office had introduced for the stagecoach industry, most of which he had committed to memory and many of which he himself had devised." See John, "Completing the Network."

32. [Ed.], "United States Post System," *DBR* 5 (Feb. 1848): 156.

33. Joseph Clay, Savannah, to Edward Telfair, Mar. 13, 1793, Telfair Papers, in *RASP*, ser. F, DU, pt. 2, r. 11, fr. 495, p. 1.

34. Andrew Johnston, Bull. St., [Columbia], to [William Johnston], Aug. 26, 1829, p. 2, Johnston Papers, SCL.

35. [Ed.], "Coaches in England," *RB* 1 (May 4, 1833): 1. See also extract from the *Quarterly Review*, "Speed of Mail Coaches and Keep of Their Horses in England," *FR* 1 (July 1833): 84.

36. From the *Macon Messenger*, "Plank Roads," *DBR* 7 (Nov. 1849): 462–63, 464. Consult also Report of the Committee of Fifteen on the Establishment of a Plankroad from Tuscaloosa to Roup's Valley, "Internal Improvements. 1. Plank Roads at the South," *DBR* 8 (May 1850): 474; [Mr. Gregg], "Plank Roads," *DBR* 11 (July 1851): 63.

37. For a brief discussion of the impact of the postal service on northern time sensibilities, see O'Malley, *Keeping Watch*, 60.

38. Compiled from [Eli Bowen], Appendix 1 of "The Post System," *DBR* 12 (Mar. 1852): 255.

39. [Eli Bowen], "The Post System," *DBR* 12 (Mar. 1852): 236, 247.

40. King Diary, Sept. 1, 1855, ser. 3, King Papers, in *RASP*, ser. J, SHC, pt. 3, r. 6, fr. 749, p. 5.

41. Cotterill, "The Telegraph in the South."

42. [Ed.], "Commercial and Agricultural Statistics," *DBR* 4 (Sept. 1847): 138.

43. William Habersham, Savannah, to Charles Manigault, Charleston, Jan. 5, 1858, New York and New Orleans Magnetic Telegraph Company; Charles Manigault, Charleston, Jan. 7, 1859, to R. Habersham, [Ga.?]; Louis Manigault, Gowrie plantation, Savannah River, to "Mon Cher Pere," [Charles Manigault], Jan. 9, 1859; Wm. Capers, Savannah River, to Louis Manigault, Gibbs St., Charleston, 1:50 P.M., June 9, 1860, American Telegraph Company; Charles Manigault, Charleston, to A. Poullaine, Savannah, May [24, 1862?], Louis Manigault Papers, in *RASP*, ser. F, DU, pt. 2, r. 5, fr. 224; r. 6, fr. 126, 127, 312, 583. On absentee planters, see Oakes, *Ruling Race*, 175, 219–20; Woodman, *King Cotton*, esp. 267, 273–74.

44. W. P. M., Washington, [D.C.], to "My dear love" [Martha Person Mangum], May 27, 1844, p. 1, Mangum Papers, vol. 13, LC; [Ed.], "Rail-Road Prospects and Progress," *DBR* 12 (May 1852): 492. See also Telegraph to Mitchell King, ca. 1857, King Papers, in *RASP*, ser. J, SHC, pt. 3, r. 4, fr. 62.

45. In 1825, for example, a total of 73 steamboats were in operation on the western rivers; in 1830 the number was 187. See Hunter, *Steamboats on the Western Rivers*, 33. Generally see the resilient classic by George R. Taylor, *Transportation Revolution*. Also useful is Phillips, *History of Transportation*.

46. [William Elliott] to Ann Elliott, Beaufort, July 20, 1823, Elliott and Gonzales Papers, ser. 1: corresp., subser. 1.3, in *RASP*, ser. J, SHC, pt. 3, r. 18, fr. 356, p. 1.

47. Grimball Diary, vol. 3, June 17, 1835, in *RASP*, ser. J, SHC, pt. 3, r. 15, fr. 611, pp. 123–24.

On the velocity of canals, see From the *Alexandria Gazette*, "Rail Roads and Canals," *FR* 1 (June 1833): 56–57; From the Proceedings of the British Association, "Resistance to Motion in Canals, in Relation to Velocity," *FR* 5 (May 1837): 28.

48. Henry C. King, Charleston, to "My Dear Father" [Mitchell King], Flat Rock P.O., Henderson Cty, N.C., King Papers, subser. 1.3, in *RASP*, ser. J, SHC, pt. 3, r. 3, fr. 627.

49. [Ed.], "British and American Steam Ships," *DBR* 9 (Nov. 1850): 549–50.

50. [Ed.], "Mobile and Ohio Railroad," *DBR* 3 (Apr. 1847): 336–37.

51. [Ed.], "Communication between New York and New Orleans," *DBR* 7 (July 1849): 45.

52. [Ed.], "Internal Improvements. Vicksburg and Jackson (Miss.) Rail-Road," *DBR* 9 (Oct. 1850): 454; Osborne, "Railway Time."

53. Freehling, *Road to Disunion*, 1:25–26; King Diary, ser. 3, Dec. 6, 1854, King Papers, in *RASP*, ser. J, SHC, pt. 3, r. 6, fr. 550, p. 6; the examples of problems faced by railways are taken from Bruce Diary, Mar. 9, 14, 31, Apr. 2, Aug. 22, 1836, Bruce Family Papers, VHS. Generally see Cotterill, "Southern Railroads"; Jack K. Williams, "Travel in Ante-Bellum Georgia"; Alvarez, *Travel on Southern Antebellum Railroads*, 40–42, 100–105. For an interesting comparison that lends weight to this argument, see Cottrell, "Of Time and the Railroader."

54. King Diary, ser. 3, July 24, 1852, p. 73, King Papers, in *RASP*, ser. J, SHC, pt. 3, r. 6, fr. 434. See also the account of railroad travel in the South in Olmsted, *Cotton Kingdom*, 44, 72.

55. Gavin Diary, Aug. 24, 1859, in *RASP*, ser. J, SHC, pt. 3, r. 10, fr. 991, p. 176.

56. For examples of published changes in schedules by various southern railroad companies, see Geo. Yonge, General Superintendent, Augusta, [Ga.], "Central Railroad. New Arrangement," *So. Cult.* 16 (July 1858): 229; Andrew Yonge, Sup't, "Augusta and Savannah Railroad Change of Schedule," *So. Cult.* 18 (Mar. 1860): 109; Geo. Yonge, "Change of Schedule on the Georgia Railroad," *So. Cult.* 21 (Sept. and Oct. 1863): 120.

57. Grimball Diary, vol. 3, June 10, 1835, in *RASP*, ser. J, SHC, pt. 3, r. 15, fr. 592–93, pp. 104–5.

58. Olmsted, *Cotton Kingdom*, 212.

59. John B. DeSaussure, Charleston, to A. H. Boykin, Plane Hill, Nov. 8, 1851, ser. 1: corresp., folder 5, Boykin Family Papers, in *RASP*, ser. J, SHC, pt. 3, r. 28, fr. 322, p. 1. On southern railroads and the factorage system generally, see Woodman, *King Cotton*, 269–73.

60. Bruce Diary, Apr. 11, Sept. 24, 1836, Bruce Family Papers, VHS. On the railroad's impact on its employees' time consciousness specifically, as harbinger of the modern age generally, see Licht, *Working for the Railroad*, esp. 73.

61. "A Hurried Visit to Newberry District," *So. Cab.* 1 (Nov. 1840): 640.

62. From the *London Mechanics Magazine*, "Further Experiments on the Liverpool and Manchester Railway, to Determine the Correctness of the Undulating Railway System," *FR* 1 (Apr. 1834): 466.

63. [Ed.], "Railway Systems and Prospects in Europe and America," *DBR* 3 (Feb. 1847): 141.

64. From the *Philadelphia Inquirer*, "Rail Road Rapidity," *FR* 2 (Dec. 1834): 455–56. See also Segal, *Technological Utopianism*, esp. 56–97.

65. Horry, *An Address Respecting the Charleston & Hamburgh Railroad*, 1, 11. Similar sentiments were echoed in an earlier report of 1828. See *Report of a Special Committee*. As did virtually every American railroad, southern companies invoked the British success as both a reason and a concrete example to follow. See Horatio Allen, *Reports to the Board of Directors*, 18. On Charleston's declining balance of trade with the Georgia and South Carolina up-country during the 1820s and the subsequent decision to build the Charleston-Hamburg line, see Starr, *One Hundred Years*, 151.

66. Stephens, " 'The Most Reliable Time.' "

67. Starr, *One Hundred Years*, 151–68.

68. First quotation in "Report of the Chief Engineer, Horatio Allen," in Horry, *Annual Report*, 12. On this and the postal service, see Stephens, " 'The Most Reliable Time,' "

esp. 4–5; Alvarez, *Travel on Southern Antebellum Railroads*, 120–21. Second quotation in [Eli Bowen], "The Post System," *DBR* 12 (Mar. 1852): 247. Biographical details on Allen may be found in Forney, *Memoir of Horatio Allen*, esp. 5, 17–19, 21. Allen died in 1889, six years after the introduction of standard time. According to an article in the *Farmers' Register* in 1833, the Charleston and Hamburg Railroad started carrying local mail as early as 1833. See [Ed.], "General Description of Hamburg and Charleston Rail Road," *FR* 1 (Oct. 1833): 261–62.

69. Unidentified, Richmond, to Jourdan Woolfok, Shane Saw Mills, [Caroline Co.], Feb. 26, 1836, Woolfok Family Papers, VHS.

70. First quotation in Horatio Allen, *Semi-Annual Report*, 5; second in [J. Ravenel], *Report*, 4–5.

71. [T. Tupper], *Semi-Annual Report*, 5–6.

72. In order see *Semi-Annual Report . . . to July, 1838*, 5–6; *Semi-Annual Report . . . Jan. 18th, 1839*, 6–9. On the post office's contract times see Bowen, *United States Post-Office Guide*, 26; Thomas Curtis Clark, *American Railway*, 314.

73. "Memorial of John Bryce and 212 Others," Apr. 9, 1838, 25th Cong., 2d sess., Doc. 325, House of Representatives. Whether the petition had the desired effect is unclear.

74. Bruce Diary, May 15, 21, 1837, Jan. 15, 1839, Bruce Family Papers, VHS.

75. On the causal relationship between technological change and an increasing, subjective awareness of the need for punctuality, there is a substantial, largely psychology-based, literature. For a nineteenth-century opinion on the connection, see George M. Beard, "Causes of Nervousness." For modern explanations consult Neustadter, "Beat the Clock"; Hay and Usunier, "Time and Strategic Action"; the various essays in Macar, Poulthas, and Friedman, *Time, Action and Cognition*; and Cross, *Quest for Time*, esp. 3–4. A useful discussion on the relationship between material culture and subjective consciousness is to be found in Isaac, "Imagination and Material Culture," esp. 401.

76. John Ball Jr. to "Dear Lucille," John Ball Sr. and John Ball Jr. Papers, Charleston District, in *RASP*, ser. F, DU, pt. 2, r. 3, fr. 472. See also James Burchell Richardson, Charleston, to Ann C. (Sinkler) Richardson, 9 OClk. P.M., May 22, 1829, in Richardson Papers, ibid., r. 14, fr. 88.

77. Mitchell King, Charleston, to David M. Gaylay, 2 PM, June 11, 1855; to Messrs Aiken & Burns, 1 PM, June 27, 1855, King Papers, ser. 1.6, Lettercopy Books, in *RASP*, ser. J, SHC, pt. 3, r. 4, fr. 783, p. 206.

78. Daniel Turner, St. Mary's Co., Ga., to Dr. and Mrs. Peter Turner, East Greenwich, R.I., Oct. 5, 1805, p. 1, Turner Papers, LC.

79. Ann Simons, Charleston, to "My Dear Mary," Apr. 25, 1809, ser. 1: corresp., folder 4, Singleton Family Papers, in *RASP*, ser. J, SHC, pt. 3, r. 30, fr. 111, p. 1.

80. M. A. J. Washburn, Saratoga Springs, to Fannie Habersham, July 27, 1858, Louis Manigault Papers, in *RASP*, ser. F, DU, pt. 2, r. 6, fr. 73.

81. James Burchell Richardson, Charleston, to Ann C. (Sinkler) Richardson, 9 OClk. P.M., May 22, 1829, Richardson Papers, in *RASP*, ser. F, DU, pt. 2, r. 14, fr. 88.

82. William Jervey, Darlington, S.C., to Josiah Smith, Charleston, July 1, 1862, in Smith Papers, in *RASP*, ser. F, DU, pt. 2, r. 13, fr. 52.

83. Wm. Elliott, Beaufort, S.C., to R. E. Elliott, Savannah, Ga., Dec. 20, 1836, King Papers, in *RASP*, ser. J, SHC, pt. 3, r. 18, fr. 895, p. 1.

84. James B. Richardson, Jamesville, to William Henry Burchell Richardson, Nov. 25, 1824, Richardson Papers, Sumter District, S.C., in *RASP*, ser. F, DU, pt. 3, r. 14, fr. 46–47, pp. 1–2.

85. Charles Manigault, Charleston, to "Mon Cher Louis," Feb. 18, 1856, Louis Manigault Papers, in *RASP*, ser. F, DU, pt. 2, r. 5, fr. 812–13.

86. Daniel Turner, St. Mary's Co., Ga., to Dr. and Mrs. Peter Turner, East Greenwich, R.I., Aug. 13, 1806, p. 3, Feb. 20, 1805, p. 2, Turner Papers, LC.

87. Diary of Rosanna Law, Jan. 5, May 23, 1853, SCDAH.

88. Bruce Diary, Aug. 2, 1839, Bruce Family Papers, VHS.

89. [Thomas Allen], "Internal Improvements. Railroads in Missouri," *DBR* 8 (June 1850): 574. See also Edmund Trewbridge Dana Myers, Speech, n.d., Myers Family Papers, VHS.

90. An alternative formulation of the in but not of argument may be found in Genovese and Fox-Genovese, *Fruits of Merchant Capital*.

91. [Ed.], "Thoughts on a Rail-Road System for New Orleans," *DBR* 10 (May 1851): 511.

92. [Ed.], "The Rail-Road System of the United States," *DBR* 13 (Dec. 1852): 574–75.

93. [Ed.], "Liability of Rail-Roads for Accidents," *DBR* 15 (Oct. 1853): 426. For some intriguing comparisons with modern America, see Robinson, "Time Squeeze."

94. King Diary, Aug. 3, 1854, King Papers, in *RASP*, ser. J, SHC, pt. 3, r. 6, fr. 764; Wm. Elliott to "Dear Emily," Sept. 14, 1858, Elliott and Gonzales Papers, ibid., r. 20, fr. 819, p. 4. On the high incidence of lost luggage see Alvarez, *Travel on Southern Antebellum Railroads*, 121.

95. "Bill of Fare," [1863], Louis Manigault Papers, in *RASP*, ser. F, DU, pt. 2, r. 6, fr. 409–10. Also see Elizabeth Doris King, "The First-Class Hotel and the Age of the Common Man."

96. Alfred Huger, Post Office [Charleston], to "My dear Wife," Jan. 1, 1858, Huger Letterbooks, Charleston District, in *RASP*, ser. F, DU, pt. 2, r. 8, fr. 225, 226, pp. 218–19. See also Rose, *Voices of the Marketplace*, 11–13.

97. Grimball Diary, vol. 1, June 19, 1833, Oct. 25, 1835, in *RASP*, ser. J, SHC, pt. 3, r. 15, fr. 420, p. 89, r. 16, fr. 81–82, pp. 25–26; [Ed.], "Speed on Western Rivers," *DBR* 13 (July 1852): 100.

98. "Agricultural Convention," *So. Ag.* 12 (June 1839): 281.

99. Ann Elliott, Beaufort, S.C., to Wm. Elliott, N.Y., July 6, 1836, Elliott and Gonzales Papers, in *RASP*, ser. J, SHC, pt. 3, r. 18, fr. 838–41, pp. 1–2.

100. "Memorial of the Internal Improvements Convention to the General Assembly of North Carolina," *FR* 7 (Feb. 1839): 98; "The Rail-Road," *So. Ro.* 3 (May 2, 1835): 142. Also see Gould, *Time's Arrow, Time's Cycle*.

101. James Johnston, M.D., "The Rail Road Steamer," *FR* 6 (Apr. 1838): 3.

102. Gavin Diary, June 23, 1856, in *RASP*, ser. J, SHC, pt. 3, r. 10, fr. 855, p. 42. See also Brewster, "Ante-Bellum Planters and Their Means of Transportation."

103. [Ed.], "Communication between New York and New Orleans," *DBR* 7 (July 1849): 46.

104. [Ed.], "Morse's Electro-Magnetic Telegraph," *DBR* 1 (Feb. 1846): 134, 139, 140.

105. [Ed.], "The Telegraph," *DBR* 16 (Mar. 1854): 253.

106. From the *Richmond Dispatch*, "Difference of Time," *So. Pl.* 18 (Oct. 1858): 636.

107. [Ed.], "The Telegraph," *DBR* 15 (Nov. 1853): 466.

108. From the *Macon Messenger*, "Observations on the Internal Improvements of the Present Age," *TF* 1 (Dec. 1835): 203. See also [Ed.], "Railroad Speed and Power," *So. Pl.* 10 (Jan. 1850): 13.

109. From the *Philadelphia Ledger*, "The Last Half Century," *So. Pl.* 11 (Apr. 1851): 117–18.

110. From the *Albany Cultivator*, "Inaccuracy in Farming," *So. Pl.* 12 (July 1852): 212; Leo Marx, *Machine in the Garden*.

111. From the *Knickerbocker Magazine*, "The Oldest Inhabitant's Opinion of Rail-Roads," *So. Pl.* 19 (Nov. 1859): 690.

112. George Fitzhugh, "Uniform Postage, Railroads, Telegraphs, Fashions, etc.," *DBR* n.s., 6 (June 1859): 657–64. Interesting comparisons to Fitzhugh's argument are in the various essays in Lewis and Griessman, *Southern Mystique*.

CHAPTER FOUR

1. Prude, *Coming of Industrial Order*, 131; Brody, "Time and Work," 18; Thompson, "Time, Work-Discipline." See also Christopher Clark, *Roots of Rural Capitalism*, esp. 258–59; Hensley, "Time, Work, and Social Context in New England"; Bruegel, " 'Time That Can Be Relied Upon.' "

2. See Bender, *Antislavery Debate*. Quotation from Wyatt-Brown, "Modernizing Southern Slavery," 28. See also Craven, *Soil Exhaustion*, esp. 137, 142–47; Gray, *History of Agriculture*, esp. 2:916. In some respects, of course, eighteenth-century slave owners thought themselves to be embarking on an age of improvement. But their impetus for doing so was different because eighteenth-century planters rarely embraced the use of clock time as a means to that end. See Chaplin, *Anxious Pursuit*; and Daniels, "Gresham's Laws," esp. 205–22.

3. Genovese, *Slaveholders' Dilemma*, esp. 5. See also Kilbride, "Slavery and Utilitarianism." Other important interpretations of the proslavery argument include Donald, "Proslavery Argument Reconsidered"; and Faust, *Sacred Circle*. On the rise of the free-wage-labor ideology in the North, see Foner, *Free Soil, Free Labor, Free Men*; Glickstein, *Concepts of Free Labor*; and, more generally, Hobsbawm, *Age of Capital*. For examples of planters who took scientific agriculture seriously, see Oakes, *Ruling Race*, esp. 166.

4. Quotations from Genovese, *Slaveholders' Dilemma*, 13. On structural impediments to southern economic development, see Genovese, *Political Economy of Slavery*. Also useful in this context are David Brion Davis, *Slavery and Human Progress*; and Shore, *Southern Capitalists*, esp. chap. 1. For parallel developments in twentieth-century Kenya, see Cooper, "Colonizing Time," esp. 239.

5. Karl Marx, *Theories of Surplus-Value*, 302–3. See also Eric Hobsbawm's excellent introduction to Karl Marx, *Pre-Capitalist Economic Formations*, esp. 47–48. Quotations from J. S., "Slavery," *So. Pl.* 1 (Sept. 1841): 157; H. C., "On the Management of Negroes—Addressed to the Farmers and Planters of Virginia," *So. Ag.* 7 (July 1834): 368. Ideally, planters would successfully inculcate "an industrious habit" among their charges and so obviate the need for the whip. See, A Retired Planter, "Reflections, &c. of a Retired Planter," *So. Ag.* 7 (Aug. 1834): 407. The quotation from Pope was inscribed on the frontispiece of a preprinted plantation journal manufactured by J. W. Randolph of Virginia. The journal was intended to facilitate "the better Ordering and Management of Plantation and Farm Business." An example is to be found in Philip St. George Cocke's Plantation Journal, 1861, Cocke Papers, VHS. See the advertisement for "Plantation Book. J. W. Randolph," *DBR* 14 (Jan. 1853): 92. On planters' almost pathological obsession with control and discipline, see Greenberg, *Masters and Statesmen*; and A Planter, "On the Management of Negroes," *FR* 4 (Jan. 1837): 574. The planter's analogy to clock-regulated ship discipline was not altogether accurate, at least for the first half of the eighteenth century. See Rediker, *Between the Devil and the Deep Blue Sea*, esp. 212–27.

6. An Overseer, "The Duty of Overseers," *So. Cult.* 2 (Oct. 16, 1844): 166; [Ed.], "Overseers, Read This!" *So. Cult.* 13 (May 1855): 158. For an overseer who followed such advice by "flog[g]ing [a hand] for not coming to his work in due time," see John Evans, Chemonie Plantation, Fla., to George Noble Jones, Feb. 9, 1848, in Phillips and Glunt, *Florida Plantation Records*, 57. Generally see Clifton, "Rice Driver."

7. See Hammond Plantation Book, Silver Bluff Plantation, Jan. 1851, Jan. 1855, in *RASP*, ser. A, LC, pt. 1, r. 14 (no frames, no pagination).

8. Unidentified newspaper clipping, ca. 1838, in McDowell Plantation Journal, n.p., n.d., SCL.

9. From the *Farmer's Guide*, "Exhortations to the Young Farmer," *So. Pl.* 11 (Dec. 1851): 375–76; [Ed.], "Profits of Agriculture," *So. Pl.* 2 (Jan. 1842): 11.

10. Clod Thumper, "Maxims for Young Farmers and Overseers," *So. Pl.* 17 (Nov. 1857): 671.

11. From the *Soil of the South*, "The Bachelor Farmer," *So. Cult.* 12 (July 1854): 208. See also William W. Minor and P. H. Goodloe, Albemarle Co., [Va.], "The Cost, Profits, and Economy of Labor," *So. Pl.* 12 (June 1852): 164.

12. Agricultural Society of Albemarle, Charlottesville, Va., Minute Book, pp. 3–4, Nov. 9, 1825, VHS; [James Henry Hammond,] "Quick Work," *FR* 4 (Dec. 1836): 458. For other

examples of this fascination with timing work and time-saving machinery, see From the *Southern Agriculturalist*, "Important to Farmers," *FR* 6 (Aug. 1838): 275; Wm. B. Harrison, "Hussey's Reaper," *FR* 9 (July 1841): 434–35.

13. [Ed.], "Samuelson's Rotary Digging Machine," *So. Cult.* 12 (Feb. 1854): 44; Edward Stabler, "Saving Clover Seed—Economy in the Use of Agricultural Machinery," *So. Pl.* 14 (Apr. 1854): 110.

14. [Ed.], "Farm Economy," *So. Cult.* 11 (Dec. 1853): 353. And see the account in Bancroft, *Slave-Trading in the Old South*, 88–89.

15. From the *Boston Cultivator*, "Early Rising," *So. Pl.* 11 (Jan. 1851): 21–22; Kollock Plantation Journals, Retreat Plantation, folder 1, vol. 1, Sat., July 1, 1837, pp. 4–5, SHC.

16. Aufhauser, "Slavery and Scientific Management," esp. 818–21. If William Sander's formulation that "economic growth increases the economic value of time" is correct, then planters' increasing concern with the value of time may well be indicative of the South's antebellum economic growth. For further details, see Sander, "Economics of Time and Community," esp. 44.

17. Jesse H. Turner, "Address to the Henrico Agricultural Society," *FR* 9 (Aug. 1841): 451.

18. "The Farmer's Guide," *So. Pl.* 18 (Oct. 1858): 640.

19. From the *Yankee Farmer*, "Time is Money," *So. Ag.* 9 (Aug. 1836): 433–34; From the *Vermont Free Press*, "Procrastination," *TF* 1 (Mar. 1835): 60; [Ed.], "Business of To-Morrow," *TF* 1 (Mar. 1835): 61; Poor Richard, "Rainy Days," *TF* 1 (Apr. 1835): 78.

20. See From the *Yankee Farmer*, "Time and Money," *So. Ag.* 9 (Aug. 1836): 433–34; [Ed.], "How to Save Time," *TF* 1 (Mar. 1838): 272; [Ed.], "Value of Time," *TF* 2 (Nov. 1837): 176; [Ed.], "Punctuality," *TF* 2 (July 1837): 104. For other examples see [Ed.], "How to Save Time," *So. Ag.* 11 (Mar. 1838): 165; Poor Richard, "Rainy Days," *TF* 1 (Apr. 1835): 78. On the time consciousness of northern colonial almanac editors, see O'Malley, *Keeping Watch*, 13–20.

21. John Forsyth, "The North and the South," *DBR* 17 (Oct. 1854): 364–65. Not all liked southern journals' tendency to reprint northern advice. It was especially frowned upon during the heightening tension of the 1850s. See [Ed.], "The Soil of the South and the Tropical Farmer," *So. Pl.* 12 (Dec. 1852): 379.

22. Olmsted, *Journey in the Seaboard Slave States*, 2:205.

23. On what planters said and what they actually did, consult Oakes, *Ruling Race*, esp. 166–67; and Faust, "Rhetoric and Ritual."

24. William Elliott, N.Y., to "My Dear Wife," Beaufort, S.C., Oct. 5, 1828, pp. 2–3, Elliott and Gonzales Papers, in *RASP*, ser. J, SHC, pt. 3, r. 18, fr. 391. A year earlier Elliott received a letter from Mr. M. Ashe of the *Southern Agriculturalist* in Charleston complaining about the need to improve the scientific basis of agriculture in the South (Letter of July 31, 1827, ibid., fr. 535).

25. William Elliott, Boston, Mass., to "My Dear Wife," Beaufort, S.C., Aug. 25, 1836, Elliott and Gonzales Papers, in *RASP*, ser. J, SHC, pt. 3, r. 18, fr. 868.

26. Elliott, Oak Lawn plantation, S.C., to "My Dear Mother," Apr. 26, 1854, ibid., r. 20, fr. 202; Elliott, Beaufort, S.C., to his son, "Dear Ralph," July 12, 1856, ibid., fr. 513–14.

27. William Elliott, Paris, to Ralph Elliott, Aug. 22, 1855, ibid., r. 20, fr. 365.

28. T. S. K., "The Factory System," *So. Ag.* n.s., 5 (Feb. 1845): 49–51.

29. A Virginian, "Yankee Improvements in Virginia," *So. Pl.* 5 (Nov. 1845): 241.

30. Georgian, "Labor-Saving Machines," *So. Cult.* 8 (Aug. 1850): 152; D. Lee, "Farm Economy and Political Economy, One and Inseparable," *So. Cult.* 10 (Oct. 1852): 289–90; Backwoods Planter, "System in Farming," *So. Cult.* 7 (June 1849): 82–83; A Lover of System, "Necessity of System," *So. Pl.* 10 (Jan. 1850): 30. See also the reprint from the *American Agriculturalist* in the *Southern Cultivator* in 1850 advising planters to "take time by the forelock" and so improve farm efficiency generally ("Take Time by the Forelock," *So. Cult.* 8 [Aug. 1850]: 126).

31. That such progressive efforts did result in profit for planters see Aufhauser, "Slavery and Scientific Management"; Conrad and Meyer, "Economics of Slavery in the Ante Bellum South"; Fogel and Engerman, *Time on the Cross*, esp. 1:59–106; Oakes, *Ruling Race*, 153–91; Metzer, "Rational Management." For interpretations stressing the barriers to industrialization in the plantation economy, see Bateman and Weiss, *Deplorable Scarcity*; and Genovese, *Political Economy of Slavery*.

32. N. Herbemont, Columbia, S.C., "An Essay on the Culture of the Grape Vine, and Making of Wine," *So. Ag.* 1 (Feb. 1828): 13; S. F. Clark, Savannah River, to Louis Manigault, [Charleston?], Sept. 30, 1853, Louis Manigault Papers, in *RASP*, ser. F, DU, pt. 2, r. 5, fr. 545, p. 1; [Ed.], "On Manufacturing in the South," *So. Ag.* 1 (Aug. 1828): 358.

33. Quotations from advertisements for cotton gins made by Clavert's of Leeds, England, and the Aberdeen Gin Factory of Mississippi, ca. 1857, in Foreign Office Papers, 84/1027, pp. 148, 155, British Public Records Office, Kew, London; From the *Mobile Register*, "Improved Cotton Gin," *So. Ag.* n.s., 5 (Feb. 1845): 79.

34. J. E. Haynes, Argyle Island, Ga., to Charles Manigault, Oct. 5, 1846, p. 2, Nov. 3, 1846, p. 1, Louis Manigault Papers, in *RASP*, ser. F, DU, pt. 2, r. 5, fr. 60, 63. Other examples are in Clifton, *Life and Labor on Argyle Island*. See also Dusinberre, *Them Dark Days*, 9.

35. Gould Diary, Oct. 29, Nov. 6, 7, 1834, p. 46, SHC.

36. Plantation Journal, Aug. 1, 7, Jan. 3, Nov. 26, 1832, Millwood and Midway Plantations, Colhoun Papers, Abbeville, Charleston, and Pendleton Districts, S.C., ser. 2, in *RASP*, ser. J, SHC, pt. 3, r. 29, fr. 516–19. See also M., "Moon-ology—Superstitions and Humbugs," *So. Pl.* 10 (June 1850): 182–83.

37. [Ed.], "Whatever Is Worth Doing, Is Worth Doing Well," *TF* 1 (Feb. 1835): 37.

38. See From the *Vermont Free Press*, "Procrastination," *TF* 1 (Mar. 1860): 60; [Ed.], " 'Business of To-Morrow,' " *TF* 1 (Mar. 1835): 61; From the *Working Farmer*, "Order and Economy on the Farm," *So. Pl.* 18 (July 1858): 439–40; From the *Southern Organ*, "Plantation Register and Account Books," *So. Cult.* 12 (Feb. 1854): 55; A Mississippi Planter, "Plantation Management," *So. Cult.* 17 (June 1859): 169–70; [Ed.], "Illustration of Early Rising," *So. Cab.* 1 (Aug. 1840): 512. On related efforts to use the slack time that plantation, slave-based agriculture inevitably invited, see Gallman, "Slavery and Southern Economic Growth," esp. 1018; Anderson and Gallman, "Slaves as Fixed Capital."

39. Cincinnatus, "General Observations on Agricultural Pursuits and Some Remedies Hinted At," *TF* 1 (Sept. 1835): 150.

40. This was not unlike the shift to personal time discipline among northern independent farmers described by Hensley, "Time, Work, and Social Context in New England," and Bruegel, " 'Time That Can Be Relied Upon.' "

41. Olmsted, *Cotton Kingdom*, 376. See Janney and Janney, *John Jay Janney's Virginia*, 30.

42. J. L., "Large Products of Small Farming," *TF* 1 (Jan. 1836): 218–19.

43. Sloan Papers and Diaries, Rich Hill, Pacolet, Spartanburg Co., S.C., vol. 1, Aug. 10, 1854, p. 9, July 7, 11, 1855, p. 26, July 19, 1857, Dec. 30, 1857, n.p., SCL. On Sloan as an upwardly mobile South Carolina up-country yeoman farmer, see Ford, *Origins of Southern Radicalism*, 78–80.

44. Cecilia, "Management of Servants," *So. Pl.* 3 (Aug. 1843): 175. See, too, Fox-Genovese, *Within the Plantation Household*, esp. 37–99. On the use of labor-saving machines in farm kitchens, see From the *American Agriculturalist*, "Economy of Labor-Saving Machines," *So. Pl.* 7 (Oct. 1847): 311.

45. From *Selected*, "Punctuality," *So. Cult.* 1 (May 10, 1843): 79. Also see Kasson, *Civilizing the Machine*, esp. 53–106.

46. "Dear Cousin" [John A. Wanes?] to Major J. D. Warren, Point Place, May's Isld., Brick House Plantation, Ashepoo, S.C., Feb. 4, 1859, box 1, folder 9, Warren Papers, SCL.

47. [George Washington], "Agricultural Letter from Gen. Washington," *So. Pl.* 2 (Oct.

1842): 217–19; [George Washington], "Washington's Agricultural Notes," *FR* 5 (Nov. 1837): 488. On Washington's time sense, see Sobel, *World They Made Together*, esp. 47, 55.

48. Senex, "Hints to Market Gardeners, &c.," *So. Ag.* 2 (May 1829): 201.

49. [R. M. T. Hunter], "Senator Hunter's Appeal to the North," *DBR* 21 (Nov. 1856): 531. Generally see R. Randall Moore, "In Search of a Safe Government," esp. 153–211. See also [Ed.], "Origin of Civilization," *DBR* 25 (Dec. 1858): 660–61.

50. [J. Harlston Read Jr.], "Slave Labor in Cities," *DBR* 26 (Mar. 1859): 600; H. N. McTyeire, D.D., "Plantation Life—Duties and Responsibilities," *DBR* 29 (Sept. 1860): 357. Worries about slaves hiring their own time were expressed in "Memorial of the Citizens of Charleston to the Senate and House of Representatives of the State of South Carolina (Charleston, 1822)," in Foner and Lewis, *Black Worker*, 1:84–85. Also see Wade, *Slavery in the Cities*.

51. "On the Management of Slaves," *So. Ag.* 6 (June 1833): 283–84, 286.

52. Faust, *Ideology of Slavery*, 244. On the eighteenth-century New England precursors to this argument, see Tise, *Proslavery*.

53. James Hamilton Couper, "Essay on Rotation of Crops," *So. Ag.* 6 (Feb. 1833): 58; J. R., "Follow Nature," *FR* 3 (Nov. 1835): 432; [Ed.], "The Laws of Nature," *TF* 3 (Sept. 1838): 224–25. See also Daniel K. Whitaker, "An Address Delivered before the Agricultural Society of South-Carolina, at the Anniversary Meeting, August 20th, 1833," *So. Ag.* 6 (Oct. 1833): 504–14, esp. 506. Generally, see Conser, *God and the Natural World*, esp. 76–77. On the secular influence of Bacon's thought in the Old South, see Faust, *Sacred Circle*, 70–86.

54. H. B. C., "A Word for Progressive Farmers," *So. Cult.* 11 (Mar. 1853): 78.

55. D. Lee, "A National Academy of Agriculture," *So. Cult.* 10 (Mar. 1852): 66; [Anon., from Clifton College, Tenn.], "Culture of Blue Grass," *TF* 2 (Jan. 1837): 3; F. H. Gordon, Bourbon, Ky., "For the Tennessee Farmer," *TF* 2 (Jan. 1837): 2–3.

56. From the *Pennsylvania Inquirer*, "Great Feat in Mowing against Time," *TF* 2 (Oct. 1837): 158.

57. "Lex Incognita," 1859, in Louis Manigault Papers, in *RASP*, ser. F, DU, pt. 2, r. 6, fr. 220.

58. J. R., "Follow Nature," *FR* 3 (Nov. 1835): 432. See also Communication from Holmesburg Co., Philadelphia, "Letter First," *FR* 3 (Jan. 1836): 536.

59. From *Life Illustrated*, " 'Protest against Early Rising,' " *So. Cult.* 18 (May 1860): 161.

60. George J. F. Clarke, "On Agricultural Prejudices," *So. Ag.* 2 (May 1829): 219. For a trenchant theoretical statement on the interdependency of clock time and natural time in industrial and capitalist societies alike, see Adam, *Timewatch*, esp. 84–106.

61. See From the *New Orleans Courier*, "A Model Southern Plantation," *So. Cult.* 10 (Mar. 1852): 88; [J. H. Fennell], "Natural Sciences," ibid., 89.

62. Genovese, *Slaveholders' Dilemma*; [Ed.], "The Black and White Races of Men," *DBR* 30 (Apr. 1861): 455. On slaveholders' long-held fears about subordinating nature and, in turn, injuring human nature, see Chaplin, "Tidal Rice Cultivation and the Problem of Slavery," esp. 30–31.

63. On southern concerns with an organically ordered, hierarchal but modern society, see Chaplin, *Anxious Pursuit*.

64. D. R. Williams, "On Upper Country Cultivation," *So. Ag.* 2 (June 1829): 262.

65. Thomas Cassells Law, "Report on Management of Slaves—Duty of Overseers and Employers," Aug. 10, 1852, Law Papers, SCL.

66. O'Malley, "Time, Work and Task Orientation."

67. Thos. Spalding, "On the Time to Plant Sea-Island Cotton," *So. Ag.* 2 (Aug. 1829): 347.

68. Russell, "Importance of System on the Plantation," *So. Cult.* 6 (Oct. 1848): 146.

69. Lawton Plantation Journal, folder 32b, ser. 2, Lawton Papers, in *RASP*, ser. J, SHC, pt. 3, r. 26, fr. 709, p. 51; S. F. Clark, [Savannah] River, to Louis Manigault, [Charleston?], Aug. 20, 1855, Louis Manigault Papers, in *RASP*, ser. F, DU, pt. 2, r. 5, fr. 755, p. 1.

70. Charles Izard Manigault, Plantation Work[book], Louis Manigault Papers, Charleston District, S.C., and Chatham County, Ga., in *RASP*, ser. F, DU, pt. 2, r. 4, fr. 930.

71. Lawton Plantation Journal, folder 32b, ser. 2, Lawton Papers, in *RASP*, ser. J, SHC, pt. 3, r. 26, fr. 694, p. 37; William Capers Sr. to [Louis Manigault], Feb. 25, 1863, Louis Manigault Papers, ser. F, DU, pt. 2, r. 6, fr. 653, p. 1. For a contemporary account of harried seasonal agriculture, see Maria Gordon (Pryor) Rice, Reminiscences, Charlotte Co., Va., p. 5, VHS.

72. "Journal of Mr. Gregory's Plantation," Greenwood Plantation Records, McPhersonville, S.C., May 5, 1861, LC; Grimball Diary, Colleton and Charleston Districts, S.C., Sept. 29, 1834, ser. 2, folder 18, vol. 3, in *RASP*, ser. J, SHC, pt. 3, r. 15, fr. 512, 557; Wickham Diary, Hickory Hill Plantation, Hanover County, Va., vol. 2, Oct. 2, 1834, VHS.

73. See the untitled communication from Westover, Aug. 20, 1883, in *FR* 1 (Nov. 1833): 321; O'Malley, "Time, Work and Task Orientation," 341–44. For a planter who kept a keen eye on nature and the weather, see Rosengarten, *Tombee*, esp. 196–97.

74. Cocke Diary, Woodland Plantation, Amelia Co., Va., June 25, 1856, Cocke Family Papers, VHS; Cobb Diary, Southampton Co., Va., Aug. 11, 1843, and "Notebook for 1843 kept by Daniel W. Cobb," Apr. 3, 1843, VHS. See also Crofts, "Southampton County Diarists in the Civil War Era."

75. Hatchett Diary, Lunenburg Co., Va., May 1, 1853, VHS. Similar remarks are in McDowell Plantation Journal, Strawberry Hill, Mar. 6–8, 1807, SCL.

76. "Notes," n.d., Diary of Charles Friend, Friend Family Papers, sec. 1, VHS.

77. Evidence suggests that some colonial planters were also concerned about the seasonal push, viewing some seasons as leisurely, others as frenetic. See Menard, Carr, and Walsh, "A Small Planter's Profits," esp. 197.

78. Genovese, *Roll, Jordan, Roll*, 289–91. See also Durrill, "Routine of Seasons."

79. Couper's comments in John D. Legare, "Account of an Agricultural Excursion Made into the South of Georgia in the Winter of 1832," *So. Ag.* 6 (July 1833): 359. That he stuck to this regimen is clear from the Couper Record Book, Hopeton Plantation, LC. Generally see Clifton, "Hopeton"; and Flanders, *Plantation Slavery in Georgia*, 101–3.

80. Miliken (Mulberry) Plantation Journals, vol. 1, SCHS. The same tendency can be discerned in other plantation journals, for example, the journal of Colleton District planter Edward Barnwell Heyward, Plantation Day Book, SCL; Connors Farm Journals, Clarendon and Lancaster Counties, S.C., SCL. Also consult Clifton, "Ante-Bellum Rice Planter."

81. From the *Alabama Planter*, "On the Management of Slaves," *DBR* 13 (Aug. 1852): 193–94.

82. "Priveleges [*sic*] of the Negroes on the Island Plantation," Richard Eppes, Code of Laws, Rules, and Regulations, ca. 1857, Eppes Family Papers, sec. 69, n.p., n.d., VHS. On Eppes, see Loth, *Virginia Landmarks Register*, s.v. "Eppes Island," 82–83.

83. Hammond Plantation Manual, 1844, Hammond Papers, in *RASP*, ser. A, SCL, pt. 1, r. 5, fr. 176, p. viii.

84. Thomas Legare Jr., "An Address before the St. Andrew's Agricultural and Police Society of James' Island, on the 7th of April, 1835," *So. Ag.* 8 (May 1835): 226, 233; Evert A. Duyckinck, "Time's Wallet," *Southern and Western Monthly Magazine and Review* 1 (Jan. 1845): 62. Southerners, after all, had a keen sense of linear time, a sense often articulated in poems. See "The Past and the Future," *So. Ro.* 3 (Jan. 10, 1835): 140.

85. On colonial southerners' familiarity with public, aural clock time, see Sobel, *World They Made Together*, 21–23; and, generally, Schafer, *Tuning of the World*, esp. 55–58. Quotation by Hammond in Genovese, *Slaveholders' Dilemma*, 95. See, too, [James Henry Hammond], "Governor Hammond's Address before the South Carolina Institute, 1850," *DBR* 8 (June 1850): 501–6. On slaveholders' selective appeals to the Middle Ages, see Genovese, "The Southern Slaveholders' Views of the Middle Ages"; and the contemporary accounts, [Ed.], "The History of the Middle Ages," *Southern and Western Monthly Magazine and*

Review 1 (June 1845): 379–80; [Ed.], "Fairy-Tales of the Middle Ages," *So. Ro.* 5 (Aug. 5, 1837): 193. Planters' use of sound had modern elements, too. Plantation journals often contained printed advice, courtesy of the publisher, regarding the speed of sound: "*Sound* passes through the air uniformly at the rate of 1142 feet in a second, or through a mile in 4 2/3 seconds." Planters, then, knew well the mathematical principles behind time obedience. Quotation in *Plantation and Farm Instruction, Regulation, Record Inventory and Account Book. For the Use of the Manager on the Estate of Philip St. George Cocke* (Richmond, Va.: J. W. Randolph, 1861), 13, Plantation Journal, 1861, Cocke Papers, VHS. On a similarly backward-looking but progressive eighteenth-century planter elite, see Chaplin, *Anxious Pursuit*, 53, 114–16.

86. On the use of the factory bell and some interesting twists in the hidden role of the clock in northern time usage, see Kulik, "Pawtucket Village and the Strike of 1824," esp. 399; and the contemporary accounts in Dublin, *Farm to Factory*, esp. 126–27. On the Janus-faced nature of southerners' attitude toward progress, see Wyatt-Brown, "Modernizing Southern Slavery," esp. 29.

87. [Mr. St. Geo. Cocke], "Plantation Management—Police," *DBR* 14 (Feb. 1853): 177–78. And see the examples in Holbrook, "A Glimpse of Life on Antebellum Slave Plantations in Texas," 370; James Benson Sellers, *Slavery in Alabama*, 59, 66–67, 79; Sydnor, *Slavery in Mississippi*, 12–13, 76–83; Joe Gray Taylor, *Negro Slavery in Louisiana*, 66–69; Gray, *History of Agriculture*, 1:546–47.

88. Agricola, "Management of Negroes," *DBR* 19 (Sept. 1855): 361–62. See also From the *Southern Agriculturalist*, "Notions on the Management of Negroes, &c.," *FR* 4 (Dec. 1836): 494–95.

89. Quotations in *Am. Sl.*, supp. ser. 1, vol. 9, Miss. narrs., pt. 4, 1552, 1550; supp. ser. 1, vol. 10, Miss. narrs., pts. 4 and 5, 2298–99; supp. ser. 1, vol. 12, Okla. narrs., 9; supp. ser. 1, vol. 8, Miss. narrs., pt. 3, 1170. Eighteenth-century slaves sometimes noticed the presence of a household clock. Thomas Jefferson apparently had one in his kitchen. See Jefferson, *Memoirs of a Monticello Slave*, 29; Sobel, *World They Made Together*, 57–58.

90. From the *Southern Agriculturalist*, "Notions on the Management of Negroes," *FR* 4 (Dec. 1836): 494; [A Northern Gentleman], "Negro Slavery at the South," *DBR* 7 (Nov. 1849): 382.

91. Foby, "Management of Servants," *So. Cult.* 11 (Aug. 1853): 226–28.

92. "Rules for Government of Plantation," John Blount Miller and John H. Furman Cornhill Plantation Book, ca. 1845, McDonald Furman Papers, in *RASP*, ser. F, DU, pt. 2, r. 9, fr. 116, 125.

93. S. H. C., "An Alarm Clock for the Plantation," *So. Cult.* 13 (July 1855): 212.

94. [Ed.], "The Sugar-Cane," *DBR* 6 (Oct. and Nov. 1848): 358. For photographic evidence of bell towers on antebellum southern plantations see Vlach, *Back of the Big House*, 42, 92, 114, 152, 199, 219.

95. [An Alabama Planter], "Plantation Life in the South—A Picture of Comfort," *So. Cult.* 18 (June 1860): 183.

96. From *Fraser's Magazine*, "Laborers in English Factories," *FR* 1 (Aug. 1833): 188–89. See also [Ed.], "A Slavery Far Worse Than Chattel," *DBR* 16 (Mar. 1854): esp. 269. British self-criticism, however, provided slaveholders with ample ammunition to indicate the wrongs of industrialization. See Cunliffe, *Chattel Slavery and Wage Slavery*.

97. Harriet Beecher Stowe, *Uncle Tom's Cabin*, 250. My thanks to Peter A. Coclanis for bringing this reference to my attention.

98. Wright, *Old South, New South*, esp. 17–19; Wright, *Political Economy of the Cotton South*, esp. 43–88. See also Metzer, "Rational Management"; Aufhauser, "Slavery and Scientific Management."

99. Olson, "Clock Time versus Real Time," 234–35. Olson's excellent study does not consider whether planters actually used clocks or watches to achieve this level of intensity.

100. Ibid., 227. See Anderson and Gallman, "Slaves as Fixed Capital."

101. Robert Collins, "Management of Slaves," *DBR* 17 (Oct. 1854): 424.

102. Olson, "Clock Time versus Real Time," 222, 235. For other examples of planters following this practice see Mark M. Smith, "Old South Time in Comparative Perspective"; John A. Calhoun, E. E. DuBose, and Virgil Bubo [June 13, 1846], "Management of Slaves," *DBR* 18 (June 1855): 718; Joseph Acklen of Louisiana, "Rules on the Management of a Southern Estate," *DBR* 22 (Apr. 1857): 380. Planters recognized that northern laborers worked fewer hours in their still shorter winter months. See [Ed.], "Education," *So. Pl.* 5 (Oct. 1845): 234–35.

103. As noted in Bonner, *History of Georgia Agriculture*, 201; and in Olson, "Clock Time versus Real Time," 235.

104. According to some recent work, although planters employed a variety of incentives and punishments to regulate their bondpeoples' productivity, "roughly 36 to 45 percent of southern slaves lived on plantations of frequent physical punishment." See Crawford, "Punishments and Rewards," 536.

105. Agricola, "Management of Slaves," *DBR* 14 (Sept. 1855): 359.

106. Flinn Plantation Book, Green River Plantation, n.d., pp. 2–3, SCL. For a very useful discussion of the profitability of keeping pregnant slave women in the field until the last moment and, conversely, the small babies that this practice produced, see Fogel, "Was the Overwork of Pregnant Women Profit Maximizing?"

107. "Labor," *FR* 2 (June 1834): 51.

108. In order see John Ball and Keating Simmons Ball Plantation Record Books, Dec. 1849, in *RASP*, ser. J, SHC, pt. 3, r. 1, fr. 44; Wickham Diary, Hanover Co., Va., vol. 7, Oct. 24, 1858, VHS. For veiled references to clock time and the task, see Joyner, "Slave Folklife on the Waccamaw Neck," 42–45.

109. Gaillard Plantation Journals, vol. 1, Mar. 27, 1844, vol. 2, Aug. 14, 1847, in *RASP*, ser. A, SCL, pt. 2, r. 1, fr. 116, 234.

110. Simms Plantation Book, May 7, 1847, SCL; Aiken Diary, Oct. 8, 1856, SCL.

111. Anon., Plantation Journal, Barnwell District, S.C., Aug. 1843, SCL.

112. From the *Charleston Courier*, "Whittemore's Cotton Gin," *So. Ag.* 8 (Sept. 1835): 477.

113. B. McBride, "Memoranda of the Culture of the Sugar Cane, and Manufacture of Sugar," *So. Ag.* 3 (July 1830): 352–53. On the precision required in the sugar refining and production process, see Gates, *Farmer's Age*, 122–28. Hemp production, centered in Kentucky, was similarly precise. See Hopkins, *History of the Hemp Industry in Kentucky*, 24–27, 132–35.

114. [Ed.], "On the Manufacture of Indigo," *So. Ag.* 1 (Nov. 1828): 478; Chaplin, *Anxious Pursuit*, 193–95. And see the eighteenth-century account, "Observations upon the Method of Manufacturing Indico," in Charles Garth Letterbook, pp. 179–80, SCDAH.

115. M. W. Philips, "Plantation Economy.—Treatment of Slaves," *So. Ag.* n.s., 6 (June 1846): 225–26; A Tennessean, "Management of Negroes—Bathing Feet," *So. Cult.* 11 (Oct. 1853): 302. This may have been a preventive treatment for tetanus.

116. Sparkman Plantation Journal, Georgetown District, S.C., folder 1, in *RASP*, ser. J, SHC, pt. 3, r. 1, fr. 670, 678; Grimball Diary, ser. 2, folder 21, vol. 4, Sept. 21, 1864, in *RASP*, ser. J, SHC, pt. 3, r. 16, fr. 396, p. 88. See Lale and Campbell, "Plantation Journal of John B. Webster," esp. 61.

117. See Philip D. Morgan, "Work and Culture"; Berlin and Morgan, *Cultivation and Culture*. On the need for the task as a way to measure the labor of slaves who might be working away from supervision, see Weir, *Colonial South Carolina*, 181. Julie Saville warns:

"Under no circumstances should antebellum task labor be likened to the task-oriented labor of a free peasantry." She is right, mainly because the antebellum task system entailed a heavy dose of clock time whereas task-oriented labor does not. See Saville, *Work of Reconstruction*, 7, n. 2.

118. Boney, *Slave Life in Georgia*, 160.

119. See, in order, R. King, "On the Management of the Butler Estate, &c.," *So. Ag.* 1 (Dec. 1828): 525; Lawton Plantation Journal, folder 32b, ser. 2, Lawton Papers, in *RASP*, ser. J, SHC, pt. 3, r. 26, fr. 716, p. 58; P. C. Weston, "Management of a Southern Plantation," *DBR* 22 (Jan. 1857): 40.

120. Walvin, "Slaves, Free Time and the Question of Leisure," esp. 7–8. Useful studies of off time and the slaves' economy are in the various essays in Berlin and Morgan, *Cultivation and Culture*, esp. pt. 3; Genovese, *Roll, Jordan, Roll*, esp. 313; on slave leisure, Betty Wood, *Slavery in Colonial Georgia*, esp. 165–68; her most recent work on the slaves' economy in Georgia, *Women's Work, Men's Work*, esp. 12–30; and Twaddle, "Wages of Slavery." On the proportion of former slaves who owned garden plots and the like, see Crawford, "Problems in the Quantitative Analysis," esp. 334.

121. Nguyen, "Spatialization of Metric Time," 45.

122. *Am. Sl.*, vol. 12, Ga. narrs., pt. 1, 241.

123. Ibid., vol. 13, Ga. narrs., pt. 3, 94–95.

124. Ibid., vol. 4, Texas narrs., pt. 2, 82.

125. Ibid., vol. 14, N.C. narrs., pt. 1, 101.

126. Ibid., vol. 10, Ark. narrs., pt. 6, 328.

127. Ibid., vol. 2, S.C. narrs., pt. 1, 53.

128. Ibid., vol. 12, Okla. narrs., supp. ser. 1, 5.

129. Ibid., vol. 5, Texas narrs., pt. 4, 8.

130. Ibid., vol. 9, Miss. narrs., supp. ser. 1, pt. 4, 1663.

131. Ibid., vol. 2, S.C. narrs., pt. 1, 327.

132. Ibid., vol. 8, Ark. narrs., pt. 1, 142.

133. Ibid., vol. 7, Okla. and Miss. narrs., 12.

134. Ibid., vol. 4, Texas narrs., pt. 1, 170–71.

135. James Henry Hammond, Silver Bluff, S.C., to W. B. Hodgson, Jan. 1, 1846, Hammond Papers, in *RASP*, ser. F, DU, pt. 2, r. 9, fr. 519, p. 1; William Elliott, Oak Lawn, to Phebe Elliott, Beaufort, Dec. 10, 1857, Elliott and Gonzales Papers, Beaufort and Colleton Districts, S.C., ser. 1, subser. 1.5, folder 47, in *RASP*, ser. J, SHC, pt. 3, r. 20, fr. 252, p. 1. On the way slavery impinged on masters' freedom, also see Schantz, "'A Very Serious Business,'" esp. 21. On romanticism, melancholy, and the sense of a ruined present in southern history, see O'Brien, *Rethinking the South*, esp. 50–51, 83.

136. "Order Overdone," *So. Cult.* 17 (Nov. 1859): 349. A similar account of clock-regulated plantation domestic affairs may be found in Curlee, "History of a Texas Slave Plantation," 113. Northerners, by contrast, seemed comfortable with similarly strict regimens. See Gara, "A New Englander's View of Plantation Life," esp. 346.

137. From *Sleeper's Agricultural Address*, "Small vs. Large Farms," *So. Pl.* 5 (Aug. 1845): 179.

138. Generally on the existence of slavery as a litmus test of white freedom, see Edmund S. Morgan, *American Slavery, American Freedom*. On this problem in the South, see Greene, "'Slavery or Independence'"; Harvey J. Jackson, "'American Slavery, American Freedom.'" See also the intriguing characterization by Weir, "South Carolinian as Extremist."

139. See Ford, *Origins of Southern Radicalism*; Hahn, *Roots of Southern Populism*; Genovese and Fox-Genovese, *Fruits of Merchant Capital*.

140. On the political drift, see Freehling, *Road to Disunion*, 1:211–566. For interpretations stressing the cultural and economic differences between North and South, see Genovese, *Political Economy of Slavery*, 28–31, 34–36; Eric Foner, *Free Soil, Free Labor, Free Men*, 38–41,

69–72; Charles A. Beard and Mary R. Beard, *Rise of American Civilization*, 2:3–10. See also Ramsdell, *Lincoln the Liberal Statesman*, 36–64; Donald, *Excess of Democracy*.

CHAPTER FIVE

1. On the marginalization of African Americans, see Moses, *Wings of Ethiopia*, 27–44. That this marginalization occurred in the area of American time sensibilities, see Horton, "Time and Cool People," 43–44. In the 1960s, Horton conducted a sociological study in which he found: "In the street, watches have a special and specific meaning. Watches are for pawning and not for telling time. When they are worn, they are decorations and ornaments of status. The street clock is informal, personal, and relaxed. It is not standardized to other clocks. In fact, a street dude may have almost infinite toleration for individual time schedules. To be on time is often meaningless, to be late an unconsciously accepted way of life. 'I'll catch you later,' or simply 'later,' are the street phrases that mean business will be taken care of, but not necessarily now." The same was true with middle-class African Americans. See ibid., 43. See also Henry, "White People's Time, Colored People's Time," 31–33.

2. On the stereotype of Colored Peoples' Time, see Herskovits, *Myth of the Negro Past*, 153; McKenzie, "Time in European and African Philosophy," esp. 84. On CPT as resistance and for hints that the term may have been spread by African Americans themselves, see Horton, "Time and Cool People," 31–50.

3. See Mark M. Smith, "Old South Time in Comparative Perspective"; Thompson, "Time, Work-Discipline"; Brody, "Time and Work."

4. On time as a cultural construct, see the suggestive remarks in Glasser, *Time in French Life and Thought*, 12. A very sensible discussion of the cultural constructions of time in African societies is by Dorthy L. Pennington, "Time in African Culture."

5. See Samuel Swain to Thomas F. Wharton, Medford, Dec. 28, 1810, and "Captain George Howeland's Voyage to West Africa, 1822–1823," in Bennett and Brooks, *New England Merchants in Africa*, 46, 126. Of course, it should be remembered that the vast majority of African American slaves were brought to the South before the ban on importation in 1808. The account was by Philip G. Hubert Jr., "The Business of a Factory," *Scribner's Magazine* 21 (Mar. 1897): 307–31. On colonization see, for example, the accounts by Beecham, *Ashantee and the Gold Coast*, 184; Mbaeyi, *British Military and Naval Forces in West African History*, 1–5; and Priestly, "Philip Quaque of Cape Coast," 102. The Portuguese had been attempting to proselytize West Africans since the fourteenth century. What impact their instructions in Christianity had on African cyclical time perspectives is difficult to ascertain. See, though, Da Mota and Hair, *East of Mina*, 3–5, 72–89; Hair, *Andre De Faro's Missionary Journey to Sierra Leone*, 37–38, 52, 59–60. On the benefits and dangers in American/African comparative history, see Jordan, "Planter and Slave Identity Formation."

6. Generally, see Mark M. Smith, "Old South Time in Comparative Perspective"; Atkins, *The Moon Is Dead!*; Edward Hall, *Dance of Life*, esp. 3–4; Davison, *Unforgiving Minute*; Genovese, *Roll, Jordan, Roll*, esp. 289.

7. Mbiti quoted in Mullin, *Africa in America*, 72. Mbiti also makes the following points: "The rising of the sun is an event which is recognized by the whole community. It does not matter, therefore, whether the sun rises at 5 a.m. or 7 a.m., so long as it rises. . . . For the people concerned, time is meaningful at the point of the event and not at the mathematical moment. . . . In western or technological society, time is a commodity which must be utilized, sold and bought; but in traditional African life, time has to be created or produced. Man is not a slave of time; instead he 'makes' as much time as he wants. . . . Those who are seen sitting down, are actually *not wasting* time, but either waiting for time or in the process of 'producing' time." Of the broader African time philosophy, Mbiti writes: "The notion of a messianic hope, or a final destruction of the world, has no place in traditional [African]

concept of history." Quotations in Mbiti, *African Religions and Philosophy*, 19, 23. Traveler and missionary accounts reaffirm Mbiti's argument. See, for example, Anna M. Scott, *Day Dawn in Africa*.

8. Quotation from McKenzie, "Time in European and African Philosophy," 81. On the role of nature in African societies see Harms, *Games against Nature*, 243–56. Heavily colonized plantation areas elsewhere in Africa, however, tended to make African and Arab laborers more sensitive to the existence of mechanical time and its relationship to work. See Cooper, *Plantation Slavery on the East Coast of Africa*, esp. 180–81; Atkins, " 'Kafir Time' "; Atkins, *The Moon Is Dead!* Of course, the Islamic requirement of midday prayer and afternoon prayer, at 2 P.M. and 4 P.M. respectively, ensured some degree of time awareness. See H. F. Smith et al., "Ali Eisami Gazirmabe of Borno," 208. Conflict over time has always been bound up with social and religious identity. On January 4, 1994, for example, in an effort to cast off Western influence, Libya abandoned the Gregorian solar calendar in favor of the Islamic lunar calendar, which was about three weeks shorter. See *Independent* (London), Wed., Jan. 5, 1994, 8. For a fine collection of essays that explore the cultural specificity of time conceptions, see Hughes and Trautmann, eds., *Time*.

9. This should not be taken to mean that Western time conceptions are exclusively linear. The influence of Christianity on time is ambiguous insofar as it has made Westerners sensitive to both the cyclical and linear nature of historical time. Plainly, however, if what Mbiti suggests is true, any linear time conception found in African American historical time consciousness is very likely derived from Western thought. On this generally see O'Malley, *Keeping Watch*, esp. 1–54; and Gould, *Time's Arrow, Time's Cycle*, esp. 10–16.

10. This should not be taken to imply that African time notions were simplistic, as the following works make clear: Wilks, "On Mentally Mapping Greater Asante"; McCaskie, "Time and the Calendar in Nineteenth-Century Asante"; McKenzie, "Time in European and African Philosophy"; Mbiti, *African Religions and Philosophy*, 15–28; G. I. Jones, "Time and Oral Tradition"; Vansina, *Children of Woot*; Ojo, *Yoruba Culture*, 201–7; and Meyerowitz, *The Akan of Ghana*, 23–31. According to Mechal Sobel, most West African societies shared this view and understanding of time, thus making it acceptable to speak of a broadly defined West African time perception. See *World They Made Together*, 18. See, too, Hilton, *Kingdom of Kongo*, 6–9, 96–99, 106–7; Law, *Slave Coast of West Africa*, 46–57; Kea, *Settlements, Trade, and Politics*, esp. 212–13.

11. In order see J. W. E. Bowen, ed., *Addresses and Proceedings . . . December 13–15, 1895*, 33; [Hugh Crow], *Memoirs of the Late Captain Hugh Crow of Liverpool*, 233; Beecham, *Ashantee and the Gold Coast*, 185; Duncan, *Travels in Western Africa*, 1:219; Park, *Travels in the Interior of Africa*, 246; Herskovits, *Myth of the Negro Past*, 153; McKenzie, "Time in European and African Philosophy," 84.

12. Whitemarsh B. Seabrook, "On the Causes of the Want of General Unsuccessfulness of the Sea-Island Planters," *So. Ag.* 7 (April 1834): 178. Another planter, H. C., made similar observations: "It is characteristic of the negro, that he lives only for to-day, and is willing to let the morrow provide for itself." It was a habit that could be solved "by a proper discipline." See "On the Management of Negroes," *So. Cab.* 1 (May 1840): 279. See also [Dr. Cartwright of New Orleans], "Dr. Cartwright on the Caucasians and the Africans," *DBR* 25 (July 1858): 47.

13. In this context see Genovese, "A Georgia Slaveholder Looks at Africa"; Horton, "Time and Cool People," 31–33. On white stereotypes of slaves, see Blassingame, *Slave Community*, 224–30. Southern savants attempted to give pseudo-scientific legitimacy to their claim that blacks were innately indolent. *Dysaethesia Aethiopica* was promoted as a medical condition peculiar to African Americans in the 1850s, the main "symptoms" of which were "torpor," "natural indolence," and "a hebetude of the intellectual faculties." See [Ed.], "Dysaethesia Aethiopica, or Hebetude of Mind and Obtuse Sensibility of Body—A Disease Peculiar to

Negroes—Called by Overseers, 'Rascality,' " *DBR* 11 (Sept. 1851): 333–35. As is well known, slaveholders and their overseers believed they could detect differences between ethnic and regional groups. Some of these differences devolved on the work ethic. As one South Carolina overseer wrote in 1855: "We are now getting some hands in the low Country and from other sections; but I prefer the Sumter negroes to any I have yet tried—The Charleston Dist negroes are slow & feeble. . . . The Darlington & Marion negroes are insolent and refractory and the Williamsburg negroes are as untamed as Bufaloes." See D. B. M. Sauvin, Manchester [S.C.], to Col. [James Burchell?] Richardson, Aug. 3, 1855, Richardson Papers, Sumter District, S.C., in *RASP*, ser. F, DU, pt. 2, r. 14, fr. 827, p. 1.

14. Other historians have made similar observations for the colonial South. In particular, see Isaac, *Transformation of Virginia*, 68, 77–78, 307; Sobel, *World They Made Together*, 1–25.

15. First two quotations in Mullin, *Africa in America*, 31. Testimony of George Nichols, [South Carolina] Council Journal, beginning Jan. 24, 1748, Legislative Journals, 1748–49, p. 90, SCDAH. For other examples see Sobel, *World They Made Together*, 30–43.

16. Sobel, *World They Made Together*, chap. 2.

17. As Abby Munro, principal of the Laing Normal and Industrial School in Mt. Pleasant, South Carolina, explained to the school's northern benefactors in 1889: "Fifteen minutes after the bells are rung, the gates are locked, each morning and there is no more passing in and out the side gates for the day. Yesterday morning, however,—was an exception. The country people use the sun for a clock, and, it was such a very cloudy, dark morning. I knew they would be deceived. They came in about fifteen minutes late, and one of them volunteered the excuse, that they hadn't seen the sun 'till yet.' " See Abby D. Munro, Mt. Pleasant, South Carolina, to "My dear Friends," [Philadelphia], Mar. 9, 1889, pp. 5–6, Munro Papers, SCL. Thanks to John Oldfield for bringing this document to my attention.

18. Thompson, "Time, Work-Discipline." See also O'Malley, "Time, Work and Task Orientation."

19. It is not apparent from the secondary literature on slave revolts whether slaves themselves attempted to coordinate their movements by the clock. There are, however, some strong hints that urban slaves, especially those involved in the 1822 Vesey conspiracy in Charleston, South Carolina, did attempt to recruit the town's public time to coordinate their meeting times. See the account in Lofton, *Denmark Vesey's Revolt*, 144. Generally, see the classic work by Aptheker, *American Negro Slave Revolts*.

20. *Am. Sl.*, vol. 12, Ga. narrs., pts. 1 and 2, 97; supp. ser. 1, vol. 12, Okla. narrs., 19.

21. Hammond, "Management of Negroes," Plantation Book, p. 32, in *RASP*, LC, r. 14, (no frames, no pagination).

22. *Am. Sl.*, supp. ser. 2, vol. 2, Texas narrs., pt. 1, 288.

23. See ibid., vol. 4, Texas narrs., pt. 3, 1082; for the slave whose mother owned a clock, supp. ser. 1, vol. 1, Ala. narrs., 212; *Records of the Committee of Claims (Southern Claims Commission)*, r. 14, "Consolidated Index of Claims," 1–262. Watch ownership might have been more common among South Carolina and Georgia low-country slaves because the task system enabled them to accumulate money and hence personal property. For one Georgia slave who claimed a watch after the war, see Philip D. Morgan, "Work and Culture," 588, n. 94. Urban slaves apparently had slightly greater access to watches as, indeed, they did to public sources of time. But of the eighteen hundred or so slaves and free blacks arrested in Charleston between December 28, 1855, and June 1, 1856, seven, or less than 1 percent, were found to have watches on them by the arresting officers. See entries for Jan. 8, 18, Mar. 16, Apr. 13, May 6, 11, 1856, in Records of Arrests and Sentences, Charleston, S.C., Charleston Library Society. Again, thanks to John Oldfield for alerting me to this source.

24. Very occasionally, slaves stole watches when running away. See advertisements for Jim, Jacob, and Tony in the *Georgia Messenger*, Nov. 15, 1848, Aug. 13, 1831, July 3, 1850; Reidy, *From Slavery to Agrarian Capitalism*, 27, 259, n. 38; Prude, "To Look Upon the 'Lower Sort.' "

For a slave who was entrusted to deliver "Mr. North's watch" (his overseer's) and so had opportunity to steal it, see Grimball Diary, Colleton and Charleston Districts, S.C., Sept., 30., 1834, in Grimball Diaries, ser. 2, folder 18, vol. 1, ser. J, SHC, pt. 3, r. 15, fr. 557, p. 69. An unusual piece of evidence which suggests that slaves owned watches is the observations of a dental surgeon writing for the *New York Day Book* in 1857. Of slaves in Fairfield, Alabama, he wrote: "I do not speak of fancy negroes, such as barbers and hotel waiters, but of plantation negroes. Many of them sport an excellent watch, keep a horse, and raise cattle." J. D. B. De Bow was only half convinced, stating that the surgeon's account contained "some free but truthful dashes." Certainly, there is little corroborating evidence. See the account in "Negro Life at the South," *DBR* 22 (June 1857): 631–32. See also Boney, *Slave Life in Georgia*, 125. Free blacks, however, could and did acquire watches. See, for example, the fascinating account in Hogan, *William Johnson's Natchez*, 453.

25. Simpson's testimony in *Am. Sl.*, vol. 11, Ark. narrs., pt. 7 and Mo. narrs., 313. Other testimony, in order, ibid., vol. 19, God Struck Me Dead (Fisk University), 104; supp. ser. 1, vol. 1, Ala. narrs., 172; testimony of Henry James Trentham in Hurmence, *Before Freedom*, 6.

26. *Am. Sl.*, supp. ser. 2, vol. 5, Texas narrs., pt. 4, 1608, 1653; supp. ser. 2, vol. 7, Texas narrs., pt. 6, 2493; supp. ser. 2, vol. 2, Texas narrs., pt. 1, 2101, 184; Olson, "Clock Time versus Real Time," 227.

27. Mark M. Smith, "Old South Time in Comparative Perspective."

28. There has been a lamentable tendency by some historians of both the left and right to sentimentalize the slave experience by overly applauding the survival of so-called African-isms during slavery. The net effect has been sometimes to understate the power and flex-ibility of the slaveholders' regime, especially during its most dynamic and resilient period in the first half of the nineteenth century. Moses has rightly warned against such sentimental-ism in *Wings of Ethiopia*, 45–64. Also appropriately sobering is Kolchin, "Reevaluating the Antebellum Slave Community." For a similar critique of the "new labor history" and northern industrialization, see McDonnell, " 'You Are Too Sentimental.' " For a sampling of the variety of useful work that has been produced on slave culture, see Owens, *This Species of Property*; Norrece T. Jones, *Born a Child of Freedom*; and Stuckey, *Slave Culture*.

29. Boney, *Slave Life in Georgia*, 108.

30. Quotations in Ball, *Fifty Years in Chains*, 118, 113. Although the lash was less than desirable as a way to enforce obedience to clock time, its use was common and, moreover, does not appear to have had, from the planters' point of view, the deleterious consequences attributed it by Genovese. According to Genovese, slaveholders "failed in deeper ways that cast a shadow over the long-range prospects for [their survival in a capitalist world market] and over the future of both blacks and whites in American society. Too often they fell back on the whip and thereby taught and learned little" (*Roll, Jordan, Roll*, 286). Certainly, the planter's use of the clock did not instill time discipline among slaves; but the clock coupled with the whip went some way toward it by imposing time obedience. See Crawford, "Pun-ishments and Rewards."

31. On the various methodological problems in using narratives of slaves and former slaves much has been written. See especially Blassingame, *Slave Testimony*, esp. xlii–lvii; Genovese, "Getting to Know the Slaves"; Yetman, "The Background of the Slave Narrative Collection"; Woodward, "History from Slave Sources," 470; and Escott, *Slavery Remem-bered*, esp. 3–17. The justification for using the slave narratives should not necessarily be that they are all the historian has. Rather, if used with care, the narratives are solid historical testimony even though they have been subject to more historical scrutiny than equally problematic sources written by whites. For an excellent defense of historians' use of the narratives see Byrd, "Gifts to Do Unnatural Things," 1–27; and the extremely useful essay by Crawford, "Problems in the Quantitative Analysis," esp. 349–50.

32. In order see *Am. Sl.*, supp. ser. 1, vol. 12, Okla. narrs., 277; supp. ser. 2, vol. 7, Texas

narrs., pt. 6, 2833; vol. 7, Okla. and Miss. narrs., 311; "De Parable of 'De Wuck Time,'" in John G. Williams, *"De Ole Plantation,"* 42.

33. *Am. Sl.*, vol. 14, N.C. narrs., pt. 1, 167–68; supp. ser. 2, vol. 9, Texas narrs., pt. 8, 3626; supp. ser. 2, vol. 4, Texas narrs., pt. 3, 1219. Lue Bradford's testimony quoted in Cade, "Out of the Mouths of Ex-Slaves," 312. On the task, see the testimony in Cade, "Out of the Mouths of Ex-Slaves," 326. On the factory see John Washington Memoir, "Memorys of the Past," r. 1, p. 66, LC; and, generally, Mark M. Smith, "Old South Time in Comparative Perspective." Consult, too, the detailed work by Dew, in particular his *Bond of Iron* and "Disciplining Slave Ironworkers."

34. *Am. Sl.*, vol. 12, Ga. narrs., pts. 3 and 4, 214; vol. 11, Ark. narrs., pt. 7, and Mo. narrs., 220; vol. 12, Ga. narrs., pt. 2, 257. Graves's testimony in Perdue, Barden, and Phillips, *Weevils in the Wheat*, 122.

35. John Washington Memoir, "Memorys of the Past," p. 55, LC; testimony of Lu Lee in *Am. Sl.*, supp. ser. 2, vol. 6, Texas narrs., pt. 5, 2298. See also "Speech of Lewis Richardson," Amherstburgh, Mar. 13, 1846, in Blassingame, *Slave Testimony*, 164.

36. Charley Williams quoted in "Plantation Ways," Botkin, *Treasury of Southern Folklore*, 587; Dave Walker's testimony in *Am. Sl.*, supp. ser. 1, vol. 10, Miss. narrs., pt. 5, 2148–49.

37. *Am. Sl.*, supp. ser. 2, vol. 3, Texas narrs., pt. 2, 797.

38. Ibid., vol. 1, Ala. . . . Wash., narrs., 81.

39. Ibid., vol. 2, Texas narrs., pt. 1, 592.

40. In order see Burton, *Memories of Childhood's Slavery Days*, 5; testimony of Betty Cofer in Hurmence, *Before Freedom*, 57. Planters' communication of time through sound may have polluted more than just African Americans' time sense. Although little work has been done on the subject, it is feasible that the African conception of sound, broadly construed, also came under attack. If, as Paul Stoller claims, there is a discrete and identifiable African sound conception that is "a dimension of experience separate from the domains of human, animal, and plant life . . . that sounds carry forces that can penetrate an object," and that "the sounds of praise-names, magical words, and sacred musical instruments create an auditory presence that can transform a person morally, politically, and magically," then planters' comparatively corporeal and certainly functional adaptation of the bell for the secular task of regulating labor may well have threatened the integrity of a purer, more spiritually defined African sound sensibility. Of course, it is possible that no such reaction occurred because there appears to have been little resistance to the appropriation of church sound and time, in the form of bells, for the secular function of ordering civic life. The subject, however, is worthy of further consideration. For some initial thoughts on the subject, see Mark M. Smith, "Time, Sound, and the Virginia Slave," and a larger work in progress, tentatively titled, "American Soundscapes." Quotations from Stoller, "Sound in Songhay Cultural Experience," 559. On African sound understandings, see Tambiah, "Magical Power of Words"; Feld, *Sound and Sentiment*. On the history of sound in Western society, consult Zukerkandl, *Sound and Symbol*; Alfred Jackson, "Sound and Ritual"; Leppert, *Sight of Sound*, esp. xix–xxvii, 50–59.

41. *Am. Sl.*, supp. ser. 2, vol. 2, Texas narrs., pt. 1, 771.

42. Ibid., supp. ser. 1, vol. 10, Miss. narrs., pt. 5, 2410; supp. ser. 2, vol. 7, Texas narrs., pt. 6, 2640. Similar examples can be found in James L. Smith, *Autobiography*, 8, 41.

43. *Am. Sl.*, supp. ser. 1, vol. 12, Okla. narrs., 346; vol. 4, Texas narrs., pts. 1 and 2, 194; supp. ser. 2, vol. 1, Texas narrs., pt. 1, 41; vol. 12, Ga. narrs., pts. 1 and 2, 323; testimony of Fannie Berry in Perdue, Barden, and Phillips, *Weevils in the Wheat*, 43.

44. *Am. Sl.*, supp. ser. 2, vol. 3, Texas narrs., pt. 2, 881.

45. For quotations and corroborative evidence see ibid., vol. 3, Texas narrs., pt. 2, 575; vol. 9, Texas narrs., pt. 8, 3489; vol. 2, Texas narrs., pt. 1, 398–99, 165; Seward, *Twenty-Two Years a*

Slave, 15. For Douglass's remarks see his *Narrative*, 29. Douglass also recalled that he was given "often less than five minutes" for his midday meal (ibid., 73).

46. *Am. Sl.*, supp. ser. 2, vol. 2, Texas narrs., pt. 1, 867. On the wage fine and whip see Mark M. Smith, "Old South Time in Comparative Perspective."

47. *Am. Sl.*, vol. 12, Ga. narrs., pts. 1 and 2, 218; Yellin, *Incidents in the Life of a Slave Girl*, 12.

48. A Mississippi Planter, "Management of Negroes upon Southern Estates," *DBR* 10 (June 1851): 625.

49. Mark M. Smith, "Old South Time in Comparative Perspective."

50. Martineau, *Retrospect of Western Travel*, 1:214; Hopley, *Life in the South*, 1:207. A virtually identical example may be found in Wilma King, *A Northern Woman in the Plantation South*, 97. Olmsted, *Cotton Kingdom*, 41. See also Genovese, *Roll, Jordan, Roll*, 363–65. On house hands as having more control over their working hours, see Crawford, "Punishments and Rewards," 544. Seemingly innocent mistakes like the following may well represent an attempt on the part of slaves to disrupt masters' affairs: "Bachus came from Wiltown last Evening—but brought no letter. There was some mistake it seems about the time of his starting." See Grimball Diary, Aug. 10, 1832, Grimball Diaries, ser. 2, vol. 1, folder 18, in *RASP*, ser. J, SHC, pt. 3, r. 15, fr. 362, p. 31. The same kind of feigned stupidity occurred with respect to time obedience, sometimes with a twist of humor: "The Negro does love to laugh at the mishaps of his white master, as evidenced by such stories as that of the new field hand who did not understand the meaning of the dinner bell. His master found him in the field still working after the bell had rung, and angrily commanded him to 'drop whatever he had in his hands' and run for the table whenever he heard it ring. Next day at noon he was carrying his master, taken sick in the fields, across a foot-log over the creek when the bell rang. He 'dropped' the white man in the water and nothing was done to him for he had only done what the master had commanded." Quoted in Herskovits, *Myth of the Negro Past*, 154. Whether or not the form of resistance noted by Martineau and Hopley was exclusively the purview of female slaves and, as such, has a gendered significance, is not clear. Doctoral work on work, time, and female slaves in the antebellum South is currently being conducted by Liese Perrin and should help clarify this issue. See Perrin, "Female Slaves and the Idea of Work." For a discussion of female resistance to slavery, see Betty Wood, "Some Aspects of Female Resistance to Chattel Slavery in Low Country Georgia."

51. "Management of Slaves, &c.," *FR* 5 (June 1837): 32.

52. On slave resistance, its various forms, and its prepolitical character much has been written. The subject is dealt with skillfully by Genovese in his *From Rebellion to Revolution* and his seminal *Roll, Jordan, Roll*, 597–660. Also useful is Boles, *Black Southerners*, esp. 177–79.

53. In order, see Yellin, *Incidents in the Life of a Slave Girl*, 87; Edward Thomas Heriot Estate, James Ritchie Sparkman Books, Dec. 30, 1854, in *RASP*, ser. J, SHC, pt. 2, r. 1, fr. 26, p. 6. Former slave testimony is in *Am. Sl.*, supp. ser. 1, vol. 4, Ga. narrs., pt. 2, 562; vol. 17, Fla. narrs., 66–67. For Fripp's "poping," see Fripp Papers, Beaufort District, S.C., Oct. 19, 1858, ser. 3, folder 10, in *RASP*, ser. J, SHC, pt. 3, r. 25, fr. 712, p. 91.

54. *Am. Sl.*, supp. ser. 1, vol. 3, Ga. narrs., pt. 1, 184; supp. ser. 2, vol. 2, Texas narrs., pt. 1, 1002; vol. 17, Fla. narrs., 67; George Skipworth, Hopewell Plantation, Ala., to "Master," Hopewell Plantation, Greene Co., Ala., July 8, 1847, in Randall M. Miller, *Letters of a Slave Family*, 157. On estimates of the proportion of black males on large plantations who were drivers, see Wilcox, "Overseer Problem."

55. Browne, *Autobiography of a Female Slave, Mattie Griffiths*, 90; *Am. Sl.*, supp. ser. 2, vol. 10, Texas narrs., pt. 9, 4228. See also Berlin and Morgan, *Cultivation and Culture*, 1–48; Joyner, *Down by the Riverside*, 51–59.

56. Quoted in Angela Y. Davis, *Women, Race and Class*, 22.

57. Hammond, "Management of Negroes," Plantation Book, pp. 16, 40, in *RASP*, LC, r. 14.

58. Testimony of Mary Dodson in *Am. Sl.*, supp. ser. 2, vol. 4, Texas narrs., pt. 3, 1211.

59. Quotations from ibid., supp. ser. 1, vol. 4, Ga. narrs., pt. 2, 650; supp. ser. 1, vol. 3, Ga. narrs., pt. 1, 127. Associations between clocks and death were incredibly common and still exist in the South. For variations on the theme described by Womble and Bunts, see Reaver, *Florida Folktales*, 66; Newman Ivey White, *Frank C. Brown Collection of North Carolina Folklore*, 7:28–29, 79; Parsons, "Folk-Lore of the Sea Islands," 214; Whitney and Bullock, "Folk-Lore from Maryland," 18–19, 45, 50; Henry C. Davis, "Negro Folk-Lore in South Carolina," 246. On clocks and African American graves and photographs thereof, see Combes, "Ethnography, Archaeology and Burial Practices among Coastal South Carolina Blacks," esp. 56–58; Conner, " 'Sleep on and Take Your Rest,' " 122; Vlach, *By the Work of Their Hands*, 43; Cates, *Early Days of Coastal Georgia*, 297. For a contemporary account of "simple monuments of affection" being placed on slave graves, see "Recollections of a Southern Matron. Chap. XI. Jacque's Funeral," *So. Ro.* 4 (Nov. 14, 1835): 4. That the placing of decorations on the deceased's grave was probably of African origin, see Harms, *River of Wealth, River of Sorrow*, 192–93. Generally see Ferguson, *Uncommon Ground*, esp. 115–17.

60. The Dahome practice is described in the Savannah Unit, Georgia Writers' Project, Works Projects Administration, *Drums and Shadows*, 231. On African American grave decoration generally, see Carrington, "Decoration of Graves of Negroes in South Carolina," 267. By the mid-twentieth century some southern whites also adopted such decorative practices. See Jeane, "Traditional Upland South Cemetery." For the opposite interpretation of this and the following evidence, see Sobel, *Trabellin' On*, esp. 125–26, 245–46.

61. See *Am. Sl.*, vol. 19, God Struck Me Dead (Fisk University), 77, 99. See also Friedman, *Enclosed Garden*, esp. 68, 72.

62. Abby D. Munro, Mt. Pleasant, S.C., to "Friends," [Philadelphia], Feb. 28, 1891, pp. 2–4, Munro Papers, SCL.

63. See testimony of Jim Barclay, *Am. Sl.*, supp. ser. 2, vol. 2, Texas narrs., pt. 1, 163.

64. Ibid., vol. 7, Miss. and Okla. narrs., 190. Hunter's testimony in Perdue, Barden, and Phillips, *Weevils in the Wheat*, 151. On Christianity as a "mystic clock," see Yellin, *Incidents in the Life of a Slave Girl*, 24.

65. *Am. Sl.*, vol. 4, Texas narrs., pts. 1 and 2, 134.

66. Robert W. Gibbes, "Southern Slave Life," *DBR* 24 (Apr. 1858): 322.

67. *Am. Sl.*, supp. ser. 2, vol. 2, Texas narrs., pt. 1, 271–72.

68. Mullin, *Africa in America*, 242, 275.

69. Lou Austin testimony in, *Am. Sl.*, supp. ser. 2, vol. 2, Texas narrs., pt. 1, 130.

70. See Browne, *Autobiography of a Female Slave*, 203; *Am. Sl.*, vol. 19, God Struck Me Dead (Fisk University), 2, 209.

71. Boney, Hume, and Zafar, *God Made Man, Man Made the Slave*, 67; Raboteau, *Slave Religion*, esp. 3–95; Sobel, *World They Made Together*, 171–232; and the useful account in Kolchin, *American Slavery*, 54–57, 141–54. But see too Suttles, "African Religious Survivals." Consult also the testimony of John Henry Beauregard Smith, who asked his interviewer in the 1930s: "Dis am de calendar. . . . Do it go back? No. It is made for de futcha and dee present" (*Am. Sl.*, supp. ser. 1, vol. 1, Ala. narrs., 370).

72. Quotations in Hurmence, *Before Freedom*, 40; testimony of Steve Jones in *Am. Sl.*, supp. ser. 2, vol. 6, Texas narrs., pt. 5, 2141. See the testimony of Waters McIntosh, who recalled: "The conk [conch] sounded at about eleven o'clock, and they knew that the long expected time had come [Freedom]," ibid., vol. 10, Ark. narrs., pts. 5 and 6, 17. On the significance of attaching clock time to important life events such as birth, death, and, in this case, freedom, see Kaiser and Engel, "Time- and Age-Awareness in Early Modern Russia"; and, for the American comparison, Fischer, *Growing Old in America*, esp. 82, who demonstrates that colonial New Englanders measured birth especially, informally, with the date, not the time, being the most precise measurement. That slaves, at least those born in the late antebellum period, often knew the time of their births is revealing. Recalled William Lee of

Virginia: "I stepped in 90 years old 6 of dis last October, 'bout 10:00 o'clock in de morning [1847]. Mother tole me dat I came to dis world 'bout 10:00 o'clock" (Perdue, Barden, and Phillips, *Weevils in the Wheat*, 194). "I was born July 4, 1862 at 2.08 in the morning at Lynchburg, Sumter County, South Carolina," remembered Waters McIntosh. So too with many others: "I was born on Thursday, in the morning at three o'clock, May the twelfth [1864]"; "Mamblelay—dat's whut de folks called our mammy—told me more'n once dat 'xactly at four o'clock on a Christmas day in 1845, I was born"; "My name is Mary Anne Gibson, and I was a Hardeman. I was bawn on July 4, 1861, at four o'clock in de afternoon. I know all of dis 'cause Massa Rutherford got it out of his Bible" (*Am. Sl.*, vol. 10, Ark. narrs., pts. 5 and 6, 17; vol. 8, Ark. narrs., pts. 1 and 2, 78; supp. ser. 2, vol. 9, Texas narrs., pt. 8, 3690; supp. ser. 2, vol. 5, Texas narrs., pt. 4, 1468). Of course, many slaves did not know the time of their birth: "I do not remember to have ever met a slave who could tell of his birthday. They seldom come nearer to it than planting-time, harvest-time, cherry-time, spring-time, or fall-time" (Douglass, *Narrative*, 21). Also useful is Jonathan Bowen, "Time- and Age-Awareness among American Slaves." The question of natal alienation is explored in Patterson, *Slavery and Social Death*.

73. *Am. Sl.*, vol. 7, Okla. and Miss. narrs., 283; supp. ser. 1, vol. 1, Ala. narrs., 70.

74. Eric Foner, *Nothing but Freedom*. See also Chapter 6 of this book.

75. See *Am. Sl.*, supp. ser. 2, vol. 9, Texas narrs., pt. 8, 3844–45. The statistical evidence is based on probate records for Charleston District and Laurens County, South Carolina, compiled from Charleston District Estate Files, microfilm roll PR-EF 053-PR-EF 057, 1883–86, Charleston County Courthouse, Probate Office, North Charleston, South Carolina; and Laurens County, Inventories, Appraisements, and Sales, 1875–89 (1880–89), 391–509, SCDAH. See Appendix, Tables A.17–A.18, A.23–A.25 for details. Herndon Bogan's testimony in *Am. Sl.*, vol. 14, N.C. narrs., pt. 1, 128; Owen, *Camp-Fire Stories and Reminiscences*, 32; Washington, *Up from Slavery*, 113, 152. For a portrait by François Fleischbein of a watch-owning *femme de couleur libre* in New Orleans, ca. 1865, see Bundy, *Painting in the South*, 243. The connection between freedom, death, and clocks is touched on in Connor, " 'Sleep on and Take Your Rest,' " 59–60, 102–3, 122. See also Foner, *Reconstruction*, 262.

76. Quotations from Kulik, "Patterns of Resistance," 230. So anxious were English laborers to combat managers' ownership of time that many clubbed together to form clock and watch societies whereby a single watch was shared among up to twenty people for twenty weeks. These laborers recommended that this practice be adopted in America in 1829. See *Twenty-Four Letters from Labourers*, 48.

77. Quoted in Puckett, *Folk Beliefs of the Southern Negro*, 53. For similar riddles, see Brewster, *Frank C. Brown Collection of North Carolina Folklore*, 1:291; Parsons, "Folk-Lore of the Sea Islands," 160–65. The ideas of work and time are also present in slave work songs, the religious connotation notwithstanding. See, for example, "Quitting Time Song," in Botkin, *Treasury of Southern Folklore*, 744–45; "Heaven Bell A-Ring," and "Every Hour in the Day," in Allen, Ware, and Garrison, *Slave Songs of the United States*, 20, 58.

78. See the story "The Clock in the Sky" by Cable in which he has a plantation mistress explain to one of her slaves why she called the stars "the clock of heaven; which gained, each night, four minutes, and only for, on the time we kept by the sun." Cable, "The Clock in the Sky," *Scribner's Magazine* 30 (1901): 330.

79. *Am. Sl.*, vol. 7, Okla. and Miss. narrs., 41; Perdue, Barden, and Phillips, *Weevils in the Wheat*, 165.

CHAPTER SIX

1. Fields, "Advent of Capitalist Agriculture," esp. 77–78. For an alternative interpretation, see Govan, "Americans below the Potomac," esp. 38–39.

2. The debate among historians on how new or how old was the postbellum South is well reviewed in Carter, "From the Old South to the New," esp. 26–31. The father of the New South thesis is C. Vann Woodward, in *Origins of the New South*. Similarly see his "Emancipations and Reconstructions." Also useful in this context is Gavin Wright, *Old South, New South*, esp. 3–50. On the idea of planter persistency, the historiographical counterpart to the New South thesis, see Wiener, "Planter Persistence and Social Change"; his *Social Origins of the New South*; Mandle, *Roots of Black Poverty*; Dawley, "E. P. Thompson and the Peculiarities of the Americans"; and Emmer, "Price of Freedom."

3. Few historians have touched on this subject. J. William Harris has. "Eighteen sixty-six was a hard year for overseers," he writes, continuing: "One of them, James Spratlin, overseer on David Crenshaw Barrow's plantation in Oglethorpe County, Georgia, kept a running record that year in the form of a diary, as he struggled to keep count of every peck of corn meal furnished to, and every hour of time lost by, black workers he supervised." Because Harris neglects to consider the presence of such a time consciousness in antebellum Georgia, his conclusion is unsubstantiated: "Overseers' letters on plantation matters before emancipation were strikingly different." See his "Plantations and Power," 246. A better treatment is Saville, *Work of Reconstruction*, esp. 51.

4. Sobel, *World They Made Together*, 21. On changes in time consciousness denoting either a reflection of social changes or initiating change much has been written. See esp. Price, "Clockwork before the Clock and Timekeepers before Timekeeping"; Cipolla, *Clocks and Culture*; Gurevich, "Time as a Problem of Cultural History"; and Elias, *Time*, esp. 39–41.

5. Fields, "Advent of Capitalist Agriculture," 75–87.

6. If several eminent historians of the Civil War experience are right in their contention that "moments of revolutionary transformation expose as do few human events the foundation upon which societies rest," then any change in time sensibilities that did occur would presumably be laid bare too. Quotation in the introduction to Berlin et al., *Freedom*, ser. 1, 3:xvi. See also Saville, *Work of Reconstruction*, 15.

7. On emancipation and its various effects on other societies, see Woodward, "Emancipations and Reconstructions"; Hahn, "Class and State in Postemancipation Societies"; Adamson, "The Reconstruction of Plantation Labor after Emancipation"; Rebecca J. Scott, *Slave Emancipation in Cuba*; and Foner, *Nothing but Freedom*.

8. Quoted in Hepworth, *Whip, Hoe, and Sword*, 49–50. See also Rodrigue, "Raising Cane," esp. 11. South Carolina planters expressed similar fears even before the emancipation fiat or the South's defeat. "After this war is over," wrote Louis Manigault in 1862, "I hear many Planters say that a new code of management, of the strictest nature will have to be established for the Government of our Negroes. It has been too slack entirely hitherto" (Louis Manigault, Charleston, S.C., to Mr. Capers, Jan. 26, 1862, Louis Manigault Papers, Charleston District, in *RASP*, ser. F, DU, pt. 2, r. 6, fr. 556, p. 2).

9. John Ball and Keating Simons Ball, Plantation Record Books, Charleston District, folder 5a, vol. 5, in *RASP*, ser. J, SHC, pt. 3, r. 2, fr. 79, p. 73.

10. See [Ed.], "Dysaethesia Aethiopica . . . ," *DBR* 11 (Sept. 1851): 333–35. The stereotype has carried over into the late nineteenth and twentieth centuries in the form of CPT, or Colored People's Time, which explicitly charges African Americans with having, in addition to a presentist orientation to work and time, a "disregard for punctuality." See Herskovits, *Myth of the Negro Past*, 153. See also McKenzie, "Time in European and African Philosophy," esp. 84. Second quotation in Dennett, *The South as It Is*, 58, 62. For evidence suggesting that these stereotypes were applied to most preindustrial lower classes by northerners and southerners, especially after the Civil War, see Foner, *Reconstruction*, 133–38. For interesting parallels with Porfirian Mexico, see Beezley, *Judas at the Jockey Club*, 78–83.

11. Untitled, *Black Republican and Office-Holder's Journal*, Aug. 1865, 2. See also Clinton, "Reconstructing Freedwomen," 314.

12. [Ed.], "Reply to Abolition Objections to Slavery," *DBR* 20 (June 1856): 660. Another "lesson" learned from British emancipation was that "left to themselves, they will not work, no matter how great may be the inducements or facilities." See [Ed.], "What Negro Fanaticism Does," *DBR* 21 (Sept. 1856): 313. And of Haitian freedmen, southern slave owners learned: "The men . . . pass much of their time in sauntering, idling. . . . Nor did this unwillingness to work arise from want of incentives, but from sheer laziness" ([Ed.], "Free Negroes in Hayti," *DBR* 27 [Nov. 1859]: 535–36). See also [Ed.], "Free Negroes in Jamaica," *DBR* 28 (Jan. 1860): 87–88. For contemporary discussions on the subject, see Dennett, *The South as It Is*, 133.

13. For a slightly different interpretation of southerners' views of other postemancipation societies, see Reidy, *From Slavery to Agrarian Capitalism*, 137; and McPherson, "Was West Indian Emancipation a Success?"

14. Hepworth, *Whip, Hoe, and Sword*, 160–61. Also see Marchinow, "Go South, Young Man!," esp. 19; and Roark, *Masters without Slaves*, 68–155.

15. Mr. [George] Fitzhugh, "Freedmen and Free Men," *DBR* after the war series (hereinafter, a.w. ser.), 1 (Apr. 1866): 416–17.

16. See Saville, *Work of Reconstruction*, esp. 110–11.

17. [A resident of St. Croix], "West India Emancipation—Its Practical Workings," *DBR* a.w. ser., 1 (June 1866): 595, 599.

18. "General Orders No. 23, Order by the Commander of the Department of the Gulf, New Orleans, February 3, 1864," "Regulations by the Superintendent of Plantations in the Treasury Department 5th Special Agency [New Orleans, February? 1864]," "[H. Styles], Testimony by the Superintendent of Plantations in the Treasury Department 3rd Special Agency before the Smith-Brady Commission, New Orleans, February 3, 1865," in Berlin et al., *Freedom*, ser. 1, 3:512–13, 527, 585. See also the wonderful detail in Litwack, *Been in the Storm So Long*, 407–8.

19. "Our Arrogance," *Cotton Planter* 5 (July 1887): 4, in the Singleton Family Papers, subser. 4.3, folder 329, in *RASP*, ser. J, SHC, pt. 3, r. 41, fr. 543. Similarly, the editors of the *Southern Cultivator* noted in 1867: "The following article, published some thirty years ago, with two or three substitutions of servant or negro for slave, which we have made, are as applicable to the negroes now as it was to them in slavery." See Hill Carter, "Management of Negroes," *So. Cult.* 25 (Aug. 1867): 250. See also "A Generation Back," *SPF* n.s., 6 (Jan. 1872): 61. One farmer's appeal to the past would be credible if it were not so utterly hypocritical. "Farmer" of Granville County, North Carolina, wrote: "The many discouragements and difficulties we have to contend with, the sudden and complete change of our labor system from the obedient, industrious slave, to the idle, improvident freedman. . . . We must change our tactics or we are lost" (Farmer, "Farm Accounts—Again," *SPF* n.s., 2 [Jan. 1868]: 35–36). Generally see Litwack, *Been in the Storm So Long*, esp. 409–10.

20. Robert Jemison [and William Jemison] Proclamation[s] to his Slaves, pp. 2, 3, SHC. For biographical details see Brewer, *Alabama*, 563.

21. On the evolution of the sharecropping system in Georgia during and after the 1870s, see Flynn, *White Land, Black Labor*, 84–114.

22. See Glymph, "Freedpeople and Ex-Masters"; Reidy, *From Slavery to Agrarian Capitalism*, 136–60; Foner, *Reconstruction*, 77–175; the useful emphasis in Saville, *Work of Reconstruction*, esp. 130–42; and Lynda J. Morgan, *Emancipation in Virginia's Tobacco Belt*, esp. chap. 2.

23. Glymph, "Freedpeople and Ex-Masters." Saville, *Work of Reconstruction*, 25–28, 45, provides compelling evidence demonstrating that northern emancipators incurred the wrath of former slaves when they insisted that freedpeople remember "that all your working time belongs to the man who hires you" (ibid., 27).

24. See generally Rifkin, *Time Wars*.

25. As Gerald David Jaynes has argued in his excellent study, *Branches without Roots*, 45: "According to most historical accounts of the period, the great majority of employers sought not only to maintain the gang labor regime but also adopted a fixed money wage payment system." For similar statements, see Ransom and Sutch, *One Kind of Freedom*, 57; Mandle, *Roots of Black Poverty*, 17. For an instance of a former master who refused to pay freedmen wages simply on the grounds that he considered "they are not worth it," see Dennett, *The South as It Is*, 82. But also consult Shlomowitz, "'Bound' or 'Free?,'" 676–77.

26. On the postwar money markets, the devastating impact of the various credit instruments used by planters, and merchants' monopoly of finance capital, see Ransom, *Conflict and Compromise*, 240–46; Ransom and Sutch, *One Kind of Freedom*, 107–70; Bensel, *Yankee Leviathan*, 238–302; and Thornton, "Fiscal Policy and the Failure of Radical Reconstruction."

27. G. A. W., "To Manage Negro Labor," *So. Cult.* 26 (July 1868): 201. See also Dennett, *The South as It Is*, 289.

28. "The Labor Question," *SPF* n.s., 6 (Nov. 1872): 671. See also Jaynes, *Branches without Roots*, 3–56.

29. W. H. Evans, Society Hill, S.C., "The Labor Question," *So. Cult.* 27 (Feb. 1869): 54–55. Virtually identical arguments were made by W. Miles Hazzard of Santee, South Carolina, in "The Labor Question," *So. Cult.* 27 (July 1869): 206–7. Others couched the benefits of wage contracts in familiar paternalist garb, arguing that teaching freedpeople the value of time and money would be of service to them. For example, the minutes of the Goodwyn Agricultural Club, North Carolina, October 29, 1870, read: "Heretofore there has been but little difficulty in procuring . . . help from among that class of freedmen who unable or unwilling to make contracts to labor by the year, were ever ready to work by the day. But this class has already become thinned by emigration. . . . The introduction of the system, as it exists in England, would be eminently beneficial to our colored population. . . . It would remove them from the slough of idleness in which they now live, inure them to labor, and they, receiving the wages, would be taught the value of money, and the prudent and judicious use of it" (C. R. Lewis, "Essay upon the Subject of Labor," *SPF* n.s., 5 [Mar. 1871]: 136). Similar sentiments in favor of the wage system and its paternalist benefits may be found in N. A. Gregory, "Discussion of the Labor Question," *SPF* n.s., 5 (Nov. 1871): 656–60; and Dennett, *The South as It Is*, 15.

30. [Ed.], "Domestic Economy," *DBR* a.w. ser., 7 (Aug. 1870): 617.

31. [Ed.], "Saving of Labor," *So. Cult.* 26 (Jan. 1868): 17.

32. From the *Hearth and Home*, "The Farm-Labor Question," *SPF* n.s., 4 (Nov. 1870): 638–39. Such sentiments were echoed in [Ed.], "In Lieu of Labor," *DBR* a.w. ser., 4 (July and Aug. 1867): 69–71.

33. South-Sider, "Practical Farming, No. 7—Economy," *SPF* n.s., 6 (Nov. 1872): 625–28.

34. Z., "Save Your Labor," *SPF* n.s., 7 (Jan. 1873): 13. Some New South planters, of course, gave eloquent testimony to their own antebellum sloth and were apparently unaware that the advice they were administering was almost four decades old. Farmers like the following felt his brethren must eschew the past, presumably because he himself had ignored the increasing move toward modernity during the late antebellum period: "We must lay aside our old habits, and old ways of thinking, and of doing things. . . . We must depend less on the hoe, and more on the plough,—must employ less manual labor, and more horse power and machinery. . . . We *must* keep a strict, and fair, and full, and accurate account of all expenditures and of all receipts; we *must* add up and balance those accounts, and find where the losses are, and where the profits are. . . . To one who has no system, who has seen no system, of farm accounts, who has never been in the habit of keeping accounts, the difficulties at the outset seem insuperable" (Farmer, "Farm Accounts—Again," *SPF* n.s., 2 [Jan. 1868]: 36–37).

35. Sinclair, "Rules for Farmers," *SPF* n.s., 2 (Mar. 1868): 164. Just as they had in the 1830s, postbellum planters sometimes looked north for advice. One article, "Farm Labor," *SPF* n.s., 4 (Mar. 1870): 131–33, for example, reprinted the minutes of a meeting of the Rochester, New York, Farmer's Club: "Although some of the remarks of the speakers have but a local application, many of them are more or less applicable to every section of our country, and especially so to ours, where the general necessity for the employment of HIRED farm labor is of so recent origin. . . . Farmers should plan their work in advance, and thus prevent loss of time. . . . In the country, the ten hour system is not regarded. In winter, farmers and laborers work less than ten hours, and in the summer more. It is important that farmers should plan their work in advance."

36. Mrs. A. M., "Household," *SPF* n.s., 5 (Feb. 1871): 93. Northern educators of southern freedmen and women evidently hoped to head off such complaints by counseling freedwomen especially on "how to keep house." If the homilies themselves were not familiar to freedwomen, the spirit certainly was: " 'A time for everything, and everything in its time,' is a good motto for the housewife. . . . 'A stitch in time saves nine' is a third motto worth remembering." See "How to Keep House," *Freedman* 5 (Mar. 1868): 12, in Morris, *Freedmen's Schools and Textbooks*, 3: n.p. This periodical was published by the American Tract Society in Boston and intended, in the best proselytizing and epistolic tradition of the Protestant work ethic, to "guide them in their mental, moral, social and political duties" (ibid., n.p.).

37. For two good studies on freedpeople's resistance consult Eric Foner, *Nothing but Freedom*, and Litwack, *Been in the Storm So Long*.

38. In order see the editorials, "Everything in Its Time," *Freedman* 5 (Apr. 1868): 16; 5 (May 1868): 20; 5 (June 1868): 24; 5 (Aug. 1868): 32; "The Alarum [*sic*]-Clock," 5 (Sept. 1868): 34. On the value of minutes, hours, and days, the "worth of a watch," and the importance of punctuality see "Days," *Freedman* 1 (June 1864): 23; "How Did it Come?" 2 (Aug. 1865): 29; "Too Late," 3 (Oct. 1866): 40; "The Know How," 4 (Oct. 1867): 38; and "Hours, Days, Weeks, Months," *Freedmen's Torchlight* (Brooklyn, N.Y.) 1 (Dec. 1866): 4. All are in Morris, *Freedmen's Schools and Textbooks*, vol. 3. On the northern education of freedpeople generally, see Reidy, *From Slavery to Agrarian Capitalism*, 169–85; Jacqueline Jones, *Soldiers of Light and Love*; Currie-McDaniel, *Carpetbagger of Conscience*.

39. Abby D. Munro, Mt. Pleasant, S.C., to "My dear Friends," [Philadelphia], Feb. 28, 1891, Jan. 14, 1886, Munro Papers, SCL.

40. Braybrooke, "Diagnosis and Remedy in Marx's Doctrine of Alienation"; Mark M. Smith, "Fugitives from Labor," 27–60.

41. Glymph, "Freedpeople and Ex-Masters," 53.

42. Obviously I am suggesting that the postbellum South could embrace a capitalist time consciousness so quickly precisely because it had undergone almost half a century of experimentation with clock time and its practical application. On the gradual evolution of such an understanding in other societies, see Thompson, "Time, Work-Discipline"; O'Malley, *Keeping Watch*; Mark M. Smith, "Old South Time in Comparative Perspective"; Dohrn-van Rossum, *History of the Hour*. For a non-Western society where the move toward clock time was similarly gradual, see Thomas C. Smith, "Peasant Time and Factory Time in Japan."

43. Horton, "Time and Cool People," 31.

44. Hepworth, *Whip, Hoe, and Sword*, 29, 173.

45. Cobb Diary, "Book's of Times," 1872, Southampton Co., Va., VHS.

46. Quoted in Saville, *Work of Reconstruction*, 22–23.

47. "Questionnaire Responses by Northern Plantation Lessees," Answers to Questions for Planters by J. H. Carter & Co., Lessees Joe Davis Plantation, Davis Bend, [Mississippi, November? 1864], in Berlin et al., *Freedom*, ser. 1, 3:857–58, 105, 257. See also Dennett, *The South as It Is*, 208, 212.

48. Z., "The Labor Question," *SPF* n.s., 7 (Jan. 1873): 12–13.

49. Glymph, "Freedpeople and Ex-Masters," 48–51. On planters' efforts to control the terms of labor in other ways see Ferleger, "Sharecropping Contracts in the Late-Nineteenth-Century South."

50. Gaillard Plantation Journal, Apr. 6, 1868, in *RASP*, ser. A, SCL, pt. 2, r. 2, fr. 690.

51. W. C. Knight, Henrico Co., Va., "Form of Contract between Planters and Laborers," *DBR* a.w. ser., 3 (Feb. 1867): 192–93. Presumably, planters made some complex calculation which enabled them to translate time lost into a proportion of the share of the crop to be deducted from each worker's share at the end of the year. John Forsyth Talbert's accounts with his laborers reveal how this system may have worked. Talbert's workers were paid both by the day (average wages were roughly twenty-five cents a day) and by shares. He was meticulous in adding up hours, even minutes, lost by freedmen for various and sundry reasons, and this lost time was then applied to his laborers' wages at the end of the year, presumably after they had received their share of the crop and deductions had been made for his workers' expenses incurred at the plantation shop. The following entry provides a good example:

Statement for Nancy's Settlement for 1867

Due her for last year 1866	[$]20.00
Wages for year 1867	[$]60.00
	[$]80.00
a/c for 1867	[$]32.97
	[$]47.03
deduction for time lost	[$]15.42
Amount in money	$ 31.61 paid

In Talbert Plantation Journals, Edgefield District, S.C., vol. 4, in *RASP*, ser. A, SCL, pt. 2, r. 2, fr. 899, 945. For similar examples see Dennett, *The South as It Is*, 81, 328.

52. "Form of Contract with Plantation Hands," *So. Cult.* 24 (Jan. 1866): 4–5. This contract was also printed as "The South Carolina Freedmen," *DBR* a.w. ser., 1 (Mar. 1866): 327.

53. "Commander of the Department of the Gulf to the Secretary of War; Enclosing, First, a Memorandum of a Contract between the United States and Planters in Two Louisiana Parishes and, Second, an Order by the Department Commander, [New Orleans, November 14, 1862]," in Berlin et al., *Freedom*, ser. 1, 3:383–84, 385. This is a good example of what Thomas C. Holt has described as northerners' efforts to reconcile telling freedpeople what it meant to be free with the demands of a bourgeois, time-oriented, democratic capitalism. See his " 'An Empire over the Mind.' "

54. See Reidy, *From Slavery to Agrarian Capitalism*, 146–48; Jaynes, *Branches without Roots*, 40–50; Crouch, *The Freedmen's Bureau and Black Texans*, 13–15, 19–30; Graham, "From Slavery to Serfdom," esp. 51–53; Mandle, *Not Slave, Not Free*, 5–20.

55. Lawton Papers, Beaufort District, S.C., ser. 2, folder 30, in *RASP*, ser. J, SHC, pt. 3, r. 26, fr. 480.

56. Agreement of Aug. 18, 1866, Bacot Family Papers, Darlington District, S.C., ser. 2, folder 4, in *RASP*, ser. J, SHC, pt. 3, r. 27, fr. 918–20, copied from a preprinted labor contract, ibid., fr. 939. Some planters dispensed with finessed legalities, stating bluntly: "Rules for Hands 1. Working consists of (10) Ten consecutive hours and 1 hour for dinner" (Moore Farm Record Book, p. 192, SCL).

57. S. C. Shelton, Asheville, N.C., Dec. 20, 1871, "Discipline on the Farm," *SPF* n.s., 6 (Feb. 1872): 73–74. Generally, see Current, *Northernizing the South*, esp. 50–82.

58. Wimbish Accounts, Mecklenburg Co., Va., in Wimbish Diary, 1843, VHS.

59. Cornhill Plantation Book of John Blount Miller and John H. Furman, Sumter District, S.C., McDonald Furman Papers, in *RASP*, ser. F, DU, pt. 2, r. 9, fr. 239, p. 27; Dabbs

Farm Time Book, Sumter Co., S.C., box 1, SCL. See also Sherfesee Farm Journal, Charleston County, S.C., pp. 306–7, 322–25, 350–59, SCL.

60. Pinckney Oakland Plantation Journal, Sumter District, S.C., in *RASP*, ser. F, DU, pt. 2, r. 9, fr. 425–26.

61. Hammond Account Book, in *RASP*, ser. A, LC, pt. 1, r. 14 (no frames, no pagination).

62. His overseer, J. C. Hankinson, kept the time cards. The entry for June 11, 1884, read: "Recd of J. C. Hankinson—Time checks [$]34.15"; and for June 30, 1884: "Recd JCH Time checks [$]34.95" See Paul Fitzsimmons Hammond Account Book, Cathwood Plantation, pp. 66, 71–72, SCL. His "Lost Time" accounts for his twenty-five laborers are on pages 170–81.

63. Mason Account Book, Fortsville, Southampton Co., Va., p. 8, VHS. Virtually identical practices may be found in the Fleet Account Book, Green Mount Plantation King and Queen Co., Va., King and Queen County Historical Society Papers, VHS.

64. Talbert Plantation Journals, Edgefield District, S.C., vol. 4, in *RASP*, ser. A, SCL, pt. 2, r. 2, fr. 932, 905.

65. Gavin Wright, *Old South, New South*, chap. 2.

66. Charles Craddock Wimbish Accounts, 1865–70, Mecklenburg Co., Va., in Wimbish Diary, 1843, VHS.

67. Mason Account Book, Fortsville, Southampton Co., Va., pp. 28–29, VHS. See also Duffer Overseer's Diary, 1866, Sylvan Hill Plantation, Charlotte Co., Va., VHS.

68. Gaillard Plantation Journal, vol. 7, Apr. 6, 1868, in *RASP*, ser. A, SCL, pt. 2, r. 2, fr. 690.

69. Talbert Plantation Journals, Edgefield District, S.C., vol. 4, in *RASP*, ser. A, SCL, pt. 2, r. 2, fr. 901.

70. *Am. Sl.*, supp. ser. 2, vol. 7, Texas narrs., pt. 6, 2806.

71. Talbert Plantation Journals, Edgefield District, S.C., vol. 4, in *RASP*, ser. A, SCL, pt. 2, r. 2, fr. 920. Similarly: "1867 G. Custin furnished his daughter Jenney to work three days in the crop for which I have given him credit for three days of the time that he has lost." See Wimbish Accounts, Mecklenburg Co., Va., in Wimbish Diary, 1843, VHS.

72. Gaillard Plantation Journal, vol. 7, Apr. 17, 1868, in *RASP*, ser. A, SCL, pt. 2, r. 2, fr. 693.

73. Lewis Plantation Records, vol. 1, folder 1, "Articles of Agreement," 1874, p. 1, SHC.

74. Quoted in Dennett, *The South as It Is*, 73. On the probable lengths of postbellum working hours, see Ransom and Sutch, *One Kind of Freedom*, 235–36.

75. See, for example, John David Smith, *An Old Creed for the New South*.

76. Dennett, *The South as It Is*, 205.

77. Quoted from the *Mobile Register and Advertiser*, Apr. 2, 1867, in Foner and Lewis, *Black Worker*, 1:353.

78. Thompson, "Time, Work-Discipline," 86. This might also help explain why freedpeople tried to find the best paying employers. See Shlomowitz, "'Bound' or 'Free?,'" 666–69.

79. See Karl Marx, *Theories of Surplus-Value*, 302–3; *Capital*, 1:1022.

80. Genovese, *Roll, Jordan, Roll*, 286, 309, 292.

81. *Am. Sl.*, vol. 10, Ark. narrs., pt. 5, 135.

82. Thompson, "Time, Work-Discipline."

83. Olmsted, *Cotton Kingdom*, 103.

EPILOGUE

1. See O'Malley, *Keeping Watch*, 96–118; Trachtenberg, *Incorporation of America*, 59.

2. See Adam, *Timewatch*, esp. 112–16.

3. O'Malley, *Keeping Watch*, chap. 3.

4. Generally see Degler, *Out of Our Past*, 188–208; Ransom, *Conflict and Compromise*, 253–83.

5. Bensel, *Yankee Leviathan*, ix.

6. For the history behind standard time see Stephens, *Inventing Standard Time*; Liggett, "History of the Adoption of Standard Time in the United States"; Zeruvabel, "Standardization of Time"; Reigel, "Standard Time in the United States." Britain began adopting standard time, though, again, at the behest of railroad companies, not the government, in 1840. But the country's size necessitated only one time zone. See Humphrey M. Smith, "Greenwich Time and the Prime Meridian"; Howse, *Greenwich Time*, esp. 33.

7. See Chapter 3 of this book.

8. Bartky, "Adoption of Standard Time"; Stephens, " 'The Most Reliable Time' "; Jones and Boyd, *Harvard College Observatory*, 159–61.

9. Bartky, "Adoption of Standard Time," 29; Stephens, "Astronomy as Public Utility"; Stephens, "Partners in Time."

10. Bartky, "Adoption of Standard Time."

11. Ibid., 48–49; O'Malley, *Keeping Watch*, 100–101.

12. O'Malley, *Keeping Watch*, 111.

13. See, for example, the *Chicago Tribune*, Nov. 18, 1883, 12.

14. Quotations from O'Malley, *Keeping Watch*, 115–16.

15. Quotation from Bartky, "Adoption of Standard Time," 49.

16. Ibid., 49–51; O'Malley, *Keeping Watch*, 123.

17. Quoted in Bartky, "Adoption of Standard Time," 26. A fuller discussion may be found in Bartky and Harrison, "Standard and Daylight-Saving Time." The protracted and uneven shift to standard time in Britain is covered in Thrift, "Owners' Time and Own Time," esp. 69–75. Also see Pawson, "Local Times and Standard Times in New Zealand."

18. Bartky, "Adoption of Standard Time," 49; O'Malley, *Keeping Watch*, 133. Many southern newspapers reported this. See, for example, *Arkansas Weekly Mansion* (Little Rock), Nov. 17, 1883, 2, Nov. 24, 1883, 2.

19. Quoted in Bartky, "Adoption of Standard Time," 52.

20. Ibid., 52.

21. *Cleveland Gazette*, Nov. 3, 1883, 2, Nov. 24, 1883, 1, Dec. 1, 1883, 3, Dec. 15, 1883, 3.

22. O'Malley, *Keeping Watch*, 127. On rural time, see Gaylord, *Life in Florida*, 33; Bartky, "Adoption of Standard Time," 54. See the brief discussion in Ayers, *Promise of the New South*, 11–13.

23. Allen's time divisions are no longer in place. At 2:00 A.M. on March 18, 1918, the new federal zones were implemented. They exist today and differ markedly from Allen's. This information and quotation in Bartky, "Adoption of Standard Time," 54–55.

24. Quoted in O'Malley, *Keeping Watch*, 135. See too the jeremiads in "The New Standard Time," *Massachusetts Ploughman and New England Journal of Agriculture*, Nov. 17, 1883, 2.

25. O'Malley, *Keeping Watch*, 139.

26. *Daily Picayune*, Nov. 17, 1883, 4.

27. *Atlanta Constitution*, Nov. 20, 1883, 7.

28. *Arkansas Weekly Mansion*, Dec. 1, 1883, 2.

29. *Plateau Gazette and East Tennessee News*, Nov. 24, 1883, 2, Dec. 1, 1883, 2, Dec. 8, 1883, 4.

30. *Courier-Journal* (Louisville), Nov. 16, 1883, 4, Nov. 18, 1883, 1.

31. *Abbeville [S.C.] Press and Banner*, Nov. 21, 1883, 2; *Newberry [S.C.] Herald*, Nov. 22, 1883, 3.

32. *Orangeburg [S.C.] Times and Democrat*, Nov. 15, 1883, 3.

33. See *Columbia Daily Register*, Nov. 20, 1883, 2; *Easley [S.C.] Messenger*, Nov. 9, 1883, 1; *Charleston News and Courier*, Nov. 14, 1883, 4; *Georgetown [S.C.] Inquirer*, Nov. 28, 1883, 4; *Carolina Spartan* (Spartanburg), Nov. 14, 1883, 3; John Hammond Moore, *Columbia and Richland County*, 235–36.

34. Quoted in the *Orangeburg [S.C.] Times and Democrat*, Dec. 6, 1883, 3. See also the remarks in Alabama's *Huntsville Gazette*, Nov. 24, 1883, 1.

35. On the whole, this resistance was never very great. Compared to the tortured history of standard time and "time violators" who refused to adopt official time in the former Soviet Union, the American shift appears very peaceful. See " 'Statutory Time' Abolished in USSR"; Löwenhardt, "Over Time."

BIBLIOGRAPHY

MANUSCRIPT COLLECTIONS

Many of the items listed below are available on microfilm in one of the following collections: Kenneth M. Stampp, ed., *Records of Ante-Bellum Southern Plantations from the Revolution through the Civil War* (Frederick, Md.: University Publications of America, 1985); *American Women's Diaries (Southern Women)* (New Canaan, Conn.: Readex Film Products, 1993), as indicated by the abbreviation *RASP* or *AWD* in parentheses following the item.

Athens, Georgia
University of Georgia Libraries, Cased Image Collection
    Donald McHood and Frances Hood, ca. 1860

Atlanta, Georgia
Emory University, Woodruff Library
    Dolly Sumner (Lunt) Burge Diaries, 1847–79 (*AWD*)

Chapel Hill, North Carolina
University of North Carolina at Chapel Hill, Southern Historical Collection, Manuscript Department, Wilson Library
    Bacot Family Papers, 1767–1887 (*RASP*)
    John Ball and Keating Simmons Ball Plantation Record Books, 1770–1871 (*RASP*)
    Boykin Family Papers, 1748–1860 (*RASP*)
    Carolyn Elizabeth (Eliza) Burgwin Clitherall Diary, ca. 1800 (*AWD*)
    John Ewing Colhoun Papers, 1774–1961 (*RASP*)
    Louis M. DeSaussure Journal, 1835–65 (*RASP*)
    Elliott and Gonzales Family Papers, 1701–1866 (*RASP*)
    John Edwin Fripp Papers, 1817–1905 (*RASP*)
    David Gavin Diary, 1855–74 (*RASP*)
    William Proctor Gould Diary, 1828–56 (microfilm)
    John Berkley Grimball Diary, 1832–83 (*RASP*)
    Robert [and William] Jemison Proclamations, 1827, 1865 (typescript)
    Mitchell King Diaries, 1855–56 (*RASP*)
    Mitchell King Papers, 1801–76 (*RASP*)
    George J. Kollock Plantation Journals, 1837–61
    Alexander Robert Lawton Papers, 1774–1897 (*RASP*)
    Alexander Robert Lawton Plantation Journal, 1810–40 (*RASP*)
    Ivey Foreman Lewis Plantation Records, 1857–1916
    Nathaniel Russell Middleton Papers, 1761–1908 (*RASP*)
    Ravenel Family Papers, 1790–1918 (*RASP*)
    Singleton Family Papers, 1759–1905 (*RASP*)
    Singleton Financial Papers, 1787–1855 (*RASP*)
    Josiah Smith Jr. Letter Book, 1771–84 (*RASP*)
    Ben Sparkman Plantation Journal, 1848–59 (*RASP*)

James Ritchie Sparkman Books, 1839–78 (*RASP*)
William Ervine Sparkman Plantation Journal, 1833–66 (*RASP*)

Charleston, South Carolina
Charleston Library Society
  Records of Arrests and Sentences, 1855–56
South Carolina Historical Society
  Allard Belin Sr. Plantation Journals, 1792–98
  Alexander Crawford Daybook, 1786–95
  Peter Manigault Letterbook, 1763–72
  Thomas Miliken Plantation Journals, 1853–57
  Robert Raper Letterbook, 1759–70 (fiche)

Columbia, South Carolina
South Carolina Department of Archives and History
  Allen and Johnston Journal, 1835–36
  Anon. Ledger, 1831–74
  James T. Barentine Ledger, 1852
  Charleston District Probate Inventories. Vol. KK, 1739–44
  Charleston District Probate Inventories. Vol. W, 1763–67
  Charleston District Probate Inventories. Vol. A, 1783–87
  Charleston District Probate Inventories. Vol. D, 1800–1810
  Charleston District Probate Inventories. Vol. H, 1839–44
  Charleston District Probate Inventories. Vol. G, 1863–67
  Council Journal, Legislative Journals, 1748–49
  P. A. Gardener Watchmaker and Jeweller's Cashbook, 1887–90
  Charles Garth Letterbook, 1775 (microfilm)
  James Anderson Johnson Ledger, 1827–63
  Laurens County Probate Inventories. Book 597, 1788–96
  Laurens County Probate Inventories. Book 598, 1802–9
  Laurens County Probate Inventories, 1837–43
  Laurens County Probate Inventories, 1862–68
  Laurens County Probate Inventories, 1875–89
  Diary of Rosanna Law, 1853 (typescript)
  James Mason Farm Accounts, 1843–44
  Misc. Records, Wills, and Inventories. Charleston District. Vol. 52, 1687–1710 (micro-film)
  John Rodgers Account Book, 1816–19
  G. D. Smith General Store Ledger, 1858–59
  John D. Smith Watchmaker's Daybook, 1836–39
University of South Carolina, South Caroliniana Library
  David Wyatt Aiken Diary, 1855–58
  Thomas Aiton & Co. Letterbook, 1802 (typescript)
  Keith Alexander Commonplace Book, ca. 1730–40 (photocopies)
  William Ancrum Letterbook, 1776–80
  Anon. Misc. Planting Records, 1849
  Anon. Plantation Journal, 1838–44
  Margaret Carson *Mental Photographs Album*, 1876–1907
  William John Connors Farm Journals, 1821–43 (microfilm)
  Eugene Whitefield Dabbs Farm Time Book, 1884–86
  Andrew Flinn Plantation Books, 1840
  Samuel Porcher Gaillard Plantation Journals, 1835–71 (*RASP*)

Michael Gramling Plantation and Account Book, 1839–58
James Henry Hammond Papers, Plantation and Account Books, 1785–1865 (*RASP*)
Paul Fitzsimmons Hammond Account Book, 1882–84
Edward Barnwell Heyward Plantation Day Book, 1851–58
William Johnston Papers, 1776–1848
Thomas Cassells Law Papers, 1852–70
Davison McDowell Plantation Journal, 1803–9 (microfilm)
Davison McDowell Plantation Journal, 1838–41 (photocopy)
John A. Moore Farm Record Book, 1886
Abby D. Munro Papers, 1881–1921
John Palmer Ledger, 1777–1807 (typescript)
Charles Pinckney Accounts, 1751–52
Louis Sherfesee Farm Journal, 1882–88
William Gilmore Simms Plantation Book, 1845–74
James F. Sloan Papers and Diaries, 1854–62
Henry Summer Journal, 1837 (microfilm)
John Forsyth Talbert Plantation Journals, 1854–68 (*RASP*)
John D. Warren Papers, 1856–85

Durham, North Carolina
Duke University, Manuscript Department, William R. Perkins Library
John Durant Ashemore Plantation Journal, 1853–59 (*RASP*)
John Ball Sr. and John Ball Jr. Papers, 1773–1892 (*RASP*)
Martha E. (Foster) Crawford Diaries, 1846–81 (*AWD*)
Robert Marion Deveaux Papers, 1758–1894 (*RASP*)
McDonald Furman Papers, 1827–73 (*RASP*)
William Gibbons Papers, 1728–1803 (*RASP*)
James Henry Hammond Papers, 1835–75 (*RASP*)
Alfred Huger Letterbooks, 1853–63 (*RASP*)
Charles Izard Manigualt Plantation Work[book], 1837–44 (*RASP*)
Louis Manigault Papers, 1776–1865 (*RASP*)
Henry L. Pinckney Oakland Plantation Journal, 1850–69 (*RASP*)
James Burchell Richardson Papers, 1803–65 (*RASP*)
Josiah Edward Smith Papers, 1753–1889 (*RASP*)
Edward Telfair Papers, 1764–1831 (*RASP*)

Kew, London, U.K.
British Public Records Office
Foreign Office Papers, FO 84/1027

New York, New York
Burns Collection, Ltd.
Physician, ca. 1860

North Charleston, South Carolina
Charleston County Courthouse, Probate Office
Charleston District Estate Files, 1883–86 (microfilm)

Richmond, Virginia
Virginia Historical Society
Agricultural Society of Albemarle, Charlottesville, Minute Book, 1817–25
Mark Alexander Diary, 1804
Benjamin Barton Letterbook, 1853–68

Benjamin Barton Papers, 1804–1913
Bernard Family Papers, 1742–1887
William R. Bernard Commonplace Book, 1847–50
John Blair Diary, 1751 (photocopy)
John Durburrow Blair Papers, 1784–1823
Richard Blow Commonplace Book, 1827–32
Blair Bolling Commonplace Book (Diary), 1810–39 (photocopy)
Bruce Family Papers, 1836–1906
John Bruce Diary, 1836–39 (typescript)
William Cabell Commonplace Books, 1769–79, 1803–22 (photocopy)
Carrington Family Papers, 1761–1954 (photocopy)
Carter Family Papers, 1651–1861
Timothy Chandler Commonplace Book, 1818–23
Christ Church (Protestant Episcopal) Papers, 1988–89
Daniel William Cobb Diary, 1843–72
Cocke Family Papers, 1770–1860
James Powell Cocke Dairy, 1836–51
Philip St. George Cocke Papers, 1854–61
Dabney Minor Cosby Account Book, 1826–54
Daughters of the American Colonists, Virginia Division, Pocahontas Chapter, Records,
    1921–57
Simeon H. Duffer Overseers' Diary, 1866
Dunn Family Papers, 1844–1946
Eppes Family Papers, 1722–1953
Richard Eppes Diary, 1852–96 (microfilm)
Friend Family Papers, 1792–1871
Grigsby Family Papers, 1745–1940
William Haynie Hatchett Diary, 1853–55
Hollywood Cemetery Co., Richmond, Records, 1847–1929
(photocopy)
King and Queen County Historical Society Papers, 1822–1955 (microfilm)
Lewis Edmunds Mason Account Book, 1865–67
Forrest D. Murden, "Post and Post-Roads in Colonial Virginia," 1941 (typescript)
Myers Family Papers, 1763–1923
George Llewellyn Nicolson Diary, [1858]–1859
Isaac Gorham Pleck Papers, 1818–59
Pleck, Wellford & Co. Papers, 1834–44
Maria Gordon (Pryor) Rice Reminiscences, ca. 1855–85
Robinson Family Papers, 1740–1887
William Smith Account Books, 1831–35
William Smith Papers, 1821–72
Jeremiah White Commonplace Book, 1721–1817
William Fanning Wickham Diaries, 1828–80
Charles Craddock Wimbish Accounts, 1865–70
Lewis Williams Wimbish Diary, 1843
Woolfolk Family Papers, 1780–1936

Savannah, Georgia
Georgia Historical Society
    McIntosh Memorandum Book, McIntosh Papers, 1799–1812

Tuscaloosa, Alabama
University of Alabama Library, W. Stanley Hoole Special Collections
  Sarah (Haynesworth) Gayle Diaries, 1827–35 (*AWD*)

Washington, D.C.
Library of Congress, Manuscript Division
  William Chamberlayne Account Book, 1788–1802
  John Chesnutt Letterbook, 1794–1805
  James Hamilton Couper Record Book, 1818–76
  Stephen D. Doar Account Books, 1851–62
  Walter Folger Collection, 1953 (typescript)
  Greenwood Plantation Records, 1854–64
  James Henry Hammond Plantation Books, 1849–58 (*RASP*)
  Historic American Buildings Survey
  Willie Person Mangum Papers, 1771–1906
  Daniel Turner Papers, 1782–1858 (microfilm)
  John Washington Memoir, n.d. (microfilm)

Winston-Salem, North Carolina
Museum of Early Southern Decorative Arts, Research Center
  American Beacon and Commercial Diary (Norfolk, Va.), 1816
  Architecture, South Carolina, Charleston
  Aufseher Collegium Minutes, 1775
  [Charleston] City Gazette Daily Advertiser, 1797
  Charleston Courier, 1806
  Clock Movements, British, n.d.
  Colonial Park Cemetery, Savannah, Georgia, n.d.
  John Fessler, n.d.
  Goldsmith Chandlee, n.d.
  Helpers Conference Minutes, 1773
  Index of Early Southern Artists and Artisans
  John McKee, n.d.
  Lynchburg Press, 1815
  Catherine Parry, 1739
  Political Examiner & Public Advertiser (Frederick, Md.), 1820
  Raleigh Minerva, 1815
  Republican Advocate, 1803
  Richmond Enquirer, 1813, 1814
  South Carolina Gazette, and Public Advertiser, 1785
  Sundial, 1709, 1858

PUBLIC DOCUMENTS

Allen, Horatio. *Reports to the Board of Directors of the South-Carolina Canal & Rail-Road Company*. Charleston, S.C.: J. S. Burges, 1831.
——. *Semi-Annual Report of the Direction of the South-Carolina Canal and Rail-road Company to the Stockholders, October 31, 1834*. Charleston, S.C.: J. S. Burges, 1834.
Bowen, Eli. *The United States Post-Office Guide*. New York: D. Appleton, 1851.
Catterall, Helen Tunicliff, ed. *Judicial Cases Concerning American Slavery and the Negro*. Vol. 2: *Cases from the Courts of North Carolina, South Carolina, and Tennessee*. New York: Negro Universities Press, 1968.

Cooper, Thomas, ed. *The Statutes at Large of South Carolina; Edited, under the Authority of the Legislature. Volume Third, Containing the Acts from 1716, Exclusive, to 1752, Inclusive.* Columbia, S.C.: A. S. Johnston, 1838.

Coxe, Tench, comp. *A Statement of the Arts and Manufactures of the United States of America for the Year 1810.* Philadelphia: A. Coleman Jr., 1814.

De Bow, J. D. B., comp. *The Seventh Census of the United States.* Washington, D.C.: Robert Armstrong, 1850.

Holloway, J. B., and Walter French, comps. *Consolidated Index of Claims Reported by the Commissioners of Claims by the House of Representatives from 1871 to 1880.* Washington, D.C.: Government Printing Office, 1892. Reel 14 of *Records of the Committee of Claims (Southern Claims Commission), 1871–1880.* Washington, D.C.: National Archives and Records Service General Services Administration, 1972.

Horry, Elias. *An Address Respecting the Charleston & Hamburgh Railroad, and the Railroad System as Regards a Large Portion of the Southern and Western States of the North American Union.* Charleston, S.C.: A. E. Miller, 1833.

——. *Annual Report of the Direction of the South Carolina Canal and Rail Road Company, to the Stockholders, May 6th, 1834.* Charleston, S.C.: W. S. Blain, 1834.

Horsey, John R., comp. *Ordinances of the City of Charleston from the 14th of September, 1854, to the 1st December, 1859; and the Acts of the General Assembly.* Charleston, S.C.: Walker, Evans, 1859.

McCord, David J., ed. *The Statutes at Large of South Carolina; Volume Seventh, Containing the Acts Relating to Charleston, Courts, Slaves, and Rivers.* Columbia, S.C.: A. S. Johnston, 1840.

——, ed. *The Statutes at Large of South Carolina; Volume the Ninth, Containing the Acts Relating to Roads, Bridges and Ferries.* Columbia, S.C.: A. S. Johnston, 1841.

Manufactures of the United States in 1860; Compiled From the Original Returns of the Eighth Census. Washington, D.C.: Government Printing Office, 1865.

Ninth Census, Vol. 3: The Statistics of the Wealth and Industry of the United States. Washington, D.C.: Government Printing Office, 1872.

[Ravenel, J.]. *Report of J. Ravenel (President), Charleston, Nov. 23, 1835 to the Stockholders of the South-Carolina C. & R.R. Company.* Charleston, S.C.: J. S. Burges, 1834.

Records of the 1820 Census of Manufactures: Schedules for North Carolina, South Carolina and Georgia. Roll 19. Washington, D.C.: National Archives Microfilm Publications, 1965.

Report of a Special Committee Appointed by the Chamber of Commerce, to Inquire into the Cost, Revenue and Advantages of a Rail Road Communication between the City of Charleston and the Towns of Hamburg & Augusta. Charleston, S.C.: A. E. Miller, 1828.

Semi-Annual Report of the Direction of the South-Carolina Canal and Rail-Road Company, to July, 1838. Charleston, S.C.: Burges & James, 1838.

Semi-Annual Report of the South-Carolina Canal and Rail-Road Company. Accepted Jan. 18th, 1839. Charleston, S.C.: A. E. Miller, 1839.

The Seventh Census of the United States: 1850. Washington, D.C.: Robert Armstrong, 1853.

Testimony of George Nichols: Executive Department Journals: Province, 1664–1774. "Proceedings of His Majestys Honorable Council of South Carolina from the 20th Day of December 1748 to the Sixteenth Day of December 1749." Comp. by James Bullock, p. 90, January 30, 1748. In *Records of the States of the United States of America: A Microfilm Compilation Prepared by the Library of Congress in Association with the University of North Carolina*, 1,870 reels, edited by William Sumner Jenkins, E.1, p. 4. Washington, D.C.: Government Printing Office, 1949–51.

[Tupper, T.]. *Semi-Annual Report of the South-Carolina Canal and Rail-Road Company. Accepted July 15th, 1839.* Charleston, S.C.: A. E. Miller, 1839.

U.S. Congress. House. Committee of Claims. *Churchwardens—Elizabeth City Parish, Vir-*

ginia, *Report No. 73, February 11, 1829*. 20th Cong., 2d sess., 1829. Washington, D.C.:
Gales & Seaton, 1829.

U.S. Congress. House. Doc. 325. *Memorial of John Bryce and 212 Others, Inhabitants of Columbia, S.C., and Vicinity, Remonstrating against the Removal of the Great Southern Mail Route, April 9, 1838*. 25th Cong., 2d sess. Washington, D.C.: Government Printing Office, 1838.

Walker, H. Pinckney, comp. *Ordinances of the City of Charleston, from the 19th of August 1844, to the 14th of September 1854; and the Acts of the General Assembly*. Charleston, S.C.: A. E. Miller, 1854.

Ward, John. *Ordinances of the City Council of Charleston*. Charleston, S.C.: W. P. Young, 1802.

CONTEMPORARY JOURNALS AND PERIODICALS

Black Republican and Office-Holder's Journal, 1865
Carolina Law Journal, 1830
Century Magazine, 1882
Cotton Planter, 1887
De Bow's Review, 1846–70
Farmers' Register, 1833–41
Freedman, 1864–68
Freedmen's Torchlight, 1866
Massachusetts Ploughman and New England Journal of Agriculture, 1883
Outlook, 1894
Rose Bud, 1832–33
Scribner's Magazine, 1897–1901
Southern Agriculturalist, 1828–46
Southern and Western Monthly Magazine and Review, 1845
Southern Cabinet, 1840
Southern Christian Advocate, 1904
Southern Cultivator, 1843–69
Southern Literary Gazette, 1828–29
Southern Planter, 1841–60
Southern Planter and Farmer, 1868–73
Southern Rose, 1835–38
Southern Rose Bud, 1834
Tennessee Farmer, 1835–39
[John Tobler]. *South Carolina Almanac for 1756*. N.p.
Virginia Literary Museum and Journal of Belles, Lettres, Arts, Sciences, &c, 1829

NEWSPAPERS

Abbeville [S.C.] Press and Banner, 1883
Arkansas Weekly Mansion (Little Rock), 1883
Atlanta Constitution (Ga.), 1883
Carolina Spartan (Spartanburg, S.C.), 1883
Charleston Courier, 1806
Charleston News & Courier, 1883
Chicago Tribune, 1883
Christian Neighbor (Columbia, S.C.), 1881
Cleveland Gazette, 1883

Columbia Daily Register, 1883
Courier-Journal (Louisville, Ky.), 1883
Easley [S.C.] Messenger, 1883
Georgetown [S.C.] Inquirer, 1883
Georgia Messenger (Macon), 1831–50
Huntsville [Ala.] Gazette, 1883
Independent (London), 1994
Manchester Weekly Telegraph (U.K.), 1994
New Orleans Daily Picayune (La.), 1883
Orangeburg [S.C.] Times and Democrat, 1883
Plateau Gazette and East Tennessee News, 1883
Rock Hill [S.C.] Herald, 1880–94
South Carolina City Gazette (Charleston), 1806–32
South Carolina Gazette (Charleston), 1732–1832
Tampa Morning Tribune, 1901
Virginia Gazette (Richmond), 1769

BOOKS, ARTICLES, DISSERTATIONS, AND UNPUBLISHED PAPERS

Abbott, H. G. *The Watch Factories of America Past and Present*. Chicago: Geo. K. Hazlitt, 1888.
Adam, Barbara. *Timewatch: The Social Analysis of Time*. Cambridge, Eng.: Polity Press, 1995.
Adams, Evelyn Taylor. *The Courthouses in Virginia Counties, 1634–1776*. Warrenton, Va.: Privately printed, 1966.
Adamson, Alan H. "The Reconstruction of Plantation Labor after Emancipation: The Case of British Guiana." In *Race and Slavery in the Western Hemisphere: Quantitative Studies*, edited by Stanley L. Engerman and Eugene D. Genovese, 457–76. Princeton: Princeton University Press, 1975.
Albright, Frank P. *Johann Ludwig Eberhardt and His Salem Clocks*. Chapel Hill: University of North Carolina Press, 1978.
Allen, William Francis, Charles Pickard Ware, and Lucy McKim Garrison, eds. *Slave Songs of the United States*. New York: Peter Smith, 1929.
Alvarez, Eugene. *Travel on Southern Antebellum Railroads, 1828–1860*. Tuscaloosa: University of Alabama Press, 1974.
"The American Manufacture of Watch Movements." In *The Annual of Scientific Discovery: or, Year-Book of Facts in Science and Art*, 65–69. Boston: Gould, Kendal, and Lincoln, 1859.
Anderson, Ralph V., and Robert E. Gallman. "Slaves as Fixed Capital: Slave Labor and Southern Economic Development." *Journal of American History* 64 (June 1977): 24–46.
Aptheker, Herbert. *American Negro Slave Revolts*. New York: International Publishers, 1970.
Armah, Kwei. *Two Thousand Seasons*. Chicago: Third World Press, 1984.
Atherton, Lewis E. *The Southern Country Store, 1800–1860*. Baton Rouge: Louisiana State University Press, 1949.
Atkins, Keletso E. " 'Kafir Time': Preindustrial Temporal Concepts and Labour Discipline in Nineteenth-Century Colonial Natal." *Journal of African History* 29 (1988): 229–44.
———. *The Moon Is Dead! Give Us Our Money! The Cultural Origins of an African Work Ethic, Natal, South Africa, 1843–1900*. Portsmouth, N.H.: Heinemann, 1993.
Aufhauser, R. Keith. "Slavery and Scientific Management." *Journal of Economic History* 33 (September 1973): 811–24.

Aveni, Anthony F. *Empires of Time: Calendars, Clocks, and Cultures*. New York: Basic Books, 1989.

Ayers, Edward L. *The Promise of the New South: Life after Reconstruction*. New York: Oxford University Press, 1992.

Bailey, Chris H. *Two Hundred Years of American Clocks and Watches*. Englewood Cliffs, N.J.: Prentice-Hall, 1975.

Bailyn, Bernard. *The New England Merchants in the Seventeenth Century*. Cambridge, Mass.: Harvard University Press, 1955.

Ball, Charles. *Fifty Years in Chains*. New York: Dover, 1970.

Bancroft, Frederic. *Slave-Trading in the Old South*. Baltimore: J. H. Furst, 1931.

Bartky, Ian R. "The Adoption of Standard Time." *Technology and Culture* 30 (January 1989): 25–56.

Bartky, Ian R., and Elizabeth Harrison. "Standard and Daylight-Saving Time." *Scientific American* 240 (May 1979): 46–53.

Bateman, Fred, and Thomas Weiss. *A Deplorable Scarcity: The Failure of Industrialization in the Slave Economy*. Chapel Hill: University of North Carolina Press, 1981.

Beard, Charles A., and Mary R. Beard. *The Rise of American Civilization*. Vol. 2. New York: Macmillan, 1927.

Beard, George M. "Causes of Nervousness." In *Popular Culture and Industrialism, 1865–1890*, edited by Henry Nash Smith, 57–70. New York: New York University Press, 1967.

Beecham, John. *Ashantee and the Gold Coast*. London: John Mason, 1841.

Beezley, William H. *Judas at the Jockey Club and Other Episodes of Porfirian Mexico*. Lincoln: University of Nebraska Press, 1989.

Behagg, Clive. "Controlling the Product: Work, Time, and the Early Industrial Revolution in Britain, 1800–1850." In *Worktime and Industrialization: An International History*, edited by Gary Cross, 41–58. Philadelphia: Temple University Press, 1988.

Bender, Thomas, ed. *The Antislavery Debate: Capitalism and Abolitionism as a Problem in Historical Interpretation*. Berkeley: University of California Press, 1992.

Bennett, Norman R., and George E. Brooks Jr., eds. *New England Merchants in Africa: A History through Documents, 1802 to 1865*. Boston: Boston University Press, 1965.

Bensel, Richard Franklin. *Yankee Leviathan: The Origins of Central State Authority, 1859–1877*. New York: Cambridge University Press, 1990.

Benson, Adolph B., ed. *The America of 1750: Peter Kalm's Travels in North America, The English Version of 1770*. Vol. 2. New York: Wilson-Erickson, 1937.

Berg, Maxine. *The Age of Manufactures: Industry, Innovation, and Work in Britain, 1700–1820*. London: Fontana Press, 1985.

Berlin, Ira. *Slaves without Masters: The Free Negro in the Antebellum South*. New York: Pantheon, 1975.

Berlin, Ira, Thavolia Glymph, Steven F. Miller, Joseph P. Reidy, Leslie S. Rowland, and Julie Saville, eds. *Freedom: A Documentary History of Emancipation, 1861–1867, Selected from the Holdings of the National Archives of the United States*. Ser. 1, vol. 3, *The Wartime Genesis of Free Labor: The Lower South*. New York: Cambridge University Press, 1990.

Berlin, Ira, and Herbert G. Gutman. "Natives and Immigrants, Free Men and Slaves: Urban Workingmen in the Antebellum American South." *American Historical Review* 88 (October 1983): 1175–2000.

Berlin, Ira, and Philip D. Morgan, eds. *Cultivation and Culture: Labor and the Shaping of Slave Life in the Americas*. Charlottesville: University Press of Virginia, 1993.

Bertelson, David. *The Lazy South*. New York: Oxford University Press, 1967.

Betts, Edwin Thomas, ed. *Thomas Jefferson's Garden Book, 1766–1824*. Philadelphia: American Philosophical Society, 1944.

Bilodeau, Francis W., and Mrs. Thomas J. Tobias, eds. *Art in South Carolina, 1670–1970.* Charleston: South Carolina Tricentennial Commission, 1970.

Blassingame, John W. *The Slave Community: Plantation Life in the Antebellum South.* Oxford: Oxford University Press, 1979.

——, ed. *Slave Testimony: Two Centuries of Letters, Speeches, Interviews, and Autobiographies.* Baton Rouge: Louisiana State University Press, 1977.

Bloch, Marc. *Feudal Society.* Translated by L. A. Manyon. Vol. 1. Chicago: University of Chicago Press, 1961.

Boles, John B. *Black Southerners, 1619–1869.* Lexington: University Press of Kentucky, 1983.

Bolick, Julian Stevenson. *A Laurens County Sketchbook.* N.p.: N.p., 1973.

Boman, Thorleif. *Hebrew Thought Compared with Greek.* Translated by Jules L. Moreau. London: SCM Press, 1960.

Boney, F. N., ed. *Slave Life in Georgia: A Narrative of the Life, Sufferings, and Escape of John Brown, a Fugitive Slave.* Savannah: Beehive Press, 1972.

Boney, F. N., Richard L. Hume, and Raifa Zafar, eds. *God Made Man, Man Made the Slave: The Autobiography of George Teamoh.* Macon, Ga.: Mercer University Press, 1990.

Bonner, James C. *A History of Georgia Agriculture, 1732–1860.* Athens: University of Georgia Press, 1964.

Bonomi, Patricia U. *Under the Cope of Heaven: Religion, Society, and Politics in Colonial America.* New York: Oxford University Press, 1986.

Bontemps, Arna, ed. *Great Slave Narratives.* Boston: Beacon Press, 1969.

Boorstin, Daniel J. *The Discoverers.* New York: Random House, 1983.

Booth, W. J. "Economies of Time: On the Idea of Time in Marx's Political Economy." *Political Theory* 19 (February 1991): 7–27.

Borst, Arno. *The Ordering of Time: From the Ancient Computus to the Modern Computer.* Translated by Andrew Winnard. Chicago: University of Chicago Press, 1993.

Botkin, B. A., ed. *A Treasury of Southern Folklore: Stories, Ballads, Traditions, and Folkways of the People of the South.* New York: Crown, 1966.

Bowen, J. W. E., ed. *Africa and the American Negro . . . : Addresses and Proceedings of the Congress on Africa Held under the Auspices of the Stewart Missionary Foundation for Africa of Gammon Theological Seminary in Connection with the Cotton States and International Exposition, December 13–15, 1895.* Miami: Mnemosyne Publishing, 1969.

Bowen, Jonathan. "Time- and Age-Awareness among American Slaves." Undergraduate HAESH diss., University of Birmingham, 1996.

Bowman, Shearer Davis. *Masters and Lords: Mid-19th-Century U.S. Planters and Prussian Junkers.* New York: Oxford University Press, 1993.

Brandon, S. G. F. "The Deification of Time." In *The Study of Time: Proceedings of the First Conference of the International Society for the Study of Time, Oberwolfach (Black Forest)— West Germany,* edited by J. T. Fraser, F. C. Haber, and G. H. Miller, 370–82. Berlin: Springer-Verlag, 1972.

Braudel, Fernand. *The Mediterranean and the Mediterranean World in the Age of Philip II.* Translated by Siân Reynolds. Vol. 1. New York: Harper & Row, 1976.

Braybrooke, David. "Diagnosis and Remedy in Marx's Doctrine of Alienation." *Social Research* 25 (Autumn 1958): 325–45.

Breen, T. H. "Of Time and Nature: A Study in Persistent Values in Colonial Virginia." In *Puritans and Adventurers: Change and Continuity in Early America,* 164–96. New York: Oxford University Press, 1980.

——. *Tobacco Culture: The Mentality of the Great Tidewater Planters on the Eve of the Revolution.* Princeton: Princeton University Press, 1985.

Brewer, W. *Alabama: Her History, Resources, War Record, and Public Men.* Montgomery, Ala.: Barrett & Brown, 1872.

Brewster, Lawrence Fay. "Ante-Bellum Planters and Their Means of Transportation." *Proceedings of the South Carolina Historical Association* 17 (1948): 15–25.

Brewster, Paul G., ed. *The Frank C. Brown Collection of North Carolina Folklore*. Vol. 1, *Games and Rhymes, Beliefs and Customs, Riddles, Proverbs, Speech, Tales and Legends*. Durham: Duke University Press, 1952.

Brody, David. "Time and Work during Early American Industrialization." *Labor History* 30 (Winter 1989): 5–46.

Brown, Richard D. "Modernization and the Modern Personality." *Journal of Interdisciplinary History* 2 (Winter 1972–73): 201–28.

———. *Modernization: The Transformation of American Life, 1600–1865*. New York: Hill & Wang, 1976.

Browne, Martha (Griffith). *Autobiography of a Female Slave, Mattie Griffiths*. New York: Redfield, 1857.

Bruegel, Martin. " 'Time That Can Be Relied Upon': The Evolution of Time Consciousness in the Mid-Hudson Valley, 1790–1860." *Journal of Social History* 28 (Spring 1995): 547–64.

Bundy, David S., comp. *Painting in the South, 1564–1980*. Richmond: Virginia Museum of Fine Arts, 1983.

Burlingame, Roger. "Technology as Cause in History." *Technology and Culture* 2 (Summer 1961): 219–29.

Burton, Annie L. *Memories of Childhood's Slavery Days*. Boston: Ross, 1909. In *Six Women's Slave Narratives*. New York: Oxford University Press, 1988.

Burton, E. Milby. *South Carolina Silversmiths, 1690–1860*. Charleston: Contributions from the Charleston Museum, 1991.

Bushman, Richard L. "American High-Style and Vernacular Cultures." In *Colonial British America*, edited by Jack P. Greene and J. R. Pole, 345–83. Baltimore: Johns Hopkins University Press, 1984.

Butler, Jon. *Awash in a Sea of Faith: Christianizing the American People*. Cambridge, Mass.: Harvard University Press, 1990.

Byrd, Alexander X. "Gifts to Do Unnatural Things: Africa and Africans in the Oral Tradition and Personal Remembrances of Former Slaves." Paper presented at the Graduate History Association Spring Symposium, University of South Carolina, Columbia, 1993.

Cade, John B. "Out of the Mouths of Ex-Slaves." *Journal of Negro History* 44 (January 1935): 312–27.

Cain, P. J., and A. G. Hopkins. *British Imperialism: Innovation and Expansion, 1688–1914*. Vol. 1. London: Longman, 1993.

Carll-White, Mary Allison. "The Role of the Black Artisan in the Building Trades and the Decorative Arts in South Carolina's Charleston District, 1760–1800." Ph.D. diss., University of Tennessee, 1982.

Carr, Lois G., and Lorena S. Walsh. "Inventories and the Analysis of Wealth and Consumption Patterns in St. Mary's County, Maryland, 1658–1777." *Historical Methods* 13 (Spring 1980): 81–104.

Carrington, H. "Decoration of Graves of Negroes in South Carolina." *Journal of American Folk-Lore* 4 (July–September 1891): 267.

Carter, Dan T. "From the Old South to the New: Another Look at the Theme of Change and Continuity." In *From the Old South to the New: Essays on the Transitional South*, edited by Walter J. Fraser Jr. and Winfred B. Moore Jr., 26–40. Westport, Conn.: Greenwood Press, 1981.

Catanzariti, John, and E. James Ferguson, eds. *The Papers of Robert Morris*. Vol. 6, *July 22–October 31, 1782*. Pittsburgh: University of Pittsburgh Press, 1984.

Cates, Margaret D. *Early Days of Coastal Georgia*. St. Simon's Island, Ga.: Fort Frederica Association, 1955.

Censer, Jane Turner. *North Carolina Planters and Their Children, 1800–1860*. Baton Rouge: Louisiana State University Press, 1984.

Chamberlain, Paul M. *It's about Time*. New York: Richard S. Smith, 1941.

Chaplin, Joyce E. *An Anxious Pursuit: Agricultural Innovation and Modernity in the Lower South, 1730–1815*. Chapel Hill: University of North Carolina Press, 1993.

——. "Tidal Rice Cultivation and the Problem of Slavery in South Carolina and Georgia, 1760–1815." *William and Mary Quarterly* 3d. ser., 49 (January 1992): 29–61.

Church, R. A. "Nineteenth-Century Clock Technology in Britain, the United States, and Switzerland." *Economic History Review* 28 (1975): 616–30.

Cipolla, Carlo. *Clocks and Culture, 1300–1700*. New York: Walker, 1967.

Clark, Christopher. *The Roots of Rural Capitalism: Western Massachusetts, 1780–1860*. Ithaca: Cornell University Press, 1990.

Clark, Gregory. "Factory Discipline." *Journal of Economic History* 54 (March 1994): 128–63.

Clark, Laura. "Williams and Victor." *Signpost (Lynchburg, Virginia, Museums System)* 2 (Fall 1987): 2.

Clark, Thomas Curtis. *The American Railway: Its Construction, Development, Management, and Appliances*. New York: Charles Scribner's Sons, 1889.

Clifton, James M. "The Ante-Bellum Rice Planter as Revealed in the Letterbook of Charles Manigault, 1846–1848." *South Carolina Historical Magazine* 74 (July 1973): 119–27.

——. "Hopeton, Model Plantation of the Antebellum South." *Georgia Historical Quarterly* 66 (Winter 1982): 429–40.

——. "The Rice Driver: His Role in Slave Management." *South Carolina Historical Magazine* 82 (October 1981): 331–53.

——, ed. *Life and Labor on Argyle Island: Letters and Documents of a Savannah River Rice Plantation, 1833–1867*. Savannah: Beehive Press, 1978.

Clinton, Catherine. "Equally Their Due: The Education of the Planter Daughter in the Early Republic." *Journal of the Early Republic* 2 (Spring 1982): 39–60.

——. "Reconstructing Freedwomen." In *Divided Houses: Gender and the Civil War*, edited by Catherine Clinton and Nina Silber, 306–19. New York: Oxford University Press, 1992.

Coakley, Robert Walter. "Virginia Commerce during the American Revolution." Ph.D. diss., University of Virginia, 1944.

Coates, A. W. Bob. *On the History of Economic Thought: British and American Economic Essays*. Vol. 1. London: Routledge, 1992.

Coclanis, Peter A. *The Shadow of a Dream: Economic Life and Death in the South Carolina Low Country, 1670–1920*. Oxford: Oxford University Press, 1989.

Cohen, Patricia Cline. *A Calculating People: The Spread of Numeracy in Early America*. Chicago: University of Chicago Press, 1982.

Cole, Arthur H. "The Tempo of Mercantile Life in Colonial America." *Business History Review* 33 (Autumn 1959): 277–99.

Combes, John D. "Ethnography, Archaeology and Burial Practices among Coastal South Carolina Blacks." *Conference on Historic Site Archaeology Papers* 2, pt. 2 (1972): 52–61.

Connor, Cynthia. "'Sleep on and Take Your Rest': Black Mortuary Behavior on the East Branch of the Cooper River, South Carolina." M.A. thesis, University of South Carolina, 1989.

Conrad, Alfred, and John Meyer. "The Economics of Slavery in the Ante Bellum South." *Journal of Political Economy* 66 (April 1958): 95–122.

Conser, Walter H. *God and the Natural World: Religion and Science in Antebellum America*. Columbia: University of South Carolina Press, 1993.

Cooper, Frederick. "Colonizing Time: Work Rhythms and Labor Conflict in Colonial Mombassa." In *Colonization and Culture*, edited by Nicholas B. Dirks, 209–46. Ann Arbor: University of Michigan Press, 1992.

———. *Plantation Slavery on the East Coast of Africa*. New Haven: Yale University Press, 1977.

Cott, Nancy F. *The Bonds of Womanhood: "Woman's Sphere" in New England, 1780–1835*. New Haven: Yale University Press, 1977.

Cotterill, Robert Spencer. "Southern Railroads." *Mississippi Valley Historical Review* 10 (March 1924): 396–405.

———. "The Telegraph in the South, 1845–1850." *South Atlantic Quarterly* 16 (April 1917): 149–54.

Cottrell, W. F. "Of Time and the Railroader." *American Sociological Review* 4 (April 1939): 190–98.

Cowan, Harrison J. *Time and Its Measurement*. Cleveland: World, 1958.

Craven, Avery O. *Soil Exhaustion as a Factor in the Agricultural History of Virginia and Maryland, 1606–1860*. Urbana: University of Illinois Press, 1926.

Crawford, Stephen C. "Problems in the Quantitative Analysis of the Data Contained in the WPA and Fisk University Narratives of Ex-Slaves." In *Without Consent or Contract: The Rise and Fall of American Slavery: Evidence and Methods*, edited by Robert W. Fogel, Ralph A. Galantine, and Richard L. Manning, 331–70. New York: W. W. Norton & Company, 1992.

———. "Punishments and Rewards." In *Without Consent or Contract: The Rise and Fall of American Slavery, Conditions of Slave Life and the Transition to Freedom, Technical Papers*, Vol. 2, edited by Robert William Fogel and Stanley L. Engerman, 536–50. New York: Norton, 1992.

Crofts, Daniel W. "Southampton County Diarists in the Civil War Era: Elliott L. Strong and Daniel W. Cobb." *Virginia Magazine of History and Biography* 98 (October 1992): 537–613.

Cross, Gary. *A Quest for Time: The Reduction of Work in Britain and France, 1840–1940*. Berkeley: University of California Press, 1989.

———. *Time and Money: The Making of Consumer Culture*. London: Routledge, 1993.

Crouch, Barry A. *The Freedmen's Bureau and Black Texans*. Austin: University of Texas Press, 1992.

[Crow, Hugh]. *Memoirs of the Late Captain Hugh Crow of Liverpool*. London: Frank Cass, 1970.

Crowley, J. E. *This Sheba, Self: The Conceptualization of Economic Life in Eighteenth-Century America*. Baltimore: Johns Hopkins University Press, 1974.

Cunliffe, Marcus. *Chattel Slavery and Wage Slavery: The Anglo-American Context, 1830–1860*. Athens: University of Georgia Press, 1979.

Cunningham, Noble E., Jr., ed. *Circular Letters of Congressmen to the Constituents, 1789–1829*. Vol. 2, Chapel Hill: University of North Carolina Press, 1978.

Curlee, Abigail. "The History of a Texas Slave Plantation, 1831–63." *Southwestern Historical Quarterly* 26 (October 1922): 79–127.

Current, Richard N. *Northernizing the South*. Athens: University of Georgia Press, 1983.

Currie-McDaniel, Ruth. *Carpetbagger of Conscience: A Biography of John Emory Bryant*. Athens: University of Georgia Press, 1987.

Curtin, Philip D. *Africa Remembered: Narratives by West Africans from the Era of the Slave Trade*. Madison: University of Wisconsin Press, 1967.

Cutten, George Barton. *The Silversmiths of Virginia (Together with Watchmakers and Jewelers) from 1694 to 1850*. Richmond: Dietz Press, 1952.

Da Mota, A. Teixeira, and P. E. H. Hair. *East of Mina: Afro-European Relations on the Gold Coast in the 1550s and 1560s, An Essay with Supporting Documents*. Madison: African Studies Program, University of Wisconsin-Madison, 1988.

Daniels, Christine. "Gresham's Laws: Labor Management on an Early-Eighteenth-Century Chesapeake Plantation." *Journal of Southern History* 62 (May 1996): 205–38.

———. "'Without Any Limitacon of Time': Debt Servitude in Colonial America." *Labor History* 36 (Spring 1995): 232–50.

Danilova, L. V. "Controversial Problems of the Theory of Precapitalist Societies." *Soviet Anthropology and Archaeology* 9 (1974): 269–328.

Davis, Angela Y. *Women, Race and Class.* New York: Random House, 1983.

Davis, David Brion. *Slavery and Human Progress.* New York: Oxford University Press, 1984.

Davis, Henry C. "Negro Folk-Lore in South Carolina." *Journal of American Folk-Lore* 27 (July–September 1914): 246–49.

Davison, Graeme. *The Unforgiving Minute: How Australia Learned to Tell the Time.* Oxford: Oxford University Press, 1994.

Dawley, Alan. "E. P. Thompson and the Peculiarities of the Americans." *Radical History Review* 19 (Winter 1978–79): 33–59.

Degler, Carl N. *Out of Our Past: The Forces That Shaped Modern America.* New York: Harper & Row, 1970.

Dennett, John Richard. *The South as It Is, 1865–1866.* 1965. Reprint. Athens: University of Georgia Press, 1986.

Dew, Charles B. *Bond of Iron: Master and Slave at Buffalo Forge.* New York: Norton, 1994.

———. "Disciplining Slave Ironworkers in the Antebellum South: Coercion, Conciliation, and Accommodation." *American Historical Review* 79 (1979): 393–418.

Ditz, Toby L. "Shipwrecked; or Masculinity Imperiled: Mercantile Representations of Failure and the Gendered Self in Eighteenth-Century Philadelphia." *Journal of American History* 81 (June 1994): 51–80.

Doerflinger, Thomas M. *A Vigorous Spirit of Enterprise: Merchants and Economic Development in Revolutionary Philadelphia.* Chapel Hill: University of North Carolina Press, 1985.

Dohrn-van Rossum, Gerhard. *History of the Hour: Clocks and Modern Temporal Orders.* Translated by Thomas Dunlap. Chicago: University of Chicago Press, 1996.

Donald, David H. *An Excess of Democracy: The American Civil War and the Social Process.* Oxford: Oxford University Press, 1960.

———. "The Proslavery Argument Reconsidered." *Journal of Southern History* 37 (February 1971): 3–18.

[Douglass, Frederick]. *Narrative of the Life of Frederick Douglass an American Slave.* New York: Signet, 1968.

Dreppard, Carl H. *American Clocks and Clockmakers.* Boston: Charles T. Branford, 1958.

Dublin, Thomas, ed. *Farm to Factory: Women's Letters, 1830–1860.* New York: Columbia University Press, 1993.

Duncan, John. *Travels in Western Africa, in 1845 & 1846, Comprising a Journey from Whydah through the Kingdom of Dahomey, to Adofoodia.* Vol. 1. London: Richard Bentley, 1847.

Durrill, Wayne K. "Routine of Seasons: Labour Regimes and Social Ritual in an Antebellum Plantation Community." *Slavery and Abolition* 16 (August 1995): 161–87.

Dusinberre, William. *Them Dark Days: Slavery in the American Rice Swamps.* New York: Oxford University Press, 1996.

Earle, Alice Morse. *Child-Life in Colonial Days.* New York: Macmillan, 1946.

———. *Home Life in Colonial Days.* New York: Grosset & Dunlap, 1898.

Eisenstadt, S. N., ed. *The Protestant Ethic and Modernization: A Comparative View.* New York: Basic Books, 1968.

Eliade, Mircea. *The Sacred and the Profane: The Nature of Religion.* Translated by Willard R. Trask. London: Harcourt Brace Jovanovich, 1959.

Elias, Norbert. *Time: An Essay.* Oxford: Basil Blackwell, 1992.

Elkins, Stanley M. *Slavery: A Problem in American Institutional and Intellectual Life.* Chicago: University of Chicago Press, 1959.

Elson, Ruth Miller. *Guardians of Tradition: American Schoolbooks of the Nineteenth Century*. Lincoln: University of Nebraska Press, 1964.

Emmer, Pieter C. "The Price of Freedom: The Constraints of Change in Postemancipation America." In *The Meaning of Freedom: Economics, Politics, and Culture After Slavery*, edited by Frank McGlynn and Seymour Drescher, 23–47. Pittsburgh: University of Pittsburgh Press, 1992.

Escott, Paul D. *Slavery Remembered: A Record of Twentieth-Century Slave Narratives*. Chapel Hill: University of North Carolina Press, 1979.

Farish, Hunter Dickinson, ed. *Journal and Letters of Philip Vickers Fithian, 1773–1774*. Charlottesville: University Press of Virginia, 1957.

Faust, Drew G. "The Rhetoric and Ritual of Agriculture in Antebellum South Carolina." *Journal of Southern History* 45 (November 1979): 541–68.

——. *A Sacred Circle: The Dilemma of the Intellectual in the Old South, 1840–1860*. Baltimore: Johns Hopkins University Press, 1977.

——, ed. *The Ideology of Slavery: Proslavery Thought in the Antebellum South, 1830–1860*. Baton Rouge: Louisiana State University Press, 1981.

Feld, Steven. *Sound and Sentiment: Birds, Weeping, Poetics, and Song in Kaluli Expression*. Philadelphia: University of Pennsylvania Press, 1982.

Ferguson, Leland. *Uncommon Ground: Archaeology and Early African America, 1650–1800*. Washington, D.C.: Smithsonian Institution Press, 1992.

Ferleger, Louis. "Sharecropping Contracts in the Late-Nineteenth-Century South." *Agricultural History* 67 (Summer 1993): 31–46.

Fields, Barbara Jeanne. "The Advent of Capitalist Agriculture: The New South in a Bourgeois World." In *Essays on the Postbellum Southern Economy*, edited by Thavolia Glymph and John Kushma, 73–94. College Station: Texas A&M University Press, 1985.

——. "Slavery, Race and Ideology in the United States of America." *New Left Review* 181 (May–June 1990): 95–118.

Fischer, David Hackett. *Albion's Seed: Four British Folkways in America*. New York: Oxford University Press, 1989.

——. *Growing Old in America*. New York: Oxford University Press, 1977.

Flanders, Ralph Betts. *Plantation Slavery in Georgia*. Chapel Hill: University of North Carolina Press, 1933.

Flynn, Charles L., Jr. *White Land, Black Labor: Caste and Class in Late Nineteenth-Century Georgia*. Baton Rouge: Louisiana State University Press, 1983.

Fogel, Robert W. "Moral Aspects of the Debate over the 'Extra Income' of Slaves." In *Without Consent or Contract: The Rise and Fall of American Slavery, Evidence and Methods*, edited by Robert W. Fogel, Ralph A. Galantine, and Richard L. Manning, 593–96. New York: Norton, 1992.

——. "Was the Overwork of Pregnant Women Profit Maximizing?" In *Without Consent or Contract: The Rise and Fall of American Slavery, Evidence and Methods*, edited by Robert W. Fogel, Ralph A. Galantine, and Richard L. Manning, 321–25. New York: Norton, 1992.

——. *Without Consent or Contract: The Rise and Fall of American Slavery*. New York: Norton, 1989.

Fogel, Robert W., and Stanley Engerman. *Time on the Cross: The Economics of American Negro Slavery*. 2 vols. Boston: Little, Brown, 1976.

Foner, Eric. *Free Soil, Free Labor, Free Men: The Ideology of the Republican Party before the Civil War*. New York: Oxford University Press, 1970.

——. *Nothing but Freedom: Emancipation and Its Legacy*. Baton Rouge: Louisiana State University Press, 1983.

——. *Reconstruction: America's Unfinished Revolution, 1863–1877*. New York: Harper & Row, 1988.

Foner, Philip S., and Ronald L. Lewis, eds. *The Black Worker: A Documentary History from Colonial Times to the Present*. Vol. 1. Philadelphia: Temple University Press, 1978.

Ford, Lacy K., Jr. *Origins of Southern Radicalism: The South Carolina Upcountry, 1800–1860*. Oxford: Oxford University Press, 1988.

Forney, M. N. *Memoir of Horatio Allen*. New York: Burr Printing House, 1890.

Foucault, Michel. *Discipline and Punish: The Birth of the Prison*. London: Allen Lane, 1977.

Fouché, Rebecca Talbery. "St. Philip's Episcopal Church, Charleston, South Carolina: The Building and Its Architectural History." M.A. thesis, University of South Carolina, 1979.

Fox-Genovese, Elizabeth. *Within the Plantation Household: Black and White Women of the Old South*. Chapel Hill: University of North Carolina Press, 1988.

Freehling, William W. *Prelude to Civil War: The Nullification Controversy in South Carolina, 1816–1836*. New York: Harper & Row, 1965.

———. *The Road to Disunion*. Volume 1: *Secessionists at Bay, 1776–1854*. Oxford: Oxford University Press, 1990.

Friedman, Gerald, and Richard L. Manning. "The Rent and Hire of Slaves." In *Without Consent or Contract: The Rise and Fall of American Slavery, Evidence and Methods*, edited by Robert W. Fogel, Ralph A. Galantine, and Richard L. Manning, 77–78. New York: Norton, 1992.

Friedman, Jean E. *The Enclosed Garden: Women and Community in the Evangelical South, 1830–1900*. Chapel Hill: University of North Carolina Press, 1985.

Furniss, Edgar S. *The Position of the Laborer in a System of Nationalism: A Study in the Labor Theories of the Later English Mercantilists*. Boston: Houghton Mifflin, 1920.

Gaines, William H., Jr. "Nerve Center of the Colonial Mails: New Post, Virginia, Alexander Spotswood's General Post Office for North America." *Virginia Cavalcade* 3 (Winter 1953): 33–36.

Gallman, Robert E. "Slavery and Southern Economic Growth." *Southern Economic Journal* 14 (April 1979): 1007–22.

Gara, Larry, ed. "A New Englander's View of Plantation Life: Letters of Edwin Hall to Cyrus Woodman, 1837." *Journal of Southern History* 18 (August 1952): 341–54.

Gates, Paul W. *The Farmer's Age: Agriculture 1815–1860*. Vol. 2, *The Economic History of the United States*. New York: Harper & Row, 1960.

Gaylord, E. N. *Life in Florida since 1886*. Miami: Mnesymone Press, 1969.

Genovese, Eugene D. *From Rebellion to Revolution: Afro-American Slave Revolts in the Making of the Modern World*. Baton Rouge: Louisiana State University Press, 1979.

———. "A Georgia Slaveholder Looks at Africa." *Georgia Historical Quarterly* 51 (June 1967): 186–93.

———. "Getting to Know the Slaves." *New York Review of Books* September 21, 1972, 16–19.

———. "Marxian Interpretations of the Slave South." In *Towards a New Past: Dissenting Essays in American History*, edited by Barton J. Bernstein, 90–126. New York: Pantheon, 1968.

———. *The Political Economy of Slavery: Studies in the Economy and Society of the Slave South*. Middletown, Conn.: Wesleyan University Press, 1989.

———. *Roll, Jordan, Roll: The World the Slaves Made*. New York: Vintage Books, 1976.

———. *The Slaveholders' Dilemma: Freedom and Progress in Southern Conservative Thought, 1820–1860*. Columbia: University of South Carolina Press, 1992.

———. "The Southern Slaveholders' Views of the Middle Ages." In *Medievalism in American Culture: Papers of the Eighteenth Annual Conference of the Center for Medieval and Early Renaissance Studies*, edited by Bernhard Rosenthal and Paul E. Szarmach, 31–52. Binghamton, N.Y.: State University of New York at Binghamton, 1989.

———. *The Southern Tradition: The Achievements and Limitations of an American Conservatism*. Cambridge, Mass.: Harvard University Press, 1994.

—. *The World the Slaveholders Made: Two Essays in Interpretation*. Middletown, Conn.: Wesleyan University Press, 1988.

Genovese, Eugene D., and Elizabeth Fox-Genovese. *Fruits of Merchant Capital: Slavery and Bourgeois Property in the Rise and Expansion of Capitalism*. New York: Oxford University Press, 1983.

—. "The Ideological Bases of Domestic Economy: The Representation of Women and the Family in the Age of Expansion." In *Fruits of Merchant Capital: Slavery and Bourgeois Property in the Rise and Expansion of Capitalism*, 299–336. New York: Oxford University Press, 1983.

Gibbs, James W. *Dixie Clockmakers*. Gretna, La.: Pelican, 1975.

Gifford, Carey Jerome. "Space and Time as Religious Symbols in Ante-Bellum America." Ph.D. diss., Claremont Graduate School, 1980.

Gitelman, H. M. "The Labor Force at Waltham Watch Factory during the Civil War Era." *Journal of Economic History* 25 (June 1965): 214–43.

Glasser, Richard. *Time in French Life and Thought*. Translated by C. G. Pearson. Totowa, N.J.: Rowman & Littlefield/Manchester University Press, 1972.

Glickstein, Jonathan A. *Concepts of Free Labor in Antebellum America*. New Haven: Yale University Press, 1991.

Glymph, Thavolia. "Freedpeople and Ex-Masters: Shaping a New Order in the Postbellum South, 1865–1868." In *Essays on the Postbellum Southern Economy*, edited by Thavolia Glymph and John Kushma, 48–72. College Station: Texas A&M University Press, 1985.

Gould, Stephen Jay. *Time's Arrow, Time's Cycle: Myth and Metaphor in the Discovery of Geological Time*. Cambridge, Mass.: Harvard University Press, 1987.

Govan, Thomas P. "Americans below the Potomac." In *The Southerner as American*, edited by Charles Grier Sellers Jr., 20–39. New York: E. P. Dutton, 1966.

Graham, Glennon. "From Slavery to Serfdom: Rural Black Agriculturalists in South Carolina, 1865–1900." Ph.D. diss., Northwestern University, 1982.

Gras, Norman S. B. *Business History of the United States about 1650 to 1950's*. Ann Arbor: Edward Brothers, 1967.

Gray, Lewis C. *History of Agriculture in the Southern United States to 1860*. 2 vols. Washington, D.C.: Carnegie Institution, 1933.

Green, Fletcher M. "Higher Education of Women in the South prior to 1860." In *Democracy in the South and Other Essays by Fletcher Melvin Green*, edited by J. Isaac Copeland, 199–219. Knoxville: Vanderbilt University Press, 1969.

Green, Robert W., ed. *Protestantism and Capitalism: The Weber Thesis and Its Critics*. Boston: D. C. Heath, 1959.

Greenberg, Kenneth S. *Masters and Statesmen: The Political Culture of American Slavery*. Baltimore: Johns Hopkins University Press, 1985.

Greene, Jack P. " 'Slavery or Independence': Some Reflections on the Relationship among Liberty, Black Bondage, and Equality in Revolutionary South Carolina." *South Carolina Historical Magazine* 80 (July 1973): 193–214.

Griffin, Frances. *Less Time for Meddling: A History of Salem Academy and College, 1772–1866*. Winston-Salem, N.C.: John F. Blair, 1979.

Gundersen, Joan Rezner. "The Double Bonds of Race and Sex: Black and White Women in a Colonial Virginia Parish." *Journal of Southern History* 52 (August 1986): 351–72.

Gurevich, L. "Time as a Problem of Cultural History." In *Cultures and Time*, edited by Louis Gardet, 229–45. Paris: UNESCO Press, 1976.

Gutman, Herbert. "Work, Culture, and Society in Industrializing America, 1815–1919." In *Work, Culture, and Society in Industrializing America*, 3–78. Oxford: Oxford University Press, 1977.

Hahn, Steven. "Class and State in Postemancipation Societies: Southern Planters in Comparative Perspective." *American Historical Review* 105 (February 1990): 75–98.

——. *The Roots of Southern Populism: Yeomen Farmers and the Transition of the Georgia Upcountry, 1850–1890*. New York: Oxford University Press, 1983.

Hair, P. E. H., ed. *Andre De Faro's Missionary Journey to Sierra Leone in 1663–1664*. N.p.: N.p., 1982.

Hall, Catherine. "The Early Formation of Victorian Domestic Ideology." In *Fit Work for Women*, edited by Sandra Burman, 15–32. New York: St. Martin's Press, 1979.

Hall, Edward. *The Dance of Life: The Other Dimension of Time*. New York: Anchor/Doubleday, 1984.

Hamer, Philip M., et al., eds. *The Papers of Henry Laurens*. Vol. 1. Columbia: University of South Carolina Press, 1968.

Hareven, Tamara K. "Synchronizing Individual Time, Family Time, and Historical Time." In *Chronotypes: The Construction of Time*, edited by John Bender and David E. Wellbery, 167–84. Stanford: Stanford University Press, 1991.

Harms, Robert. *Games against Nature: An Eco-Cultural History of the Nunu of Equatorial Africa*. New York: Cambridge University Press, 1987.

——. *River of Wealth, River of Sorrow: The Central Zaire Basin in the Era of the Slave and Ivory Trade, 1500–1891*. New Haven: Yale University Press, 1981.

Harris, Barbara J. *Beyond Her Sphere: Women and the Professions in American History*. Westport, Conn.: Greenwood Press, 1978.

Harris, J. William. "Plantations and Power: Emancipation on the David Barrow Plantations." In *Toward a New South? Studies in Post–Civil War Southern Communities*, edited by Orville Vernon Burton and Robert C. McMath Jr., 246–64. Westport, Conn.: Greenwood Press, 1982.

Harrison, Mark. "The Ordering of the Urban Environment: Time, Work and the Occurrence of Crowds, 1790–1835." *Past and Present* 110 (February 1986): 134–68.

Hay, Michael, and Jean-Claude Usunier. "Time and Strategic Action: A Cross-Cultural View." *Time and Society* 2 (September 1993): 313–34.

Henry, Jules. "White People's Time, Colored People's Time." *Trans-action* 2 (March–April 1965): 31–33.

"Henry Laurens." *Hunt's Merchants Magazine*, November 1844, 439–44.

Hensley, Paul B. "Time, Work, and Social Context in New England." *New England Quarterly* 65 (December 1992): 531–59.

Hepworth, George H. *The Whip, Hoe, and Sword; or the Gulf-Department in '63*. Boston: Walker, Wise, 1864.

Herskovits, Melville J. *The Myth of the Negro Past*. Boston: Beacon Press, 1958.

Hewitt, Nancy A. "Beyond the Search for Sisterhood: American Women's History in the 1980s." *Social History* 10 (October 1985): 299–317.

Higginbotham, A. Leon, Jr. *In the Matter of Color: Race and the American Legal Process, the Colonial Period*. New York: Oxford University Press, 1978.

Hilton, Anne. *The Kingdom of Kongo*. Oxford: Clarendon Press, 1985.

Hindle, Bruce, and Stephen Lubar. *Engines of Change: The American Industrial Revolution*. Washington, D.C.: Smithsonian Institution Press, 1986.

Hitt, Susie Juanita. *Some Colonial Churches in the Thirteen Original Colonies Organized before 1800*. N.p.: N.p., ca. 1976.

Hobsbawm, Eric J. *The Age of Capital, 1848–1875*. London: Weidenfeld and Nicholson, 1975.

——. "Introduction: Inventing Traditions." In *The Invention of Tradition*, edited by Eric Hobsbawm and Terence Ranger, 1–14. Cambridge: Cambridge University Press, 1992.

Hodgson, Adam. *Letters from North America, Written during a Tour in the United States and Canada.* Vol. 1. London: Hurst, Robinson, 1824.

Hogan, William Ransom, ed. *William Johnson's Natchez: The Ante-Bellum Diary of a Free Negro.* Baton Rouge: Louisiana State University Press, 1993.

Hoke, Donald R. *Ingenious Yankees: The Rise of the American System of Manufactures in the Private Sector.* New York: Columbia University Press, 1990.

Holbrook, Abigail Curlee. "A Glimpse of Life on Antebellum Slave Plantations in Texas." *Southwestern Historical Quarterly* 76 (April 1973): 361–83.

Holifield, E. Brooks. *Gentlemen Theologians: American Theology in Southern Culture, 1795– 1860.* Durham: Duke University Press, 1978.

Hollan, Catherine B. "John Gaither, Silversmith." *Journal of Early Southern Decorative Arts* 9 (November 1983): 32–51.

Holt, Thomas C. " 'An Empire over the Mind': Emancipation, Race, and Ideology in the British West Indies and the American South." In *Region, Race, and Reconstruction: Essays in Honor of C. Vann Woodward*, edited by J. Morgan Kousser and James M. McPherson, 283–307. New York: Oxford University Press, 1982.

Hooker, Richard J., ed. *The Carolina Backcountry on the Eve of the Revolution: The Journal and Other Writings of Charles Woodmason, Anglican Itinerant.* Chapel Hill: University of North Carolina Press, 1953.

Hopkins, James F. *A History of the Hemp Industry in Kentucky.* Lexington: University of Kentucky Press, 1951.

Hopley, Catherine Cooper. *Life in the South from the Commencement of the War, Being a Social History of Those Who Took Part in the Battles, from a Personal Acquaintance with Them in Their Own Homes from the Spring of 1860 to August 1862.* Vol. 1. New York: Augustus M. Kelley, 1971.

Horkheimer, Max. *Critique of Instrumental Reason.* New York: Seabury, 1974.

Horton, John. "Time and Cool People." In *Black Experience: Soul*, edited by Lee Rainwater, 43–54. New Brunswick, N.J.: Transaction Books, 1978.

Howard, E. "American Clocks and Watches." In *One Hundred Years of American Commerce*, edited by Chauncey M. DePew, 2:540–43. New York: D. O. Haynes, 1895.

Howard, Robert A. "Interchangeable Parts Reexamined: The Private Sector of the American Arms Industry on the Eve of the Civil War." *Technology and Culture* 19 (October 1978): 633–49.

Howse, Derek. *Greenwich Time and the Discovery of the Longitude.* Oxford: Oxford University Press, 1980.

Hughes, Diane Owen, and Thomas R. Trautmann, eds. *Time: Histories and Ethnologies.* Ann Arbor: University of Michigan Press, 1995.

Hunter, Louis C. *Steamboats on the Western Rivers: An Economic and Technological History.* Cambridge, Mass.: Harvard University Press, 1949.

Hurmence, Belinda, ed. *Before Freedom: 49 Oral Histories of Former North and South Carolina Slaves.* New York: Penguin, 1990.

Ingold, Tim. "Work, Time and Industry." *Time and Society* 4 (February 1995): 5–28.

Innes, Stephen. *Creating the Commonwealth: The Economic Culture of Puritan New England.* New York: Norton, 1995.

Isaac, Rhys. "Imagination and Material Culture: The Enlightenment on a Mid-18th-Century Virginia Plantation." In *The Art and Mystery of Historical Archaeology: Essays in Honor of James Deetz*, edited by Anne Elizabeth Yentsch and Mary C. Beandry, 401–23. Boca Raton, Fla.: CRC Press, 1992.

——. *The Transformation of Virginia, 1740–1790.* New York: Norton, 1982.

Jackson, Alfred. "Sound and Ritual." *Man* n.s., 3 (June 1968): 292–300.

Jackson, Harvey J. " 'American Slavery, American Freedom' and the American Revolution in the Lower South: The Case of Lachlan McIntosh." *Southern Studies* 19 (Spring 1980): 81–93.

Jacoby, Mary Moore, ed. *The Churches of Charleston and the Lowcountry*. Columbia: University of South Carolina Press, 1994.

Jaffee, David. "Peddlers of Progress and the Transformation of the Rural North, 1760–1860." *Journal of American History* 78 (September 1991): 511–35.

Janney, Werner L., and Asa Moore Janney, eds. *John Jay Janney's Virginia: An American Farm Lad's Life in the Early 19th Century*. McLean, Va.: EPM Publications, 1978.

Jaynes, Gerald David. *Branches without Roots: Genesis of the Black Working Class in the American South, 1862–1882*. New York: Oxford University Press, 1986.

Jeane, Donald D. "The Traditional Upland South Cemetery." *Landscape* 18 (Winter 1969): 39–41.

Jefferson, Isaac. *Memoirs of a Monticello Slave. As Dictated to Charles Campbell in the 1840s by Isaac, One of Thomas Jefferson's Slaves*. Charlottesville: University of Virginia Press, 1951.

Jerome, Chauncey. *History of the American Clock Business for the Past Sixty Years, and Life of Chauncey Jerome, Written by Himself*. New Haven: N.p., 1860.

John, Richard. "Completing the Network." Unpaginated manuscript in author's possession.

———. "The Imagined Community." Unpaginated manuscript in author's possession.

———. "The Postal System, the 'Public Sphere,' and the Social Construction of Time and Space in the Early Republic." Paper presented at the Annual Meeting of the Organization of American Historians, Atlanta, April 14, 1994.

Johnson, Michael P. "Planters and Patriarchy: Charleston, 1800–1860." *Journal of Southern History* 44 (1980): 45–72.

Johnson, Paul E. *A Shopkeeper's Millennium: Society and Revivals in Rochester, New York, 1815–1877*. New York: Hill & Wang, 1978.

Jones, Bessie Zaban, and Lyle Gifford Boyd. *The Harvard College Observatory: The First Four Directorships, 1839–1919*. Cambridge, Mass.: Harvard University Press, 1971.

Jones, G. I. "Time and Oral Tradition with Special Reference to Eastern Nigeria." *Journal of African History* 7 (1965): 153–60.

Jones, Gareth Stedman. *Outcast London: A Study in the Relationship between Classes in Victorian Society*. Oxford: Clarendon Press, 1971.

Jones, Jacqueline. *Soldiers of Light and Love: Northern Teachers and Georgia Blacks, 1865–1873*. Chapel Hill: University of North Carolina Press, 1980.

Jones, Norrece T., Jr. *Born a Child of Freedom, Yet a Slave: Mechanisms of Control and Strategies of Resistance in Antebellum South Carolina*. Hanover, N.H.: Wesleyan University Press, 1990.

Jordan, Winthrop D. "Planter and Slave Identity Formation: Some Problems in the Comparative Approach." *Annals of the New York Academy of Sciences* 292 (June 1977): 35–40.

———. *White over Black: American Attitudes toward the Negro, 1550–1812*. Chapel Hill: University of North Carolina Press, 1968.

Joyner, Charles W. *Down by the Riverside: A South Carolina Slave Community*. Urbana: University of Illinois Press, 1984.

———. "Slave Folklife on the Waccamaw Neck: Antebellum Black Culture in the South Carolina Lowcountry." Ph.D. diss., University of Pennsylvania, 1977.

Julien, Carl, and Daniel W. Hollis, eds. *Look to the Rock: One Hundred Ante-Bellum Presbyterian Churches of the South*. Richmond: John Knox Press, 1961.

Kaiser, Daniel H., and Peyton Engel. "Time- and Age-Awareness in Early Modern Russia." *Comparative Studies in Society and History* 35 (October 1993): 824–39.

Kasson, John F. *Civilizing the Machine: Technology and Republican Values in America, 1776–1900.* New York: Grossman, 1976.

Kea, Ray A. *Settlements, Trade, and Politics in the Seventeenth-Century Gold Coast.* Baltimore: Johns Hopkins University Press, 1982.

Kerber, Linda. "Separate Spheres, Female Worlds, Woman's Place: The Rhetoric of Women's History." *Journal of American History* 75 (June 1988): 9–39.

Kern, Stephen. *The Culture of Time and Space, 1880–1914.* London: Weidenfeld and Nicholson, 1983.

Kessler-Harris, Alice. *Out to Work: A History of Wage-Earning Women in the United States.* New York: Oxford University Press, 1982.

Kett, Joseph, and Patricia McClung. "Book Culture in Post-Revolutionary Virginia." *Proceedings of the American Antiquarian Society* 94 (April 1984): 94–147.

Kilbride, Daniel. "Slavery and Utilitarianism: Thomas Cooper and the Mind of the Old South." *Journal of Southern History* 59 (August 1993): 469–86.

King, Elizabeth Doris. "The First-Class Hotel and the Age of the Common Man." *Journal of Southern History* 23 (May 1957): 173–88.

King, Wilma, ed. *A Northern Woman in the Plantation South: Letters of Tryphena Blanche Fox.* Columbia: University of South Carolina Press, 1992.

Klein, Rachel N. *Unification of a Slave State: The Rise of the Planter Class in the South Carolina Backcountry, 1760–1808.* Chapel Hill: University of North Carolina Press, 1990.

Kolchin, Peter. *American Slavery, 1619–1877.* New York: Hill & Wang, 1993.

———. "Reevaluating the Antebellum Slave Community: A Comparative Perspective." *Journal of American History* 70 (December 1983): 579–601.

Kolko, Gabriel. "Max Weber on America: Theory and Evidence." *History and Theory* 1 (1961): 243–60.

Kulik, Gary. "Patterns of Resistance." In *American Workingclass Culture: Explorations in Labor and Social History*, edited by Milton Cantor, 209–40. Westport, Conn.: Greenwood Press, 1979.

———. "Pawtucket Village and the Strike of 1824: The Origins of Class Conflict in Rhode Island." In *Material Life in America, 1600–1800*, edited by Robert Blair St. George, 385–406. Boston: Northeastern University Press, 1988.

Kulik, Gary, Roger Parks, and Theodore Z. Penn. *The New England Mill Village, 1790–1860.* Cambridge, Mass.: MIT Press, 1982.

Lale, Max S., and Randolph B. Campbell, eds. "The Plantation Journal of John B. Webster, February 17, 1858–November 5, 1859." *Southwestern Historical Quarterly* 84 (July 1980): 49–77.

Landes, David S. "Debate." *Past and Present* 116 (August 1987): 192–99.

———. *Revolution in Time: Clocks and the Making of the Modern World.* Cambridge, Mass.: Harvard University Press, 1983.

Lane, Frederic C. "Meanings of Capitalism." *Journal of Economic History* 29 (March 1969): 5–12.

Larson, John Lauritz. " 'Bind the Republic Together': The National Union and the Struggle for a System of Internal Improvements." *Journal of American History* 74 (September 1987): 363–87.

[Laurens County Historical Society]. *The Scrapbook: A Compilation of Historical Facts about Places and Events of Laurens County, South Carolina.* Laurens, S.C.: Laurens County Historical Society, 1982.

Law, Robin. *The Slave Coast of West Africa, 1550–1750: The Impact of the Atlantic Slave Trade on an African Society.* Oxford: Clarendon Press, 1991.

Le Goff, Jacques. "Labor Time in the 'Crisis' of the Fourteenth Century: From Medieval

Time to Modern Time." In *Time, Work, and Culture in the Middle Ages*, translated by Arthur Goldhammer, 43–52. Chicago: University of Chicago Press, 1980.

———. "Merchant's Time and Church's Time in the Middle Ages." In *Time, Work, and Culture in the Middle Ages*, translated by Arthur Goldhammer, 29–42. Chicago: University of Chicago Press, 1980.

Leone, Mark P. "The Georgian Order as the Order of Merchant Capitalism in Annapolis, Maryland." In *The Recovery of Meaning: Historical Archaeology in the Eastern United States*, edited by Mark P. Leone and Parker Potter Jr., 235–61. Washington, D.C.: Smithsonian Institution Press, 1988.

Leppert, Richard. *The Sight of Sound: Music, Representation, and the History of the Body*. Berkeley: University of California Press, 1993.

Lerner, Gerda. "The Lady and the Mill Girl: Changes in the Status of Women in the Age of Jackson, 1800–1840." In *A Heritage of Her Own: Toward a New Social History of American Women*, edited by Nancy F. Cott and Elizabeth H. Pleck, 182–96. New York: Simon and Schuster, 1979.

Levy, Babette M. "Early Puritanism in the Southern and Island Colonies." *Proceedings of the American Antiquarian Society* 70, pt. 1 (April–October 1960): 69–348.

Lewis, David B., and B. Eugene Griessman, eds. *The Southern Mystique: The Impact of Technology on Human Values in a Changing Region*. Tuscaloosa: University of Alabama Press, 1977.

Licht, Walter. *Working for the Railroad: The Organization of Work in the Nineteenth Century*. Princeton: Princeton University Press, 1983.

Liggett, Barbara. "A History of the Adoption of Standard Time in the United States, 1869–1883." M.A. thesis, University of Texas, 1960.

Litwack, Leon F. *Been in the Storm So Long: The Aftermath of Slavery*. New York: Vintage Books, 1980.

Lofton, John. *Denmark Vesey's Revolt: The Slave Plot That Lit a Fuse to Fort Sumter*. Kent: Kent State University Press, 1983.

Loth, Calder, ed. *The Virginia Landmarks Register*. Charlottesville: University Press of Virginia, 1986.

Löwenhardt, John. "Over Time: Time and Politics in the USSR." *Soviet Geography* 28 (November 1987): 656–65.

Ludwig, Alan I. *Graven Images: New England Stonecarving and Its Symbols, 1650–1815*. Middletown, Conn.: Wesleyan University Press, 1966.

Lukács, Georg. *History and Class Consciousness*. Boston: MIT Press, 1973.

Luraghi, Raimondo. *The Rise and Fall of the Plantation South*. New York: New Viewpoints, 1978.

Lynd, Staughton. "On Turner, Beard, and Slavery." *Journal of Negro History* 48 (October 1963): 235–50.

Macar, F., V. Poulthas, and W. J. Friedman, eds. *Time, Action and Cognition: Towards Bridging the Gap*. Dordrecht: Kluwer Academic, 1992.

McCaskie, Thomas C. "Time and the Calendar in Nineteenth-Century Asante: An Exploratory Essay." *History in Africa* 7 (1980): 179–200.

McCurry, Stephanie. *Masters of Small Worlds: Yeoman Households, Gender Relations, and the Political Culture of the Antebellum South Carolina Low Country*. New York: Oxford University Press, 1995.

McDonnell, Lawrence T. " 'You Are Too Sentimental': Problems and Suggestions for a New Labor History." *Journal of Social History* 17 (1983–84): 629–46.

Macey, Samuel L. *Clocks and the Cosmos: Time in Western Life and Thought*. Hamden, Conn.: Archon Books, 1980.

McKendrick, Neil. "Josiah Wedgewood and Factory Discipline." *Historical Journal* 4 (1961): 30–55.

McKenzie, Earl. "Time in European and African Philosophy." *Caribbean Quarterly* 19 (September 1973): 77–85.

McMillen, Sally G. *Southern Women: Black and White in the Old South.* Arlington Heights, Ill.: Harlan Davidson, 1992.

McPherson, James M. "Was West Indian Emancipation a Success?: The Abolitionist Argument during the American Civil War." *Caribbean Studies* 4 (July 1964): 28–34.

Mailer, Norman. "The Political Economy of Time." In *Cannibals and Christians*, 321–55. New York: Dell, 1966.

Main, Gloria L. "Probate Records as a Source for Early American History." *William and Mary Quarterly* 3d ser., 32 (January 1975): 89–99.

Mandle, Jay R. *Not Slave, Not Free: The African American Economic Experience since the Civil War.* Durham: Duke University Press, 1992.

——. *The Roots of Black Poverty: The Southern Plantation Economy after the Civil War.* Durham: Duke University Press, 1978.

Marchinow, William P., Jr. "Go South, Young Man! Reconstruction Letters of a Massachusetts Yankee." *South Carolina Historical Magazine* 80 (January 1979): 18–35.

Martineau, Harriet. *Retrospect of Western Travel.* Vol. 1. New York: Harper & Brothers, 1838.

Marx, Karl. *Capital: A Critique of Political Economy.* Vol. 1. Translated by Ben Fowkes. New York: Vintage Books, 1976.

——. *Grundisse: Foundations of the Critique of Political Economy (Rough Draft).* Translated by Martin Nicolaus. London: Penguin, 1973.

——. *Pre-Capitalist Economic Formations.* Edited by Eric J. Hobsbawm, translated by Jack Cohen. New York: International Publishers, 1965.

——. *Theories of Surplus-Value.* Vol. 4 of *Capital. Part II.* Moscow: Progress Publishers, 1968.

Marx, Leo. *The Machine in the Garden: Technology and the Pastoral Ideal in America.* New York: Oxford University Press, 1964.

Mathews, Donald G. *Religion in the Old South.* Chicago: University of Chicago Press, 1977.

Mayr, Otto, and Carlene E. Stephens. *American Clocks.* Washington, D.C.: Smithsonian Institution Press, 1990.

Mbaeyi, Paul Megha. *British Military and Naval Forces in West African History, 1807–1874.* New York: NOK Publishers, 1978.

Mbiti, John S. *African Religions and Philosophy.* New York: Heinemann, 1971.

Medford, Edna Greene. " 'There was so many degrees in slavery . . .': Unfree Labor in an Antebellum Mixed Farming Community." *Slavery and Abolition* 14 (August 1993): 35–47.

Menard, Russell R., Lois Green Carr, and Lorena S. Walsh. "A Small Planter's Profits: The Cole Estate and the Growth of the Early Chesapeake Economy." In *Material Life in America, 1600–1800*, edited by Robert Blair St. George, 185–202. Boston: Northeastern University Press, 1988.

Merrill, Michael. "Putting 'Capitalism' in Its Place: A Review of Recent Literature." *William and Mary Quarterly* 3d ser., 52 (April 1995): 315–26.

Metzer, Jacob. "Rational Management, Modern Business Practices, and Economies of Scale in the Ante-Bellum Southern Plantations." *Explorations in Economic History* 12 (April 1975): 123–50.

Meyerowitz, E. L. *The Akan of Ghana: Their Ancient Beliefs.* London: Faber and Faber, 1958.

Miers, Earl Schenck, ed. *When the World Ended: The Diary of Emma Le Conte.* New York: Oxford University Press, 1957.

Miles, Robert. *Capitalism and Unfree Labour: Anomaly or Necessity?* London: Tavistock, 1987.

Miller, Charles A. *Jefferson and Nature: An Interpretation*. Baltimore: Johns Hopkins University Press, 1988.

Miller, Perry. *Errand into the Wilderness*. Cambridge, Mass.: Belknap Press of Harvard University Press, 1956.

Miller, Randall M., ed. *Letters of a Slave Family*. Ithaca: Cornell University Press, 1978.

Mitman, Carl W. "Watchmakers and Inventors." *Scientific Monthly* 25 (July 1927): 58–64.

Moore, Barrington, Jr. "The American Civil War: The Last Capitalist Revolution." In Moore, *Social Origins of Dictatorship and Democracy: Lord and Peasant in the Making of the Modern World*, 111–58. Boston: Beacon Press, 1966.

Moore, John Hammond. *Columbia and Richland County: A South Carolina Community, 1740–1990*. Columbia: University of South Carolina Press, 1993.

Moore, N. Hudson. *The Old Clock Book*. New York: Tudor, 1937.

Moore, R. Randall. "In Search of a Safe Government: A Biography of R. M. T. Hunter." Ph.D. diss., University of South Carolina, 1993.

Moran, Gerard T. "Conception of Time in Early Modern France: An Approach to the History of Collective Mentalities." *Sixteenth Century Journal* 12 (Winter 1981): 3–20.

Morgan, C. Octavious S. *List of Members of the Clockmakers' Company: From the Period of Their Incorporation in 1631 to the Year 1732*. Exeter: William Pollard, 1883.

Morgan, Edmund S. *American Slavery, American Freedom: The Ordeal of Colonial Virginia*. New York: Norton, 1975.

——. "The Puritan Ethic and the American Revolution." *William and Mary Quarterly* 3d ser., 24 (January 1967): 3–43.

Morgan, Lynda J. *Emanicipation in Virginia's Tobacco Belt, 1850–1870*. Athens: University of Georgia Press, 1992.

Morgan, Philip D. "Work and Culture: The Task System and the World of Lowcountry Blacks, 1700 to 1880." *William and Mary Quarterly* 3d ser., 39 (April 1982): 563–99.

Morris, Robert C., ed. *Freedmen's Schools and Textbooks*. Vol. 3. New York: AMS Press, 1980.

Moses, Wilson Jeremiah, Jr. *The Wings of Ethiopia: Studies in African-American Life and Letters*. Ames: Iowa State University Press, 1990.

Mullin, Michael. *Africa in America: Slave Acculturation and Resistance in the American South and British Caribbean, 1736–1831*. Urbana: University of Illinois Press, 1992.

Mumford, Lewis. *Technics and Civilization*. New York: Harbinger, 1963.

Murphy, J. J. "Entrepreneurship in the Establishment of the American Clock Industry." *Journal of Economic History* 26 (1966): 169–86.

Neustadter, Roger. "Beat the Clock: The Mid-20th-Century Protest against the Reification of Time." *Time and Society* 1 (September 1992): 379–98.

Nguyen, Dan Thu. "The Spatialization of Metric Time: The Conquest of Land and Labour in Europe and the United States." *Time and Society* 1 (1992): 29–50.

Norton, Mary Beth. "The Evolution of White Women's Experience in Early America." *American Historical Review* 89 (June 1984): 593–619.

Novak, William J. "Public Economy and the Well-Ordered Market: Law and Economic Regulation in 19th-Century America." *Law and Social Inquiry* 18 (1993): 1–32.

Nyland, Chris. "Capitalism and the History of Worktime Thought." *British Journal of Sociology* 37 (December 1986): 513–34.

Oakes, James. *The Ruling Race: A History of American Slaveholders*. New York: Knopf, 1983.

——. *Slavery and Freedom: An Interpretation of the Old South*. New York: Knopf, 1990.

O'Brien, Michael. *Rethinking the South: Essays in Intellectual History*. Baltimore: Johns Hopkins University Press, 1988.

Ojo, J. Afolabi. *Yoruba Culture: A Geographical Analysis*. London: University of Ife and University of London Press, 1966.

Olmsted, Frederick Law. *The Cotton Kingdom: A Traveller's Observations on Cotton and Slavery in the American Slave States.* (1861). Edited by Arthur M. Schlesinger. New York: Knopf, 1953.

———. *A Journey in the Seaboard Slave States in the Years 1853–1854 with Remarks on Their Economy.* 2 vols. 1856. Reprint. New York: G. P. Putnam's Sons, 1904.

Olson, John F. "Clock Time versus Real Time: A Comparison of the Lengths of the Northern and Southern Agricultural Work Years." In *Without Consent or Contract: The Rise and Fall of American Slavery, Technical Papers.* Vol. 1, edited by Robert W. Fogel and Stanley L. Engerman, 216–40. New York: Norton, 1992.

O'Malley, Michael. *Keeping Watch: A History of American Time.* New York: Viking Penguin, 1990.

———. "Time, Work and Task Orientation: A Critique of American Historiography." *Time and Society* 1 (September 1992): 341–58.

Osborne, Thomas R. "Railway Time: The Railways and the Standardization of Time." Paper presented at the Southeastern Nineteenth Century Studies Association Annual Conference, Lexington, Kentucky, April 7–9, 1994.

Outland, Robert B., III. "Slavery, Work, and the Geography of the North Carolina Naval Stores Industry, 1835–1860." *Journal of Southern History* 62 (February 1996): 27–56.

Owen, Dock. *Camp-Fire Stories and Reminiscences.* Greenwood, S.C.: Index Publishing Co., n.d.

Owens, Leslie Howard. *This Species of Property: Slave Life and Culture in the Old South.* New York: Oxford University Press, 1976.

Pace, Antonio, ed. *Luigi Castiglioni's Viaggio: Travels in the United States of North America, 1785–87.* Syracuse, N.Y.: Syracuse University Press, 1983.

Padgug, Robert A. "Problems in the Theory of Slavery and Slave Society." *Science and Society* 40 (1976): 3–27.

Paolucci, Gabriella. "The Changing Dynamics of Working Time." *Time and Society* 5 (June 1996): 145–67.

Park, Mungo. *Travels in the Interior of Africa.* New York: Hippocrene Books, 1983.

Parsons, Elsie Clews. "Folk-Lore of the Sea Islands, South Carolina." *Memoirs of the American Folk-Lore Society* 16 (1923): 214–16.

Patterson, Orlando. *Slavery and Social Death: A Comparative Study.* Cambridge, Mass.: Harvard University Press, 1982.

Pawson, Eric. "Local Times and Standard Time in New Zealand." *Journal of Historical Geography* 18, no. 3 (1992): 278–87.

Peacock, James L. "The Southern Protestant Ethic Disease." In *The Not So Solid South: Anthropological Studies in a Regional Subculture*, edited by J. Kenneth Morland, 107–15. Athens: University of Georgia Press, 1971.

Pease, Jane H. "A Note on Patterns of Conspicuous Consumption among Seaboard Planters, 1820–1860." *Journal of Southern History* 35 (August 1969): 381–93.

Pelzer, Louis. "Pioneer Stage-Coach Travel." *Mississippi Valley Historical Review* 23 (June 1936): 1–26.

Pennington, Dorthy L. "Time in African Culture." In *African Culture: The Rhythm of Unity*, edited by Molefi Kete Asante and Kariamu Welsh Asante, 123–40. Westport, Conn.: Greenwood Press, 1985.

Pennington, Estill Curtis. *Look Away: Reality and Sentiment in Southern Art.* Spartanburg, S.C.: Saraland Press, 1989.

Perdue, Charles L., Jr., Thomas E. Barden, and Robert K. Phillips, eds. *Weevils in the Wheat: Interviews with Ex-Virginia Slaves.* Charlottesville: University Press of Virginia, 1976.

Perrin, Liese. "Female Slaves and the Idea of Work." Ph.D. diss., University of Birmingham, in progress.

Pessen, Edward. "How Different from Each Other Were the Antebellum North and South?" *American Historical Review* 85 (December 1980): 1119–49.

Phillips, Ulrich Bonnell. *A History of Transportation in the Eastern Cotton Belt to 1860*. New York: Octo Press, 1968.

———. "The Slave Labor Problem in the Charleston District." In *Plantation, Town and Country: Essays on the Local History of the American Slave South*, edited by Elinor Miller and Eugene Genovese, 7–28. Urbana: University of Illinois Press, 1975.

Phillips, Ulrich Bonnell, and James David Glunt, eds. *Florida Plantation Records from the Papers of George Noble Jones*. St. Louis: Missouri Historical Society, 1927.

Pollard, Sidney. "Factory Discipline in the Industrial Revolution." *Economic History Review* 2d ser., 16 (1963): 254–71.

Post, Charles. "The American Road to Capitalism." *New Left Review* 133 (May–June 1982): 30–52.

Potter, David. *People of Plenty: Economic Abundance and the American Character*. Chicago: University of Chicago Press, 1954.

Pred, Allan. "Production, Family, and Free-Time Projects: A Time Geographic Perspective on the Individual and Societal Change in Nineteenth-Century U.S. Cities." *Journal of Historical Geography* 7 (1981): 3–36.

Price, Derek da Solla. "Clockwork before the Clock and Timekeepers before Timekeeping." In *The Study of Time II*, edited by J. T. Fraser and N. Lawrence, 367–80. Berlin: Birkhaüser, 1975.

Priestly, Margaret. "Philip Quaque of Cape Coast." In *Africa Remembered: Narratives by West Africans from the Era of the Slave Trade*, edited by Philip D. Curtin, 102. Madison: University of Wisconsin Press, 1967.

Prown, Jonathan, Ronald Hurst, and Sumpter Priddy III. "Fredricksburg Clock Cases, 1765–1825." *Journal of Early Southern Decorative Arts* 17 (November 1992): 55–119.

Prude, Jonathan. *The Coming of Industrial Order: Towns and Factory Life in Rural Massachusetts 1810–1860*. Cambridge: Cambridge University Press, 1983.

———. "To Look Upon the 'Lower Sort': Runaway Ads and the Appearance of Unfree Laborers in America, 1750–1800." *Journal of American History* 78 (June 1991): 124–59.

Puckett, Newbell Niles. *Folk Beliefs of the Southern Negro*. Chapel Hill: University of North Carolina Press, 1926.

Raboteau, Albert J. *Slave Religion: The "Invisible Institution" in the Antebellum South*. New York: Oxford University Press, 1978.

Radford, John P. "The Charleston Planters in 1860." *South Carolina Historical Magazine* 77 (October 1976): 227–35.

Ramsdell, James G. *Lincoln the Liberal Statesman*. New York: Dodd, Mead, 1947.

Randolph, Mary. *The Virginia House-Wife*. Columbia: University of South Carolina Press, 1984.

Ranft, Charles F. "The Colonial Post Office, 1710–1789." *Johns Hopkins University Circular: Notes in History*, May 1906, 86–89.

Ransom, Roger L. *Conflict and Compromise: The Political Economy of Slavery, Emancipation, and the American Civil War*. New York: Cambridge University Press, 1989.

Ransom, Roger L., and Richard Sutch. *One Kind of Freedom: The Economic Consequences of Emancipation*. New York: Cambridge University Press, 1977.

Rawick, George P., ed. *The American Slave: A Composite Autobiography*. 41 vols. Westport, Conn.: Greenwood Press, 1972–79.

Reaver, J. Russell, ed. *Florida Folktales*. Gainesville: University Presses of Florida, 1988.

Rediker, Marcus. *Between the Devil and the Deep Blue Sea: Merchant Seamen, Pirates, and the Anglo-American Maritime World, 1700–1750*. New York: Cambridge University Press, 1993.

Reidy, Joseph P. *From Slavery to Agrarian Capitalism in the Cotton Plantation South: Central Georgia, 1800–1880*. Chapel Hill: University of North Carolina Press, 1992.

Reigel, Robert E. "Standard Time in the United States." *American Historical Review* 33 (1927): 84–89.

Rezsoházy, Rudolf. "The Concept of Social Time: Its Role in Development." *International Social Science Journal* 24, no. 1 (1972): 26–36.

Rice, Howard C., Jr. *Travels in North America in the Years 1780, 1781 and 1782 by the Marquis de Chastellux*. Vol. 2. Chapel Hill: University of North Carolina Press, 1963.

Rifkin, Jeremy. *Time Wars: The Primary Conflict in Human History*. New York: Henry Holt, 1987.

Roark, James L. *Masters without Slaves: Southern Planters in the Civil War and Reconstruction*. New York: Norton, 1977.

Robinson, John P. "The Time Squeeze." *American Demographics* 2 (February 1990): 30–33.

Rodgers, Daniel T. *The Work Ethic in Industrial America 1850–1920*. Chicago: University of Chicago Press, 1978.

Rodrigue, John C. "Raising Cane: From Slavery to Free Labor in Louisiana's Sugar Parishes, 1862–1880." Paper presented at the Annual Meeting of the St. George Tucker Society, Atlanta, June 1994.

Roediger, David S., and Philip S. Foner. *Our Own Time: A History of American Labor and the Working Day*. London: Verso, 1989.

——. "Time, Republicanism, and Merchant Capitalism: Consciousness of Hours before 1830." In *Our Own Time: A History of American Labor and the Working Day*, 1–19. London: Verso, 1989.

Rogers, George C., Jr. "Changes in Taste in the Eighteenth Century: A Shift from the Useful to the Ornamental." *Journal of Early Southern Decorative Arts* 8 (May 1982): 1–23.

——. *Charleston in the Age of the Pinckneys*. Columbia: University of South Carolina Press, 1980.

Rogers, George C., Jr., and David R. Chesnutt, eds. *The Papers of Henry Laurens*. Vol. 5, *September, 1765–July 31, 1768*. Columbia: University of South Carolina Press, 1976.

Rose, Anne C. *Voices of the Marketplace: American Thought and Culture, 1830–1860*. New York: Twayne, 1995.

Rosengarten, Theodore. *Tombee: Portrait of a Cotton Planter with the Journal of Thomas B. Chaplin (1822–1890)*. New York: William Morrow, 1986.

Rothenberg, Winifred B. "The Emergence of a Capital Market in Rural Massachusetts, 1730–1838." *Journal of Economic History* 44 (December 1985): 789–91.

Rutland, Robert A., ed. *The Papers of George Mason, 1725–1792*. Vol. 1, *1749–78*. Chapel Hill: University of North Carolina Press, 1970.

Ryan, Mary P. *Women in Public: Between Banners and Ballots, 1825–1880*. Baltimore: Johns Hopkins University Press, 1990.

Sander, William. "The Economics of Time and Community." *Review of Social Economy* 42 (April 1984): 44–49.

Savannah Unit, Georgia Writers' Project, Works Projects Administration. *Drums and Shadows: Survival Studies among the Georgia Coastal Negroes*. Spartanburg, S.C.: Reprint Co., 1974.

Saville, Julie. *The Work of Reconstruction: From Slave to Wage Laborer in South Carolina, 1860–1870*. Cambridge: Cambridge University Press, 1995.

Saxton, Robert, ed. *Mental Photographs: An Album for Confessions of Tastes, Habits, and Convictions*. New York: Henry Holt, 1875.

Schafer, R. Murray. *The Tuning of the World: Toward a Theory of Soundscape Design*. Philadelphia: University of Pennsylvania Press, 1980.

Schantz, Mark S. "'A Very Serious Business': Managerial Relationships on the Ball Plantations, 1800–1835." *South Carolina Historical Magazine* 88 (January 1988): 1–22.

Scheele, Carl H. *A Short History of the Mail Service*. Washington, D.C.: Smithsonian Institution Press, 1970.

Schoepf, Johann David. *Travels in the Confederation [1783–1784]*, edited and translated by Alfred J. Morrison, vol. 2. Philadelphia: Bergman, 1968.

Schwartz, Nancy L. "Labor, Politics, and Time in the Thought of Karl Marx." Ph.D. diss., Yale University, 1976.

Scott, Anna M. *Day Dawn in Africa: or, Progress of the Prot. Epis. Mission at Cape Palmas, West Africa*. New York: Negro Universities Press, 1969.

Scott, Ann Firor. *The Southern Lady: From Pedestal to Politics, 1830–1930*. Chicago: University of Chicago Press, 1970.

Scott, Rebecca J. *Slave Emancipation in Cuba: The Transition to Free Labor, 1860–1899*. Princeton: Princeton University Press, 1985.

Segal, Howard P. *Technological Utopianism in American Culture*. Chicago: University of Chicago Press, 1985.

Sellers, Charles. *The Market Revolution: Jacksonian America, 1815–1846*. New York: Oxford University Press, 1991.

Sellers, Hazel Crowson. *Old South Carolina Churches*. Columbia, S.C.: Crowson, 1941.

Sellers, James Benson. *Slavery in Alabama*. Tuscaloosa: University of Alabama Press, 1950.

Seward, Austin. *Twenty-Two Years a Slave, and Forty Years a Freeman; Embracing a Correspondence of Several Years, While Resident of Wilberforce Colony, London, Canada West*. New York: Negro Universities Press, 1968.

Shackel, Paul A. *Personal Discipline and Material Culture: An Archaeology of Annapolis, Maryland, 1695–1870*. Knoxville: University of Tennessee Press, 1993.

Shlomowitz, Ralph. "'Bound' or 'Free'? Black Labor in Cotton and Sugar Cane Farming, 1865–1880." In *Without Consent or Contract: The Rise and Fall of American Slavery, Conditions of Slave Life and the Transition to Freedom, Technical Papers*, Vol. 2, edited by Robert William Fogel and Stanley L. Engerman, 665–86. New York: Norton, 1992.

Shore, Laurence. *Southern Capitalists: The Ideological Leadership of an Elite, 1832–1885*. Chapel Hill: University of North Carolina Press, 1986.

Simms, William Gilmore. *The Charleston Book: A Miscellany in Prose and Verse*. Spartanburg, S.C.: Reprint Co., 1983.

Simons, Albert, and Samuel Lapham, eds. *The Early Architecture of Charleston*. Columbia: University of South Carolina Press, 1970.

Sinha, Manisha. "The Counter-Revolution of Slavery: Class, Politics and Ideology in Antebellum South Carolina." Ph.D. diss., Columbia University, 1994.

Smith, H. F., et al. "Ali Eisami Gazirmabe of Borno." In *Africa Remembered: Narratives by West African Slaves from the Era of the Slave Trade*, edited by Philip D. Curtin, 208. Madison: University of Wisconsin Press, 1967.

Smith, Humphrey M. "Greenwich Time and the Prime Meridian." *Vistas in Astronomy* 20 (1976): 220–22.

Smith, James L. *Autobiography of James L. Smith*. New York: Negro Universities Press, 1969.

Smith, Jane Webb. "'A Large and Elegant Assortment': A Group of Baltimore Tall Clocks, 1795–1815." *Journal of Early Southern Decorative Arts* 13 (November 1987): 33–103.

Smith, John David. *An Old Creed for the New South: Proslavery Ideology and Historiography, 1865–1918*. Athens: University of Georgia Press, 1985.

Smith, Jonathan Z. "A Slip in Time Saves Nine: Prestigious Origins Again." In *Chronotypes:*

The Construction of Time, edited by John Bender and David E. Wellbery, 67–76. Stanford: Stanford University Press, 1991.

Smith, Marion B. "South Carolina and the *Gentleman's Magazine*." *South Carolina Historical Magazine* 95 (April 1994): 102–29.

Smith, Mark M. "American Soundscapes: Listening to Class, Power, and Culture" (work in progress).

———. "Counting Clocks, Owning Time: Detailing and Interpreting Clock and Watch Ownership in the American South, 1739–1865." *Time and Society* 3 (October 1994): 241–59.

———. "Fugitives from Labor: Alienation and Resistance in the American Slave South." M.A. thesis, University of South Carolina, 1991.

———. "Old South Time in Comparative Perspective." *American Historical Review* 101 (1996): 1432–69.

———. "The Political Economy of Time in the American South: The Evolution of a Southern Time-Consciousness, 1700–1900." Ph.D diss., University of South Carolina, 1995.

———. "Time, Slavery and Plantation Capitalism in the Ante-Bellum American South." *Past and Present* 150 (February 1996): 142–68.

———. "Time, Sound, and the Virginia Slave." In *New Directions in Virginia African American History*, edited by John D. Saillant. New York: Garland, forthcoming.

Smith, Thomas C. "Peasant Time and Factory Time in Japan." *Past and Present* 111 (May 1986): 165–97.

Smith, Warren B. *White Servitude in Colonial South Carolina*. Columbia: University of South Carolina Press, 1961.

Smith, William H. "The Colonial Post-Office." *American Historical Review* 21 (January 1916): 258–75.

Sobel, Mechal. *Trabellin' On: The Slave Journey to an Afro-Baptist Faith*. Westport, Conn.: Greenwood Press, 1979.

———. *The World They Made Together: Black and White Values in Eighteenth Century Virginia*. Princeton: Princeton University Press, 1987.

Sokoloff, Kenneth L. "Inventive Activity in Early Industrial America: Evidence from Patent Records, 1790–1846." *Journal of Economic History* 48 (December 1988): 813–50.

Soltow, Lee. *Distribution of Wealth and Income in the United States in 1798*. Pittsburgh: University of Pittsburgh Press, 1989.

Spruill, Julia Cherry. *Women's Life and Work in the Southern Colonies*. New York: Norton, 1972.

Stampp, Kenneth M. *The Peculiar Institution: Slavery in the Ante-Bellum South*. New York: Vintage, 1989.

Starr, John W., Jr. *One Hundred Years of American Railroading*. New York: Dodd, Mead, 1929.

"'Statutory Time' Abolished in USSR." *Soviet Geography* 32 (March 1991): 190–95.

Stephens, Carlene E. "Astronomy as Public Utility: The Bond Years at the Harvard College Observatory." *Journal for the History of Astronomy* 21 (1990): 21–35.

———. *Inventing Standard Time*. Washington, D.C.: Smithsonian Institution Press, 1983.

———. "'The Most Reliable Time': William Bond, the New England Railroads, and Time Awareness in 19th-Century America." *Technology and Culture* 30 (January 1989): 1–24.

———. "Partners in Time: William Bond & Son of Boston and the Harvard College Observatory." *Harvard Library Bulletin* 35 (Fall 1987): 351–81.

Stewart, Mary E. "The Flight of Time." In *The Charleston Book: A Miscellany in Prose and Verse*, edited by William Gilmore Simms, 53. Spartanburg, S.C.: Reprint Co., 1983.

Stoller, Paul. "Sound in Songhay Cultural Experience." *American Ethnologist* 11 (August 1983): 559–70.

Stoney, Samuel Gaillard. "Nicholas De Longuemare: Huguenot Goldsmith and Silk Dealer in Colonial South Carolina." *Transactions of the Huguenot Society of South Carolina* 55 (1950): 38–69.

Stott, Richard B. *Workers in the Metropolis: Class, Ethnicity, and Youth in Antebellum New York City*. Ithaca: Cornell University Press, 1990.

Stowe, Harriet Beecher. *Uncle Tom's Cabin or, Life among the Lowly*. Cambridge, Mass.: Library of America, 1982.

Stowe, Steven M. "The Not-So-Cloistered Academy: Elite Women's Education and Family Feeling in the Old South." In *The Web of Southern Social Relations: Women, Family, and Education*, edited by Walter J. Fraser Jr., R. Frank Saunders Jr., and Jon L. Wakelyn, 90–106. Athens: University of Georgia Press, 1985.

——. "Seeing Themselves at Work: Physicians and the Case Narrative in the Mid-Nineteenth-Century American South." *American Historical Review* 101 (February 1996): 41–79.

Stowell, Marion Barber. *Early American Almanacs: The Colonial Weekday Bible*. New York: Burt Franklin, 1977.

Strodtbeck, Fred L., and Marvin B. Sussman. "Of Time, the City, and the 'One-Year Guaranty': The Relations between Watch Owners and Repairers." *American Journal of Sociology* 61 (January 1956): 602–9.

Stuckey, Sterling. *Slave Culture: Nationalist Theory and the Foundations of Black America*. New York: Oxford University Press, 1987.

Suttles, William C., Jr. "African Religious Survivals as Factors in American Slave Revolts." *Journal of Negro History* 56 (April 1971): 97–104.

Sydnor, Charles Sackett. *Slavery in Mississippi*. New York: D. Appleton-Century, 1933.

Tambiah, S. J. "The Magical Power of Words." *Man* n.s., 3 (June 1968): 175–208.

Taylor, George R. *The Transportation Revolution, 1815–1861*. New York: Rinehart, 1951.

Taylor, Joe Gray. *Negro Slavery in Louisiana*. New York: Negro Universities Press, 1969.

Thomas, Keith. "Work and Leisure." *Past and Present* 29 (December 1964): 50–66.

Thomas, Sidney Albert. *A Historical Account of the Protestant Episcopal Church in South Carolina 1820–1957*. Columbia, S.C.: R. L. Bryan, 1957.

Thompson, E. P. *The Making of the English Working Class*. London: Penguin, 1963.

——. "Time, Work-Discipline and Industrial Capitalism." *Past and Present* 38 (December 1967): 56–97.

Thornton, J. Mills, III. "Fiscal Policy and the Failure of Radical Reconstruction in the Lower South." In *Region, Race, and Reconstruction: Essays in Honor of C. Vann Woodward*, edited by J. Morgan Kousser and James M. McPherson, 349–94. New York: Oxford University Press, 1982.

Thrift, Nigel. "Owners' Time and Own Time: The Making of a Capitalist Time Consciousness, 1300–1880." In *Space and Time in Geography: Essays Dedicated to Torsten Hägerstrand*, edited by Allen Pred, 56–84. Lund Studies in Geography. Series B. Human Geography No. 48. Gleerup: Royal University of Lund, 1981.

Tise, Larry E. *Proslavery: A History of the Defense of Slavery in America, 1701–1840*. Athens: University of Georgia Press, 1987.

Touchstone, Blake. "Planter and Slave Religion in the Deep South." In *Masters and Slaves in the House of the Lord: Race and Religion in the American South, 1740–1870*, edited by John B. Boles, 99–126. Lexington: University Press of Kentucky, 1988.

Townsend, George E. *Almost Everything You Wanted to Know about American Watches and Didn't Know Who to Ask*. Vienna, Va.: Privately printed, 1970.

Trachtenberg, Alan. *The Incorporation of America: Culture and Society in the Gilded Age*. New York: Hill & Wang, 1982.

Train, Arthur, Jr. *The Story of Everyday Things*. New York: Harper & Brothers, 1941.

Turner, Robert P., ed. *Lewis Miller, Sketches and Chronicles: The Reflections of a Nineteenth Century Pennsylvania German Folk Artist*. York, Pa.: Historical Society of York County, 1966.

Twaddle, Michael, ed. "The Wages of Slavery: From Chattel Slavery to Wage Labour in Africa, the Caribbean and England." *Slavery and Abolition* 14 (April 1993): 1–226.

Twenty-Four Letters from Labourers in America to Their Friends in England. London: Edward Rainford, 1829.

Tyack, George S. *A Book about Bells*. London: William Andrews, 1939.

Ulrich, Laurel Thatcher. *Good Wives: Image and Reality in the Lives of Women in Northern New England, 1650–1750*. New York: Knopf, 1982.

——. "Housewife and Gadder: Themes of Self-Sufficiency and Community in Eighteenth-Century New England." In *"To Toil the Livelong Day": America's Women at Work, 1780–1980*, edited by Carol Groneman and Mary Beth Norton, 21–34. Ithaca: Cornell University Press, 1987.

Vansina, Jan. *The Children of Woot: A History of the Kuba Peoples*. Madison: University of Wisconsin Press, 1978.

Vickers, Daniel. "Competency and Competition: Economic Culture in Early America." *William and Mary Quarterly*, 3d ser., 47 (January 1990): 3–29.

"Virginia Watch Papers." *Virginia Historical Society Occasional Bulletin* 19 (October 1969): 7–10.

Vlach, John Michael. *Back of the Big House: The Architecture of Plantation Slavery*. Chapel Hill: University of North Carolina Press, 1993.

——. *By the Work of Their Hands: Studies in Afro-American Folklife*. Charlottesville: University Press of Virginia, 1991.

Wade, Richard C. *Slavery in the Cities: The South, 1820–1860*. New York: Oxford University Press, 1964.

Waldo, Leonard. "The Mechanical Art of American Watchmaking." *Journal of the Society of Arts* 34 (May 21, 1886): 740–51.

Walker, F. W. *The Romance of Church Bells*. London: Elliot Stock, 1938.

Wallace, David D. *South Carolina: A Short History, 1520–1948*. Columbia: University of South Carolina Press, 1961.

Wallerstein, Immanuel. "American Slavery and the Capitalist World Economy." *American Journal of Sociology* 81 (March 1976): 1199–1213.

Walsh, James P. "Holy Time and Sacred Space in Puritan New England." *American Quarterly* 32 (Spring 1980): 79–95.

Walvin, James. "Slaves, Free Time and the Question of Leisure." *Slavery and Abolition* 16 (April 1995): 1–13.

Washington, Booker T. *Up from Slavery: An Autobiography*. New York: Young People's Missionary Movement of the United States and Canada, 1901.

Watterson, Henry. "Oddities of Southern Life." *Century Magazine* 23 (April 1882): 884.

Waugh, Albert E. *Sundials: Their Theory and Construction*. New York: Dover, 1973.

Weber, Max. *The Protestant Ethic and the Spirit of Capitalism*. Translated by Talcott Parsons. London: Unwin University Books, 1970.

Weir, Robert M. *Colonial South Carolina: A History*. Millwood, N.Y.: KTO Press, 1983.

——. "The Role of the Newspaper Press in the Southern Colonies on the Eve of the Revolution: An Interpretation." In *The Press and the American Revolution*, edited by Bernard Bailyn and John B. Hench, 89–150. Boston: Northeastern University Press, 1981.

——. "The South Carolinian as Extremist." *South Atlantic Quarterly*, December 1975, 86–103.

Wenzel, Peter. "Pre-Modern Concepts of Society and Economy in American Pro-Slavery

Thought: On the Intellectual Foundations of the Social Philosophy of George Fitzhugh." *Amerika Studies* 27 (1987): 157–75.

White, Carla. "The Bells of Fincastle." *Journal of the Roanoke Historical Society* 6 (Winter 1970): 37–39.

White, Newman Ivey, ed. *The Frank C. Brown Collection of North Carolina Folklore.* Vol. 7, Wayland D. Hand, ed., *Popular Beliefs and Superstitions from North Carolina.* Durham: Duke University Press, 1964.

Whitney, Annie Weston, and Caroline Canfield Bullock. "Folk-Lore from Maryland." *Memoirs of the American Folk-Lore Society* 18 (1925): 18–50.

Whitney, Philip. "Shenandoah Valley Clockmakers." *Winchester–Frederick County Historical Society* 1 (December 1986): 13–21.

Wiener, Jonathan M. "Planter Persistence and Social Change: Alabama, 1850–1870." *Journal of Interdisciplinary History* 7 (Autumn 1976): 235–60.

———. *Social Origins of the New South: Alabama, 1860–1885.* Baton Rouge: Louisiana State University Press, 1978.

Wilcox, Nathaniel T. "The Overseer Problem: A New Data Set and Method." In *Without Consent or Contract: The Rise and Fall of American Slavery, Evidence and Methods*, edited by Robert W. Fogel, Ralph A. Galantine, and Richard L. Manning, 84–108. New York: Norton, 1992.

Wilentz, Sean. *Chants Democratic: New York City and the Rise of the American Working Class, 1788–1850.* New York: Oxford University Press, 1984.

Wilks, Ivor. "On Mentally Mapping Greater Asante: A Study of Time and Motion." *Journal of African History* 33 (1992): 175–90.

Williams, Jack K. "Travel in Ante-Bellum Georgia as Recorded by English Visitors." *Georgia Historical Quarterly* 33 (September 1949): 191–205.

Williams, John G. *"De Ole Plantation."* Charleston, S.C.: Walker, Evans & Cogswell, 1895.

Wood, Betty. *Slavery in Colonial Georgia, 1730–1775.* Athens: University of Georgia Press, 1984.

———. "Some Aspects of Female Resistance to Chattel Slavery in Low Country Georgia, 1763–1815." *Historical Journal* 30, no. 3 (1987): 603–22.

———. *Women's Work, Men's Work: The Informal Slave Economies of Lowcountry Georgia.* Athens: University of Georgia Press, 1995.

Wood, Peter H. *Black Majority: Negroes in Colonial South Carolina from 1670 through the Stono Rebellion.* New York: Norton, 1975.

Woodfin, Maude H., ed. *Another Secret Diary of William Byrd of Westover, 1739–1741.* Richmond: Dietz Press, 1942.

Woodman, Harold D. *King Cotton and His Retainers: Financing the Cotton Crop of the South, 1800–1925.* Columbia: University of South Carolina Press, 1990.

Woodward, C. Vann. "Emancipations and Reconstructions: A Comparative Study." In *The Future of the Past*, 145–64. New York: Oxford University Press, 1989.

———. "History from Slave Sources." *American Historical Review* 79 (April 1974): 470–72.

———. *The Origins of the New South, 1877–1913.* Baton Rouge: Louisiana State University Press, 1951.

———. *The Political Economy of the Cotton South: Households, Markets, and Wealth in the Nineteenth Century.* New York: Norton, 1978.

———. "The Southern Ethic in a Puritan World." In *American Counterpoint: Slavery and Racism in the North-South Dialogue*, 13–46. New York: Oxford University Press, 1971.

Wright, Gavin. *Old South, New South: Revolutions in the Southern Economy since the Civil War.* New York: Basic Books, 1986.

Wright, Richardson. *Hawkers and Walkers in Early America: Strolling Peddlers, Preachers,*

Lawyers, Doctors, Players, and Others, from the Beginning to the Civil War. Philadelphia: J. B. Lippincott, 1927.

Wyatt-Brown, Bertram. "Modernizing Southern Slavery: The Proslavery Argument Reinterpreted." In *Region, Race, and Reconstruction: Essays in Honor of C. Vann Woodward,* edited by J. Morgan Kousser and James M. McPherson, 27–50. New York: Oxford University Press, 1982.

Yellin, Jean Fagan, ed. *Incidents in the Life of a Slave Girl Written by Herself by Harriet A. Jacobs.* Cambridge, Mass.: Harvard University Press, 1987.

Yetman, Norman R. "The Background of the Slave Narrative Collection." *American Quarterly* 19 (Fall 1967): 534–53.

Zerubavel, Eviatar. *The Seven Day Circle: The History and Meaning of the Week.* New York: Free Press, 1985.

———. "The Standardization of Time: A Sociohistorical Perspective." *American Journal of Sociology* 88 (1982): 1–23.

Zukerkandl, Victor. *Sound and Symbol: Music and the External World.* Translated by Willard R. Trask. Princeton: Princeton University Press, 1958.

INDEX

67–68, 70; and industrial time, 6–7, 15, 41, 67, 95, 117, 212 (n. 3); and workers' accommodation to managers' time, 7, 10, 11, 175; and workers' resistance to managers' time, 11, 250 (n. 76); manufacturing of timepieces and sundials, 19, 22–24, 33; and merchants, 66, 67–68; and stagecoaches, 75, 81; compared to South, 95, 117, 175; and efficient farming, 97. *See also* Greenwich mean time

Brody, David, 6, 94

Brown, John (slave), 122

Brown, Richard D., 12

Bruce, John (railroad president), 81, 85, 87

Bruegel, Martin, 35

Bruin, Madison (slave), 124

Bunts, Elizabeth (slave), 147

Burge, Dolly Sumner, 59

Burr, Esther, 57

Butler, Benjamin F., 168

Byrd, William (slave), 141

Cabell, William (planter), 28, 71

Cable, George Washington, 152

Cain, Louis (slave), 140

Camden and Amboy Railroad, 82, 179

Carrington, William Cabell (planter), 52

Carroll, Cora (slave), 139–40

Carson, Margaret, 62

Carter, George (merchant), 65

Carter, Landon, 65

Cemeteries, 50–51

Chamberlayne, William (planter), 71

Chandler, Timothy (planter), 51

Charleston, S.C., 19–23, 26, 44–46, 51–56, 58–59, 65–66, 77–78, 80, 81, 86, 89, 104, 105–6, 178; district and city, 29–30, 220 (n. 85); timepiece ownership in, 30–36, 48, 220 (n. 92); city time, 47–48, 56

Charleston and Hamburg railroad, 82–83, 232–33 (n. 68); and standardizing time, 83

Chicago, 180, 181

Churches, 44, 179–80, 183; medieval, 16, 65; and aural time in eighteenth- and nineteenth-century South, 17–20, 41, 65, 139. *See also* Sound: and time; Time and time consciousness: and religion; Time and time consciousness: medieval conception of; Time and time con-

sciousness: and urban public order and coordination

Civil War, 19, 32, 45, 135, 154–55, 168; and rise of nation state, 178, 180

Clay, Joseph (merchant), 75

Cleveland, 181

Clitherall, Carolyn Burgwin, 58

Clocks and watches, 17; as modern, 3, 12, 14; ownership of, 7, 11, 15–16, 18, 20, 30–36, 150–51, 216 (n. 4); as representing power, 14; public clocks, 17–20, 139, 179–80, 183; accuracy of, 18, 21; repair and assembly of, 19, 22–23, 26–29, 80, 144; ornamental value of, 20–22, 217 (n. 21); technical aspects of, 21; taxes and tariffs on, 21–23; sale and advertising of, 21–23, 27–28; import and export of, 21–26, 33–34, 37–38, 116; and peddlers, 22–23, 28; and miscellaneous equipment, 23–24; and southern makers of, 24–29, 218–19 (nn. 52, 53, 63); and manufacturing of by region, 25–27; and immigrants, 26–27; ownership levels among rural and urban southerners compared, 30–37; ownership among nonslaveholders, 31–33, 221 (n. 97); cost of, 33–35; ownership among slaveholders, 33–37; and northern manufacturing of, 34, 116, 131; ownership levels of North and South compared, 35–36; sentimental value of, 51; household, 58, 60, 112, 113, 125, 162–63, 240 (n. 89); and travel, 80; as prizes, 96; alarm clocks, 116, 163, 164; export of to West Africa, 131; nautical clock, 227–28 (n. 77). *See also* Churches; Courthouses

Coates, Charles (slave), 144

Cobb, Daniel William (planter), 47, 110, 165

Cocke, James Powell (planter), 110

Cofer, Betty (slave), 140

Cole, Harrison (slave), 140

Coleman, William (slave), 141–42

Colhoun, John Ewing (planter), 102

College of Charleston, 54. *See also* Education: of southern white children

Collins, Bill (slave), 141

Collins, Robert (planter), 118–19

Colored Peoples' Time (CPT), 18, 130, 132, 163–64, 165, 243 (n. 1), 251 (n. 10)

Colquitt, Martha (slave), 123–24

McCormick, Stephen (farmer), 97
McGillery, Lee (slave), 136
McKee, John (clock maker), 25
McKim, J. G. (planter), 165
McWhorter, William (slave), 124
Mangum, Willie Person (U.S. senator), 77
Maine, 60, 184; Bangor, 181–82; Bath, 182
Manigault, Charles (planter), 47, 72, 77, 102
Manigault, Charles Izard (planter), 110
Manigault, Henry, 58
Manigault, Heyward (planter), 28–29
Manigault, Louis (planter), 52, 54, 72, 101
Manigault, Peter, 30
Martineau, Harriet, 142
Marx, Karl, 15, 164; on slavery and capital-
    ism, 1, 93, 95, 174; on time and capital-
    ism, 11, 212 (n. 4)
Marx, Leo, 92
Maryland, 25; Fredericktown, 23; Balti-
    more, 76–77
Mason, George, 49
Mason, James (farmer), 72
Mason, Lewis Edmunds (planter), 171, 172
Massachusetts, 92
Mbiti, John, 131–32
Mercantilism, 5
Merchants, 4, 40, 101; British, 21, 65–68;
    European, 22, 63, 66; southern, 22–23,
    32, 42, 63–67, 70, 73, 75–76, 81, 102, 125,
    228 (n. 144); medieval, 42, 63, 65, 227
    (n. 132); northern, 63–65, 131, 227
    (n. 135); African, 131. See also Planters,
    antebellum: and merchants
Merrit, Susan (slave), 140
Michigan: Detroit, 181–82; Port Huron, 182
Middleton, Alicia, 59
Midwives, 60
Miliken, Thomas (planter), 111
Miller, John Blount (planter), 170
Ministers, 43, 52
Mississippi, 88, 103, 113, 114, 121, 124,
    139–40, 149, 166; Jackson, 79; Vicksburg,
    79; Natchez, 144, 152
Missouri, 135; Hannibal, 139
Montgomery, Laura (slave), 113
Mooreman, Mattie (freedwoman), 175
Moravians, N.C., 45
Morgan, Edmund S., 41
Mosley, John (freedman), 173
Moultrie, J. L. (Rev.), 96

Moye, Calvin (slave), 137
Mullin, Michael, 149
Mumford, Lewis, 39, 212 (n. 4)
Munro, Abby D. (teacher), 148, 163–64, 245
    (n. 17)

Nebraska, 182
New Jersey, 52, 66
New Orleans, 25, 74, 78, 88, 89, 91, 158, 180,
    182
New York, 52, 54, 65, 77, 78, 88, 178, 184;
    New York City, 179–80
New-York and New-Orleans Magnetic
    Telegraph Company, 77
Nichols, George (slave), 133
Nicolson, George Llewellyn (planter), 46
Nonslaveholders: and timepiece owner-
    ship, 31–33, 221 (n. 97)
North, 2, 52, 63, 64, 70, 73, 78, 94; urban,
    2, 6–7, 15, 18; rural, 2–3, 212 (n. 3); and
    democratic capitalism, 7; compared to
    South, 7, 15, 92, 95, 100–101, 107, 126, 151,
    175; colonial, 12; and timepiece industry,
    22, 23–26; industrial-capitalist time con-
    ception, 38, 41, 94–95, 98, 100, 164; and
    wage labor, 71, 175; and travel, 80, 82, 83,
    91. See also Time and time conscious-
    ness: and factories
North Carolina, 23, 26–27, 78, 89, 107,
    138, 150, 170; Hillsborough County, 20;
    Winston-Salem, 45; Wilmington, 84–85;
    Raleigh, 85
Northerners: as teachers of freedpeople,
    148, 163–64; postbellum views of black
    labor, 155; racial stereotypes, 155, 163–64;
    counseling postbellum planters on
    proper use of time to regulate freed
    labor, 157–58, 168–69, 174, 252 (n. 23); as
    postbellum plantation lessees, 166
Nott, J. C., 153
Nyland, Chris, 5–6

Ohio, 181–82, 184; Cincinnati, 182; Dayton,
    182
Oklahoma, 140, 150
Oliver, Mark (slave), 124
Olmsted, Frederick Law, 2, 81, 99, 103, 143,
    176
Olson, John F., 118–19
O'Malley, Michael, 11, 35–36, 42, 109

compared to wage labor, 105–6, 118–19; urban, 106, 138–39; compared to freedom, 158–59